Negotiating Langua

"This volume is about educators who create and negotiate multilingual spaces in their classrooms, fostering their learners' academic empowerment. The wisdom encompassed in these essays is tellingly international in scope, usefully pedagogical in orientation, and solidly grounded in the authors' decades of experience."

Nancy H. Hornberger, from the Foreword

"This book offers a combination of bottom-up, top-down, and 'side-by-side' analyses of language planning and policy in practice. It also provides a unique, comparative lens on the field of teacher preparation—an especially timely contribution in light of the growing impact of transmigration and globalization in education systems around the world."

Teresa McCarty, Arizona State University

Educators are at the epicenter of language policy in education. This book explores how they interpret, negotiate, resist, and (re)create language policies in classrooms. Bridging the divide between policy and practice by analyzing their interconnectedness, it examines the negotiation of language education policies in schools around the world, focusing on educators' central role in this complex and dynamic process.

Each chapter shares findings from research conducted in specific school districts, schools, or classrooms around the world and then details how educators negotiate policy in these local contexts. Discussion questions are included in each chapter. A highlighted section provides practical suggestions and guiding principles for teachers who are negotiating language policies in their own schools.

Kate Menken is Assistant Professor of Linguistics at Queens College of the City University of New York (CUNY), and a Research Fellow at the Research Institute for the Study of Language in an Urban Society at the CUNY Graduate Center.

Ofelia García is Professor in the Ph.D. programs in Urban Education and Hispanic an   nguages at the Graduate Center of the City Un

Negotiating Language Policies in Schools

Educators as Policymakers

Edited by
Kate Menken
Ofelia García

 Routledge
Taylor & Francis Group

NEW YORK AND LONDON

First published 2010
by Routledge
270 Madison Avenue, New York, NY 10016

Simultaneously published in the UK
by Routledge
2 Park Square, Milton Park, Abingdon, Oxon OX14 4RN

Routledge is an imprint of the Taylor & Francis Group, an informa business

© 2010 Taylor and Francis

Typeset in Minion by Book Now Ltd, London
Printed and bound in the United States of America on
acid-free paper by Walsworth Publishing Company, Marceline, MO

Library of Congress Cataloging-in-Publication Data
Negotiating language education policies: educators as
policymakers/edited by Kate Menken, Ofelia García.
    p. cm.
Includes bibliographical references and index.
1. Languages, Modern—Study and teaching—Cross-cultural
studies. 2. Language policy—Study and teaching—Cross-cultural
studies. I. Menken, Kate, 1968– II. García, Ofelia.
PB1.N44 2010
379.2′4—dc22   2009037234

ISBN10: 0–415–80207–5 (hbk)
ISBN10: 0–415–80208–3 (pbk)
ISBN10: 0–203–85587–6 (ebk)

ISBN13: 978–0–415–80207–9 (hbk)
ISBN13: 978–0–415–80208–6 (pbk)
ISBN13: 978–0–203–85587–4 (ebk)

Dedication

We dedicate this book to the teachers in our lives: our personal teachers, Stephen and Ricardo, the teachers in our family, Mary and Emmy, as well as the many wonderful teachers with whom we have worked. We are also grateful for the chance we have here, as former teacher and student, who are now colleagues and co-editors, to continue to learn from and with each other.

Acknowledgements

We thank Naomi Silverman and the entire editorial team at Routledge for preparing and publishing this book. We also thank Nelson Flores, a doctoral student in Urban Education at the Graduate Center of the City University of New York, as well as teacher and language policymaker, for his work compiling our indexes.

Contents

Foreword

Nancy H. Hornberger

Not long ago, I sat in class at the University of Limpopo with Sepedi-speaking students enrolled in their final year of a three-year undergraduate program taught through the medium of both English and Sepedi, officially Sesotho sa Leboa, one of nine African languages recognized in South Africa's Constitution of 1993. This innovative program in Contemporary English and Multilingual Studies (CEMS) was founded in 2003 by Professors Esther Ramani and Michael Joseph in direct and creative response to the openings afforded by South Africa's multilingual language policy (Granville et al., 1998; Joseph & Ramani, 2004, 2006; Ramani et al., 2007). CEMS is to date South Africa's only bilingual university-level program in English and an African language. My fieldnote from that day reads:

> Toward the end of today's Language and Thought class, Professor Michael and I step outside to warm ourselves in the sun while the three students present (Delinah, Elizabeth, Sibongile) confer among themselves, freely code-switching in Sepedi and English, as to which of six child language development paradigms introduced in class last week best corresponds to a short text excerpt by K.C. Fuson 1979 describing a caretaker's interaction with a child. Earlier in today's class we engaged intensively in activities designed by Michael to deepen our understanding of Vygotskyan private speech and prepare the students to engage in their third-year research project exploring Sepedi-speaking children's private speech: today's activities included writing silently and then discussing our own uses of private speech, gauging various data sources such as diaries, interviews, and questionnaires along a likert scale of soft to hard data, and now consideration of this case in terms of Vygotskyan, Piagetian, Hallidayan, Behaviorist, and Chomskyan paradigms, among others.
>
> As Michael and I step outside, we are immediately approached by a broadly smiling young woman who turns out to be one of the first CEMS graduates, Mapelo Tlowane, who has caught sight of her professor and comes over to greet him warmly. She reports she's doing well, her language consulting business started jointly with fellow CEMS-graduate Thabo is picking up, and she's recently had two job interviews in the translation and communication field.

She glowingly states she feels well-prepared and ready for whatever challenges this work might bring, exuding a contagious enthusiasm and confidence that visibly light up the faces of the current CEMS students when Michael invites her in to the class to greet them. After her brief visit of a few minutes, the three students return to their academic task with renewed energy and focus, and perhaps a strengthened conviction of the value of language-oriented research and study. (Limpopo, 5 August 2008)

This volume is about educators, like Esther and Michael, who create and negoti-ate multilingual spaces in their classrooms, fostering their learners' academic empowerment. The wisdom encompassed in these essays is tellingly international in scope, usefully pedagogical in orientation, and solidly grounded in the authors' decades of experience. Through their various accounts, we see how teachers and administrators implement classroom language policies where multilingualism is nationally recognized and promoted from the top-down—as currently in Chile, Israel, Peru, South Africa, and South Asia; but also where it is not. We further learn how teachers—whether in China, Ethiopia, France, Lebanon, the U.K., or the U.S. for example—negotiate classroom language practices in the face of local multilin-gual repertoires that may disrupt whatever top-down policies are in place, whether monolingual or multilingual. All teachers are language policymakers in the classroom and the focus in this volume is a qualitative one on the kinds and complexities of multilingual language policies they make.

Mother-tongue based bilingual primary education, administrators' and teachers' interpretations of language education policies, English as an additional language classroom teaching, student teachers' experiences in multilingual class-rooms, national trilingual policies as enacted in secondary schools, and *de facto* policies for contested languages are just some of the multilingual learning possi-bilities and challenges the authors in this volume document in abundance, in classroom spaces all around the world. They evince a conviction, which I share, that nothing can be more important worldwide than the work educators do and nothing more important in that work than the decisions and practices they take up around language in the classroom. Language is, after all, omnipresent in class-rooms not only as subject and medium of instruction, but also as our very means of expression, of identity and knowledge construction. The decisions and actions educators take around language have profound implications for learners' futures.

My own first multilingual classroom experience came almost half a century ago in California when my fifth grade teacher created space and time for Spanish in our monolingual English public elementary school classroom. Miss Lohnberg instituted voluntary, early morning, before-school Spanish lessons, using audio-lingual materials and methods she herself created on the inspiration of a summer course she had attended in those early days of audio-lingual language teaching. Retrospectively, that first foreign language learning experience was indeed pro-found for me, an early step in what was to become a life-long trajectory of lan-guage learning, intercultural communication and educational linguistics pursuits.

In that work, and through various metaphors—from creating successful contexts for biliteracy to bottom-up language planning, from unpeeling and slicing the language policy onion to opening up implementational and ideological spaces for multilingual education, from activating Indigenous voices to saving Indigenous languages—I have sought to foreground and theorize the fundamental importance of recognizing, incorporating, building on and extending the language repertoires learners bring to the classroom. Key in all this, though, as the authors here so convincingly show us, is the crucial role of educators in their classrooms and the decisions and choices they make about language use, both their own and their students'. It is their language policies, after all, that have the power to affirm or undermine the language and intellectual resources learners bring to the classroom, and thereby to empower or constrain them as future citizens of our global and gloriously multilingual world.

Note

1 I am grateful to Esther Ramani and Michael Joseph for inviting me to sojourn with them, and to the Fulbright Senior Specialist program for sponsoring my visit. A postscript: Esther and Michael inform me that Mapelo has since joined the CEMS faculty as junior lecturer.

References

Granville, S., Janks, H., Mphahlele, M., Reed, Y., Watson, P., Joseph, M., & Ramani, E. (1998). English with or without g(u)ilt: A position paper on language in education policy for South Africa. *Language and Education, 12*(4), 254–272.

Joseph, M., & Ramani, E. (2004). Academic excellence through language equity: A new bilingual degree (in English and Sesotho sa Leboa). In H. Griesel (Ed.), *Curriculum responsiveness: Case studies in higher education* (pp. 237–261). Pretoria: South African Universities Vice-Chancellors Association.

Joseph, M., & Ramani, E. (2006). English in the world does not mean English everywhere: The case for multilingualism in the ELT/ESL profession. In R. Rubdy & M. Saraceni (Eds.), *English in the world: Global rules, global roles* (pp. 186–199). London: Continuum.

Ramani, E., Kekana, T., Modiba, M., & Joseph, M. (2007). Terminology development versus concept development: Insights from a dual-medium BA degree. *Southern African Linguistics and Applied Language Studies, 25*(2), 207–233.

Chapter 1

Introduction

Kate Menken and Ofelia García

A diverse array of language education policies are put into practice in schools around the world, yet little research exists about the complex process of language policy implementation within educational contexts. At each level of an educational system, from the national ministry or department of education to the classroom, language education policies are interpreted, negotiated, and ultimately (re)constructed in the process of implementation. Both in countries with highly centralized educational systems and in those with decentralized systems, where language policies in education are explicit or in others where they are covert (Shohamy, 2006), the policy implementation process is defined by its dynamism; ultimately, a language education policy is as dynamic as the many individuals involved in its creation and implementation.

Educators are at the epicenter of this dynamic process, acting on their agency to change the various language education policies they must translate into practice. As Cochran-Smith (2003) so aptly noted, this is part of what she terms the "unforgivable complexity of teaching," a reality we both acknowledge and embrace in this volume. Regardless of the type of policies or the educational context in which a policy text comes to life in the classroom, there is typically space for policy negotiation in classroom practice, as it is ultimately educators— particularly classroom teachers—who are the final arbiters of language policy implementation. As such, policies often have different results from those intended by policymakers.

In spite of this dynamism and complexity, however, most language policy research remains national in scope, focusing on top-down policies and analyzing written policy statements (Kaplan & Baldauf, 1997; Ricento, 2005; Spolsky, 2004), overlooking the central role of classroom practitioners. Researchers in language policy are just beginning to explore questions of agency and local resistance (Canagarajah, 2004). Policy documents are thus presented as static and dead (Shohamy, 2006), without significant attention paid to the ways that they actually come to life in the classroom.

In this book, we dive into the complex and often contradictory arena of policy implementation. The purpose of this book is to bridge the gap between research and practice by exploring the negotiation of language education policies in schools around the world and to provide educators with deeper understandings of this process to guide their implementation of language policies in schools and classrooms. Using research conducted at the level of local school districts, schools, or classrooms as their point of departure, contributors to this edited volume examine how language education policies come to life in schools. Specifically, researchers contributing to this edited volume were asked to go into schools and classrooms to answer the following research question within their different contexts:

- How are language education policies interpreted, negotiated, resisted, and (re)created in classrooms?

We find that entirely new policies are often created in the process of policy negotiation and enactment in schools. Thus, in this book, we argue that implementation by definition involves policymaking, with educators acting as policymakers. Likewise, we find it insufficient to discuss a language policy as singular, but rather in this volume we discuss language education policies in the plural.

The New Wave of Language Education Policy Research: A Focus on Agency in Implementation

According to Spolsky (2004), language policy encompasses all of the "language practices, beliefs and management of a community or polity" (p. 9); the field examines such topics as which language(s) will be official or national languages, which language(s) will be taught in school, as well as ideologies about language. Because schools are primary sites for the implementation as well as contestation of language policies (Cooper, 1989; Corson, 1999), in this volume we focus specifically on language education policies.[1]

Within the evolution of the field of language policy, earlier research focused first on top-down national language planning and the resolution of language "problems" (Fishman, 1979; Haugen, 1972), and more recent critical approaches explored the ways that language policies can create and/or perpetuate social inequities (Corson, 1999; Phillipson, 1992; Phillipson & Skutnabb-Kangas, 1996; Tollefson, 1991). Characterizing these approaches as neoclassical and critical, respectively, Ricento and Hornberger (1996, p. 408) noted that both obfuscate the complexity of the policy process. As they write,

> None offers a model that can predict the consequences of a particular policy or show a clear cause/effect relationship between particular policy types or configurations and observed (often undesirable, from the perspective of critical theorists) outcomes.

In other words, little attention was previously paid to understanding how a given policy was actually implemented and any changes it may have undergone in the implementation process. Moreover, the neoclassical and critical research approaches have been criticized for underestimating human agency in policymaking (Canagarajah, 2005; Hornberger & Johnson, 2007; Ramanathan, 2005).

To highlight the complexity of language education policy with a spotlight on the critical role of educators within the process of policy creation and implementation, Ricento and Hornberger (1996) offered a metaphor of language planning and policy as a multilayered "onion." The layers they explored, ordered from the outer layers to the center, include legislation and political processes (at the outer layers), states and supranational agencies, institutions, and classroom practitioners (at the heart of the onion). Within this construct, agents across national, institutional, and interpersonal levels are engaged in a process wherein they interact with and are impacted by one another to enact language policies (Ricento & Hornberger, 1996, p. 419).

This book is part of a newer wave of language education policy research that refocuses our attentions from governments to local school administrators, teachers, students, parents, and community members—the so-called bottom of the educational policy structure—and which views language policies as far more multidimensional than written policy statements. Now that the onion is over a decade old, we still see the urgent need to heed the call for a more multilayered and textured exploration of language education policies. A central tenet of this volume, which unifies its diverse chapters, is the view that language policies cannot be truly understood without studying actual practices. As described in our conclusion, the authors of this volume thus *stir* the metaphorical onion.

About This Book

Although as editors we did not request that authors contributing to this volume prescribe to a specific methodology, most used qualitative methods in their explorations of how language education policies are negotiated by teachers at the classroom level. Hornberger and Johnson (2007) in fact promoted what they called the "ethnography of language education policy" to extend research in this area. As they write,

> [E]thnographies of language policy offer unique insights into LPP [language planning and policy] processes through thick descriptions of policy interpretation and implementation at the local level. Historical and intertextual analyses of policy texts can capture the confluence of histories, attitudes, and ideologies that engender a language policy but, alone, cannot account for how the creation is interpreted and implemented in the various contextual layers through which a language policy must pass. (Hornberger & Johnson, 2007, p. 511)

For the authors whose chapters appear in this book, qualitative methods were favored as the most effective to delve into language education policy implementation, to gain the rich understandings of language policy processes that we sought.

From the contributions of the authors in this volume, we find that language policies can be explicit or implicit, *de facto* or planned, and that educators at the

local level hold as much responsibility for policymaking as do government officials. Just as a policy statement can either open up or restrict "ideological and
implementational" spaces in schools for multilingualism (Hornberger, 2005), so
too can educators either carve out or close off these spaces. Although teachers can
simply serve as what Shohamy (2006, p. 78) termed "'soldiers' of the system who
carry out orders by internalizing the policy ideology and its agendas," they are
often found instead to play a far more powerful and active role, changing and
redefining policies, or creating entirely new ones.

In this way, we move beyond top-down, bottom-up, or even side-by-side divisions to a conceptualization of language policy as a far more dynamic, interactive,
and real-life process (García, 2009). Hence the authors use terms like *policy appropriation* (Johnson & Freeman, [this volume]), *negotiation* (Creese, [this volume]),
interpretation (Valdiviezo, [this volume]), *contestation* or *resistance* (Shohamy,
[this volume]), *challenges* (Bloch et al., [this volume]; Mohanty et al., [this
volume]), *responsiveness* (Berryman et al., [this volume]), and *reconstruction*
(Zakharia, [this volume]). Within this perspective, "policy implementation" and
"policymaking" go hand in hand.

In our view, variations in policy implementation are not a problem that creators
of language policies should avoid. Instead, we need to gain deeper understandings
of this variation so that we can offer theoretical constructs that will help educators
negotiate this complex terrain when faced with their own policy decisions.

Organization of This Book

Contributors to this volume come from all over the world and share in this book
their findings from classroom research within the different regional contexts in
which they specialize. A striking finding that cuts across the chapters of this
volume is that educators *always* seem to negotiate the language education policies
they enact in their schools, even in countries where the ideological and implementational spaces for resistance or change are small. A distinction between the
chapters can be drawn, however, in the driving force(s) that guide educators' decisions about how to implement policy. These fall into two main categories, into
which we have divided the book chapters. In some cases, authors analyzed internal, individual forces—how teachers' or school administrators' prior experiences
or personal identity shaped their interpretations and enactment of language policies. In other cases, authors analyzed external forces shaping educators' language
policy negotiations, based on the situation or context (e.g., political, community,
region, etc.) within which their school or district is nested. These two forces—
internal and external—are dialectical in that educators are shaped by their situations as they, in turn, influence them; also, these external and internal forces are
not mutually exclusive. However, they offer a helpful a way for thinking about
how educators ultimately translate policies into classroom practice.

Unlike research in language policy, there already exists a significant body of
research about general education policy implementation, which offers helpful
information for our purposes. Our findings and the divisions we use to organize

this book are supported by this research. Stemming from the field of organizational science, "sense-making theory" explores how educators negotiate complexity and contradictions in the workplace and analyzes why some top-down policies are implemented when others are not. There are now some very recent examples of research in this area being applied to deepening our understandings of language education policies as well (e.g., Palmer & Lynch, 2008; Palmer & Snodgrass, 2009).

Spillane, Reiser, and Gomez (2006) draw on research in human cognition to contribute to research in education policy implementation. As they write,

> Cognitive frames have been used in studies of policy implementation in education to investigate how various dimensions of human sense-making influence implementation. Some of this work concentrates on implementing agents' prior knowledge (Cohen & Weiss, 1993) and the analogies that implementing agents draw between new ideas and their existing understandings (Spillane, 2000). Other work concentrates on how aspects of social situations—including organizational and community history (Lin, 2000; Yanow, 1996), organizational segmentation and professional expertise (Spillane, 1998b), professional discourse (Hill, 2000), and formal and informal networks (Coburn, 2001a)—influence implementing agents' sense making. (Spillane et al., 2006, pp. 48–49)

As these authors indicate, individual as well as social cognition influence the choices educators make.

In other words, individuals use their prior knowledge and experiences to interpret new information based on what they already know. Thus educators will understand a new policy or approach differently from one another, based on what they—as individuals—know and believe already. Whereas the role of individual sense-making accounts for certain aspects of implementation, other research shows how an individual's situation or social context can also greatly affect policy implementation. For instance, teachers or school administrators work in schools that are typically within local school districts, nested in states or regions, within a country. Educators are also part of cultural communities outside of school, perhaps have other professional affiliations, are members of wider society, citizens of the country in which they reside, and so on. Each of these will pressure educators in distinct ways and influence how they negotiate and ultimately enact policies (Spillane et al., 2006).

Book Contents

The chapters in this book are, therefore, divided into two main sections, according to the approach to policy implementation research taken by the authors. Part I includes Chapters 2–8, in which authors examine how educators' negotiation of language education policies is guided by their personal experiences or identity (individual forces). Part II includes Chapters 9–14, in which educators' negotiation of language education policies is influenced by their context/community/situation (social forces).

The chapters of this book span all seven continents; accordingly, though the chapters are written in English, English is an additional language for most of the contributing authors. Two chapters involve research in Africa (Ethiopia and South Africa), two in the Middle East (Lebanon and Israel), two in South America (Peru and Chile), two in North America (United States), one in Australia/Oceania (New Zealand), two in Europe (United Kingdom and France), and two in Asia (China and India).

Part I: Negotiation of Language Education Policies Guided by Educators' Experiences or Identity (Individual)

Chapter 2 (Johnson & Freeman) examines differing individual interpretations of federal, state, and local education policies in the United States by three school administrators in the School District of Philadelphia, through action-oriented ethnography of language policy in combination with policy discourse analysis. The chapter highlights the powerful roles of administrators and teachers in policymaking and how these policy actors can either create or curtail possibilities for multilingual education.

Chapter 3 (Creese) explores two different UK policies: (1) personalized learning, a pedagogical approach focused on each student's individualized needs, and (2) the inclusion paradigm, whereby students with special needs such as those learning English as an additional language (EAL) are in the same classroom with native English speakers and instructed by two teachers—a subject-area teacher and a trained EAL teacher. Drawing on detailed transcripts of classroom interactions in two different London secondary schools, Creese shows how the teachers involved implement these two policies. She finds that though the policies are in some ways complimentary and promising for EAL learners, they fail to counter uneven power dynamics between teachers and beliefs in transmission and whole class teaching over other approaches.

Chapter 4 (Hélot) examines how two student teachers negotiate paradoxical Ministry of Education policy in France that on one hand promotes foreign language learning, but on the other hand, in practice, promotes monolingual French instruction for students who speak languages other than French at their residence. The student teachers draw on their differing personal backgrounds, language attitudes, and proficiencies, to create new language policies in the preprimary schools where they teach that embrace multilingualism while reflecting the paradoxes of national policy.

Chapter 5 (Valdiviezo) employs ethnographic methods to analyze four Quechua teachers' interpretations of Bilingual Intercultural Education Policy in Peru, within three different indigenous communities in the Peruvian Andes. Valdiviezo shows how contradictory national language education policy is reflected in contradictions in implementation, as teachers are found to both challenge and reproduce the marginalization of Quechua, according to their prior experiences and beliefs.

Chapter 6 (Bloch, Guzula, & Nkence) explores the efforts of three Xhosa teachers in two schools in the Western Cape to implement South Africa's Language in Education Policy, which promotes bilingualism, and also new regional policy that favors balanced language and literacy instruction. The authors find that the Xhosa teachers are moving from English-dominant instruction to Xhosa, despite challenges such as limited materials and government support, as well as teachers' own beliefs about mother-tongue instruction.

Chapter 7 (English & Varghese) shows how teachers in Washington State (United States) negotiate Eastlake local school district policy that is restrictive of multilingualism, in a state that on paper advocates bilingual education. In this case, much like the educational model described in Chapter 3 (Creese), an English as a second language (ESL) teacher is partnered with primary school classroom teachers in two different schools; in this case, one ESL teacher must work with many different classroom teachers, limiting the possibility to actually meet the students' needs. However, the authors focus on the efforts of one classroom teacher who, because of her personal experiences and identity, works closely with the ESL teacher to improve the quality of schooling for the English learners in her classroom.

Chapter 8 (Zhang & Hu) documents the responses of three English-language teachers in Shenzhen to the top-down promotion of communicative English-language teaching in mainland China through new pedagogical reform, Task-Based Language Teaching. The authors found that the teachers enacted the reform very differently, according to such factors as the teachers' beliefs about language teaching, their understandings of the reform, their perceptions of the students' learning needs, and school-level support for the reform.

Part II: Educators' Negotiation of Language Education Policies Influenced by Situation/Context/Community (Social)

Chapter 9 (Berryman, Glynn, Woller, & Reweti) highlights the critical role of community involvement in its investigation of the implementation of the Māori Education Strategy, a policy of the government of New Zealand that promotes Māori language and culture and was adopted in response to pressures from the Māori community, who used their political influence to shape current language education policy within this context of language revitalization. The authors' interview data from a Māori immersion school show symbiosis between school and local community context and how instruction in this case is culturally responsive and reflective of a Māori worldview.

Chapter 10 (Zakharia) shows how teachers working within a context of political conflict and postwar reconstruction in Lebanon reconstruct foreign, colonial languages into local, relevant languages through critical pedagogy that brings in pressing current sociopolitical concerns. Zakharia uses ethnographic methods to examine how four English and French teachers implement Lebanese language education policy, wherein Arabic, English, and French are all media of instruction, at a Shi'i school in Beirut.

Chapter 11 (Shohamy) offers three instances of resistance to Israel's top-down language education policy which requires Hebrew, Arabic, and English instruction and offers written support for multilingualism in other languages as well. Shohamy shows how situational factors result in resistance by Jewish Hebrew speakers to learning Arabic, the establishment of Arabic-Hebrew bilingual schools to counter this resistance and promote cross-cultural exchange, and the teaching of English at earlier grades as a result of parental pressures.

Chapter 12 (Ambatchew) examines the implementation of Ethiopia's 1994 language education policy, which promotes monolingual mother-tongue instruction at the early grades, and ambitiously allows for every language in the country to become a medium of instruction. Due to great linguistic diversity on the ground, however, teachers in Addis Ababa are found instead to code-switch for students who do not speak Amharic; similar variation exists when parents change their national identity or relocate to other places to ensure their students attend schools with the language medium they desire.

Chapter 13 (Mohanty, Panda, & Pal) analyzes the efforts of teachers and school administrators to implement language educational policies in highly multilingual India, involving constitutional provisions for mother-tongue instruction; the three-language formula (the use of a regional language or mother tongue, Hindi and/or English, and an additional modern Indian language in all schools); and the National Curricular Framework that also calls for mother-tongue instruction. Through their investigation of educational practices in Orissa and Delhi, the authors discover how educators resist policies as a result of what they term a *double divide* between English and the major regional languages, and between the regional languages and minority languages.

Chapter 14 (Galdames & Gaete) studies 2004 policy by the Chilean Ministry of Education to use extensive professional development for teachers to move native-language literacy instruction away from traditional skills-based, decoding approaches to a balanced literacy approach, whereby reading comprehension and literacy in context are also incorporated. However, Galdames and Gaete find that the policy fails to recognize the sociohistorical context and is thus typically not accepted by teachers who remain attached to the education traditions that preceded it.

Each chapter of this book outlines the language education policies being negotiated in each context and then details how educators enact those policies in schools. At the end of each chapter, the authors provide a set of discussion questions and/or ideas for action research projects to facilitate further understandings of the chapter contents. The book concludes with Chapter 15, which analyzes the contributions of this edited volume to the field, and also Chapter 16, which offers to educators a set of principles to guide their work as policymakers.

Note

1 As further detailed in our conclusion, Cooper (1989) introduced the term "language acquisition planning" into the literature in recognition of the central role of education

in language policy. Kaplan and Baldauf (1997) used the term "language in education policy" (LiEP), whereas Shohamy (2003, 2006) used "language education policy." These terms are used interchangeably by the authors who have contributed to this volume.

References

Canagarajah, S. (2005). *Reclaiming the local in language policy and practice.* Mahwah, NJ: Lawrence Erlbaum.

Cochran-Smith, M. (2003). The unforgivable complexity of teaching: Avoiding simplicity in an age of accountability. *Journal of Teacher Education, 54*(1), 3–5.

Cooper, R. L. (1989). *Language planning and social change.* Cambridge, UK: Cambridge University Press.

Corson, D. (1999). *Language policy in schools: A resource for teachers and administrators.* Mahwah, NJ: Lawrence Erlbaum.

Fishman, J. A. (1979). Bilingual education, language planning, and English. *English World-Wide, 1,* 11–24.

García, O. (2009). *Bilingual education in the 21st century: A global perspective.* Malden, MA and Oxford: Wiley/Blackwell.

Hornberger, N. (2005). Nichols to NCLB: Local and global perspectives on U.S. language education policy. *Working Papers in Educational Linguistics, 20*(2), 1–17.

Hornberger, N., & Johnson, D. (2007). Slicing the onion ethnographically: Layers and spaces in multilingual language education policy and practice. *TESOL Quarterly, 41*(3), 509–533.

Haugen, E. (1972). *Ecology of language.* Stanford: Stanford U. Press.

Kaplan, R., & Baldauf, R. (1997). *Language planning: From practice to theory.* Philadelphia, PA: Multilingual Matters.

Palmer, D., & Lynch, A. (2008, September). A bilingual education for a monolingual test? The pressure to prepare for TAKS and its influence on choices for language of instruction in Texas elementary bilingual classrooms. *Language Policy, 7,* 217–235.

Palmer, D., & Snodgrass, V. (2009). *Bilingual teachers respond to the TAKS: Access to curriculum for English learners in Texas.* Paper presented at the American Educational Research Association conference. San Diego, CA.

Phillipson, R. (1992). *Linguistic imperialism.* Oxford, UK: Oxford University Press.

Phillipson, R., & Skutnabb-Kangas, T. (1996). English only worldwide or language ecology? *TESOL Quarterly, 30*(3), 429–452.

Ramanathan, V. (2005). Rethinking language planning and policy from the ground-up: Refashioning institutional realities and human lives. *Current Issues in Language Planning, 6*(2), 89–101.

Ricento, T. (2005). *An introduction to language policy: Theory and method.* Oxford, UK: Wiley-Blackwell.

Ricento, T., & Hornberger, N. (1996). Unpeeling the onion: Language planning and policy and the ELT professional. *TESOL Quarterly, 30*(3), 401–427.

Shohamy, E. (2003). The issue: Implications of language education policies for language study in schools and universities. Lead article in Perspective, *Modern Language Journal, 88*(ii), 277–286.

Shohamy, E. (2006). *Language policy: Hidden agendas and new approaches.* London: Routledge.

Spillane, J., Reiser, B., & Gomez, L. (2006). Policy implementation and cognition: The role of human, social, and distributed cognition in framing policy implementation. In

M. Honig (Ed.), *New directions in education policy implementation* (pp. 47–64). Albany, NY: State University of New York Press.

Spolsky, B. (2004). *Language policy (Key topics in sociolinguistics).* Cambridge, UK: Cambridge University Press.

Tollefson, J. (1991). *Planning language, planning inequality: Language policy in the community.* London and New York: Longman.

Part I

Negotiation of Language Education Policies Guided by Educators' Experiences or Identity (Individual)

Chapter 2

Appropriating Language Policy on the Local Level

Working the Spaces for Bilingual Education

David Cassels Johnson and Rebecca Freeman

Educators in the United States who want to promote bilingualism face many challenges including English-focused legislation on the federal and state level and widespread confusion, conflict, and controversy about bilingual education. Not only have anti-bilingual education initiatives passed in California, Arizona, and Massachusetts but also the current federal educational policy—the *No Child Left Behind Act* (NCLB)—ignores the value of bilingualism and bilingual education and instead focuses on English language acquisition. Despite this focus on English, we argue that School District language policy and empowered educators, should and *can* promote bilingualism. Our focus is on the power of administrators, teachers, and action-oriented researchers working collaboratively to develop research-based, pedagogically sound, and contextually appropriate language policies and programs for bilingual learners.

Based on several years of ethnographic and discourse analytic research in the linguistically and culturally diverse School District of Philadelphia (SDP), this chapter illustrates how educators' beliefs about the needs of language learners interact with their interpretations of evolving federal, state, and local language policies. We show how educators who are committed to promoting the development of languages other than English on the local level can and do create ideological and implementational space for bilingual education. We also show how educators can and do have the power to obfuscate that possibility and restrict the reality of bilingual education. This discussion shows the dynamic, interrelated processes of language policy appropriation on the local level and suggests ways that educators and researchers can collaborate to promote bilingual education.

Evolving Conceptualizations of Language Policy in Education

Much of the scholarship on language policy has focused on the restrictive power of policies. Critical models emphasize how language policies subjugate linguistic minorities and how the state can use language policy to perpetuate systems of social inequality (e.g., Pennycook, 2006; Tollefson, 1991, 2002). Yet these critical approaches have been criticized for implicitly reifying a top-down perspective and underestimating the power of human agency (Davis, 1999; Hornberger & Johnson, 2007; Ricento & Hornberger, 1996).

Anthropological and sociological work on educational policy tends to *fore-ground* human agency. For example, Levinson and Sutton (2001) propose a socio-cultural approach that not only recognizes the power in authorized policy but also emphasizes policy *appropriation* when the "temporarily reified text is circulated across the various institutional contexts, where it may be applied, interpreted, and/or contested by a multiplicity of actors" (p. 2). Levinson, Sutton, and Winstead (2007) challenge the traditional portrayal of the division between policy formation and implementation in which those in power legislate directives to be implemented by practitioners.

"Implementation" implies that policy directives are necessarily and predictably implemented when, instead, even overt anti-bilingual education policies are *appropriated* in a variety of ways (see Stritikus & Wiese, 2006). Thus, we adopt the word appropriation because it highlights the powerful role of educators in the language policy process. We are particularly interested in the tension between structure and agency in language policy research and practice and between the power of policies to sculpt and/or normalize educational practices and the power of educators to appropriate policy in creative and unpredictable ways. As many have noted (Freeman, 2004; Hornberger & Johnson, 2007; Johnson, in press b; Skilton-Sylvester, 2003; Stritikus, 2002), educators play a vital role in dynamic, interrelated language policy processes, and they are not merely "implementers" of some monolithic doctrine. Still, language policies are capable of hegemonically setting discursive boundaries on what is educationally normal or feasible.

The tension between structure and agency is reflected in Ball's framework (1993, 2006) in which he offers two conceptualizations of policy: A *policy as text* orientation rejects the quest for understanding authorial intentions in policy and instead emphasizes the variety of ways a particular policy text is interpreted and put into action. On the other hand, a *policy as discourse* orientation reemphasizes the potential power of educational policies to set boundaries on what is educationally feasible. Whereas a plurality of readings and interpretations are possible, "[W]e need to appreciate the way in which policy ensembles . . . exercise power through the production of truth and knowledge as discourses" (Ball, 1993, p. 16). Although Ball proffers two opposing conceptualizations of educational policy, both are useful and not necessarily in conflict, and, again, though it is important to respect the power of language policy agents, it is equally important to respect the power of discourses that language policies can engender, instantiate, and perpetuate.

Hornberger (2002) introduced the idea of *implementational* and *ideological* spaces to describe how local educational practitioners take advantage of spaces in language policy for multilingual education (Hornberger 2002, 2005; Hornberger & Johnson, 2007; Johnson, in press b). We recognize the ability of language policies to hegemonically define the limits of what is educationally normal and/or possible—and the ability of schools themselves to restrict the educational and social possibilities of students—and language policy research should investigate this. Still, even within ostensibly restrictive language policies, there is often *implementational space* that local educators and language planners can work to their advantage and *ideological space* in schools and communities, which opens educational and social possibilities for bilingual learners and potentially challenges dominant/hegemonic educational discourses (see Freeman, 2004; Johnson, 2004; Stritikus & Wiese, 2006).

The Ethnography of Language Policy: An Action-Oriented Approach

Although the conceptualizations of language policy have grown increasingly rich, Ricento (2000) pointed out that research has tended to fall short of fully accounting for precisely how microlevel interaction relates to the macrolevels of social organization. Newer research is beginning to dissolve this gap in the literature (Freeman, 2004; Johnson, 2007, 2009; Menken, 2008; Stritikus, 2002; Stritikus & Wiese, 2006), and our action-oriented approach to language policy continues in this spirit. Our goal as researchers is to explore micro–macro connections in how language policies are interpreted and appropriated in schools, and our goal as activists is to collaborate with practitioners to develop the ideological spaces and work the implementational spaces for promoting bilingualism.

The ethnography of language policy conceptualizes language policy as a *process* that begins with a potentially heterogeneous text that is interpreted and appropriated in unpredictable ways by agents who appropriate, resist, and/or change dominant and alternative policy discourses (see Johnson, 2009). This conceptualization is benefited by methods that combine critical discourse analyses of policy discourse (Bakhtin, 1986; Fairclough, 1989, 1995) with ethnographic research of some local context. Critical analyses of language policy text (and language policy as discourse) are essential; however, (a) because intentions, goals, and outcomes are impossible to predict on the basis of policy text alone, and (b) because the texts mean very little without human agents, data collection must be based in an ethnographic understanding of some local context. Furthermore, because language policy processes are multilayered and play out across multiple contexts, the ethnography of language policy is necessarily multisited. Thus, we agree with Levinson et al. (2007) that multiple ethnographers looking at the same policy provide a depth of coverage that a single ethnographer cannot.

This chapter draws on 10 years of action-oriented ethnographic research (1995–2005) in schools and communities throughout the SDP. From 1995–2000, Freeman focused her ethnographic and discourse analytic research on different actors (teachers and administrators), contexts (classrooms, schools, and homes), and texts (school and district language policies) that explicitly worked to promote bilingualism. She investigated how language ideologies about Spanish and English structured opportunities for students in the predominantly Puerto Rican community in north Philadelphia. From 2000 to 2004, Freeman worked as the lead consultant on a federal grant to develop 10 dual-language programs in the dominant multilingual communities in Philadelphia (including but not limited to Spanish and English in north Philadelphia), and she continued her ethnographic and discourse analytic research throughout this phase.

Johnson joined Freeman in the district in 2002 and conducted 3 years of ethnographic research on bilingual education language policy and program development. Their involvement in action-oriented research projects on bilingual program development engendered participant observation, audio and videotaping, and collection of fieldnotes and relevant site documents in multiple school and community contexts. For the sake of data triangulation, multiple formal and informal interviews were conducted with bilingual teachers, administrators, and state and federal policymakers. These ethnographically collected data were compared with critical discourse analyses of federal, state, and local language policy texts and discourse.

The School District of Philadelphia

According to data for the 1999–2000 academic year, there were approximately 203,000 students who attended SDP schools: 63% African American, 20% Caucasian, 12% Latino, and 5% Asian. Approximately 10% of the students were designated English language learners, and in 2005 more than 14,000 were receiving English language (ESOL) or bilingual services[1]; according to educators who work in the district today, the number of English learners is growing dramatically. Though almost 50% of these learners speak Spanish, the SDP also serves large populations of Khmer, Vietnamese, Chinese, and Russian speakers, and increasing numbers of students from Sudan, Somalia, and other African countries.

There is an important distinction in the layers of SDP institutional authority between what educators call downtown and the field. "Downtown" refers both to the physical downtown administrative building for the district as well as the administrators who work therein. "The field" refers to the educators in schools—especially teachers but also principals—who are charged with implementing whatever policies downtown enacts. One central (downtown) administrative office oversees all ESOL/bilingual programs, and the administrators who work in the ESOL/bilingual office are responsible for acquiring and distributing federal money for language education and for developing language policy and programs for the whole district.

Federal and State Educational Policy for Bilingual Learners

The NCLB, and particularly the high-stakes testing requirements, have restricted access to bilingual education (Menken, 2008; Menken & Shohamy, 2008) and the language policy embedded within NCLB, Title III, has been criticized for transforming bilingual education into English-focused programs (Wiley & Wright, 2004; Wright, 2005). However, even though the policy appears to be a hegemonic attempt to marginalize bilingual education, there is conflict and dissent, both among educators *and* among the policy's creators.

Beginning in 1968, federal funding for the education of English language learners was distributed through competitive grants under Title VII of the *Elementary and Secondary Education Act* (ESEA). Title VII, otherwise known as the *Bilingual*

Education Act (BEA), began as a policy designed to transition bilingual learners into all English instruction, yet later drafts increasingly made room for native language maintenance and developmental bilingual education (see Wiese & Garcia, 2001). In 2002, Title III replaced Title VII in the new version of the ESEA, which was given the new name, NCLB. Title III subsequently became the preeminent federal U.S. language in education policy and its vigorous focus on English language acquisition (over bilingualism) fomented concern that developmental bilingual education would be phased out in favor of transitional or English-only pedagogical approaches (Wiley & Wright, 2004).

While the shift from Title VII to Title III suggests an ideological shift at the federal level with focused discourse on English language education, the congressional debates leading up to NCLB's enactment reveal competing discourses and texts. The first version of NCLB (House Resolution 1 or HR 1) abandoned most of the language in Title VII, diverting all attention to English language education and strictly prohibiting any more than 3 years of bilingual education. However, when HR 1 was sent to the Senate, the Senate's version reinserted much of the language *verbatim* from Title VII, injecting the policy with an explicit focus on the benefits of bilingualism and bilingual education. What was finally adopted in Title III was a compromise of the two versions of the bill, with much of the language from Title VII remaining intact with renewed emphasis on English language acquisition, creating a heterogeneous mixture of old and new policy text (see Johnson, 2007, in press a).

When congress had completed development of NCLB, both opponents *and supporters* of bilingual education celebrated it as a victory. Not only did NCLB's creators disagree about its intentions, but federal administrators responsible for its implementation echo the emphasized "flexibility" in NCLB text (105 instances of the word "flexibility" appear) and argue that school districts have complete freedom to implement the language education programs of their choosing. For example, Brinda Sea,[2] the director of the State Consolidated Grant Division[3] at the Office of English Language Acquisition, avers that the federal Department of Education does not promote or prefer any particular method and is, in fact, prohibited from doing so: "We stay completely out of it" (May 24, 2006). Such overt "flexibility" may ring hollow if the *de facto* results of NCLB are that bilingual programs are dismantled anyway; however, such heterogeneity both in the NCLB policy text and discourse represents implementational space for bilingual education.

State Educational Policy in Pennsylvania

While Title VII monies were administered in the form of competitive grants for which school districts applied, Title III instead requires Departments of Education at the state level to oversee the distribution of funds that are administered as an allocation and no longer as a competitive grant. Therefore, state language policy has become increasingly important in language program choice. The primary language policy in Pennsylvania education policy is entitled "Educating students with limited English proficiency (LEP) and English language learners (ELL)" and states:

Districts have the option of choosing which program to implement. . . . All programs must include ESL classes and must be based on sound educational and second language acquisition theory. Placing them in remedial reading and speech therapy classes does not constitute a program. Neither does placing them in all English classrooms without the benefit of ESL instruction and modification of classroom content. Students must have meaningful access to the academic content classes in order for them to achieve the academic standards. (PABEC 22, PA Code 4.26, 4)

This passage emphasizes district choice with regard to language education program type but strictly prohibits submersion without "ESL instruction and modification." The policy goes on to list the types of programs that provide meaningful access to content knowledge, including "transitional, developmental, and dual-language programs."[4]

In terms of official policy, Pennsylvania policy does not place any restrictions on bilingual education that are not already contained in Title III of NCLB and, in fact, one might argue (as some in the School District of Philadelphia do) that it allows schools to make any programmatic decisions they choose. This interpretation of the policy is supported by interviews with the Title III director for the Pennsylvania Department of Education who describes Title III as "vague" and asserts that school districts have the right, and can be funded for, language programs of their choosing (interview, December 6, 2005).

Analyzing policy intentions on the basis of policy text alone is a questionable endeavor. The discourse perpetuated in analyses of NCLB suggests that it is an English-focused monolith, yet both its creators and federal implementers interpret its intentions differently, and the policy text itself is a layering of old and new policy language (much of which is lifted verbatim from the previous law) creating a heterogeneous document. The question becomes: How do educators interpret and appropriate the varying policy texts and discourses?

Language Policy Development and Appropriation in the School District of Philadelphia

Inspired by Ball's (1993, 2006) notions of policy as text and discourse discussed above, we focus on language policy in the SDP from 2000 to 2004. Our chronological discussion first illustrates how Title VII interacted with Title III within the SDP, with attention to how the texts were interpreted and acted upon by agents involved in a dual-language initiative. Then we highlight how federal and state language policy interacted with the development and implementation of the official SDP language policy. Throughout this discussion, we show how actors identify and work different ideological and implementational spaces to promote bilingualism.

The Dual-Language Initiative

In November 2000, the SDP was awarded a 5-year Title VII systemwide grant, which functioned as an important language policy text. The grant writer, Emily Dixon-Marquez, was then a director in the ESOL/bilingual office and had been a lead actor in the education of bilingual learners for years. A centerpiece of the Title VII grant was the dual-language initiative, with the goal "To improve and expand Bilingual Education Programs to include Dual-Language Programs to provide students the opportunity to develop full proficiency in two languages." Ten elementary schools in the major bilingual communities in Philadelphia were targeted (seven Spanish, one Chinese, one Russian, and one Vietnamese). The grant defined dual language as two-way immersion, that is, as an additive bilingual program that (a) targets balanced numbers of English speakers and speakers of a partner language who learn together in integrated classes, (b) provides at least 50% and up to 90% of content-area instruction through the partner language, and (c) aims for bilingualism, biliteracy, academic achievement in two languages, and positive intergroup understanding and relations.

Dixon-Marquez and Freeman (the lead consultant) launched the dual-language initiative in February 2001 in one region of north Philadelphia because they had longstanding relationships with bilingual educators in this community. They aimed to build bridges between downtown and the field by developing *language-planning teams* of administrators, teachers, and community members who collectively would have or develop the authority and expertise to make decisions about the language education of bilingual learners. At the first planning meeting, administrators and teachers from the three target schools in this region expected Freeman (an "expert in the field") and Dixon-Marquez ("from downtown") to tell them exactly how to implement a dual-language program. However, because Freeman and Dixon-Marquez saw the administrators and teachers as important agents of change, they made explicit their expectation that the teams take ownership of the dual-language planning process. Over time, and in very different ways, these three dual-language planning teams embraced the opportunity to develop programs that they believed were appropriate for their students and community. They read the literature, visited other programs, talked to their parents and teachers, and developed coherent visions of dual-language programs for their schools (see Freeman, 2004, for details).

By June 2002, these teachers were clearly directing the dual-language initiative. After one dual-language meeting, Freeman writes:

> The TWI teachers want to demonstrate how their students are developing literacies in Spanish and English in the different TWI programs.... Teachers want to be able to share data with parents, educators, and other stakeholders about how their students are developing biliteracies through these programs. At the same time, the teachers have become concerned that the assessment tools that they are currently using to assess literacy development in Spanish are biased toward English. The teachers have decided that they need to a) collect data that demonstrates students' writing development through Spanish and English over

time, and b) develop valid assessments for student writing. They realize that these two tasks need to be addressed at the same time, so they have decided to collect student writing three times a year starting in October, and they will develop a task force to create valid assessments. (fieldnotes, June 2002)

The teachers, in collaboration with Freeman and inspired by Elizabeth Howard's work on the CAL/CREDE biliteracy development project (e.g., Howard & Sugarman, 2007) identified the following two action research questions to guide their inquiry:

How do students develop literacies in Spanish and English through their experiences in our TWI programs?

How can we assess students' bilingual and biliteracy development over time? What kinds of evidence can we provide to stakeholders of that development?

Teachers from these three schools began their work on this action research project during their summer dual-language professional development, and their work structured monthly "Dual Language Teachers Talking" meetings throughout the following 2 school years. The topics for these meetings (e.g., writing workshops, anchor papers, writing portfolios) were developed by the teachers on the basis of their ongoing assessments of their professional development needs, and one or two different teachers led each meeting.

By the fall of 2003, seven schools were either planning or had launched Spanish–English dual-language programs in the early elementary grades. However, the definition of dual-language education was evolving district-wide, reflecting different ways that the language-planning teams on one hand, and dual-language researchers on the other, interpreted the term "dual language." For example, some teams realized that their programs led to subtractive bilingualism and thus embraced two-way immersion as their definition of "dual language." However, target schools in another region that had one-way developmental programs already in place, maintained their programs, and resisted the notion that the term "dual language" should exclusively refer to two-way immersion programs. Dixon-Marquez and Freeman were thus forced to broaden their notion of "dual language" as a cover term for both two-way immersion for ELLs and English speakers, and one-way developmental programs exclusively for ELLs (like Cloud, Genesee, & Hamayan, 2000; but unlike Lindholm-Leary, 2001).

The dual-language planners' priorities in 2003, like educators across the country, were strongly influenced by the passage of NCLB. Although many in the district and across the country interpreted Title III of NCLB to be English-only legislation, Dixon-Marquez and Freeman regularly highlighted the passages in Title III that provide implementational space for bilingual education. For example:

[T]he flexibility to implement language instruction educational programs, based on scientifically based research on teaching limited English proficient children, that the agencies believe to be the most effective for teaching English. (Title III, Section 3102.9)

As an observer to this process, Johnson (2007) noted that both Dixon-Marquez and Freeman emphasized the flexibility of Title III and research (especially the Collier & Thomas studies, 1997, 2002) that support dual-language programs. They also emphasized that although schools are only held accountable for English language development and academic achievement in English, Title III does explicitly endorse development of the native language of ELLs (Section 3202.3).

The ideological space that fostered the dual-language programs in the SDP had macrolevel policy support—it was engendered by a Title VII grant and Dixon-Marquez included these programs in her Title III application for which she received funding—but it was perpetuated by collaboration between bilingual educators in the field and downtown administrators. Johnson (in press b) describe this language policy collaboration, generated during the dual-language initiative and carried over to the development of the SDP language policy, as an example of an *egalitarian discourse community* of language policy developers, highlighting (a) how educational researchers, like Freeman, can work with administrators and teachers to develop programs that promote additive bilingualism; (b) how administrators (like Dixon-Marquez) can empower teachers to become active participants in the language policy process; and (c) how such a discourse community can create an ideological space in which additive bilingualism is championed and implementational spaces for developmental bilingual education are developed, even within ostensibly restrictive federal language policies. Although language policy development is never *purely* egalitarian—and indeed, in the SDP, downtown often wields more power than the field—Dixon-Marquez and Freeman distributed policy power by championing teacher expertise and illuminating implementational spaces in NCLB for developmental bilingual education.

The SDP Language Policy

The ideological space sustained by Freeman, Dixon-Marquez, and the discourse community surrounding the dual-language initiative carried over to the genesis of the SDP language policy. In the fall of 2002, the newly appointed chief executive officer of the SDP asked that a language policy be developed and the ESOL/bilingual office led the way who, in turn, recruited Freeman and Johnson to help facilitate the formulation process. We worked closely with Dixon-Marquez and the head of ELL programs in the South Region of the SDP, Maggie Chang, who had also been an integral part of the dual-language initiative. Our goal was to develop a school district language policy that would help build inchoate programs and institutionalize the language education programs already in existence.

The beginnings of this process included a 2-day "language policy retreat" in Chinatown, Philadelphia. Approximately 50 people, representing different levels of institutional authority in the SDP (central, regional, and school-based administrators and teachers) and multilingual communities throughout Philadelphia attended the retreat. The guiding mission statement emphasized bilingualism as a resource:

> The School District of Philadelphia acknowledges that we live in an increasingly multicultural/multilingual global society. The diverse cultures of students are a well-spring of resources. . . . [T]he District firmly believes that administrators, teachers, students, parents, and community partners, working together in an environment of mutual respect, can bring about positive changes necessary to ensure our youth equality of education.

Besides the clear language as resource orientation (Ruiz, 1984) the mission statement provides policy text support for promoting an environment in which community and school district members from all levels of institutional authority have input.

During the retreat, participants were divided into task forces—teams responsible for different pieces of the language policy, including assessment and accountability, bilingual education, heritage language, world language, ESOL, community connections, and special education. Freeman encouraged the different groups to take ownership of *their* part of the policy; she did not *instruct* the groups on what to write—although, if they asked, she was quick with a suggestion—but *encouraged* them to "pick the issues" they felt were most important (Johnson, 2007). Because of the conflict and controversy surrounding bilingual education, before, during, and after the retreat, a brief mention of the overall recommendations from the Bilingual Education Task Force (headed by Maggie Chang) is in order. They write in April 2003: "We prefer that the SDP endorses Dual Language (DL) (One-way DBE and TWI[5]) because research shows that TBE[6] does not promote language parity between ELLs and their English counterparts."

The ideological space fostered during the dual-language initiative was becoming instantiated in the form of an official, district-wide, language policy. However, the development of the policy was somewhat interrupted because, in the fall of 2003, the entire central district administration was reconfigured. Maggie Chang, who had been a regional leader, became officer (now a cabinet-level position) of the ESOL/bilingual office, and she fired all of her original staff. Many of those same staff were rehired, although tensions and mistrust remained. Emily Dixon-Marquez was no longer to be directly involved with bilingual education and soon thereafter left her position. Lucía Sanchez, a former Pennsylvania Department of Education administrator, was hired to be the new director of Bilingual Education and ESOL.

Three Perspectives on SDP Language Policy

Formulation of the language policy document became a highly contested process, with Sanchez taking the lead. The ideological space created by the discourse community that promoted developmental bilingual education and egalitarian language policy development began to disappear in favor of more traditional authoritarian methods. The following excerpts from Johnson's interviews with Dixon-Marquez, Chang, and Sanchez provide three perspectives on language policy interpretation and appropriation and highlight the tension between structure and agency, between the power of policy as discourse and the power of agents to find implementational space in policy text, and between championing many different voices as potential agents in language policy and silencing those voices.

Emily Dixon-Marquez

As mentioned, Emily Dixon-Marquez was a grant writer in the SDP who had worked on both Title VII and Title III grants. She had a long history in the School District as a principal and later as the head of the ESOL/Bilingual Office and was a staunch advocate for bilingual education. She worked closely with Chang, Freeman, and Johnson on earlier versions of the language policy and was integral to its development. She reflects on the history and development of bilingual education in Philadelphia and the interaction between Title III, Pennsylvania policy, and SDP practice:

> [T]he fact that the state of Pennsylvania has no bilingual education law means that anything that's ever been done by this district has been done at the will and the grace of the district—not under the gun—so the policies have been much looser because we're not responding to state regulations . . . it's when you have regulations at the state level that you then have to come up with the policies in a district that meet those (regs)—and we've never had that driving us . . . there's an emphasis on English language acquisition [in NCLB] but it doesn't mean that's all they're going to fund—we haven't changed our programs dramatically—we're pretty much going to do what we've been doing. (April 11, 2003)[7]

Dixon-Marquez interprets Title III text as emphasizing English language education for ELLs but feels the barriers being set, at least in Pennsylvania, do not preclude one-way and two-way developmental programs in Philadelphia schools. Perhaps because she does not feel "under the gun" or because she refuses to bow to ideological shifts in federal language policy text, Dixon-Marquez has not been discouraged from continuing the goal of supporting multilingualism in Philadelphia schools. She argues that neither Title III nor Pennsylvania language policy stand in the way of the SDP developing the programs of their choosing. If anything, NCLB has enlivened her passion. Later in the interview, she argues that Title III distributed *more* money per student to the SDP than under the Bilingual Education Act, and this money can be used to fund developmental bilingual education in the SDP.

Maggie Chang

Maggie Chang is a Chinese American, bilingual in English and Chinese, who wants the same for her children. As mentioned, Maggie Chang was the head of the retreat focus group responsible for the policies on bilingual education. Following the retreat, Johnson conducted an interview with Maggie, then a regional administrator in charge of all ESOL and bilingual programs in southwest Philadelphia (including many Vietnamese, Cambodian, and Chinese students). Chang's office was full of lively plants, Chinese art, and texts promoting linguistic pluralism (a button prominently displayed said, "Down with Unz"[8]). When asked why bilingual education is a good thing, she refers to her children—third-generation

Chinese Americans—and the opportunity that bilingual education represents to develop bilingualism and biliteracy.

In the following, Johnson references the newly titled Office of English Language Acquisition in the U.S. Department of Education, which had previously been the Office of Bilingual Education, and Chang reflects on the space for bilingual education in NCLB:

> *Johnson*: What about, they've changed the name of one of the offices—well the bilingual education act now is title three and it's called English language acquisition whatever—and they seemed to have changed the names of stuff so that when you read through the policy the focus seems to be on English.
>
> *Chang*: Well, you're absolutely right (I can't remember) where I was reading and (?)—the focus was on English and I was trying to find at least a phrase in there that at least addressed the native language of a heritage speaker in terms of (?)—I remember seeing that, you're absolutely right but I don't know that part very well. (November 4, 2003)

Chang's response suggests that though she is cognizant of a potential shift in federal language policy, she is not especially focused on the shift. Buttressed by the ideological space that supported bilingualism through the dual-language initiative, she went about her business, promoting (especially Chinese/English) additive bilingual education without worrying about the implementational spaces for such programs in Title III of NCLB. In other words, for Maggie, local policy discourses that promoted additive multilingualism trumped macropolicy discourses that privileged English.

The interviews with Chang and Dixon-Marquez suggest that the ideological space created and sustained in the dual-language initiative and much of the development of the SDP language policy was resistant to Title III's English-only discourse for two reasons. First, Chang's comments suggest that she was not focused on Title III (at the time) as a driving force in the development of SDP language policy. Second, as Dixon-Marquez' comments show, the downtown administrators who were cognizant of Title III's demands, were not swayed by its English-focused discourse. Dixon-Marquez and Chang both interpret Title III and Pennsylvania policy as completely open to whatever the SDP influenced their development of language policy and bilingual programs in the SDP.

Lucía Sanchez

Lucía Sanchez took the position in the SDP as director of ESOL and bilingual programs in the fall of 2003 after a stint as the ESL/bilingual advisor for the Pennsylvania Department of Education.[9] Johnson's relationship with Sanchez developed out of his work with a project intended to align the various Spanish–English bilingual programs across all grade levels. Freeman and Dixon-Marquez begot this project and Freeman led the first two meetings; however, when Sanchez became director of ESOL and bilingual programs in the SDP, she took over these meetings. Still, she invited Johnson to attend, recruited him as a note taker, and often sought his opinion on the process. Sanchez's ideas about bilingual education—what programs should look like, who they were for, and so on—differ markedly from the additive beliefs among SDP administrators discussed above. In an interview, Sanchez reflects on who bilingual education is for:

> When you talk about bilingual education, in many research-based models, it is uh—considered a way to help children, or assist students who are second language learners, to acquire English—The problem we have seen historically with bilingual education is that—somehow even students who are born . . . in the United States have been placed in bilingual education programs just . . . because, even though they're native speakers of English, they come in with some gaps with their linguistic development due to maybe speaking another language at home or even *hearing* another language at home. (tape recorded interview, June 13, 2005)

What Sanchez calls bilingual education is a programmatic model intended to eventually transition ELLs into mainstream classrooms and is not intended for native English speakers. Some native English speakers may develop "gaps with their linguistic development" perhaps because they are exposed to a second language at home; however, these students are not good candidates for bilingual education. Sanchez's belief about what the research says influences her conceptualization of what bilingual education *is* and who it is for; it does *not* include developmental or additive programs.

Sanchez actively supports transitional bilingual education programs for students whose first language is not English and argues that the research shows that transitional bilingual education is a way to help children acquire English and then transition into the mainstream. These students, later, can opt for heritage language literacy instruction, which she feels will still give them the opportunity to become bilingual and biliterate. Sanchez's interpretation of the "research" accommodates (or vice versa) her interpretation of Title III:

> Title III was created to improve English language acquisition programs by increasing the services or creating situations where the students would be getting supplemental services to move them into English language acquisition situations. (tape recorded interview, June 13, 2005)

Sanchez interprets the goals of "bilingual education" and Title III as the same—eventual transition of ELLs into English-only classrooms. Whereas Freeman and Dixon-Marquez find implementational space for additive bilingual education in Title III, Sanchez sees the policy as restrictively focused on English proficiency. Because of these beliefs, Sanchez began to dissolve some of the ideological space created by Dixon-Marquez and Freeman and sustained by an egalitarian discourse community.

Sanchez's impact is perhaps felt in the final draft of the SDP language policy, which includes the following policy statement:

> The policy of the School District of Philadelphia is to ensure English Language Learners have equitable access to educational opportunities by providing them with high quality, rigorous instruction and appropriate services in accordance with the distinctive linguistic and socio-cultural needs of this group. . . . In addition, they (ELLs) should have access to programs of instruction which help them to maintain and develop proficiency in their home language(s) to the greatest degree possible.

Though this passage certainly leaves open the possibility for different types of bilingual programs, it is not the actively prodevelopmental bilingual education document that was first drafted at the language policy retreat. Indeed, like many policies, this one passed through a mediation process that had the following effects: (a) The new policy only applies to ELLs, thus obfuscating the possibility for two-way immersion programs, and, (b) By appropriating the NCLB phrase, "to the greatest degree possible," the policy does not *commit* to developmental bilingual education programs.

Still, the policy makes no real restrictions on the development of language education programs, and what might be warranted is an analysis of the implementation of this policy; however, the 2004 version of the policy exists as a remnant of a bygone ideological space in the SDP—an interesting document on the SDP website that had no real power. New administration in the SDP led to new language ideologies and language policy beliefs, and it is these beliefs that dominated and continue to dominate the new ideological space in the SDP.

This new ideological space is characterized by the transition of bilingual learners into English-only instruction and a greater division in language policy power between downtown and the field, with Sanchez taking a more authoritative role in appropriating federal and statewide language policies as well as developing internal SDP policy. However, Sanchez's philosophies and methods have met resistance. At a bilingual education teacher meeting at which Sanchez explained the new bilingual program policy in the SDP, one teacher questions the transitional policies:

Teacher: Who or where did the decision make . . . come from to (transition students)?

Sanchez: Because, because, number 1, we looked at all the programs that are effective based on Krashen's research—and the beginning of title three of the no child left behind act, which is long, and there's nothing we can do to change that (tape recorded, January 1, 2005)

Whereas Dixon-Marquez sees "the research" as support for the dual-language initiative and both she and Freeman interpret Title III text as flexible, Sanchez portrays the research, here embodied by Krashen[10] and Title III, as setting rigid standards to which SDP language policy, and the teachers, must adapt. Later in the meeting, Sanchez emphasizes Krashen's role as a *linguist* and a *scientist*. By conferring language policy decisions to Krashen and Title III, Sanchez deflects responsibility for her decision to shift SDP language policy to outside experts and outside language policy, both of which rigidly dictate a transitional bilingual language policy—and "there's nothing they can do to change that." By legitimating Krashen's decision-making ability because of his standing as a linguist and a scientist, the teachers are stripped of their expertise and agency in making language policy decisions—because they are neither linguists nor scientists. Thus, through Sanchez, Title III and the SDP language policy exert their power as policy as discourse; that is, she appropriates these policies to shape what is educationally "feasible" in the SDP.

Conclusion

Though great strides have been made in critical conceptualizations of language policy, less work has been done on how active language policy agents interpret and appropriate macrolevel policy texts. Such critical perspectives of language policy, with which we agree, should be tempered with a focus on local agency. Educators make choices, and though these choices may be constrained by language policies that tend to set boundaries on what is allowed and/or what is considered "normal," the line of power does not flow linearly from the pen of the policy's signer to the choices of the teacher. The negotiation at each institutional level can create the opportunity for reinterpretations and unpredictable policy appropriation.

In order to maintain bilingual education in the United States, both educators and researchers need to recognize their own power and take advantage of the implementational spaces in NCLB and other macrolevel policies. In our study, spaces are worked in the following ways: (a) SDP administrators find flexibility within Title III and Pennsylvania language policy, and, therefore, locate implementational space; (b) policy interpreters and developers in the SDP incorporate educational research to support their interpretations of Title III and Pennsylvania Policy as having implementational space for developmental or transitional bilingual education; and (c) language planning teams work collaboratively to foster an ideological space that champions developmental bilingual education.

Traditional and dichotomizing conceptualizations of top-down and bottom-up policymaking that delimit the various layers through which language policy develops and dichotomize divisions between policy "creation" and "implementation" obfuscate the varied and unpredictable ways that educators, as active language policy agents, interact with the policy process. Analyzing appropriation of language policy conceptualizes policy as a process in which a variety of readings of a policy text engender a variety of interpretations and appropriations, thus taking the focus off of homogenous orientations, ideologies, and goals. Focusing on policy intentions anthropomorphizes an inorganic and potentially ideologically inconsistent document and obscures the variety of interpretations by focusing on singular intentions. Such a focus also suggests that it is *possible* to understand the policy creators' intentions even though this is, in fact, impossible.

A reconceptualization of language policy is needed if researchers really believe in the power of discourse because they, themselves, help to *develop those discourses*. Focusing exclusively on the subjugating power of policy (including NCLB) helps perpetuate the conceptualization of language policy as a necessarily monolithic mechanism for educational hegemony and helps reify these critical conceptualizations as disempowering realities. Though one could argue that academics have had a relative lack of influence on language policy processes in the United States, this could very well change, and if academia is to play any sort of pivotal role, we have to develop theoretical orientations to language policy that emphasize local agency and what Giroux calls radical pedagogy (1983).

This requires a paradigmatic shift both in how we study language policy and how we interact with policy processes. We have proposed that teams of educators and researchers who understand both the local context and the larger body of research can develop language education policies and programs that promote multilingualism, even within the confines of NCLB. A critical examination of NCLB text and discourse reveals a heterogeneous document whose creators disagree on its goals. By working collaboratively, researchers and educators can identify, open, and work those ideological and implementational spaces for multilingual education within and across the multiple levels of institutional authority (see Freeman, 2004). We have also proposed that such a reconceptualization of policy is benefited by the ethnography of language policy as one way to study language policy creation, interpretation, and appropriation across the various layers of language policy development (cf. Hornberger & Johnson, 2007).

Language policy research needs to investigate how local communities engage in democratic policymaking within an *egalitarian discourse community* that maintains developmental bilingual education. Our 10+ combined years of ethnographic work in the School District of Philadelphia has taught us that, though researchers and educators can, together, create ideological spaces that work the implementational spaces in language policy, these spaces are ephemeral and can close. Thus, we need to shift our action-oriented research questions from, "How are policies mechanisms of power?" to "How is power distributed throughout the language policy process?" to "How can bilingual educators take ownership of the policy process?"

Discussion Questions

1   What language policy texts are drawn on in your context?
2   What agents—teachers, principals, administrators, and so on—play a key role in language policy appropriation?
3   How do those agents appropriate those language policy texts?

4   What spaces for promoting multilingualism can you identify in those contexts?
5   How might you work those spaces?
6   How can we assess students' bilingual and biliteracy development over time?
7   What kinds of evidence can we provide to stakeholders of that development?

Notes

1   ESOL = English to Speakers of Other Languages. ESOL programs teach English and do not incorporate native language instruction. Bilingual education programs use two languages for instructional purposes.
2   While the institutional names are real, all quoted research participants are given pseudonyms.
3   This federal department is responsible "for the administration of new formula grants and for providing technical assistance to State and Local educational agencies."
4   Transitional bilingual programs exclusively target English language learners and aim for rapid transition to English instruction and academic achievement in English; the native language (e.g., Spanish) is used to promote content learning in the early years of the program. Developmental bilingual programs also target ELLs, but they aim for additive bilingualism, biliteracy, and academic achievement in two languages (these programs are sometimes called one-way developmental or maintenance bilingual programs). Dual language here is being used as a synonym for two-way immersion programs that target ELLs and English speakers, and aim for additive bilingualism, biliteracy, and academic achievement in two languages.
5   DBE: Developmental bilingual education; TWI: Two-way immersion bilingual education
6   TBE: Transitional bilingual education
7   Transcription notes
     ( )   transcription doubt
     (?)   unclear utterance
     . . .   ellipsis
     [ ]   author comments
     -       short pause
     =   latching
     Italics emphatic stress
8   This is a reference to the anti-bilingual education movement organizer, Ron Unz, who has successfully spearheaded English-only educational policies in California, Arizona, and Massachusetts, but was unsuccessful in Colorado.
9   While in the Pennsylvania Department of Education, Sanchez was responsible for reviewing Title III applications. She reviewed and approved the application submitted by Dixon-Marquez. Therefore, when Sanchez took the position in the SDP, she became responsible for managing Title III monies that she had originally approved.
10   It should be noted that Krashen is an active champion of developmental bilingual education that is not reflected in Sanchez' interpretation of his research (see Krashen, 1996).

References

Bakhtin, M. (1986). *Speech genres and other late essays*. Austin, TX: Texas University Press.
Ball, S. J. (1993). What is policy? Texts, trajectories and toolboxes. *Discourse, 13*(2), 10–17.
Ball, S. J. (2006). *Education policy and social class: The selected works of Stephen J. Ball.* London and New York: Taylor & Francis.
Cloud, N., Genesee, F., & Hamayan, E. (2000). *Dual language education: A handbook for enriched education*. Boston, MA: Heinle & Heinle.

Collier, V., & Thomas, W. P. (1997). *School effectiveness for language minority children.* Washington, DC: National Clearinghouse for Bilingual Education.

Collier, V. P., & Thomas, W. P. (2002). *A national study of school effectiveness for language minority students' long-term academic achievement.* Santa Cruz, CA: Center for Research on Education, Diversity & Excellence (CREDE), University of California at Santa Cruz.

Davis, K. A. (1999). Dynamics of indigenous language maintenance. In T. Huebner & K. A. Davis (Eds.), *Sociopolitical perspectives on language policy and planning in the USA* (pp. 67–97). Amsterdam/Philadelphia, PA: John Benjamins Publishing Company.

Fairclough, N. (1989). *Language and power.* London and New York: Longman.

Fairclough, N. (1995). *Critical discourse analysis: The critical study of language.* London and New York: Longman.

Freeman, R. D. (2004). *Building on community bilingualism.* Philadelphia, PA: Caslon.

Giroux, H. A. (1983). *Theory and resistance in education: A pedagogy for the opposition.* New York: Bergin & Garvey.

Hornberger, N. H. (2002). Multilingual language policies and the continua of biliteracy: An ecological approach. *Language Policy, 1*(1), 27–51.

Hornberger, N. H. (2005). Nichols to NCLB: Local and global perspectives on U.S. language education policy. *Working Papers in Educational Linguistics, 20*(2), 1–17.

Hornberger, N. H., & Johnson, D. C. (2007). Slicing the onion ethnographically: Layers and spaces in multilingual language education policy and practice. *TESOL Quarterly, 41,* 3.

Howard, E. R., & Sugarman, J. (2007). *Realizing the vision of two-way immersion: Fostering effective programs and classrooms.* Washington, DC and McHenry, IL: Center for Applied Linguistics and Delta Systems.

Johnson, D. C. (2004). Language policy discourse and bilingual language planning. *Working Papers in Educational Linguistics, 19,* 73–97.

Johnson, D. C. (2007). *Language policy within and without the School District of Philadelphia.* Unpublished doctoral dissertation, University of Pennsylvania, Philadelphia, PA.

Johnson, D. C. (in press a). The relationship between applied linguistic research and language policy for bilingual education. *Applied Linguistics.*

Johnson, D. C. (in press b). Implementational and ideological spaces in bilingual education language policy. *International Journal of Bilingual Education and Bilingualism.*

Johnson, D. C. (2009). Ethnography of language policy. *Language Policy, 8,* 139–159.

Krashen, S. D. (1996). *Under attack: The case against bilingual education.* Culver City, CA: Language Education Associates.

Levinson, B. A. U., & Sutton, M. (Eds.). (2001). *Policy as practice: Toward a sociocultural analysis of educational policy.* London: Ablex Publishing.

Levinson, B. A. U., Sutton, M., & Winstead, T. (2007). *Education policy as a practice of power: Ethnographic methods, democratic options.* Paper presented at the 28th Annual Ethnography in Education Research Forum, Philadelphia, PA.

Lindholm-Leary, K. J. (2001). *Dual language education.* Bristol, UK: Multilingual Matters.

Menken, K. (2008). *English learners left behind: Standardized testing as language policy.* Clevedon, UK: Multilingual Matters.

Menken, K., & Shohamy, E. (Eds.). (2008, September). No Child Left Behind and U.S. language education policy. *Thematic Issue of Language Policy, 7*(3).

Pennycook, A. (2006). Postmodernism in language policy. In T. Ricento (Ed.), *An introduction to language policy: Theory and method* (pp. 60–76). Malden, MA: Blackwell Publishing.

Ricento, T. (2000). Historical and theoretical perspectives in language policy and planning. *Journal of Sociolinguistics, 4*(2), 196–213.

Ricento, T., & Hornberger, N. H. (1996). Unpeeling the onion: Language planning and policy and the ELT professional. *TESOL Quarterly, 30*(3), 401–427.

Ruiz, R. (1984). Orientations in language planning. *NABE Journal, 8*(2), 15–34.

Skilton-Sylvester, E. (2003). Legal discourse and decisions, teacher policymaking and the multilingual classroom: Constraining and supporting Khmer/English biliteracy in the United States. *International Journal of Bilingual Education and Bilingualism, 6*(3 & 4), 168–184.

Stritikus, T. (2002). *Immigrant children and the politics of English-only.* New York: LFB Scholarly Publishing LLC.

Stritikus, T., & Wiese, A. M. (2006). Reassessing the role of ethnographic methods in education policy research: Implementing bilingual education policy at local levels. *Teachers College Record, 108,* 1106–1131.

Tollefson, J. W. (1991). *Planning language, planning inequality: Language policy in the community.* London: Longman.

Tollefson, J. W. (Ed.). (2002). *Language policies in education: Critical issues.* Mahwah, NJ: Lawrence Erlbaum.

Wiese, A. M., & Garcia, E. E. (2001). The bilingual education act: Language minority students and U.S. federal educational policy. *International Journal of Bilingual Education and Bilingualism, 4,* 229–248.

Wiley, T. G., & Wright, W. E. (2004). Against the undertow: Language-minority education policy and politics in the "age of accountability". *Educational Policy, 18*(2), 142–168.

Wright, W. E. (2005). *Evolution of federal policy and implications of No Child Left Behind for language minority students.* Tempe, AZ: Arizona State University.

Chapter 3

Two-Teacher Classrooms, Personalized Learning and the Inclusion Paradigm in the United Kingdom

What's in it for Learners of EAL?

Angela Creese

Introduction

> In looking at the ways in which power is constructed through language and in interaction, actors can begin to see themselves as agents who have the power to transform practices and not merely as recipients of already decided upon norms. (Hornberger & Skilton-Sylvester, 2000, p. 100)

This quote offers those of us working in educational contexts a positive and proactive view of the way in which we shape our classrooms. It emphasizes the ability of practitioners to change and transform settings. It asks us to think locally and consider how our own practices as teachers and researchers will figure in the lives of the students we work with. The need to research the local social practices of classroom participants in bringing about change is also made by Denos, Toohey, Neilson, and Waterston (2009). They describe how a group of teacher researchers transform their own practices, understandings and workplaces in a 'quest for equity'. In the process of belonging to a Teacher Action Research Group (TARG) they describe finding a new vocabulary to articulate different possibilities for students who are particularly likely to suffer under current education structures. These include students such as those who are English language learners as well as those with special and additional needs. In common with Hornberger and Skilton-Sylvester's quote above, Denos et al.'s research shows how teachers can work against imposed 'slots and categories' which damage the 'vibrant and multifaceted' young people with whom they work (Denos et al., 2009, p. 47). Teachers as agents of change are also dealt with in Skilton-Sylvester's (2002) work on linguistically diverse classrooms. She focuses on the relationship between prevailing ideologies and the agency of teachers. In a carefully crafted and detailed micro-analysis, she reveals the subtler workings of teachers accepting and challenging the legal policies that are handed down to them. Despite a prevailing *language-as-a problem* (Ruiz, 1984) orientation in schools, Skilton-Sylvester (2002) showed how teachers can work towards more equitable educational policies and practices for linguistically diverse students. What emerges from her research is the way different teachers create different classroom policies of their own, depending on their underlying ideologies.

All three pieces of research described here view teachers as policymakers engaged in what Schiffman (1996) has called 'the covert and implicit language policy' of educational practice. These action research and ethnographic studies emphasize the need to research the minutiae of interactional practices in classrooms and understand these in relation to the ideologies that pervade educational language policy. They illustrate how cultural reproduction is framed locally (Erickson, 1990) and make the point that in a macro-ideological order, which is increasingly hostile to multi-lingualism and multi-culturalism (Blackledge, 2005; Rassool, 2008) the documenting of teachers as agents-of-change offers an important alternative discourse. In other words, in describing the local and iterative micro orders of our classroom practices, teachers and researchers can voice different constructions of bilingualism and multilingualism (García, 2005; Hornberger, 2001) while building solidarity, confidence and strength in the process.

This is not to present an overly naïve and innocent view of "bottom-up change" (Ricento & Hornberger, 1996). Education, like other social structures, reproduces inequalities and continues to make available discourses of power to those already most able to take them up. Inequalities are sustained and the same groups of young people continue to fail. Moreover, the policy cake can be cut two ways. Not only is it possible that conservative and illiberal language and educational policy can be usurped by determined teachers in their quest for educational equity in working with linguistically diverse students as the three studies above demonstrate. But it is also possible that progressive and liberal policies are dead-ended by teachers tired of just one more initiative for change. For example, Shohamy (2006, p. 79) has described how teachers can serve as soldiers of the system carrying out orders without questioning policy and the ideologies and agendas behind it.

Language Policy in Education

We can expect some ambiguity from teachers in their discourses and practices around policy and change and a huge variability of views in the ways teachers talk about policy and practice. Ricento (2006, p. 19) argued that we need to acknowledge the mundane everyday practices which shape societal domains, whereas Blommaert points out that language planning is not only about the 'authoritative metadiscourses' preferred in a society (Blommaert, 1999, p. 3). Instead we might consider the study of language policy as the study of discursive activities or as policy into practice (Shohamy, 2006). Corson (1999) has argued that research exploring language policy has largely ignored the school as a site where language planning is actualized within schools practices.

We now know that it's not possible to deliver a strategy or a policy in the public arena in a straightforward way. As Yanow (1996) observed, the relationship between policy and implementation outcome is not necessarily linear and straightforwardly top-down. Ball (1997, p. 270) argued that we need a much more localized understanding of how policy works:

The prevailing, but normally implicit view is that policy is something that is 'done' to people. As first-order recipients 'they' 'implement' policy, as second-order recipients 'they' are advantaged or disadvantaged by it. I take a different view. . . . That is, . . . policies pose problems to their subjects, problems that must be solved in context. Solutions to the problems posed by policy texts will be localised and should be expected to display 'ad hocery' and messiness. Responses indeed must be 'creative'.

Thus, individually and collectively teachers within their school communities will operate policy according to their local contexts, experiences and values, even where there is a strong element of statutory compliance. They will interact with policy not in a one-to-one reading of what is required, but in an interactive frame which involves their own interpretation within their own localized communities (Leung & Creese, 2008).

The ad hoc, uncoordinated, haphazard and often competing nature of language policy creation is also recorded in Menken's research (2008). She shows how language tests become de facto language policies, necessitating individuals "at every level of the educational system" to negotiate unplanned language policymaking (2008, p. 171). Menken describes how the US national policy, the "No Child Left Behind" Act, is funnelled down through the system from the national to the classroom level. She notes that 'Teachers are the final arbiters of policy implementation' (p. 174). She goes on to describe how teachers' ideological orientations drive their practices, making them language policymakers too.

Education and Language Policy for English Language Learners in England

Inclusive education for all has been stressed as a cornerstone in British education policy for school-aged children over many years. The educational policies of inclusion have emerged from a constellation of views that has coalesced into sets of publicly espoused ideological perspectives, policy and professional discourses.[1] As a consistent educational policy since at least the 1980s, inclusion has shaped decisions, values and the practices of classroom life. The inclusion of English as an additional language (EAL) learners into this paradigm is designed to allow them open access to a full and rich curriculum. The inclusion paradigm stands in direct opposition to withdrawal approaches, which are viewed as exclusionary and discriminatory and as offering an impoverished curriculum. Inclusion policies are viewed as progressive, promoting equal opportunities and recognizing individual differences. The government argues that

Educational inclusion is more than a concern about any one group of pupils such as those pupils who have been or are likely to be excluded from school. . . . It pays particular attention to the provision made for and the achievement of *different groups* of pupils within a school. (bold as in the original; OFSTED, 2000, p. 4)

The different groups mentioned in the above quote include EAL students. Other groups include pupils with special educational needs, gifted and talented pupils, and "'looked after' children" (OFSTED, 2004, p. 4). According to policy then, students who need support to learn EAL are entitled to the same and equal opportunities as all children in the mainstream but are also recognized as needing different and specific provisions to raise levels of achievement. The dilemma of how to best cater for difference is summarized by Norwich (1994, p. 296):

> This can be seen as posing a dilemma in education over how difference is taken into account—whether to recognize differences as relevant to individual needs by offering different provision, but that doing so could reinforce unjustified inequalities and is associated with devaluation; or whether to offer a common and valued provision for all but with the risk of not providing what is relevant to individual needs.

This dilemma is faced by teachers working with young people learning EAL who attempt to reconcile both common and individual needs. On the one hand, teachers recognize the common needs of all children in linguistically diverse classrooms through celebrating their multilingualism, and, on the other hand, they recognize that such a celebratory discourse does not address EAL students' individual and specific needs. However, addressing such individual linguistic and cultural needs in the mainstream classroom can result in marginalization (Creese, 2005b).

New Policy Initiatives for Inclusion

Alongside the policy of inclusion, partnerships and collaboration runs a counter discourse—that of educational competition, target setting and school "league tables"[2] in which school performances are published nationally. In other words, the setting of targets and standard descriptors is not particular to the United States alone. In the United Kingdom, too, there is increased central government control, performance targets and pressure for inter-school competition. A national curriculum and national strategies at both primary and secondary levels have been put in place and are driven by transmission models of teaching (Pollard & James, 2004).

In this climate, some groups of children do not thrive. Indeed, the government itself recognizes an over-representation of particular groups of pupils resulting in persistent attainment gaps (Department for Education and Skills; DfES, 2006), and notes:

> It seems clear to us that the education system will not achieve the next 'step change' in raising standards simply by doing more of the same: a new approach is required. (p. 7)

One group viewed as persistently under-attaining are EAL students. A professional forum for teachers working with students of EAL (National Association for

Language Development in the Curriculum; NALDIC, 2008) summarizes the government's attainment figures for 2006–2007, which show that EAL learners do worse than native English speakers at all stages of their education. Moreover, NALDIC reports that "official figures show the number of pupils speaking other languages has increased by a third since the main expansion of the European Union in 2004, from 10.5 per cent to 14.4 per cent this year" (no page). Many of these young people will be learning English as an additional language.

The government's response to addressing these persistent attainment gaps is, in part, the introduction in 2004 of the new initiative, "Personalised Learning" (DfES, 2004). In 2006 these ideas were extended in the government's vision of teaching and learning over the next 20 years:

> Personalising learning means, in practical terms, focusing in a more structured way on each child's learning in order to enhance progress, achievement and participation. All children and young people have the right to receive support and challenge, tailored to their needs, interests and abilities. This demands active commitment from pupils, responsiveness from teachers and engagement from parents. (DfES, 2006, p. 3)

This quote fits with the inclusion paradigm with its stress on common as well as individual needs. We see mention of "all children" having the right to tailored needs, whereas mention is also made of 'each child's' progress. We also see the emphasis placed on learning rather than teaching and on teaching responsiveness rather than curriculum transmission. The government's literature describes personalized learning (PL) as emphasizing the child's needs rather than the curriculum targets and adds that "a child's chances of success" should not be related to "his or her socio-economic background, gender or ethnicity" (DfES, 2006, p. 5). The government links the PL agenda to social justice issues and suggests it as a way forward to addressing issues of disadvantage and lack of success in the education system.

Despite its seemingly progressive social justice agenda, the policy itself makes it clear that "Most categorically, PL is not about a return to 'child-centred education'" (DfES, 2007, no page). Rather, although PL conjures up images of a progressive era and "strikes a chord of harmony with its interlocutors in the professions" (Hartley, 2009, p. 430), it actually has its roots in contemporary consumerism (Hartley, 2007, 2008, 2009). According to Hartley, this new kind of consumerism positions the consumer not as passive, selecting only what is on offer, but views the consumer as active and shaping provision from below. In terms of schooling, parents, pupils and schools are encouraged to be "co-authors" and "co-producers" of the "product" itself (Hartley, 2007, 2008, 2009). We see this reflected in the DfES quote above which demands "active commitment from pupils, responsiveness from teachers and engagement from parents" (DfES, 2006, p. 3). According to Hartley, marketing theory has moved away from mass marketing responses to the meeting of individual needs and the tailoring of specific responses. New "solution spaces" are re-configured, cutting across existing structures and processes (Hartley, 2009). Flexibility, light-footedness and a quick response become the preferred response to meeting needs. We can see this discourse foregrounded in recent government policy statements on personalization.

Using this approach, the curriculum no longer needs to be viewed as a set of compartmentalized subject content to be covered in formal lesson time, but instead an entire planned learning experience for young people, including lessons, events, routines of the school, the extended school day and activities that take place out of school. Schools are using this flexibility in a range of ways (Department for Children, Schools and Families; DCSF, 2008, p. 42).

Hartley's analysis shows the liminality in the personalization policy documents in which a space is created to index two different discourses: one which indexes the softer and seemingly enlightened and progressive period of the 1960s through its use of language such as "dialogue", "collaborative relationships", "strengthening the relationship between learning and teaching", whereas a second discourse indexes the competition and consumerism of the present day through language such as "rigorously", "impact", "rapid response" and "relentless focus".

The recent education policy documents on personalization do not mention language or EAL pupils directly. However, Leung (2007) has pointed out its potential importance. Leung asks for language to be added to the list of backgrounds alongside gender and ethnicity and suggests that PL can be used to address the needs of EAL learners in the mainstream. Leung's argument is that EAL has always been seen as a learning rather than teaching issue because of the nature of supporting bilingual EAL learners across all curriculum subjects. EAL has long been seen as support for learning rather than a subject to be taught—the how rather than the what of the curriculum (Creese 2005b, 2006; Davison, 2006). Leung argues that this places the EAL professional in an advantageous position in terms of experience in student-centred approaches. He suggests that the new vision of PL gives teachers a license to "back off a little bit from the centrally prescribed curriculum" (Leung, 2007, p. 16) to work more with the student experience.

> We ought to say, if EAL is at all personalised in any sense of the word, you've got to conceptualise EAL from the point of view of the *students'* own experience and how *they* experience the English language in the curriculum context. (Leung, 2007, p. 17, italics as in original)

However, alongside the hope expressed by Leung, there is also caution. Pollard and James (2004) speak of the "learner" as under-conceptualized in the PL agenda. They also give the following warning:

> It has been argued that an unintended consequence of recent policies has been to undermine motivation for some pupils, which in turn has caused annual gains in performance to level off. This means that the new concept of Personalised Learning is likely to generate scepticism in some circles. Does it represent genuine new thinking about how teaching and learning can most effectively take place? By drawing attention to the personal, and to learning rather than teaching, it enlists a softer vocabulary than that of targets, performance and delivery. . . . If this issue is left unresolved there is a risk of the DfES being

accused of "spin" by a sceptical teaching profession. (Pollard & James, 2004, p. 24)

In the remaining sections of this chapter, I wish to explore the themes of PL in two-teacher classrooms in which subject curriculum teachers and specialist EAL teachers work together. Interestingly, the PL policy documents mention teacher collaboration explicitly, including drawing on the expertise of "subject specialists to supplement the work of the class teacher" (DfES, 2006, p. 33). The relationship between specialist teachers such as EAL and the curriculum subject teacher is, therefore, very much envisioned in the PL provision. Indeed, teaching partnerships have had long-term policy support as an educational intervention in addressing the needs of young people learning EAL in school classrooms (Department of Education and Science; DES, 1985; OFSTED, 2004).

In what follows, I will present two data sets from two different London secondary schools in which EAL teachers and subject teachers worked together. There are in fact a range of collaborative relationships which subject teachers and EAL teachers form with one another in British schools. I set these out in detail elsewhere (Creese, 2005b). In this chapter I use data from two types of collaboration. The first reflects a collaboration which can be described as "support teaching" in which two teachers work together in the same classroom but with little prior planning. In this type of collaboration teachers usually target different groups of students. The EAL teacher tends to work with students learning EAL, whereas the subject teacher works with the "rest of the class". In this scenario the EAL teacher is often working with small groups on different materials. In support collaborations the EAL teacher rarely takes the whole class and whole-class teaching remains the job of the subject teacher, who provides whole-class plenaries on the subject curriculum. A second type of teacher collaboration is partnership teaching. Here, both the EAL teacher and subject teacher plan before class. Classroom activities explicitly aim to work in language learning and language awareness. In this type of teacher collaboration both teachers work with all students at different times. Clearly there are many permutations of these types of teacher collaboration and the boundaries between support and partnership are not exact. Moreover, teachers work differently with different colleagues. Both research and policy endorse partnerships as the ideal approach to teacher collaboration because teachers working in partnerships keep EAL issues central to school processes and structures. When teachers work only in support mode, EAL becomes marginalized and hidden in the school systems (Creese, 2005b).

In the data below, the first data set illustrates teachers broadly working in support mode, and the second data set illustrates teachers working broadly in partnership mode. In both examples, the teacher collaboration is between non-bilingual EAL teachers and subject curriculum teachers. Although I have researched the difference between bilingual and non-bilingual EAL teachers and their collaboration with subject teachers in mainstream contexts (see Creese, 2004), this is beyond the scope of this chapter.

The first data set looks at two interactions and presents classroom transcripts of two teachers working in the same classroom with separate students as is typical in support mode. The first transcript is the subject teacher working with an individual student learning EAL in a geography classroom. The second transcript is an EAL teacher working with a different EAL student in the same geography classroom. I analyse the two interactions with a view to understanding how we might conceptualize PL in paired teacher–student interaction. The second data set looks at the bigger institutional picture of teachers working together in secondary schools and shows how teachers' specialist expertise positions them differently in the classroom. I use this data to critique the PL agenda, arguing that it must be seen as part of a larger and more powerful discourse, which continues to endorse teaching as transmission.

Personalized Interactions in Two-Teacher Classrooms

The two extracts which follow come from two teachers working in the same geography class in the year prior to students' national GCSE[3] examinations. The EAL teacher has prioritized this class and has been encouraging the geography teacher to work with EAL students. However, despite these good intentions we will see that the two teachers find little opportunity or will to collaborate in the planning for language learning/awareness. The teachers are wearing a small microphone for data-recording purposes and are moving around the class, working with individual students. The class is made up of 50% new-to-English 15-year-old students. This is a rather unusual scenario reflecting heavy migration from mainland Turkey at the time of data collection. Some students in the class are bilingual and do not require EAL support, whereas others are advanced learners of EAL and still others still are monolingual English speakers. The class is ethnically and linguistically diverse. The particular extracts below record two teachers working with two different newly arrived students. Neither of these two teachers speaks Turkish, which is the first language of the students they are working with. This reflects the typical arrangement in English schools where the majority of EAL teachers are not bilingual in a community language of the classroom. In fact, there is a Turkish speaking teacher who works at other times with the same class but not reported on here (Creese, 2005a). The geography topic is *Climate/Seasons* and the students are learning to read and interpret graphs. The data were collected ethnographically (see Creese, 2005b). The data extracts represent typical exchanges between teachers and students in this class. In the extracts that follow the curriculum subject teacher is shown as ST, student(s) as S and the specialist EAL teacher as EALT.

Geography Teacher Working with Student Learning EAL

ST: Join the dots to give a line graph. Join.
S: Yeah.

ST: Join with crosses. That is our line. It is our line graph. OK. Bars. This is a bar. A rectangle is a bar. These are all what we call a bar graph. OK. You done that? Now we have got to look at the climate. Look at this and think. Seasons are winter and summer. Yes? Seasons equals winter, spring, summer, autumn.

S: Weather.

ST: Weather, yes it goes up and down. So it is a season. Winter, summer, spring. We have our winter holidays, summer holidays. In England. In Turkey, it is hot in summer and cold in winter?

S: Yeah.

ST: In the rainforests, it is?

S: Cold in winter.

ST: Is it cold? (Pause) It is hot all the time, isn't it? 26 degrees centigrade is hot, isn't it? We don't need sweaters and it is hot in January, February, March, April, May, June, every month. Every month it is high. 26, 27 it is always high. So we can say there is no seasons. The rainforests don't, do not, do not have seasons. We can write these sentences out. The temperatures, are they hot or are they cold?

S: Hot?

ST: Yeah. So we write this out. Write it on the paper. You can put the title, climate in Brazil. OK? (B5).

Even a brief analysis of this transcript shows the ST asks a limited range of question types and is focused on curriculum transmission through making statements about the topic. The ST asks eight questions.

1   You done that?
2   Yes?
3   It is hot in summer and cold in winter?
4   In the rainforest, it is?
5   Is it cold?
6   It is hot all the time, isn't it?
7   The temperatures, are they hot or are they cold?
8   OK?

All eight questions are display questions in which the teacher is predominantly checking understanding of specific curriculum knowledge. That is, the teacher's questions require the student to display his or her understanding of the topic according to the teacher's agenda. The grammatical construction of the questions includes the following: declarative sentences with rising intonation, tag questions, simple grammatical "BE" questions (e.g., Is [BE] it cold?). All questions are formed so that the student need only give a one-word answer. The total range of possible answers to these questions is the following: yes, no, hot or cold. The geography teacher mostly appears focused on curriculum transmission.

- This is a bar.
- A rectangle is what we call a bar.

- These are what we call a bar graph.
- Seasons are winter and summer.
- Seasons equals winter, spring, summer, autumn.
- Weather, yes it goes up and down. So it's a season. Winter, summer, spring.
- We have our winter holidays, summer holidays. In England. In Turkey, it is hot in summer and cold in winter.
- 26 degrees centigrade is hot, isn't it?
- We don't need sweaters and it is hot in January, February, March, April, May, June, every month.
- Every month it is high.
- So we can say there is no seasons.
- The rainforests don't, do not, do not have seasons.

Also of interest is the use of the imperative to get the bilingual student to act.

- Join the dots to give a line graph. Join.
- Join with crosses.
- Look at this and think.
- Write it on the paper.

Richardson Bruna (2007) argued that the use of the imperative in teacher student interaction can position the student as incompetent. In the interaction above it appears to allow the teacher to give direct commands, which do not require further negotiation. Moje, Ciechanowski, Kramer, Carrillo, and Collazo (2004, as cited in Richardson Bruna 2007, p. 254) called for "school policies to reflect an understanding that learning for non-dominant students is more than just about acquiring content knowledge itself; it is about acquiring the ability to "navigate and negotiate the oral and written texts of multiple Discourse and knowledge communities." It is important that students learning EAL have access to pedagogies that allow them to negotiate meaning in their classroom interactions. The imperative is a command and would appear to shut down such opportunities. The interaction between teacher and student suggests a teaching rather than learning agenda in the sense that the subject teacher feels under pressure to transmit the curriculum rather than work with what the student brings to the context. It provides few negotiation opportunities, teacher responsiveness is minimal and there is little which feels "personalized" about this. In an interview extract the teacher explains the pressure he feels under:

> They [*EAL students*] are just so demanding in terms of time, you either teach them or you don't and if you teach them nobody else gets a look in, or the amount of time they have from me is so minimal that it is not fair on anybody. . . . Yes, I am always conscious that they want more time. . . . On the other hand, you are aware that the lesson is coming to an end in 5 minutes time, you want to do an overall summary for everybody and often it is much quicker to say well, that is the answer, and do it for them. (Geography teacher, Sinchester School)

The interview extract shows the teacher stressing the importance of the whole-class plenary. The need to address "the many" and to offer a summary of subject

knowledge as well as provide answers to save time is a pressure that subject teachers report as common (see Creese, 2005a, 2006, for further discussion). The quote
reveals the teacher's lack of concern with a need to consider language and
language learning/teaching in his geography class.

We now turn to look at an interaction in the same class between an EAL teacher
and a different student. We will see that the teacher focuses on the student's individual needs through attention to the student's language and understanding of
the subject area.

EAL Teacher Working with EAL Student

EALT: What you must do now, you need the book, we look at this. Now can you
          tell me, in summer, let's look at the questions here. The rainforests do or
          don't have seasons as we know them?

S: Don't.

EALT: What is a season, seasons?

S: (laughs as she tries to explain) Spring, summer.

EALT: Yeah, brilliant, great. OK. Temperatures are cool or hot all year round?

S: Hot.

EALT: We are not talking. Of course we are talking of Brazil now, yes?

S: Yes.

EALT: OK. You remember where Brazil is?

S: Hmm.

EALT: Good. Err, there is rain all month. Now what you have to do is, how much
          rain is there every year in England, in London?

S: 80?

EALT: 8, 80, this is?

S: (laughs) 800.

EALT: Thank you. Now what we have got to say is there is 800 millilitres of rain
          in London, how much rain is there in Brazil, do you know? How do you
          find out how much there is?

S: You have to look at the temperature.

EALT: Not temperature.

S: At the rain.

EALT: And what must you do to the rainfall?

S: You have to look.

EALT: What do you think you have to do to see how much there is for the whole
          year? This is how much rain there is in this month.

S: 340.

EALT: And what month is that?

S: January.

EALT: So if you want to find out how much rain there is every month, what do
          you have to do?

S: You have to look at all these number.

EALT: Not look at all these numbers, what is the word that we say.

S: [not clear]
EALT: If you were to take 340, 360, what would you be doing?
S: Oh, times.
EALT: No, not times. What is that number, I mean symbol? It is not times it is?
S: Add.
EALT: So you must add those numbers, OK?

Immediately we can see that the EALT asks many more questions than the ST in the first classroom transcript. The EALT asks 19 questions. Some of these are as follows:

1   What is a season, seasons?
2   How do you find out how much there is?
3   And what must you do to the rainfall?
4   So if you want to find out how much rain there is every month, what do you have to do?
5   What is the word we have to say?
6   If you were to take 340, 360, what would you be doing?
7   What is that number, I mean symbol?

All 19 questions are display questions. However, the grammatical construction of these questions is much more varied than in the ST's extract. The full range of question types is used in this interaction and includes YES/NO questions, WH questions, tag questions and declaratives with rising intonation. Clearly noticeable is how much longer the actual questions are and how much more grammatically complex they are. Also of note is that at least five of the questions are open and require the student to move beyond a one-word answer. In addition there is a greater range of topics covered by the closed questions. Possible answers include yes, no, hot (number), month (mathematical symbol). Unlike the imperatives used by the subject teacher, the teacher of EAL uses more interrogatives. Rather than transmitting facts to the student, the EAL teacher uses his questions to guide the student through the task. His questions are used to check comprehension of the key term "season", to get the student to define a season, to establish that some places have constant temperatures, to check that the student understands the location of Brazil, to check that the student can read a graph/figure, to check knowledge of numbers in English and key mathematical symbols. This is achieved not through the declarative but building the narrative through questions.

In terms of the PL agenda, we might argue that the EAL teacher is responding to the child's individual needs in a more nuanced way. Teacher responsiveness is a key feature of PL, and this interaction seems to provide evidence of this. Indeed comparisons between the two teachers' interaction show different levels of teacher responsiveness (Jarvis & Robinson, 1997; Mercer, 1994, 1995; Mercer & Littleton, 2007) in terms of opportunities to extend and negotiate with students. Jarvis and Robinson suggest a teacher is responsive when "through her minute-by-minute choice of contingent response to what pupils have said, she uses what the pupils say, and builds on it" (Jarvis & Robinson 1997, p. 219).

Another aspect of PL according to government policy is variety of pedagogic approaches:

> Creating a coherent learning environment where children and young people will experience the range of approaches and opportunities that will enable them to increase their competence as self-motivated learners. (DfES, 2007, p. 8)

Indeed, there is a range of pedagogies at play in this two-teacher classroom with evidence of pedagogies of transmission and facilitation used by different teachers. The analysis highlights the importance of pedagogies of facilitation for students of EAL and the importance of time, questioning and negotiation for language and subject learning. We might consider this as one example of personalized learning. However, in the next data set I will show the difficulty of sustaining such an approach within schools that come to view it as remedial despite its educational merits. In the second data set that follows, I explore institutional discourses around EAL through a focus on teacher collaboration and show partnership teachers in an uphill battle to counter the hegemony of transmission pedagogies. I argue that PL cannot operate from anything other than a deficit perspective unless the educational landscape takes a less competitive orientation.

Addressing Individual and Common Needs in Two-Teacher Classrooms

In this section I focus on how teacher collaborations attempt to address the common and collective needs of EAL learners in the classroom and consider how the PL agenda might support this inclusive policy aim. As shown earlier, governments have supported the concept of teaching partnerships to provide an inclusive environment for different groups of students seen at risk of under achieving. In the following extracts, we look at one pair of collaborating teachers who describe their collaboration as in partnership mode. Typically these two teachers work with all students in the class with both participating in whole-class plenary teaching as well as working with pairs, groups and individual students. The first data extract comes from a humanity teacher describing her relationship with the EAL teacher she works with. AC is the interviewer and ST is the subject teacher. The "Susan" and "Miss Smith" referred to in the interview extract is her partner EAL teacher.

AC: Do you, do think that the children see you as equal?
ST: No, no, they do know but there is not a stigma of Susan talking to somebody.
AC: How do they know?
ST: Because they know I am a humanities teacher and they know that Susan is a language support [EAL] teacher so that is how they know. At the beginning we actually put an awful lot of effort with things like, they were coming up to me to get their toilet notes signed and I would say go to Miss Smith and

we made an awful lot of effort in the beginning to make sure that at the end of the lesson we both said you have done very well. We would both "dismiss" [the class], so you know we made a huge effort at the beginning so that they knew, and there was one incident at the beginning where I was on a course and most of the year group were out and there were four kids in so she sat with them and they were playing cards and one of them got a bit naughty and Susan sort of corrected him, tried to control him and he said to her, "you are not my bloody teacher, you know, Miss Potter is my teacher, you're not," and she told me about it and we both went to him and we said to him and you are not coming back into our lesson you know until you have apologized. And he actually did try to come in when Susan was away once and I said no you are not coming in until you do and so we were quite fastidious about doing that sort of thing which I think helped but they do still [see me as different], because I am a humanities teacher. (Interview data)

In this extract, we see how partnership teachers are consciously aware of the need to break down the structures that get built up around "support" and "subject" teaching. These teachers worked at presenting themselves in particular ways in the classroom and attempt to stand against the structural inequalities that have sprung up around support work. We see some of these points enacted in the following observational fieldnotes of the two teachers working together in class:

The ST teacher starts the class with "Now what Miss Smith and I will do is help you." Again the two teachers are using "we". The teachers are doing the same activities. Both teachers are sorting out material for students. Both teachers move around the class and approach all groups easily. They make eye contact a lot. The subject teacher does administration work like writing a slip when a student wishes to leave the class and dealing with visitors to the class. When the subject teacher leaves, there is no difference in the class noise level and the class does not seem to have noticed. When she returns the two teachers spend time at the front answering students' questions. When the bell goes the two teachers are in the front. The subject teacher is doing class-fronted discipline. She is the one that dismisses students individually. (Fieldnotes)

In these fieldnotes we see the teachers using "we" to present their joint approach. Both appear responsible for the materials and work with all students. The humanities teacher appears to be responsible for overall class administration and discipline, but the low noise level stays the same when she leaves the class. However, despite their effort to perform "equality," we will see in the transcript which follows that students interpret their teachers' statuses differently. There are three students and the humanity teacher in the following extract:

S1: Miss, what have you got that for (referring to the tape recorder)?
ST: Because she wants to err . . . record what I am saying and what Miss Smith is saying and then she can play it back and she can see if there is a difference between the two of us.

S1:   There is.

S2:   Yeah I think there should be a difference.

S3:   Miss, you're the better teacher aren't you?

S2:   So we can see it in different ways.

ST: Say what you mean?

S2:   [Not audible]

ST: So you mean it gives you a bit of variety.

S2:   But Miss, teachers might have different ideas about work and like.

ST: Hold on a second. (To the whole class) Er . . ., it's getting far too noisy in here.

S2:   I said like if I don't understand and Miss Smith explains to me and I still don't understand and I call you over and you tell me a different thing, like two different things.

ST: So we see it from two different ways you mean?

S3:   But you're the proper teacher aren't you?

ST: Well, no. We are both proper teachers.

S3:   She's like a help.

ST: No, that's not true.

S3:   That's what it's like because when you are both in, you are like the proper one.

S1:   Yeah.

ST: Yeah, but sometimes Miss Smith takes the lesson doesn't she?

S1:   Yeah, but that's because . . .

ST: When I am not.

S2:   Yeah that's because she is still a proper teacher because Miss Smith takes class as well. She still qualifies as a teacher. (Classroom recording)

In this extract we see the importance that both the subject teacher and the students give to whole-class teaching. "Taking the class" is what makes a real teacher according to the students in the above extract. In this particular collaboration, both the EAL and subject teacher make sure they speak to the whole class from the front of the room. This is typical of the partnership mode of collaboration and less frequent when teachers work in support mode. The importance of the plenary and summarizing subject knowledge is a similar point to that made by the geography teacher in an earlier transcript. Subject knowledge and curriculum transmission is what constitutes a proper teacher. Miss Smith (EALT) might be able to say "it in a different way" but when both teachers are in class and explanations on subject content are needed, Miss Potter (ST) is the proper teacher and Miss Smith is only there to help. In fact both Miss Smith and Miss Potter are qualified teachers with the EAL teacher having seniority over the subject teacher. However, a specialism which works across the curriculum to support learning is not seen as important as one which is tied to a curriculum specialism and the national examinations which test it. A specialism such as EAL which is linked to a particular group of young people with "different" needs is constructed by students as marginal and as having little to do with them. In another partnership pairing, my fieldnotes record the following:

Jeanette (the EAL teacher) tells me that Year 11 Technology erupted yesterday and got out of control. She had been disciplining a student for his involvement in pushing over one of the EAL students—Zeyneb. One of the non-EAL students, Ciğdem, bilingual herself, got involved and challenged Jeanette. "Who do you think you are? You can't tell us what to do. You are only here to teach *them*."

These fieldnotes illustrate how the EAL teacher is viewed as not having the same authority as other teachers in disciplining students. The extract also points to how more English-proficient students engage in positioning less proficient EAL students in an "us" and "them" discourse. The data are reminiscent of Talmy's research (2004, p. 164), which describes "linguicism" at work in "the public teasing and humbling of lower L2 English proficient students by their more proficient classmates". My data too illustrate the "Othering" of EAL students by students and the marginalization of the teachers who work with them (Creese, 2002, 2004, 2005a, 2005b, 2006). The way EAL teachers are marginalized in the mainstream is indicative of the "Othering" of EAL students. Data show that students understood and reproduced the deficit label associated with additional needs. Students, therefore, played their part in constructing EAL students into hierarchies of social and educational failure in the mainstream. As Bartlett (2007, p. 218) reminded us, educational success and failure exist as particular models at particular times in specific contexts and their "persistence depends in part on on-going social practice across chains of events".

Conclusion

In this chapter, I have used two data sets to consider the PL agenda. On the one hand, I have argued it offers promise through its support for facilitative and negotiated pedagogies and focus on individual interests and needs. On the other hand, I have questioned its feasibility, arguing that it is likely to fail in countering more powerful discourses of transmission and competition. In doing so, I have shown some of the potential difficulties associated with PL and partnership teaching. The data show EAL as a category continues to be attached to notions of deficit.

In our schools, diversity is at once celebrated while also qualified in practice as difficult and problematic. Pennycook (2000) reminded us not to view language teaching and learning in decontextualized ways. His view is that classrooms, "both in themselves and in their relationship to the world beyond their walls, are complex social and cultural spaces . . . socio-political spaces that exist in a complex relationship to the world outside" (p. 89).

In this chapter, I have argued that to understand language and education policy, research needs to consider the mundane interactions of classrooms. My particular angle has been to consider the inclusion paradigm and PL in two-teacher classrooms and the opportunities they afford for EAL students.

There is some encouragement to be offered through developments in personalized learning. Data show personalized approaches can offer alternative pedagogic approaches for "different groups". The transcript of the EAL teacher and student interacting showed more opportunities for questioning, extending ideas and time to talk. The teacher was able to offer encouragement to the student beyond the unrelenting focus on the cognitive and transmission aspects of curriculum exchange. However, data also show that PL must exist in a context in which transmission pedagogies and whole-class teaching count for more than facilitative one-to-one teacher–student interactions. Discourses of educational inclusion do not have as much currency as discourses of educational competition. Pedagogies of facilitation do not have the same profile as pedagogies of transmission. Working with students in groups or in pairs is not as powerful as the whole-class plenary. Students, like teachers, are aware of such hierarchies. Their challenge to EAL teachers as not real teachers or "their" teachers show such awareness. Despite their teachers' attempts at implementing inclusion, social justice and equality, students are able to read other messages behind the inclusive rhetoric.

The policy of PL can only be understood in the context that created a need for it. This recent policy initiative has been proposed by the government in a climate that emphasizes performativity and competition. PL has been put in place to deal with the failures of this approach. The introduction of PL is a recognition that the system continues to fail large groups of students. Only a real sea change in education policy offers hope, one which supports a range of pedagogies and sees an emphasis on individual learning as healthy and productive, and one which counters the privileging of whole-class teaching and transmission pedagogies. Otherwise PL is in danger of becoming another policy perpetuating the deficit label attached to "failing groups". As Hartley (2008) argued,

> The current appeal of personalisation may turn partly upon its conceptual vagueness, for there seems to be something for most people to agree with. Nor, importantly, does it offer much to disagree with. . . . For the most part, it is a policy which is ahead of the evidence; a policy which arguably turns more on the values of ministers. (Hartley, 2008, p. 378)

Discussion Questions

1   Concepts such as PL and inclusion can be interpreted in different ways. Identify the ways in which terms such as these have been interpreted in your school in relation to provisions for English language learners.
2   Consider how terms such as inclusion might militate against those they intend to include. What are the local factors which work for and against implementing inclusive approaches in your school?
3   Planning PL depends on an understanding of pedagogy. Policy documents describe creating coherent learning environments through a range of approaches. What is the range of pedagogic approaches used in your school for increasing opportunities for English language learners?

4   Focus on a classroom in which more than one adult works with English language learners. Can you identify differing pedagogic approaches in the different roles the teachers and classroom assistants have? Are there qualitative distinctions in the way different adults interact with young people? Do these provide different opportunities for learning?

Notes

1 Department of Education and Science (DES), 1985; Department for Education and Skills (DfES), 2002; Office for Standards in Education (OFSTED), 2001; Qualifications and Curriculum Authority (QCA), 2000; Teacher Training Agency (TTA), 2000.
2 Every year the Department for Children, Schools and Families publishes information on the achievement and attainment of pupils in all schools. These are known as "league tables". They allow parents to compare how their local school is doing against the national average using National Curriculum tests at different age levels.
3 General Certificate of Secondary Education is the examination which 16-year-olds take in different curriculum subjects at the end of their 11th grade in secondary school in England and Wales.

References

Ball, S. J. (1997). Policy sociology and critical social research: A personal review of recent education policy and policy research. *British Educational Research Journal, 23*(3), 257–274.

Bartlett, L. (2007). Bilingual literacies, social identification, and educational trajectories. *Linguistics and Education, 18,* 215–231.

Blackledge, A. (2005). *Discourse and power in a multilingual world.* Amsterdam: John Benjamins.

Blommaert, J. (1999). The debate is open. In J. Blommaert (Ed.), *Language ideological debates* (pp. 1–38). Berlin: Walter de Gruyter.

Corson, D. (1999). *Language policy in schools.* London: Lawrence Erlbaum.

Creese, A (2002). The discursive construction of power in teacher partnerships: Language and subject specialists in mainstream schools. *TESOL Quarterly, 36*(4), 597–616.

Creese, A. (2004). Bilingual teachers in mainstream secondary school classrooms: Using Turkish for curriculum learning. *International Journal of Bilingual Education and Bilingualism, 7*(2 & 3), 189–203.

Creese, A. (2005a). Is this content-based language teaching? *Linguistics and Education, 16,* 188–204.

Creese, A. (2005b). *Teacher collaboration and talk in multilingual classrooms.* Clevedon, Avon: Multilingual Matters.

Creese, A. (2006). Supporting talk? Partnership teachers in classroom. *International Journal of Bilingual Education and Bilingualism, 9*(4), 434–453.

Davison, C. (2006). Collaboration between ESL and content teachers: How do we know when we are doing it right? *International Journal of Bilingual Education and Bilingualism, 9*(4), 454–475.

Denos, C., Toohey, K., Neilson K., & Waterston, B. (2009). *Collaborative research in multilingual classrooms.* Clevedon, Avon: Multilingual Matters.

Department for Children, Schools and Families (DCSF). (2008). *Personalised learning— A practical guide.* Nottingham, UK: DCSF publications.

Department of Education and Science (DES). (1985). *Education for all: The report of the committee of inquiry into the education of children from ethnic minority groups* (The Swann Report). London: HMSO.

Department for Education and Skills (DfES). (2002). *Key Stage 3 national strategy—Grammar for writing: Supporting pupils learning EAL*. London: Author.

DfES. (2004). *A national conversation about personalised learning*. (Ref. 0919). Nottingham, UK: Author.

DfES. (2006). *2020 Vision: Report of the teaching and learning in 2020 review group*. London: Author.

DfES. (2007). Primary and secondary national strategies: Pedagogy and *personalisation* (London, DfES). Retrieved June, 2008, from http://www.canterbury.ac.uk/education/tf-mentors/themes/SKandPedagogy/documents/NSPamphlet.pdf

Erickson, F. (1990). Qualitative methods. In R. L. Linn & F. Erickson (Eds.), *Research in teaching and learning* (Vol. 2, pp. 77–194). New York: MacMillan Publishing Company.

García, O. (2005). Positioning heritage languages in the United States. *Modern Language Journal, 89*, 601–605.

Hartley, D. (2007). Personalisation: The emerging 'revised' code of education? *Oxford Review of Education, 33*(5), 629–642.

Hartley, D. (2008). Education, markets and the pedagogy of personalisation. *British Journal of Educational Studies, 56*, 365–381.

Hartley, D. (2009). Personalisation: The nostalgic revival of child-centred education. *Journal of Education Policy, 24*(4), July, 423–434.

Hornberger, N. H. (2001). Multilingual literacies, literacy practices, and the continua of biliteracy. In M. Martin-Jones & K. Jones (Eds.), *Multilingual Literacies: Reading and writing in different worlds* (pp. 353–367). Amsterdam: John Benjamins.

Hornberger, N. H., & Skilton-Sylvester, E. (2000). Revisiting the continua of biliteracy: International and critical perspective. *Language and Education, 14*, 96–122.

Jarvis, J., & Robinson, M. (1997). Analysing educational discourse: An exploratory study of teacher response and support to pupils' learning. *Applied Linguistics, 18*(2), 212–228.

Leung, C. (2007). Personalised EAL. *NALDIC Quarterly, 5*, 16–20.

Leung, C., & Creese, A. (2008). Professional issues in working with ethnolinguistic differences: Inclusive policy in practice. In D. E. Murray (Ed.), *Planning change, changing plans: Innovations in second language teaching* (pp. 155–173). Ann Arbor, MI: The University of Michigan Press.

Menken, K. (2008). *English learners left behind*. Clevedon, Avon: Multilingual Matters.

Mercer, N. (1994). Neo-Vygotskian theory and classroom education. In B. Stierer & J. Maybin (Eds.), *Language, literacy and learning in educational practice* (pp. 92–110). Clevedon, Avon: Multilingual Matters/Open University.

Mercer, N. (1995). *The Guided construction of knowledge*. Clevedon, Avon: Multilingual Matters.

Mercer, N., & Littleton K. (2007). *Dialogue and the development of children's thinking: A sociocultural approach*. London: Routledge.

Moje, E. B., Ciechanowski, K. M., Kramer, K., Carrillo, R., & Collazo, T. (2004). Working toward third space in content area literacy: An examination of everyday funds of knowledge and Discourse. *Reading Research Quarterly, 39*(10), 38–70.

National Association for Language Development in the Curriculum (NALDIC). (2008). Retrieved July, 2008, from http://www.NALDIC.org.uk/index.cfm

Norwich, B. (1994). Differentiation: From the perspective of resolving tensions between basic social values and assumptions about individual differences. *Curriculum Studies, 2*(3), 289–308.

OFSTED. (2000). *Evaluating educational inclusion: Guidance for inspectors and schools: Managing the ethnic minority achievement grant: Good practice in secondary schools* (HMI 2172). London: Author.

OFSTED. (2001). *Inspecting English as an additional language: 11–16 with guidance on self-evaluation.* London: Author.

OFSTED. (2004). *Managing the ethnic minority achievement grant: Good practice in primary schools* (HMI 2072). London: Author.

Pollard, A., & James, M. (Eds.). (2004). *Personalised learning: A commentary by the teaching and learning research programme* (TLRP and ESRC). Retrieved June 10, 2008, from www.tlrp.org

Pennycook, A. (2000). The social politics and the cultural politics of language classrooms. In J. K. Hall & W. G. Eggington (Eds.), *The sociopolitics of English language teaching* (pp. 89–103). Buffalo, NY: Multilingual Matters.

Qualifications and Curriculum Authority (QCA). (2000). *A language in common: Assessing English as an additional language.* London: Author.

Rassool, N. (2008). Language policy and education in Britain. In S. May & N. H. Hornberger (Eds.), *Encyclopedia of language and education: Language policy and political issues in education* (2nd ed., Vol. 1, pp. 267–284). New York: Springer Science+Business Media LLC.

Ricento, T. (2006). Language policy: Theory and practice: An introduction. In T. Ricento (Ed.), *An introduction to language policy: Theories and method* (pp. 10–23). Oxford: Blackwell Publishing.

Ricento, T. K., & Hornberger, N. H. (1996). Unpeeling the onion: Language planning and policy and the ELT professional. *TESOL Quarterly, 30*(3), 401–427.

Richardson Bruna, K. (2007). Traveling tags: The informal literacies of Mexican newcomers in and out of the classroom. *Linguistics and Education, 18,* 232–257.

Ruiz, R. (1984). Orientations in language planning. *NABE Journal, 8*(2), 15–34.

Schiffman, H. (1996). *Linguistic culture and linguistic capital.* New York: Routledge.

Shohamy, E. (2006). *Language policy: Hidden agendas and new approaches.* London & New York: Routledge.

Skilton-Sylvester, E. (2002). Should I stay or should I go? Investigating Cambodian women's participation and investment in adult ESL programs. *Adult Education Quarterly, 53*(1), 9–26.

Talmy, S. (2004). Forever FOB: The cultural production of ESL in a High School. *Pragmatics, 14*(2/3), 149–172.

Teacher Training Agency (TTA). (2000). *Raising the attainment of minority ethnic pupils: Guidance and resource materials for providers of initial teacher training.* London: Author.

Yanow, D. (1996). *How does a policy mean? Interpreting policy and organizational actions.* Washington, DC: Georgetown University Press.

Chapter 4

"Tu Sais Bien Parler Maîtresse!"

Negotiating Languages other than French in the Primary Classroom in France

Christine Hélot

Language Policies in France

France is a country well known for its long history of language legislation and for its highly centralized administration and education system. Several researchers have analysed how French has been institutionalized as the common national language (Ager, 1999; Le Nevez, 2006; Sanders, 1996), and how, in the process, minority languages have been vitiated (Grillo, 1989; May, 2001; Williams, 1991). As recently as 1992 an amendment was added to the French constitution stating explicitly yet again that the language of the Republic is French (Journal Officiel, 1992), and in 1994 the Toubon law made the use of French obligatory in five domains: education, employment, the media, commerce and public meetings. More recently again (May 22, 2008), when the Parliament voted almost unanimously for the inclusion of regional languages in the Constitution (France 3.fr., 2008, 10/06),[1] the Académie Française instantly asked (unanimously also) for the withdrawal of this amendment, using the traditional arguments of regional languages posing a threat to the unity of the nation and encouraging the development of '*communautarisme*' (L'Express, 2008, 24/07).

In the more specific domain of educational language policies, I have explained (Hélot, 2007) how despite the influence of European policies promoting multilingualism,[2] more efficient approaches for language learning, and the valuing of linguistic and cultural diversity, 'foreign' language teaching in France remains a major source of dissatisfaction, and European evaluations confirm the poor level of oral skills of a majority of French students (Bonnet & Levasseur, 2004). Yet the general inspector responsible for the teaching of foreign languages (Goullier, 2006) argues that France is a model for Europe as far as valuing linguistic and cultural diversity because a wide choice of languages are offered in the curriculum.[3] However, as I have analysed elsewhere (Hélot & Young, 2005) promoting diversification is not synonymous with valuing diversity; offering many different languages in the curriculum is a good strategy to fight the hegemony of the English language but it does not guarantee that bilingualism or multilingualism is acknowledged or valued or linguistic diversity supported. Since 2000, efforts on the part of the Ministry of Education to improve language education in France have focused mainly on dominant European languages and on developing bilingual education in some regional languages. Despite the strong incentive to use the Common European Framework of Reference for Languages (Council of Europe, 2001a) and the European Language Portfolio (Council of Europe, 2001b), practice in the classroom has remained centred on written skills and based on the native speaker as the ideal model; when students start learning a second language, the teaching approaches are kept separate and language teaching is contained within the space of the classroom. In other words, languages are seen as school disciplines like maths or history and their teaching is not envisaged as a possibility to change language use in the school. Because of a long history of top-down educational policies, it seems unimaginable in France to think in terms of a school developing a holistic approach to language policies as proposed for example by the European project *Ensemble* (Camillieri Grima, 2007; Young & Hélot, 2007).

Furthermore, as I have explained before (Hélot, 2003, 2007), the categorization of languages into denominations such as *foreign*, *regional* and *languages of origin* has created a hierarchy which keeps the minority languages spoken by people of immigrant background very much in limbo. Other researchers (Zirotti, 2006) have pointed out the lack of political will to address the issue of immigration languages and have shown how bilingualism acquired in the home context is ignored by policymakers and stigmatized by many teachers. I have tried to analyse the paradox of policies that put so much effort into making future citizens better speakers of second languages and at the same time ignore the rich linguistic and cultural competence of many bilingual pupils (Hélot, 2006; Hélot, Hoffmann, Scheidhauer, & Young, 2006; Hélot & Young, 2002). It is somewhat ironical that some bilingual pupils become monolingual through schooling and are later expected to become bilingual again but in a language other than their own.

One should also add that marginalization does not affect only immigration languages. The language varieties used nowadays by young French people in their everyday life are also stigmatized and seen as a threat to the supposed purity of the written standard. Two very successful films illustrate this point: *L'Esquive* (2004) and the recent winner at the Cannes film festival *Entre les murs* (2008). Both films portray the growing gap between the language of the street and the language of the school. In a sense, both films show that dedicated teachers of French can make their inarticulate students aware of the beauty of the French language. But they also give a stereotypical image of youth language and reinforce the idea that the classical standard written variety is the only legitimate form of speech. Though this situation tends to be seen by politicians and the larger public as a major educational problem, what the two films uncover in my opinion is the power of ideologies in framing beliefs about language, in ways of conceptualizing language and of understanding the complex relationship between language, identity and power.

Clearly, there is a reluctance to move away from ideological positions entrenched in the belief that the one-language/one-nation model is the only viable one for a country like France and French schools have remained bastions of linguistic norms, of beliefs in the universal value of the French language and culture, and of prejudice against any non-standard variety. Nowhere more than in the education system have such ideologies been so pervasive and particularly difficult to debunk. As explained by Le Nevez (2006, p. 75), the language ideology that informs language policy in France and popular opinion on the role and status of French in society can broadly be described, following Pennycook (2004), as foundationalist 'because of the way in which they reproduce beliefs about the systematicity, normativity and prior ontological status of languages as discrete, reified, pre-formed objects'. Le Nevez (2006, p. 67) identified six significant features of foundationalist ideology[4] and his analysis clearly helps to understand why it is so difficult to shift the monolingual habitus of French schools and to make teachers aware of their attitudes and representations not only towards the French language, but also towards language learning and teaching and towards diversity, be it linguistic, cultural, ethnic, religious etc.

Though recent work on language ideologies (Blommaert, 2006; Jaffe, 1999; Watts, 1999) and poststructuralist research[5] propose different approaches to the framing and contextualization of linguistic diversity, the question remains of how to 'translate' this body of knowledge for teacher education. How can one make teachers aware of the fact that seeing languages as 'finite, stable, standardised, rule governed instruments of communication' (Ricento, 2006, p. 14) is a constructed belief, that thinking that monolingualism is normal also reflects a conceptualization of language being linked to one people and one territory which was constructed politically. In other words, how can one make teachers aware of the power of ideologies because as expressed by García, Skutnabb-Kangas and Torres-Guzmán (2006, p. 37):

> Attitudes values and beliefs about language are always ideological and involved in systems of domination and subordination of different groups. Schools are, in their work of teaching the standard national languages, responsible for one of the most prevalent linguistic ideologies—constructing a unidirectional link between language and ethnicity. And so, language ideologies are responsible for the closing of spaces for multilingual practices in schools.

The Context of the Study

This chapter focuses on two French student teachers, MGR and DB,[6] working in a pre-primary school 1 day a week as part of their teaching placements. It should be made clear here that in France pre-primary education is widespread for children aged from 3 to 6 and takes place in '*école maternelle*'; as its name indicates, *école maternelle* works very much like a school and cannot be compared to a playgroup or a kindergarten. The national curriculum (Ministère de l'Éducation Nationale (Ministry of National Education) [MEN], 2008) sets very clear teaching and learning objectives from the beginning of schooling and the Ministry of Education encourages parents to school their children as early as possible. This education is free in public schools, and, in 2006/2007, 23.4% of children aged 2 to

3 attended pre-primary school, the percentage becoming 100% for children aged 3 to 4 (RERS, 2007).

Pre-primary teachers are educated together with primary teachers in university institutes of education called IUFM[7] where they are taught a common curriculum for all levels. At the time of study, the two trainee teachers concerned had completed a first university degree and had successfully passed a very competitive state exam called a 'concours'. They were attending an obligatory, professional, 1-year course at the IUFM and at the end of that year were confirmed as certified teachers. As part of their final certification they were required to write up a short research project related to their pedagogical experience during their weekly placement.

Because a major part of their studies is very academic in nature[8] and their initial professional education so short, so crammed and so weighed down by constant evaluations and because, on the whole, student teachers are learning their profession on the job during their teaching placements, some researchers have argued for the development of an approach on the basis of reflective practice (Perrenoud, 2001). The approach chosen at IUFM of Alsace requires asking trainees to reflect in writing on one or two pedagogical questions they would like to investigate, in relation to their practice during their 1-day-a-week placement in a school.

As a professor of English at IUFM, one of my responsibilities is to supervise several student teachers for their writing project. This supervision is linked to several visits in schools with feedback discussions, and I have always considered this structure as one of the spaces where it is possible to adopt a more critical approach to teacher education and to encourage students to understand the value of research. Because at the time of study trainees were allocated a tutor on a random basis, I was MGR's referent tutor and had a lot of opportunities to discuss her work with her, but in the case of DB, he was assigned another tutor. I agreed, however, to meet him on several occasions and to answer his questions relating to bilingualism (orally and through e-mail).

Although the format of supervision of research projects is set out clearly in the curriculum, obviously the process can vary according to different supervisor's research interests. Therefore, the purpose of this study is not to compare the two students' research projects but rather to analyse how they each reflected on their teaching practice in relation to very young pupils who started school without any knowledge of the school language (French). The analysis is made on the basis of a series of interviews carried out by myself during the year 2007–2008, and on their respective research projects, which dealt in both cases with the pedagogical strategies necessary to implement with very young emergent bilinguals.

The learning situation for both these student teachers during their 1-day-a-week placement was constrained by many factors: although they had very little pedagogical experience aside from having observed experienced teachers for one week, like their peers, they were on their own in charge of a class of almost 30 children from 8 a.m. till 4 p.m., and from the very beginning of the year. Another constraint came from the fact that this system has been devised to give a free day to head teachers who have administrative duties; thus, the student teachers were replacing an experienced teacher, had to comply with a set time table and with their teaching approaches expected to be not too different from those of the regular teacher. Moreover, they had to implement the very ambitious objectives set out in the national curriculum in view of their evaluation on which their final qualification also depended. These constraints meant that the spaces for innovation, for creativity and the development of an alternative approach to teaching and learning were rather limited. However, most trainees say they like being in a classroom and feel that it is where they are learning their future profession most efficiently.

The main reason for this lies in the content of the curriculum they must follow and the format through which it tends to be delivered. Apart from their 1-day-a-week placement, student teachers attend 3-hour courses at IUFM from 9 a.m. to 5 p.m. every day, leaving them very little time for reading or research. On the whole, these courses deal with the didactics of the school subjects they have to teach (French, mathematics, social sciences, science, technology, arts, music, PE and a foreign language). The approach favoured by most teacher educators tends to focus on the didactics of each school subject and very little cross-disciplinary work is proposed apart from the insistence on the French language. A 24-hour course on the didactics of a 'foreign' language is also obligatory and students in Alsace only have a choice between English and German. Again, considering the wider issues of language education, using an ecological approach to all the languages taught in a school and spoken by pupils is not easy because of its rather disciplinary nature. However, during the year 2006–2007, with another colleague professor of English at IUFM of Alsace,[9] we managed to offer a 6-hour course on linguistic and cultural diversity, which dealt with bilingualism and the support of second language acquisition in school.

Finally, before describing the research, the socio-linguistic landscape of the region in which it took place should be briefly sketched. As a border region with Germany, Alsace has had a long and troubled history: it was part of Germany between 1870 and 1918 and was annexed again during the Second World War. Now a French region, Alsace can be said to be part of a Germanic sphere of influence because of its linguistic and cultural heritage. This is clearly visible in the use of Alsatian, the local language, spoken by a small minority of older people living mostly in rural areas. Alsatian is one of the many varieties of standard German and is part of the identity of the region even if fewer and fewer people speak it. As distinct from HochDeutsch, Alsatian has been recognized as one of the regional languages of France in the same way as Breton, Catalan, Corsican and others (Cerquiglini, 2003). However, as I have explained elsewhere (Hélot, 2007), the notion of 'regional' language in Alsace is ambiguous, because in 1982 local educational authorities decided that standard German and not Alsatian should be the language taught in schools (Huck, 1999). This has meant that as distinct from the rest of France, German is taught as a second language in most primary schools in Alsace (from age 7) and is the only language which can be offered in bilingual education provision in the region.

Furthermore, Alsace has always been the site of much language contact and, as the seat of several European institutions, Strasbourg, its main city, has become very cosmopolitan. The city also counts a high level of immigrants (12.9%, Institut National de la statistique et des études économiques: National Institute for Statistics and Economic Research [INSEE], 2001[10]) who come mainly from North Africa (25%), Turkey (13%) and Germany (10%). More recently, most migrants to Alsace came from Turkey, Morocco and Germany. Thus, it is not surprising to find in most classrooms throughout the city and its surroundings pupils who speak many languages other than French. It is not uncommon either for German parents who live in France or near the border to school their children in France in the hope that they will become bilingual.

The Research

This research is part of a wider project looking at ways of including intercultural education and the issue of linguistic and cultural diversity in the curriculum for initial teacher education at primary level (Hélot & Benert, 2006; Hélot et al., 2006; Hélot, 2009). I am particularly concerned with developing a culture of plurilingualism and pluriculturalism among future primary teachers and in addressing issues of discrimination and institutional racism, which tend to remain marginalized in a curriculum based on content knowledge. Former publications have analysed educational language policies (Hélot, 2003; Hélot & Young, 2006) and the ideology of bilingual education in France (Hélot, 2007, 2008). Analysis of a 3-year school project using the language awareness approach has shown how teachers working collaboratively with parents can transform their monolingual classrooms into a multilingual and multicultural space where bilingual children who speak minority languages can find their own voice (Hélot & Young, 2003, 2006; Young & Hélot 2003, 2007). Ongoing work on children's literature and multilingual authors with student teachers involved in a bilingual programme (French/German) investigates further the monolingual ideology prevalent in bilingual education and analyses the relationship between language mixing, translation, languaging (García, 2009) and identity (Benert & Hélot, 2008, 2009).

Here I propose to analyse the way the two student teachers have recreated their own language policies in their classrooms during the year 2007–2008 at the very beginning of their teaching experience. My analysis is based on their description of the way they negotiated the use of French and of the first language of their pupils, that is, on their analysis of their choice of language strategies with very young pupils entering school. It should be made clear at the outset that these two student teachers were not aware of the notion of language policies, but they both knew of the clear agenda in the national curriculum to start teaching a foreign language from age 7 and that, as explained above, there is no choice in Alsace but to choose German. Both saw the priority given to the French language as 'normal' and part of their main teaching objectives, along with building some early competence for the acquisition of numeracy. Both were confronted with multilingualism in their classroom by the presence of pupils who spoke languages other than

French and both had a personal experience of bilingualism and language learning. The formal teaching input they received on these issues during the year was minimal, a 3-hour module in the case of DB, on how to include the notion of linguistic diversity in the teaching of French, and in the case of MGR, some input on the didactics of German as a foreign language.

Student teacher MGR was female and French, a good linguist who spoke Alsatian, fluent German and had a good command of English. She writes in her essay that she is passionate about foreign languages; thus, she chose to participate in the student exchange programme organized between IUFM Alsace and the University of Southampton (United Kingdom). She explains, 'This destination interested me specifically because of the importance of immigration in that country' (MGR, 2008, p. 12). During her 3 weeks teaching in a primary school in Southampton, she explored the various policy documents and pedagogical strategies used to support second language learners and she noticed that teachers in the United Kingdom spend a lot of time teaching about different cultures and encourage pupils to speak about their family and home cultures.

She spent every Monday in a pre-primary school in a village in the vicinity of Strasbourg. Her class consisted of 25 children aged between 2 and 3. She had a teaching assistant (untrained) for part of the morning when the children were regrouped for more formal learning sessions. Two young boys not yet 3 years old were the subject of her essay, neither having a word of French on starting their schooling. There was a German boy whose parents had just moved to Alsace and who spoke only German, and the second boy had a Thai mother and an Alsatian father who spoke English together.

Student teacher DB was male, of dual nationality (Turkish and French), bilingual and a rare example of what one would consider a success story in the French education system. Very few student teachers come from ethnic minority background, even fewer from the Turkish community. DB shared with me on several occasions his personal experiences of discrimination both at primary and secondary school. As a young Turkish boy whose mother wore a hijab and did not speak a word of French, DB felt torn between his home values and school where he sensed the negative attitudes of some of his teachers towards the fact that he spoke Turkish at home. Before deciding to become a teacher, DB had held an administrative post and he was the president of the Turkish association in his hometown in Alsace. He had inside knowledge of the Turkish community in Alsace, of their very precarious living conditions previous to immigration and an understanding of their attitudes towards education and the learning of French. Paradoxically, this type of knowledge is not specifically valued for teacher education, when it is precisely the very lack of such information about immigrant communities that prevents teachers from being sensitive to the needs of their pupils. In 2003, DB founded a new Franco-Turkish association for young Turkish people born in France and having difficulties negotiating their two cultures.[11] He still works as a school mediator and translator for the schools in his hometown.

Every Monday, DB was in charge of a pre-school class of 23 children aged 3 to 5 in a school in the vicinity of Strasbourg. This school was part of a number of schools in Alsace that offer bilingual education in German and French. DB's class, however, was not a bilingual class, which means that the pupils' parents did not make the choice of bilingual education for their children. DB decided to write his essay about two Turkish-speaking pupils, one girl aged 3 in his class whose parents did not speak French, and another girl aged 7 in a colleague's classroom. This older pupil was repeating first grade and neither of the two girls spoke nor participated in any activities in class. Her teacher and the pedagogical team had been unsuccessful in making contact with the girl's parents.

DB also participated in an international programme organized by the IUFM of Alsace. He spent a week in a prestigious French school in Turkey attended by Turkish-speaking and French-speaking children residing in Ankara. DB was keen to find out about the strategies used by the French teachers in Ankara to develop the oral skills of the Turkish-speaking children in their second language.

Both student teachers had a similar problematic for their reflective piece of writing, that is, how could they help their very young bilingual[12] pupils to participate in school activities and to start 'appropriating knowledge and competences in order to successfully acquire the basic skills required in their first year of elementary education' (MEN, 2008, p. 12). Their questioning was directly linked to the curriculum which insists that even at this very young age children should be placed in learning situations and stresses the importance of the acquisition of the French language: 'the essential objective of pre-primary schooling is the acquisition of a rich and structured oral language, comprehensible to others' (MEN, 2008, p. 12). Though DB was more focused on this point and the need to develop the school language with children speaking Turkish at home, MGR framed her reflection within the notions of plurilingualism and interculturalism. Influenced by her theoretical readings (Kramsch, 2002), she had a more socio-cultural approach and stressed the notion of socialization. In other words, she was well aware that the schooling of children at age 2 poses specific problems for all children irrespective of their home language.

This said, both student teachers were very sensitive to the special needs of their non-French-speaking pupils (as they saw them) and their linguistic as well as affective needs. They both saw the relationship with parents as central to the pupils' integration. Both reported a marked difference in the behaviour of their pupils after they had taken the time to talk to their parents. Both were keen to offer parents some support in relation to their understanding of the French school system. In other words, both these beginner teachers showed a great sense of responsibility as well as a highly ethical approach to their pupils and their parents. What they lacked and had to learn on the job was the pedagogical knowledge relating to second language acquisition by young learners, and the theoretical knowledge about bilingualism and language education in general.

Negotiating Different Languages in the Classroom

Although the two student teachers were faced with a language situation for which they were not prepared, they felt obliged to break the rule of using only French in their classroom. It should be said that the longstanding policy of using French and only French in the classroom is not inscribed into strict rules sent to schools; it is no longer necessary because such a rule has become part of the collective unconscious. This is why MGR and DB had not planned at first to use languages other than French. On their first Monday in class, when they discovered that some of the children did not know French, they both assumed that these pupils being immersed in the school language would acquire French more or less automatically. The myth of learning a second language through being immersed in that language still prevails in France, in particular where early learners are concerned, and this is reinforced by the National Programmes for Pre-school (MEN, 2007, p. 88): 'With very young children, it is not necessary to provide specific teaching in French as a second language. The communicative situations linked to life in the classroom are in most cases quite sufficient as long as they happen in a context where plurilingualism is not denigrated and the child is called upon to express himself.' The inherent contradiction of such a statement always has to be pointed out to student teachers. Young children who do not speak the school language cannot express themselves even if called upon because they do not have the linguistic means to understand what is wanted of them, and even less to speak back. The silencing of bilingual pupils in normative monolingual classrooms is a well-known fact, and both trainees did notice it and were concerned enough to do something about it.

This is how DB (2008, p. 4) describes the moment he decided to use Turkish with his pupil LH:

> I began to explain to group after group the work to be done and I asked one child in each group to repeat the instructions. Once the children were settled, I checked that all was going well and I moved to the group where LH was sitting in order to observe her. Having understood nothing neither the work to be done nor the instructions, I asked another pupil to repeat the instructions for her. He did, then two other children repeated them again, but LH still did not understand. In this precise case the non-mastery of French is beginning to cause problems in terms of comprehension and of participation in learning activities. It is difficult to ask a pupil to do schoolwork if she does not have any knowledge of the French language. Therefore it is normal for the teacher to find strategies for the child to understand. Perhaps the child can make a special effort to understand if the teacher stays close by and gives her personal support, but it is not easy for the teacher who also has to look after all the other pupils. And then LH is at a loss, and she is excluded from her group and sometimes her friends make remarks because she does not understand, and she gets even angrier. At that moment, being bilingual myself, I decided to intervene and to use Turkish, since I shared this language with the pupil. I wanted to know whether she was capable of doing her schoolwork if I gave her the instructions in Turkish.[13]

I shall not analyse this testimony in detail but I would like to make several points: first, DB believes that repetition or rephrasing will eventually lead to understanding, which might eventually work with a young first language (L1) speaker but not with a second language (L2) learner. Second, he feels he has to justify himself for using his native language with his pupil, when to an outsider it would seem the most normal thing to do, particularly in this case when DB not only shares a language but also a common experience with this little girl. When I asked him why he did not use Turkish with her from the outset, my question took him by surprise. He had not been aware he had internalized a covert policy forbidding the use of the home language. The last sentence of the quote also reveals his doubt towards the child's capabilities, as if he needed to have some tangible proof that language is the barrier to her understanding and not some other reason.

I think DB's position towards Turkish in his professional space is an example of how the French education system reproduces a monolingual ideology. DB is married and has a child, and his home language is Turkish. As a primary teacher in France, he functions like a monolingual French teacher and only when asked specifically to help Turkish-speaking children will he use his bilingual bicultural skills. In the case of the second pupil he analysed in his essay, the 7-year-old-child was in serious danger of what is referred to in France as 'échec scolaire'. Repeating the first year of schooling is only imposed on children supposed to perform very poorly and whose parents are not vocal enough to prevent it. It has been shown to have disastrous consequences for the subsequent schooling of pupils, but many teachers still believe in this practice.

DB's encounter with the parents through Turkish made a meeting possible between them, and the regular teacher, and helped the teacher to understand the pupil's silence in class, which totally transformed the situation. The little girl started speaking in French at school, although in a very low voice, but it was enough of an event for all the other pupils to rush to DB in the schoolyard and inform him. DB's mediating skills were recognized by the teacher who then made some efforts at giving extra exercises for the child to do at home with her parents, although these were exercises in French and no special support in her home language was offered. In other words, the very valuable Turkish-speaking skills DB brought to the school were treated as a one-off resource and nothing changed as far as helping bilingual children maintain their home language.

Far from blaming DB here, I would like to stress the importance of making young teachers aware of the importance of maintenance and support of the home language(s) of bilingual pupils. To this effect the TESSLA[14] project and website were developed (Hancock, Hermeling, Landon, & Young, 2006) by IUFM Alsace and the University of Edinburg in Scotland. And because all minority-language-speaking pupils cannot avail of specialized classes in their L1,[15] having a bilingual teacher in the school could make all the difference for many pupils who struggle with their acquisition of the school language. But again, it is not enough to have one bilingual teacher in a school to change attitudes towards minority languages. The whole school team needs to be informed about bilingual language acquisition and, more importantly, needs to go beyond their prejudice towards immigration languages and the beliefs that using the first language will harm the acquisition of the school language.

DB himself is the very example that it is possible to succeed in the French education system, while growing up speaking two languages, one of them Turkish. But it is difficult for him to feel legitimate when he uses Turkish in the classroom because he does not yet have the necessary understanding of the workings of language ideologies, while he has real experience of language discrimination. Even if his knowledge of Turkish was a definite asset and he really did transform the learning situation of two pupils, it did not empower him to change the attitudes of his colleagues towards bilingualism. He remained as someone who solved a 'problem', he modelled a successful mediation with Turkish parents, but he was powerless to change the school policy towards a minority language spoken by an immigrant community.

The situation of MGR is totally different. The languages she used in her class, German and Alsatian, are spoken by many people both in the community and on the other side of the border a few kilometres away. As explained above, Alsatian is not taught in schools and is felt to be a low-prestige variety, but German is highly regarded and strongly supported in education from very early on. Thus, even though her pupils are younger than the required age for learning German (age 7), proposing activities in this language is considered legitimate by the school authorities and favourably looked upon by most parents.

However, it should be made clear here that the use of German was brought upon by the presence of a German-speaking pupil in the class. MGR did not teach a specific class of German as a foreign language during a specific slot 1 hour a week; she used German as an authentic medium of communication and included the language in everyday activities like greetings and story telling.[16] Thus German had a real space and function in her class. With her Thai-speaking pupil the situation was more difficult because she did not have any language she could share with him. Like DB, she looked for strategies for her pupils to feel included, focussing on the affective dimension in learning[17] and on developing comprehension skills. She wrote: 'I did not want this difference of language to become a difficulty for them, at the very moment they discover what it is like to be at school' (MGR, 2008, p. 18).

Like DB she approached the parents and even made the effort to learn a few words of Thai from her pupil's mother so that she could include the Thai language in the multilingual greetings she used every morning. She also designed two special vocabulary booklets[18] with pictures and the corresponding words in French for the parents to help their children learn classroom language. She clearly saw bilingualism as an asset—she quotes some of the work of Cummins (2001)—and advised the Thai mother to keep speaking her language with her child, despite the contradictory advice of the Alsatian grandmother. In fact, what she did was to create a multilingual space, where the home languages of two pupils entered the space of the classroom and became part of the linguistic experience of all the pupils. She explained in her conclusion that 'whereas this linguistic difference could have been a hindrance to the socialisation of the children, I have the impression it has helped to build it faster. Now the children themselves teach me beautiful lessons about learning to live together. Now some

of them ask me spontaneously how to say this or that in T's language (German)'
(MGR, 2008, p. 21).

This last point shows that from a very young age and even in a schooling situation, children are aware of linguistic differences and curious about language and languages. As reported by both student teachers, their pupils asked a lot of questions once it had been explained that some children in the class did not know French, and they changed attitudes towards their peers, becoming more open and tolerant. They were also very impressed by their teachers using different languages in class, and hence the remark quoted in the title by a little girl in MGR's class when she heard her switching to German to explain something the German pupil had not understood: 'Teacher, you can speak so well!,' the 3-year-old exclaimed spontaneously her eyes full of admiration. As to DB, he relates how the story of his using Turkish in his class went round the school and how at break time in the playground several Muslim boys would gather around wanting to befriend him.

These two case studies argue for the importance of developing language awareness activities from the start of schooling and even with very young learners. Many researchers have shown that addressing questions relating to language use and to the multiplicity of language systems through pedagogical activities enable children to make sense of their linguistic environment (Candelier, 2003; Hélot & Young, 2003, 2006; Moore, 1995; Perregaux, 1998). As I have analysed elsewhere, such an approach also prevents pupils from being confined into one language only, as happens within the early foreign-language-learning model, which tends to always favour English at the expense of other languages. Furthermore, the language awareness model can help to transform the monolingual classroom into a multilingual space where all the languages in the class—as well as the school language—are explored, shared and given a chance to thrive. Both DB and MGR described in their essays how their (emergent) bilingual pupils found their voice once they felt reassured their teacher shared their language and once they had seen their teacher addressing their parents in their home language.

The case of the Thai pupil is interesting from the point of view of language choice and to a certain extent of language policy. MGR explained:

> M's parents have decided to choose French as the first language for their little boy as his mother is also learning French. I advised them all the same not to abandon Thai. The school will look after the development of his competence in French, but it won't be able to do anything for his competence in Thai, a language which is part of his family history. Thus I wanted to give a place in class to the language of this little boy's mother. So I started to ask his mother to translate a few simple words for me, which could find their place in the everyday life of the class: thank you, hello, enjoy your meal etc., and surprise, she brought me a small conversation guide in Thai! Then she taught me the pronunciation (difficult!) of these few words, in front of the admiring look of several children, M. included. (MGR, 2008, p. 14)

It is not surprising that M's family have decided that French should be the first language of their child even though his mother's French is limited and she has always spoken Thai with her son. M lives in a plurilingual family: he hears English at home when his parents speak together and Alsatian at his grandparents'. MGR felt from her discussions with M's mother and grandmother that the grandmother presided over her Thai daughter-in-law and was intent on her grandchild learning French. It was also important for her to tell the school authorities his first language would be French! The main reasons for this could be fear of school failure lest the child's French was not up to a supposed standard and a wish to reassure the teacher that the family was aware of the importance of the school language.

Interestingly, our young student teacher departed from a long tradition in the French teaching profession of advising bi-or multi-lingual parents not to use their first language with their children and to concentrate on the acquisition of French. Relying on the theoretical readings I had given her and my supervision of her work, she felt confident enough to give advice on retaining the use of the mother's language, Thai, at home. What should be stressed here is that she backed her advice by using Thai with her whole class, thus giving more legitimacy to this language. She was also very clear about the fact that it is sufficient to acquire French in the school context and that it would be a great loss for the child to lose a language that was part of his heritage.

On the level of policy, she can be said to have transformed the monolingual habitus of the school and to have offered new possibilities for the multilingual classroom. She showed that she was comfortable with languages other than French, those she knew, and more importantly, those she did not know, for example, Thai. She gave support to bilingual pupils and their parents, and she even designed pedagogical activities to educate her monolingual pupils to understand linguistic and cultural diversity. She was clearly acting as a change agent for her class and for her school because she showed her experienced colleagues it was possible to see bilingualism as an asset rather than as a problem. Despite being a beginner teacher, her academic qualifications and her scientific knowledge gave her a certain legitimacy, which was further backed by my position as tutor and university researcher.

DB's position within his school was far more difficult than MGR's because of the low status of the Turkish language and because of prevailing negative attitudes of teachers towards the Turkish community, related specifically to the very issue of language maintenance. Indeed, for many reasons we shall not develop here the rate of maintenance of the home language in Turkish families is very high.[19] Contact between Turkish families and schools is made difficult by the lack of knowledge on the part of teachers about Turkish culture and little understanding of the experience of economic migration. Turkish parents tend to feel somewhat in awe of teachers and are shy to approach them, particularly when they do not speak French. Moreover, it is not usual in French schools to translate school rules or letters for parents who do not know French, with most teachers believing that if you live in France you should learn French and some resenting Turkish women who survive without learning the language thanks to their close-knit community.

Though DB has found his own way to help his community by doing militant work within an association, it is more difficult for him to feel confident about asserting the need to use Turkish in his class and at school in general. This is the reason why he used Turkish to help two Turkish-speaking pupils, but did not devise activities in this language for the rest of the class. He could, for example, have taught the whole class a short Turkish song or nursery rhyme, but he would have had to justify this activity on pedagogical grounds. He could also have exposed himself to criticism from parents suspecting him of teaching 'his' language, that is, a language that is not part of the curriculum, and this could seriously undermine his chances of being evaluated positively.

However, DB was also an agent of change in the sense that he helped two Turkish-speaking children to find their voice in class, and he showed concretely to an experienced teacher that it is essential and possible to communicate with Turkish parents. Through his choice to use Turkish in his class, he also became a role model for many children in the school. There are so few teachers in France who come from immigrant communities[20] that pupils of North African or Turkish background would be very sensitive to a teacher sharing their language and their identity. Indeed DB related to me how one young boy came to him in the school yard and asked if it were true he was Turkish, if it were true he spoke Turkish in the class, and whether he was a Muslim; on the positive replies of DB the boy added: 'Are you one of us, then?' DB was shocked by the question and felt very strongly that as a French teacher in '*l'école de la République*', he should not encourage divisiveness. Through his ability to be in the middle, and because of his life experience as a bilingual, he was able to gain the confidence of this pupil and at the same time to offer him an alternative worldview, illustrating García et al.'s (2006, p. 10) statement: 'Those of us whose life experience—often not schools—has made us bilingual or multilingual also have multiple ways of using our languages, to voice an alternative worldview and a critical perspective. We have multiple associations, visions and voices, developed through our ability to be in the middle'.

Conclusion

Through the analysis of the reflective process of the two trainees I hope to have shown that even in a very centralized, hierarchical and monolingually biased education system, teachers can be key agents in the educational process from the beginning of their career. Both student teachers in this study decided their pupils had a right to have their home language acknowledged and valued. They understood that these children needed their mother tongue as well as the school language to build their future and that they should not have to abandon one language at the expense of the other. Let us not forget that their pupils were very young and vulnerable—being schooled at age 2 or 3 in a language one has hardly ever heard before must be a very frightening experience. The two student teachers were well aware that this first experience of schooling and first encounter with a teacher could have a very powerful effect on children's whole school career, on their attitudes to learning and their experience of socialization.

The extent to which both trainees could negotiate language policies in everyday classroom activities and support the maintenance and development of languages other than French was limited by various constraints, but their pedagogical choices did have a tangible effect in the lives of the children concerned and their parents. The reason why it was easier for MGR than for DB to create ideological and implementational space for multilingual education lies in the remaining discriminatory attitudes towards a minority language like Turkish. In the educational sphere, the resistance to Turkish is linked to its high level of maintenance at home and the belief it is hindering the acquisition of the school language. Whereas DB is the very counterexample to this, he could not, on his own, dispel entrenched prejudice even when his pedagogical interventions solved learning difficulties. The institutional and ideological mechanisms of power prevented him from becoming an efficient agent of change at a larger level than the classroom. All the same, he is a social activist outside of the school context, and even if he is expected to keep these activities separate from his teaching profession, he will no doubt negotiate both professional responsibilities and make his mark.

I think both student teachers did 'exert educational effort' and built further on the diversity of languages their pupils brought to the classroom and they went 'beyond acceptance or tolerance to cultivation of children's diverse languages and culture resources' (García et al., 2006, p. 14). It is obvious much more needs to be done to support linguistically diverse students in the mainstream classroom through their whole schooling, but the choices of languages and language strategies the two trainees made for their pupils need to be understood within their wider socio-political environment.

Discussion Questions

1   Why should bi/multilingual children be able to use their home language(s) at school?
2   How can mainstream teachers support the L1 of their bilingual pupils in class?
3   Is it possible for teachers to include languages they do not know in their pedagogical activities? How and where can they find help?
4   Should the L1 of bilingual pupils be taught in separate spaces or included in the everyday activities of the mainstream classroom?
5   How can one integrate linguistic and cultural diversity within the teaching of the school language and within the teaching of other school subjects?
6   How can one develop an integrated or holistic approach to language education, that is, make links between the school language, second languages, home languages and develop in pupils an awareness of the way language(s) work in society?
7   Is it enough to change attitudes towards minority languages and cultures in your class?

Notes

1 This amendment is part of a more general reform of French institutions and was passed on 24 July 2008. The clause that regional languages are part of France's heritage was included in Article 75 of the Constitution. However, this does not mean that the government intends to ratify the European Charter for Regional and Minority Languages of

the Council of Europe: http://www.coe.int/T/E/Legal_Affairs/Local_and_regional_ Democracy/Regional_or_Minority_languages/

2 For the European Commission see http://europa.eu/languages/en/home and http://ec. europa.eu/education/programmes/newprog/index_en.html
   For the Council of Europe: http://www.coe.int/t/dg4/linguistic/

3 Overall, 13 foreign languages and 13 regional languages are offered but the average per school is a choice of 4. See Goullier (2006): media.education.gouv.fr/file/37/4/3374.pdf accessed on July 17, 2008.

4 They can be summarized as follows: the belief that (a) languages are finite, stable, standardized, rule-governed instruments of communication; (b) that they express a privileged link between a people and a territory and a sense of national identity and that monolingualism is the norm; (c) that some languages are endangered because of a hierarchy in languages; (d) that one can promote or protect minority languages; (e) that languages exist in relation to one another and can influence one another; (f) that language theory is universal and exists beyond ideology, and thus that socio-linguistics is a neutral science.

5 See Pennycook (2004) and Le Nevez (2006) for a summary and analysis of this research.

6 These two student teachers cannot be considered as representative of their cohort because few of their colleagues would be interested in second-language education, and even fewer would be bilingual, and very rare are those who come from an ethnic minority background, particularly Turkish. However, most student teachers would be in the same pedagogical situation with one or several emergent bilingual children in their classrooms. I wish to thank most sincerely Mado Grundler-Reck (MGR) and Dinger Budus (DB) who agreed to answer my questions and who gave me permission to quote from their research project for this study.

7 IUFM: 'Institut Universitaire de Formation des Maîtres.' Created in 1989 to improve teacher education, these institutes have been very polemical. In October 2008, some of them became fully integrated in universities, as is the case for the IUFM of Alsace (in the east of France) described here. From September 2010, students wishing to become teachers will need to have a master's degree and a state certification exam, which can be prepared either at an IUFM or in another university department or in both (see www.alsace.iufm.fr).

8 As explained earlier, teachers study at a university for 3 years in any subject they may choose. Then they usually study for 1 year for a very competitive exam, which gives them a first teaching certification. Curriculum for this state exam is very academic and includes all subjects taught at primary school and some didactics. It is only during the following year that the approach becomes more professional and directly linked to pedagogical questions and the management of a classroom. The two student teachers in this study have followed this educational path, which is the only one possible if one wants to be a certified teacher.

9 Andrea Young: andrea.young@iufm.unistra.fr

10 This is much higher than the national figure of 5.6% (INSEE, 2001).

11 The main problems related by DB concern schooling difficulties, arranged marriages and girls being discouraged from studying after the age of 16.

12 I am using the term *bilingual* here because I consider these children as 'emergent bilinguals' (García, Kleifgen, & Falchi, 2008). The way they would be referred to in French tends to always have negative connotations, for example: non-French speakers, of foreign origin, migrants, alloglots, allophones and so on. I use the term *bilingual* purposefully with student teachers, in order to make them attentive to the notion of emergent bilingualism and thus induce a more positive outlook towards these pupils.

13 Translated from French into English by the author of this chapter.

14 See www.tessla.org, a website dedicated to Teacher Education for the Support of Second Language Acquisition.

15 See Hélot (2007) for more information on the provision of mother tongue classes at primary level in France.
16 For example, she read the children the story of Hansel and Gretel in French, and then asked the German mother to come and tell the story in German.
17 One part of her essay is entitled 'Welcoming the Child Along with His Personal History' (Grundler-Reck, 2008, p. 12)
18 Both booklets were designed specifically for each bilingual pupil and had a bilingual title page as in: 'Petit dictionnaire pour T/Kleines Wörterbuch für T.'
19 See the excellent thesis of Gonac'h, J. (2008).
20 It is impossible to give statistics because using ethnic criteria in France is illegal.

References

Ager, D. (1999). *Identity, insecurity and image. France and language.* Clevedon, Avon: Multilingual Matters.

Benert, B., & Hélot, C. (2008). Tomi Ungerer : Homo Viator. Three languages and four stories to consider the notion of identity. *Grengänge 14, Heft, 28,* 167–188. Leipzig: Leipziger Universität.

Benert, B., & Hélot, C. (2009). Translation and otherness. In V. Lalagianni (Ed.), *Children literature studies and literary theory today* (pp. 49–61). *Neohelicon, Acta Comparationis Literarum Universalis.* Dordrecht, The Netherlands: Springer.

Blommaert, J. (2006). *Language policy and national identity. An introduction to language policy.* Malden, MA: Blackwell.

Bonnet, G., & Levasseur, J. (2004). *Évaluation des competences en anglais des élèves de 15 et 16 ans dans sept pays européens. Note d'évaluation DEP, 00-04. Direction de l'évaluation et de la prospective* [Evaluation of the competence in English of 15 and 16 year-old students in seven European countries]. Paris: Ministère de l'éducation.

Budus, D. Dinger (2008). *Comment aider un enfant issu de l'immigration et ne maîtrisant pas la langue française, à entrer dans les apprentissages en maternelle ? Écrit réflexif, IUFM Alsace* [How can one help a migrant pupil without any knowledge of French to start learning at kindergarten level ?]. Unpublished manuscript.

Camillieri Grima, A. (Ed.). (2007). *Whole school language profiles and policies.* Graz: European Centre for Modern Languages, Council of Europe. Retrieved April 22, 2009, from http://www.ecml.at/mtp2/Ensemble/html/Ensemble_E_Results.htm

Candelier, M. (2003). *L'éveil aux langues à l'école primaire. EVLANG : Bilan d'une innovation* [Language awareness at primary school. EVLANG: evaluation of a pedagogical innovation]. Bruxelles: De Boeck.

Cerquiglini, B. (2003). *Les langues de France* [The Languages of France]. Paris: PUF.

Council of Europe. (2001a). *Common European framework of reference for languages: Learning, teaching, assessment.* Retrieved April 22, 2009, from http://www.coe.int/T/DG4/Linguistic/CADRE_EN.asp

Council of Europe. (2001b). *European language portfolio.* Retrieved April 22, 2009, from http://www.coe.int/t/dg4/portfolio/default.asp?l=e&m=/main_pages/welcome.html

Cummins, J. (2001). *Negotiating identities: Education for empowerment in a diverse society.* Los Angeles, CA: Association for Bilingual Education.

France 3.fr. (2008, 10/06). *Les langues régionales dans la constitution.* Retrieved July 20, 2008, from http://culture.france3.fr/patrimoine/actu/43300400-fr.php

García, O. (2009). *Bilingual education in the 21st century. A global perspective.* Malden and Oxford: Wiley/Blackwell.

García, O., Kleifgen, J., & Falchi, L. (2008). *From English language learners to emergent bilinguals* (Equity Matters: Research Review No. 1). New York: A Research Initiative of the Campaign for Educational Equity. Retrieved April 15, 2009, from http://www.tc.columbia.edu/i/a/document/6468_Ofelia_ELL__Final.pdf

García, O., Skutnabb-Kangas, T., & Torres-Guzmán, M. E. (Eds.). (2006). *Imagining multilingual schools. Language in education and glocalisation.* Clevedon, Avon: Multilingual Matters.

Gonac'h, J. (2008). Bilinguisme et bilittéracie chez des jeunes de la 2ème generation de migrants. Le cas de Lycéens et d'étudiants d'origine turque en France et en Angleterre. Thèse de doctorat, Rouen: Université de Rouen, France (Unpublished). [Bilingualism and biliteracy in young migrants of the second generation. A Case study in France and England of secondary school and university students of Turkish background. Doctoral Thesis from the University of Rouen, France.]

Goullier, F. (2006). *L'apport du système éducatif français à la dynamique européenne dans l'enseignement des langues. La Revue de l'inspection générale 03: Existe-t-il un modèle éducatif français?* [What the French education system brings to the dynamics of foreign language teaching in Europe] Retrieved Nov 6, 2009, from http://media.education.gouv.fr/file/37/4/3374.pdf

Grillo, R. (1989). *Dominant languages: Language and hierarchy in Britain and France.* Cambridge, UK: Cambridge University Press.

Grundler-Reck M. (2008). *Le plurilinguisme à l'école maternelle, un atout pour la classe, une ressource d'apprentisage. Écrit réflexif: IUFM Alsace* [Plurilingualism at kindergarten level: A learning resource for the classroom]. Unpublished manuscript.

Hancock, A., Hermeling, S., Landon, J., & Young, A. (Eds.). (2006). *Building on language and diversity with young children. Teacher education for the support of second language acquisition.* Zürich: LIT Verlag.

Hélot, C. (2003). Language policy and the ideology of bilingual education in France. *Language Policy, 2*(3), 255–277.

Hélot, C. (2006). Bridging the gap between prestigious bilingualism and the bilingualism of minorities: Towards an integrated perspective of multilingualism in the French education context. In M. Ó Laoire, (Ed.), *Multilingualism in educational settings* (pp. 15–32). Tübingen: Stauffenburg Verlag.

Hélot, C. (2007). *Du bilinguisme en famille au plurilinguisme à l'école* [From bilingualism in the family to plurilingualism at school]. Paris: L'Harmattan.

Hélot, C. (2008). Mais d'où est-ce qu'il sort ce bilinguisme ? La notion de bilinguisme dans l'espace scolaire français [Where does this bilingualism come from? The notion of bilingualism in the French education context]. In J. Erfurt, G. Budach, & M. Kunkel (Eds.), *Zweisprachig lehren und lernen. Ziele, Konzepte und Erfahrungen* (pp. 55–80). Frankfurt: Peter Lang.

Hélot, C. (2009). La formation des enseignants en contexte plurilingue [Teacher Education in plurilingual context]. In J. Vernaudon & V. Fillol (Eds.), *Vers une école plurilingue dans les collectivités françaises d'Océanie et de Guyanne. Cahiers du Pacifique Sud Contemporain, Hors Série 1* (pp. 251–270). Paris: l'Harmattan.

Hélot, C., & Benert, B. (2006). Comment penser la notion d'interculturel dans la formation des enseignants du premier degré en France. Analyse de trois notions: l'étranger, la rencontre, l'autre [Rethinking the notion of intercultural education in primary teacher education in France: Analysis of three notions: foreignness, encounter and otherness]. In A. Akkari et al. (Eds.), *Approches interculturelles dans la formation des enseignants: Impacts, stratégies, pratiques et expériences. Revue des HEP de Suisse Romande et du Tessin nº 4* (pp. 77–102). CDHEP: Neuchâtel, Suisse.

Hélot, C., Hoffmann, E., Scheidhauer, M. L., & Young, A. (Eds.) (2006). *Écarts de langues, écarts de cultures. À l'école de l'Autre* [Mind the gap: Difference in language(s) and culture(s) at school]. Frankfurt: Peter Lang.

Hélot, C., & Young, A. (2002). Bilingualism and language education in French primary schools: Why and how should migrant languages be valued? *International Journal of Bilingual Education and Bilingualism, 5*(2), 92–112.

Hélot, C., & Young, A. (2003). Education à la diversité linguistique et culturelle : Le rôle des parents dans un projet d'éveil aux langues en cycle 2. Numéro spécial de la revue LIDIL (Linguistique et Didactique des Langues). In D.L. Simon & C. Sabatier (Eds.), *Le plurilinguisme en construction dans le système éducatif : contextes, dispositifs, acteurs en situation formelle d'apprentissage* (pp. 187–200). [Educating children to linguistic and cultural diversity: the role of parents in a language awareness project at primary school. Special issue of the journal LIDIL edited by D.L. Simon & C. Sabatier: Developing plurilingualism in the education system: contexts, models, and actors in institutional settings.] Université Stendhal, Grenoble, France: LIDIL (Linguistique et Didactique des langues).

Hélot, C., & Young, A. (2005). Language education and diversity: Policy and practice at primary level in France. *Journal of Language, Culture and Curriculum, 18*(3), 242–257.

Hélot, C., & Young, A. (2006). Imagining multilingual education in France: A language and cultural awareness project at primary level. In O. García & al. (Eds.), *Imagining multilingual schools. Languages in education and glocalisation* (pp. 69–90). Clevedon, Avon: Multilingual Matters.

Huck, D. (1999).Quelle langue régionale en Alsace [Which regional language in Alsace?]. In L. Dabène (Ed.), *Les langues régionales: Enjeux sociolinguistiques et didactiques* (pp. 43–60). LIDIL n 20, LIDILEM, Université Stendhal, Grenoble, France.

Institut National de la statistique et des études économiques: National Institute for Statistics and Economic Research (INSEE) (2001). *Les étrangers en Alsace. Chiffres pour l'Alsace, Revue n° 4. Septembre 2001.* Retrieved February 2, 2009, from http://www.insee .fr/

Jaffe, A. (1999). Locating power: Corsican translators and their critics. In J. Blommaert (Ed.), *Language ideological debates* (pp. 39–66). Berlin: Mouton de Gruyter.

Journal Officiel. (1992). *Débats Assemblée Nationale* (1018–1022). Retrieved May, 12, 1992, from www.journal-officiel.gouv.fr

Kramsch, C. (2002). *Language acquisition and language socialization: Ecological perspectives* (Advances in Applied Linguistics Series). New York: Continuum International.

Le Nevez, A. (2006). Language diversity and linguistic identity in Brittany: A critical analysis of the changing practice of Breton. Unpublished doctoral dissertation, University of Technology, Sydney, Australia.

L' Express (2008, July). *Pour ou contre les langues régionales dans la Constitution.* Retrieved July 24, 2008, from http://www.lexpress.fr/actualite/politique/pour-ou-contre-les-langues-regionales-dans-la-constitution_512991.html

Loi Toubon. (1994). Website of the Ministry of Culture presenting the law and its applications. Retrieved July 16, 2008, from http://www.culture.gouv.fr/culture/dglf/lois/presentation_loi.htm

May, S. (2001, June 19). *Language and minority rights. Ethnicity, nationalism and the politics of language.* Harlow, Essex: Pearson Education.

Ministère de l'Éducation Nationale (Ministry of National Education) MEN. (2007). *Qu'apprend-on à l'école maternelle. Les programmes 2007–2008.* SCEREN, CNDP. Paris: XO Éditions.

Ministère de l'Éducation Nationale (Ministry of National Education) MEN. (2008). Horaires et programmes d'enseignement de l'école primaire. Numéro Hors Série. *Bulletin Officiel de L'éducation Nationale et du Ministère de l'Enseignement Supérieur et de La Recherche*, n 3, 2008. Paris: SCEREN, CNDP.

Moore, D. (1995). *L'éveil aux langues. Notions en Questions 1* [Language Awareness. Notions in Question 1]. CREDIF/LIDILEM, Paris: Didier Erudition.

Pennycook, A. (2004). Perfomativity and language studies. *Critical Enquiries in Language Studies*, 1(1), 1–26.

Perregaux, C. (1998). Esquisse d'un nouveau monde [A sketch for a new world]. In J. Billiez (Ed.), *De la Didactique des langues à la didactique du plurilinguisme* [From the didactics of languages to the didactics of plurilingualism] (pp. 291–298). Grenoble: CDL, LIDILEM.

Perrenoud, P. (2001). *Développer la pratique réflexive dans le métier d'enseignant* [Developing reflexive practice for teachers] [Professionnalisation et raison pédagogique]. Paris: ESF.

RERS. (2007). *Repères et références statistiques sur les enseignements, la formation et la recherche*. Paris, France: Ministère de l'Education Nationale [Ministry of Education and Research].

Ricento, T. (2006). *Theoretical perspectives in language policy. An introduction to language policy*. Malden, MA: Blackwell.

Sanders, C. (Ed.). (1996). *French today. Language in its social context*. Cambridge, UK: Cambridge University Press.

Watts, R. (1999). The Ideology of dialect in Switzerland. In J. Blommaert (Ed.), *Ideological debates* (pp. 67–104). Berlin: Mouton de Gruyter.

Williams, C. H. (Ed.). (1991). *Linguistic minorities, society and territory*. Clevedon, Avon: Multilingual Matters.

Young, A., & Hélot, C. (2003). Language awareness and / or Language learning in French primary schools today. *Journal of Language Awareness*, 12(3 & 4), 236–246.

Young, A., & Hélot, C. (2007). Parent power: Parents as a linguistic and cultural resource at school. In A. Camilleri Grime (Ed.), *Promoting linguistic diversity and whole-school development* (CELV; Centre européen des langues vivantes, Graz, Autriche) (pp. 19–34). Strasbourg: Conseil de l'Europe. Retrieved April 21, 2009, from http://www.ecml.at/mtp2/Ensemble/html/Ensemble_E_Results.htm

Zirotti, J. P. (2006). *Enjeux sociaux du bilinguisme à l'école. Langage et Société n° 116. Langues en contact et plurilinguisme* [The social dimension of bilingualism at school] (pp. 73–92). Paris: Maison des Sciences de l'Homme.

Chapter 5

"Angles Make Things Difficult"

Teachers' Interpretations of Language Policy and Quechua Revitalization in Peru

Laura Alicia Valdiviezo

Introduction: Bilingual Intercultural Policy and Indigenous Revitalization

This chapter explores bilingual teachers' interpretations of indigenous language revitalization in the Bilingual Intercultural Education (BIE) policy through their uses and teaching of the Quechua language in the context of the Peruvian rural classroom. A pre-Incan language traditionally developed as an oral language, Quechua survived three centuries of Spanish colonization,[1] where it was first designated *lingua franca* for part of the South American Andes (including territories in Argentina, Bolivia, Chile, Colombia, Ecuador, and Peru) and later condemned to systemic elimination.

Only recently, homogenizing language policies, which in the past mandated the imposition of Spanish as a national language and the subsequent eradication of indigenous languages, have shifted in favor of policies that recognize linguistic diversity as a source of national wealth. BIE is a national policy enacted in the mid-1990s that was developed as law on the basis of principles of diversity and pluralism for democracy. Figure 5.1 summarizes the official BIE language policy in Peru as stated in Article 20 of the *Ley General de Educación* (2003).

BIE as official language policy represents a rhetorical shift that now welcomes the linguistic diversity of Peru, where approximately 90 indigenous languages (including Quechua) coexist with Spanish and several high-status foreign languages (e.g. English, Italian, Hebrew, Japanese, Korean, etc.). Whereas past educational policy mandated the linguistic homogenization of Peru as a Spanish-speaking nation, official BIE law now guarantees instruction in the mother tongue and fosters the development and practice of indigenous languages (Ley General de Educación, art. 20, 2003).

It is relevant to note that despite the fact that BIE was established as a national education policy, since its implementation, BIE's management has mainly focused on the cultural and linguistic revitalization of indigenous people (Valdiviezo, 2006). The focus on indigenous peoples has placed BIE policy at the center of discussions surrounding the elevation of the status and practice of historically suppressed languages in Peru, where Quechua in its distinct varieties is the primary language of roughly 30% of the country's population.

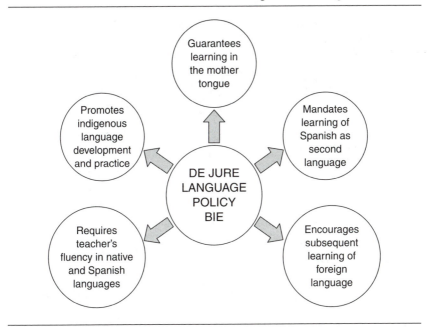

Figure 5.1 Official Language Policy in BIE

Clearly, the official written policy of BIE shows important changes toward the inclusion and revitalization of indigenous languages and cultures; however, further analysis has revealed that serious contradictions remain in its design. Among those contradictions, which I have examined elsewhere (Valdiviezo, 2009):

- BIE's design has emphasized an apolitical discourse of harmonious coexistence that neutralizes a violent history of acculturation and racist social practices affecting indigenous and other ethnic minorities in Peru.
- The policy neglects a mandate supporting teacher preparation and the development of BIE as pedagogy, elements at the root of any substantial educational reform.
- Though the policy states the need for indigenous contribution in its design, indigenous people have not actually partaken in the preparation or decisions concerning official BIE policy.
- Although the official policy's goal is to maintain indigenous languages and raise their status to a level equal to Spanish, only indigenous peoples are required to learn Spanish, whereas learning indigenous languages is not mandated for Spanish speakers. (Hornberger, 2000)

The contradictions in the design of the official BIE law have shaped BIE's irony as a *de jure* policy of indigenous revitalization that promotes harmonious coexistence of all *without* the true voice or participation of marginalized indigenous people and that officially mandates schools to conduct bilingual maintenance

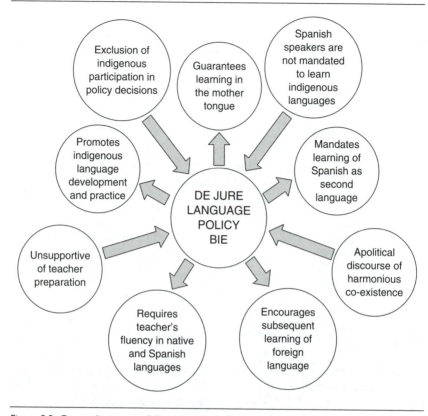

Figure 5.2 Contradictions in Official Language Policy—BIE

(indigenous language/Spanish) instruction where all languages are equal but *only* *Spanish* is mandatory. Figure 5.2 highlights the policy's contradictions.

BIE policy contradictions have had little effect on combating social practices of indigenous marginalization. Deficit notions, prevailing in Peruvian society, construct indigenous languages and their speakers as fundamentally inferior to speakers of Spanish and nonindigenous languages. When enacted in BIE schools, deficit notions have precluded indigenous knowledge and input while providing a characteristically mainstream Spanish curriculum to Quechua speakers. Within this approach, the indigenous language is conceived and treated as static, in isolation from indigenous cultures, while ignoring crucial implications of the complex and inseparable language–culture relations (Al-Khatib & Al-Ali, 2005; Fishman, 1994). Thus, Quechua language and cultures[2] have remained marginalized in the BIE program.

In this linguistically diverse environment shaped by the conflicting influences of contradictory *de jure* language revitalization policy and prevailing exclusionary social practices against indigenous languages and cultures, I conducted an ethnographic study of bilingual teachers and their implementation of BIE in rural schools in the southern Peruvian Andes. I engaged in this study with perspectives shaped by my prior experience as a bilingual Spanish/English teacher who is of Quechua, Afro-Peruvian, and Spanish descent, and my scholarly interest in schools as not only sites of social reproduction but also as loci of social change. In this research, I pay attention to the teachers' interpretations of a policy that, beyond its rhetoric of linguistic inclusion and revitalization and its grave contradictions, ought to support institutional and social transformation to include indigenous peoples, cultures, and languages. Thus, one of the questions that brought me to the research presented in this chapter is how do teachers in indigenous schools interpret BIE within institutions that have traditionally enacted contradictory *de jure* policy and social practices that marginalize indigenous language speakers? Moreover, echoing the theme of this volume, in my study I focus on teachers not only as interpreters of BIE but also as political actors who can challenge and transform official policy through local practices. Therefore, the other questions I pose here are as follows: How are BIE teachers revitalizing Quechua in their classrooms? Are teachers challenging the status quo or are they marginalizing the indigenous language?

My argument is grounded in the premise that as policy actors in the field, teachers are fundamental to the design and implementation of any reform and, as such, deserve critical attention and support, particularly from educators and policymakers. I frame the teachers' views and teaching practices of Quechua revitalization as ground-up policy and focus the present discussion on BIE teachers' interpretations of the specific law of *préstamos lingüísticos*, or linguistic term borrowing, a law of Quechua language maintenance and development (Figure 5.3). Specifically, I argue first that in a context where grave contradictions within *de jure* BIE policy have done little to affect social practices that dwarf Quechua revitalization, bilingual teachers must implement this policy without institutional support and thereby reproduce exclusionary social practices. Second, I argue that while teachers may reproduce Quechua exclusion, at the same time they are able to contest official policy and to create policy from the ground up. Thus, in spite of the barriers generated by ill-designed *de jure* and prevailing exclusionary social practices, BIE teachers are in fact central to the improvement of indigenous revitalization efforts.

A Study of Bilingual Teachers in the BIE Program

The data presented in this chapter were collected through individual interviews with BIE teachers, classroom and school observations, teaching and classroom documents, and teacher surveys. In addition, among the participants in the overall study that consisted of teachers, trainers, and officials at the Ministry of Education (MOE), this chapter highlights data from several of my interactions with Américo, Juán, Nancy, and Yolanda concerning their views and practices teaching in the Quechua language. Their perspectives illustrate the wide range of responses among the participants in the overall study. Américo, Juán, Nancy, and Yolanda, respectively, taught in schools located in three indigenous communities that were part of my study: Pachaqtusan, Ruphay, and Chama.[3] The four participants included in this chapter were bilingual Quechua-Spanish speakers, with only Juán self-identifying as a native Quechua speaker. Nancy, Yolanda, and

Orthography Norms for the Quechua Language

When reading and writing in the Quechua language, it is necessary to consider the following norms approved at the Workshop for Quechua and Aymara Writing in October, 1983:

a. When adding suffixes of any type to one Quechua root word, no modification or letter omission should take place, even in cases when phonetic assimilation has taken place in the oral use of the word.

b. Use accents only when Quechua words alter their natural accent in interrogatory and exclamatory sentences.

c. Follow the norms of Spanish writing when using capital and small letters, including the use of especial writing of ch, aa, th, etc.

d. Texts written in Quechua follow universal punctuation norms utilized in written languages. Question marks and exclamation points should be utilized at the beginning and end of the sentence, being careful of not denaturalizing the sentence intonation.

e. Concerning term borrowing [sic]. It has been agreed upon that [borrowing would take place] only in cases where there is no equivalent for the term borrowed in any of the varieties of the target language, and only after exhausting all possibilities for term rescue and creation that respect the internal norms of the language.

Figure 5.3 Legal Base for the Use of the Quechua Alphabet

Source: *Nuestro Tesoro; Texto Auto-Instructivo de lectura y escritura quechua,* pp. 31–32 (Cabrera Huamán, 2004).

Américo explained that they grew up understanding Quechua, which was either spoken by their parents or older members of their family at home or was utilized in their town. They added that they spoke Spanish first and that they learned to speak the indigenous language later. Like BIE teachers in general, Yolanda, Nancy, and Juán had been schooled in Spanish and learned to read and write in the indigenous language through BIE in-service workshops, whereas Américo took Quechua as a special elective course in college. At the time of my study in 2004, the above teachers had taught in BIE schools for several years. Yolanda was in the BIE program for 9 years, Juán for 8 years, Américo for 7 years, and Nancy had been a BIE teacher for 4 years.

The following section presents BIE teachers' interpretations of indigenous language revitalization through their views and use of the BIE policy of *préstamos lingüísticos* in the indigenous classrooms of Pachaqtusan, Ruphay, and Chama. The four teachers featured in this chapter represent diverse perspectives and practices in BIE, which illustrate how BIE teachers took up BIE policy in different and sometimes contradictory ways. Through their genuine efforts to implement BIE's goal of Quechua revitalization in a complex environment shaped by a contradictory *de jure* policy, with little support or recognition, these BIE teachers reproduced indigenous exclusion but also created effective practices of Quechua revitalization.

Findings: BIE Policy and Teachers' Interpretations of Quechua Revitalization in the Indigenous Classroom

In accordance with language policy promoting the development and practice of indigenous languages for their revitalization (Ley General de Educación, 2003), the official policy concerning the use and teaching of Quechua in BIE is the result of the official standardization of its alphabet, syntax, punctuation, and vocabulary— along with those of other indigenous languages—by linguists from prestigious universities and language institutions during a national conference that took place in 1983. Efforts toward Quechua standardization present significant challenges, considering the several distinct, locally rooted varieties of the language, which contrast with an established written system of it that—began initially by Spanish priests in the 16th century—was highly influenced by the linguistic features of Castilian Spanish. Much of the present Quechua standardization debate involves contentious issues regarding the authenticity of local varieties, including Quechua utilized by rural and urban speakers (King & Hornberger, 2006). The challenges of Quechua standardization have in turn shaped the efforts of Quechua revitalization in the BIE schools I studied.

When I conducted my study in 2004, BIE teachers shared language materials available to them, including a Quechua alphabet and a manual of Quechua that included the BIE language policy as delineated in the national conference of 1983 and enacted as official law in 1985.

A cohort of BIE teachers and a trainer had participated in the preparation of the Quechua manual that reproduces the official 1985 and current law regarding the Quechua alphabet, punctuation norms of the language, "borrowing" from Spanish, and "creating" new words in Quechua. BIE teachers participating in my study used this manual as a reference for their instruction. Teachers' take on this language policy reveal the inconsistencies in the policy as well as teachers' own resourcefulness when implementing language revitalization efforts with little preparation or support.

BIE language policy mandates that the linguistic norms delineated for the indigenous language ought to respect the natural structure of the language (Cabrera Huamán, 2004), whereas it mandates that the use of capital letters, question marks, and exclamation points follow universal linguistic norms (Norms 4.3.b, 4.3.c, and 4.3.d in Figure 5.3). According to my observations of teacher practices, the teachers' utilization and teaching of the indigenous language in the classrooms appeared to be consistent with the official norms regarding the alphabet, the syntax, and punctuation in Quechua (December 2004, fieldnotes). During Quechua instruction, BIE teachers across schools and classrooms capitalized words and used punctuation following the same norms as those that apply to the Spanish language. Exclamation points and question marks would be placed at the beginning and end of sentences or expressions, such as in the example: "¡Racchi llaqtayta!" Thus, teachers' interpretations of official language policy in this respect did not seem to change or challenge any official norm. There were, however, other instances where teachers' interpretations of language policy revealed conflicting notions concerning the status and the revitalization of Quechua. In such instances, as evidenced in the analysis presented below, teachers' views in the BIE program echoed a deficit approach to Quechua as a language that lacked academic vocabulary to denote scientific concepts. This approach not only restricted all value to Spanish, nonindigenous language, and culture but also undermined the recognition of indigenous (Quechua) knowledge as a legitimate way to conceive the world. Therefore, it is reasonable to ask the question: How did teachers with a deficit view of the indigenous language interpret and apply *de jure* BIE language policy in this case?

Norm *e* in Figure 5.3 shows BIE policy specification on *préstamos lingüísticos* or linguistic term borrowing. The norm states that linguistic borrowing should take place only in cases where there is no Quechua equivalent to a term, meaning that a Spanish term should be added to the Quechua vocabulary when such a term is lacking in the indigenous language (Norm 4.3. e in Figure 5.3). Though term borrowing is a common practice that applies to most languages around the world, the first part of the following analysis shows that from the perspective of language revitalization in the BIE program, *préstamos lingüísticos* became problematic as Spanish tended to overtake Quechua teaching in cases where teachers' deficit views of the Quechua language prevailed. In addition, the analysis points at a range of reasons behind teachers' constructed notions of Quechua deficit concerning their teaching, including their lack of training or preparation to teach in Quechua, the teachers' own lack of knowledge of academic Quechua vocabulary in math and science, and the perceived linguistic limitations of contemporary Quechua, the Quechua spoken in rural communities.

"Neither the Children Nor the Teachers Are Prepared for This": The Use of Préstamos Lingüísticos

Al inicio me pareció una cosa sencillísima. ¡Uy yo hablo quechua, mis niños hablan quechua, va a ser una maravilla esto! Pero cuando regresé de la capacitación, no era tal, no era solamente el hablar quechua, había que saber escribir…. At the beginning I thought it was the simplest thing: "I speak Quechua, my students speak Quechua. This is going to be wonderful!" But when I came back from training, this was not so. This was not only about speaking Quechua; we also had to write it. Because, speaking is speaking, a very different thing is to write. Now we had to teach our students the scientific topics and some expressions like, for example: "doubles" and "fractions," and words that we did not know in Quechua. We were always mixing Quechua with Spanish and we had been told in training that we shouldn't mix and that we needed to recover the Quechua language, the Quechua words. All that has been somewhat difficult to do, hasn't it? (Yolanda, Chama, November 18, 2004, interview transcript)

The task that BIE teachers had to fulfill by teaching, reading, writing diverse academic subject areas in the indigenous language was far greater than simply speaking Quechua in the BIE classroom. Without specific training involving a pedagogy of Quechua revitalization, *de jure* BIE policy placed on teachers the task of inserting the indigenous language in school solely through the translation of Spanish curriculum into Quechua. Although speaking and understanding the spoken language was not a major issue for either native Quechua speakers or for teachers who had learned Quechua as a second language, BIE teachers in this case were unprepared to deal with the complexities of bilingual teaching beyond ideas of literal content translation from one language into another, as teachers found that some concepts did not have a direct translation into the Quechua language.

Moreover, neither the law of 1985 (shown in Figure 5.3 above) nor training itself addressed specific issues of terminology, leaving teachers with no informed basis for their decisions, hence adding to the BIE policy's inconsistencies the demands of teaching Spanish mainstream science and math concepts in Quechua. As shown in Yolanda's quote above, teachers were aware of the weaknesses of this approach, which fell short of its goal of recovering Quechua.

"How Could We Say 'Arch' in Quechua?" The Creation of Quechua Terms for Instruction

> Se utilizaba el castellano para esos términos [que no sabíamos . . .]. Y pues más era en castellano que se estaba hablando y recuerdo mucho en las reuniones que tuvimos, siempre nos decían que deben hacer así o ¡¿cómo hacemos esto?!. . . We used Spanish for those terms [we did not know] and that way we ended up speaking more Spanish in the classroom. Also, I remember a lot about the meetings we had, we discussed how to do this and how do we do that?! We asked ourselves: "How could we say arch in Quechua?" "Arkuta, arkucha" "And is that the way we are going to speak?" Then another teacher would say "arku nispa," which means: "arch is how it is called" or "it is called arch." Things weren't done right. (Yolanda, Chama, November 28, 2004, interview transcript)

Similar to other teachers in my study, Yolanda stated that the lack of Quechua terminology in math and science constituted a problem for teaching in a BIE program, a maintenance bilingual program, which mandated that students develop their mother tongue (Quechua) and Spanish equally. *De jure* BIE policy stated that the solution to the lack of terminology in the indigenous language was for teachers to assume the *creación* or creation of new terms when they could not find the vocabulary to teach in Quechua (Norm 4.3.e in Figure 5.3). Beyond stating that this creation process should follow the internal norms of the native language, the mandate did not specify how this process of word creation was going to take place. Moreover, as Yolanda also expressed, trainers did not address such processes and teachers took upon themselves the negotiation of word creation to express math concepts in the indigenous language, as explained in the following. Based on their own experiences and assumptions, some BIE teachers like Yolanda engaged in word creation as the most feasible way to solve the problem of the lack of Quechua terminology and in order to continue teaching in Quechua as the target language. Thus, this process of teachers figuring out the policy on their own, which Yolanda noted to be not the "right" way, was neither acknowledged nor supported institutionally.

The process of terminology creation in Quechua was also problematic in terms of indigenous language revitalization because teaching in the indigenous language continued to focus on the translation of Spanish concepts into new terms in Quechua and utilized mainstream concepts with no place for indigenous world-views or knowledge. Additionally, term creation in Quechua was not always successful, particularly among teachers in the fourth, fifth, and sixth grades. Because of the shift in course emphasis between the lower and the upper grades, which included teaching more "science" courses than literacy courses, teachers felt most affected by the challenges of term borrowing or creation in the upper grades. Juán, a fifth-grade teacher in Ruphay, explained this during an interview:

Juán: Tan fácil es enseñar EBI en los primeros grados, hasta tercero porque may-ormente es producción de textos, creación de textos, que es más fácil en la oralidad [sic], pero en la parte científica, al menos en lógico matemático, con las ecuaciones, los ángulos, eso se dificulta…. It is so easy to teach BIE in the early grades because it is mainly about text production, text creation where literacy is easier. But for science and mathematical logic, [concepts] such as "equations" and "angles" make things difficult. In fifth and sixth grade especially we have to talk about science, and we [teachers] require special training in that. The students need to learn vocabulary in Quechua for words like for example "angle" and "vector," but neither the children nor the teachers are prepared for this.

LV: Then do you teach math mostly in Spanish?

Juán: Yes, mainly in Spanish. We worked on addition, subtraction, and multiplication in Quechua, but fractions, exponentials, those are a bit more difficult in Quechua, so we are working on those themes in Spanish.

LV: And how do children respond to that?

Juán: Of course they don't respond as quickly, do they? Students have difficulties because we don't have the terms we need to teach. We don't know thoroughly the Quechua terms for mathematics. (Juán, Ruphay, October 29, 2004, interview transcript)

Echoing Yolanda's view, Juán explains that one of the practices that teachers utilized first to address their difficulties in finding Quechua vocabulary for academic and technical terms was borrowing terms from Spanish, and mixing the languages during instruction—even though this was mandated to take place primarily in the indigenous language. Given that term borrowing became a very complicated practice, especially for teaching the upper grades, teachers like Juán decided to rely on Spanish to teach most science and math lessons, even when acknowledging that indigenous students did have more difficulty learning those subjects in Spanish. As shown thus far, these practices defeated the purpose of the BIE policy of language revitalization.

Teachers' interpretations of a contradictory *de jure* policy of Quechua revitalization were far from simplistic. Their take on BIE policy concerning indigenous language revitalization through the use of *préstamos lingüísticos* exposed inconsistent teacher views. Classroom practices sustaining deficit views of Quechua vocabulary for instruction coexisted with nostalgic beliefs about the purity of the ancient Quechua of the Incas.[4] In the first case, whereas this perception was linked to the conceptualization of BIE as a program that is intended to revitalize the Quechua language, the goal of language "rescue" echoed nostalgic and static views of Quechua as a language for which any intrinsic value rested on a glorious past, not on its present, as Américo's comment shows below.

"Those Terms the Incas Knew Were Lost": Notions of Quechua's Past and Status

Al menos yo, hablando por mí, viendo los restos arquitectónicos inca por decir, y las construcciones que muestran pues grandiosidad en nuestros [sic] trabajos, pienso que también han tenido un idioma.... At least speaking for myself, by seeing the architectonic remains of the Incas and the constructions that show grandeur in their work, I think that the Incas also had a language. Quechua in those times must have been quite rich so the Incas could build walls of different magnitudes and do that with such symmetry. With time, most certainly, those terms [that] the Incas knew were lost. Then, I think that it is because of this that the educational policy is recovering the language. We are, I think, in that process of recovery. (Américo, Chama, November 15, 2004, interview transcript)

Like Américo, some BIE teachers saw the need to rescue old cultural values together with those sophisticated terms in Quechua, which had been lost with the passing of time. In several instances, teachers connected the notion of lost language terms to lost cultural values. Such was the case of Juán who, during an individual interview, explained that the objective of BIE was to rescue what he called "our culture, the way our ancient people were, their beliefs, their dances, their music, all of which ... globalization is changing and losing" (Juán, Ruphay, October 2004, interview notes). Whether teachers attributed the loss of the indigenous "culture" to globalization, colonization or other factors, BIE teachers tended to refer to a "glorious" ancient past and language as opposed to a present indigenous people or, for that matter, to the present-day Quechua language, which seemed to fall under the deficit gaze as a language that had lost the knowledge and sophistication it had in a distant past.

Américo's beliefs about the Quechua language conveyed common conceptions of Quechua's past connection to the Incas, an elite ruling class, detached from the marginalized Quechua speakers of a complex and problematic present. As part of social practices of indigenous exclusion, these views silenced the value and recognition of contemporary Quechua and its speakers. For Américo, as quoted above, BIE would rescue Quechua from the past; however, the Quechua of the present and its people were rarely imagined as part of those efforts. Because the value of the indigenous language was placed on its past, the Quechua language of the present remained marginal to revitalization.

In the complex environment of the BIE program, static views of the indigenous language coexisted with perceptions on the other side of the spectrum that

expressed the significance of Quechua as a vibrant language of present-day indigenous peoples. Certainly, some teachers believed that the process of language recovery related, not to rescuing a language from the past, but to the act of valuing and
incorporating the Quechua spoken by the indigenous people in the community surrounding the BIE school. In this way, as the following analysis shows, teachers' interpretation of *de jure* BIE policy of *préstamos lingüísticos* also contested exclusionary
social practices against the indigenous language, by engaging in word rescuing that
validated Quechua cultures and language in the indigenous school.

"Once We Used it in the Classroom, There Was No Other Way, it Became Part of it!" Rescuing the Indigenous Language

Nancy showed me how in her math class she incorporated a new Quechua
math concept she heard from the children. According to Nancy, it was a
mathematical term commonly used among the Quechua farmers in the area
to name a specific amount of potatoes, which did not have an equivalent in
the Spanish language. She told me smiling: "Once we used it in the classroom,
there was no other way, it became part of it!" (Nancy, Pachaqtusan, June 8,
2004, interview notes)

In Nancy's interpretation of *de jure* BIE policy of rescuing the Quechua language, the use of the indigenous language in the BIE classroom implied reaching
out to learn local terms from the indigenous community. During my observations
in schools, other teachers who had expressed strong support for the BIE program,
in particular regarding Quechua revitalization, regularly consulted older students,
who in turn would talk to family members to find or define terms that could be
applicable to school subject areas (October 27, 2004, interview notes). Taking
advantage of their close relationships with parents and the community, teachers
were proactive in their objective of bringing contemporary Quechua into the
classroom. These BIE teachers placed the value of the indigenous language in the
present and saw in the indigenous community the resource for Quechua revitalization. Their proactive efforts incorporated the knowledge of the indigenous
community in BIE and transformed their teaching practice.

Typically, teachers who shared Nancy's take on revitalization policy found that
local Quechua concepts denoted a particular indigenous worldview that had no
direct translation into Spanish. Incorporating local Quechua terms in instruction
was coherent with BIE policy, as Nancy also stated in a later conversation
(Pachaqtusan, July 2004, fieldnotes). For teachers like Nancy, who openly advocated for Quechua revitalization, it was inevitable that the Quechua terms that
teachers learned from the community or that students brought to the classroom
were going to become part of the academic vocabulary. Moreover, in this effort,
local indigenous practices were actively incorporated when BIE teachers created
space in their lessons for a student's Quechua storytelling (Ruphay, August 2004,
fieldnotes) or when they invited parents to school to lead Quechua rituals for the

Pachamama or mother earth celebration (Pachaqtusan, October 2004, fieldnotes). By engaging in such practices BIE teachers not only expanded the academic Quechua vocabulary but also the curriculum to include views and practices that reflected the local indigenous culture.

BIE teachers across schools also engaged in critical conversations with their colleagues about the BIE policy and program. Interestingly, these were not structured events but informal exchanges among teachers. Often, when sharing meals, teachers had lively conversations where they exchanged jokes, farming tips, and their views on the BIE program. When their conversations centered on the bilingual program, teachers typically discussed ways of teaching certain lessons; expressed their concerns about parental support to the program; questioned possible agendas behind BIE policy; or envisioned the impact of BIE on Quechua status and utilization beyond the indigenous community (December 2004, fieldnotes). I participated in these critical conversations through my fieldwork at the different schools. Particularly in the community of Pachaqtusan, teachers enjoyed discussing and challenging one another about diverse issues related to the program. One of the concepts the teachers discussed was the use of Quechua archaisms for instruction in relation to the functionality of local Quechua outside the specific indigenous community. Archaisms were defined as words, often dictionary terms, no longer, if ever, used among native Quechua speakers. What I examine in the following section depicts one of the ways in which teachers engaged in critical conversations.

"Why Teach Archaisms to the Children?" Teachers' Critical Views of Language Policy

That cold evening several of us came to the teacher residence to chat. . . . Unexpectedly for me, the conversation focused on Quechua archaisms and local Quechua vocabulary. Nancy mentioned that she had talked recently to a former student and found out the community words for "potato" and "window." The principal, who was also a teacher in the school, responded that those local Quechua words were not going to be found in Quechua books and dictionaries and thus would have no use outside their community. Teachers began to compare the utility of local words to Quechua archaisms, which were "found in dictionaries." One teacher asked, "Why teach archaisms to the children? What is the purpose?" Nancy said that teaching both [localisms and archaisms] would broaden the students' vocabulary. They would learn "more than one way to name things." (teacher conversation, Pachaqtusan, May 20, 2004, fieldnotes)

Teachers contrasted their views of BIE policy and practice while critically questioning the actual implications of both outside the classroom. In spite of being supportive of BIE, for example, the school principal wondered about the practical applications of incorporating and learning local Quechua words in school, as those local words were likely of no utility beyond the community. In a later interview, the school principal acknowledged his own ambivalent position toward maintaining the Quechua language in the program, because even if children develop their mother tongue in school, what they will need to speak *fuera de su communidad* [outside their community] is Spanish (teacher interview, Urubamba, October 2004, interview notes). As shown in the quote above, teachers also understood the implications of teaching and learning Quechua under a different light by challenging deficit views about learning the indigenous language. They stated that while archaisms were neither used nor known by the native speakers of the community, if used in the classroom setting, archaisms were aimed to expand the students' Quechua vocabulary by teaching more than one way to name an object that the students already knew how to name using their regional version of the language. In a later conversation, Nancy spoke about the implications of BIE and Quechua teaching as something for generations to come (Pachaqtusan, July 2004, fieldnotes). By improving the students' knowledge and appreciation of their own language, BIE could further elevate the societal status of Quechua in the future.

Teachers' critical thinking about the BIE policy and program was a way of constructing new views and practices, a way of creating policy from the ground up. For some BIE teachers, archaisms in the Quechua language had limited function and thus relevance. It was in the everyday Quechua words that teachers like Nancy found genuine pedagogical value. The incorporation of everyday Quechua terms in the classroom was an action thought to be coherent with BIE, a policy where the language of the community is acknowledged, validated, and ultimately, revitalized. This position challenged deficit views that placed Quechua as a language of low status and low functionality beyond the rural community. However, during discussions surrounding word creation, teachers' critical conversations were not acknowledged or voiced as a valid practice of BIE policy innovation at the institutional level.

In spite of their lack of preparation, teachers engaged in innovative approaches to transform BIE policy into classroom practice. However, teachers' critical discussions and teaching received little support, which altogether undermined their efforts to revitalize and elevate the status of the indigenous language in the classroom. As teachers tried to implement BIE in their schools, they acknowledged the great dimensions of the challenges they faced against an outside world that continued to promote deficit perspectives and exclusionary practices against Quechua language, cultures, and peoples. It is through the recognition of the centrality of teachers as policy actors and the support of teachers' innovative views and practices that BIE policy and program efforts for revitalization may in fact begin to curtail marginalization and engender just social practices influencing traditionally underserved peoples and their communities.

Final Remarks

This chapter reveals that teachers held diverse interpretations (understandings and practices) that both recreated and challenged social practices that marginalize

Quechua. In a context of grave inconsistencies within *de jure* BIE policy, prevailing marginalization of indigenous languages, and lack of training on pedagogical approaches to language revitalization, BIE teachers reproduced Quechua marginalization through their teaching. However, as policy actors, they were also able to contest indigenous marginalization and to create policy from the ground up, showing that BIE teachers are in fact central to the improvement of indigenous revitalization efforts.

BIE teachers showed compliance with the language policy in cases where the norms regulated the alphabet, syntax, and punctuation in Quechua. In general, BIE teachers' views and actions also revealed contradictions of the official language policy. Whereas the norms of Quechua in BIE—such as those expressed in the law of *préstamos lingüísticos*—required that teachers "rescue" the Quechua indigenous language, these norms, as *de jure* policy, also placed on teachers the responsibility to "create" Quechua terms for academic content. A deficit approach framed Quechua as lacking math and science vocabulary for Spanish concepts and engaged teachers in practices that focused on the translation of mainstream Spanish concepts for Quechua instruction while negating the incorporation of Quechua knowledge in the curriculum.

The practice of word creation in Quechua took place as a process where decisions were made in response to immediate needs and where teachers perceived of the Quechua language as deficient. As noted by Yolanda, the practice of word creation was encouraged as a strategy to BIE language revitalization where teachers created Quechua terms based on the immediate need to represent nonindigenous concepts and worldviews. In opposition to what was suggested to them in training and the policy concerning mixing languages during instruction, BIE teachers tended to utilize *préstamos lingüísticos* often, particularly to make up for missing technical terms during science and math instruction. Because of the great difficulty of finding equivalent academic language in Quechua, teachers like Juán opted for shifting the language of instruction primarily to Spanish despite being aware of the serious difficulties that his Quechua students had in understanding the lessons in Spanish.

The deficit perspective discussed above clearly showed the understanding that the revitalization of the indigenous language implied a recovery of a glorious indigenous past, unrelated to the indigenous peoples and Quechua of present times, as revealed in America's views. Views and actions of language recovery and language creation, *préstamos lingüísticos*, in this perspective echoed societal practices of Quechua marginalization, thus reproducing indigenous exclusion by limiting efforts to revitalize the indigenous language and utilizing, instead, more Spanish for instruction.

Deficit perspectives of Quechua coexisted with more proactive positions where teachers would look for "new" terms for Quechua instruction within the indigenous community. In this way, teachers in the BIE program contested ill-defined *de jure* BIE policy concerning indigenous language revitalization. In spite of their lack of training, BIE teachers like Nancy who felt strongly about revitalizing the Quechua language engaged in innovative practices by reaching out to the indigenous community to learn local terms and knowledge to incorporate in her teaching. By using local concepts and incorporating indigenous practices in their teaching, these teachers acknowledged the value of Quechua language and cultures and of implementing indigenous revitalization in their classrooms. As policy actors, teachers not only engaged in innovative teaching practices but also in discussing the BIE critically. They interpreted revitalization as the incorporation of Quechua concepts from the local community for academic instruction in school. As opposed to the process of Quechua word creation, the practice of local concept incorporation constituted an explicit validation of Quechua in the classroom and the actual inclusion of indigenous practices and worldviews in the BIE schools.

Moreover, BIE teachers reveal to us the complexities and contradictions surrounding practitioners as language policy actors in the field, facing the challenges posed by society and institutions whose actions serve to undermine the revitalization of the indigenous cultures and languages. BIE teachers' practices and beliefs show the possibilities for change through their ground-up contributions to BIE language revitalization in particular and to language education policy in general. It is because of the contributions shown in this chapter that teachers in the field deserve special attention from educators and policy designers alike. Without that attention, possibilities to truly inform and improve policy and practice of language revitalization get lost.

Discussion Questions

1   Based on the BIE language policy information presented in Figure 5.2 in this chapter draw a diagram showing the main norms regarding language use and revitalization.

2   What are *de jure* language policies and social practices (*de facto* policies) in your state or country, and how do they compare to BIE language policies in Peru?

3   Discuss with a partner how BIE teachers' ideas about indigenous language revitalization are different or similar to your own.

4   What language education policies of your state or country would you support and which ones would you challenge? As a teacher working with multilingual students, how could your teaching practices support or challenge language education policy?

5   This activity requires at least three different small groups. The first group will write a paragraph stating a policy that supports language revitalization or native-language development (you may use the policy discussed in this chapter or other policies you know about as models). The second group will prepare and role-play in a skit depicting a specific teaching activity that will reproduce the policy written by group one as the policymakers intended. The third group will prepare and role-play in a skit depicting a specific teaching activity that opposes the policy. The first group will observe the skits and state

how the language education policy was supported or opposed. Members of the second and third group will recommend changes or additions to improve the *de jure* policy and its implementation.

6   Use a videotape of a lesson (which could be your own) to observe the implementation of language policy in the classroom. As explained in this chapter, language education policy is not implemented exclusively in language classes but also in science and other subject areas. Identify one instance from your observation that supports local official language education policy. As a policy actor, what practices would you change or what would you maintain to support the policy mandates? In order to challenge this policy, what practices would you change or maintain?

Notes

1   Peru was a Spanish Colony, the Viceroy of Peru, from 1532 to 1821.
2   I use the word *cultures* referring to Quechua cultures instead of *culture*, to denote my understanding of Quechua communities and Quechua speakers who, like speakers of other languages, are part of dynamic and changing societies. I use the word *culture* only when representing the participants' views and words.
3   I use pseudonyms for the names of communities included in my ethnography. In the case of the participants, none opposed the use of their first names in the publications or presentations that resulted from this study.
4   Although Quechua originated in the central Andes, before the development of the Inca civilization in the southern Peruvian Andes (12th century AD), it is commonly identified as the language of the Incas.

References

Al-Khatib, M. A., & Al-Ali, M. N. (2005). Language and cultural maintenance among the Gipsies of Jordan. *Journal of Multilingual and Multicultural Development, 26*(3), 187–215.

Cabrera Huamán, T. (2004). *Nuestro tesoro; texto auto-instructivo de lectura y escritura Quechua* [Our treasure; self-instructive text for Quechua reading and writing]. Fundación HOPE, Holanda–Perú.

Fishman, J. (1994). The truth about language and culture (and a note about its relevance to the Jewish case). *International Journal of the Sociology of Language 109*, 83–96.

Hornberger, N. H. (2000). Bilingual education policy and practices in the Andes: Ideological paradox and intercultural possibility. *Anthropology and Education Quarterly 31*(2), 173–201.

King, K. A., & Hornberger, N. H. (2006). Quichua as Lingua Franca. *Annual Review of Applied Linguistics 26*, 177–194.

Ley General de Educación. (2003). *Principios de la Educación* [Education Law (2003). Principles of Education]. Retrieved March 17, 2009, from http://www.minedu.gob.pe/normatividad/leyes/ley_general_de_educacion2003.doc

Valdiviezo, L. A. (2006). Interculturality for Afro-Peruvians: Towards a racially inclusive education in Peru. *International Education Journal, 7*(1), 26–35.

Valdiviezo, L. (2009). Bilingual intercultural education in indigenous schools: An ethnography of teacher interpretations of government policy. *International Journal of Bilingual Education and Bilingualism, 12*(1), 61–79.

Chapter 6

Towards Normalizing South African Classroom Life

The Ongoing Struggle to Implement Mother-Tongue Based Bilingual Education

Carole Bloch, Xolisa Guzula, and Ntombizanele Nkence

Introduction

In this chapter we describe some of the language and literacy issues facing a group of primary school teachers in Cape Town, who are language policy implementation pioneers. Their task is to challenge the present classroom linguistic situation by beginning to implement mother-tongue (MT)- based bilingual education[1] in primary schools of the Western Cape Province of South Africa in which Afrikaans, Xhosa and English are the three major languages.

Xolisa Guzula and Ntombizanele Nkence, two early language and literacy specialists in the PRAESA Early Literacy Unit, are mentoring these teachers' efforts, with guidance from Carole Bloch, the unit coordinator. This work is part of The Three R's Project, a 5-year development research project involving a consortium of organizations that are collaborating with the South African National Department of Education to improve literacy and mathematics education. PRAESA is a multilingual education project, which has worked on language planning and policy implementation issues in education in South Africa and on the African continent since it's inception in 1992.

Nelli, Lumka, Sibongile[2] and their colleagues are teachers who can be said to represent many teachers in present-day South Africa. The schools where they work provide typical present-day manifestations of the segregated schools legislated for African-language-speaking and 'coloured' children[3] under the apartheid system, although various language permutations exist. As with most other teachers on the African continent, they teach in a multilingual society where many languages are spoken by the population and where individuals often speak more than one language. However, it was only after the fall of the apartheid regime in 1994 that the South African constitution gave official status to Xhosa, the MT of these teachers, as well as eight other African languages. This was a significant democratic policy movement, as it put indigenous African languages and sign language on an equal footing (at least on paper) with English and Afrikaans, the only two official languages during the apartheid years. Under apartheid, all government and other official business was conducted in English or Afrikaans, or in the two languages bilingually. African languages, though cherished and used in home and community spheres, suffered from a 'static maintenance syndrome' (Alexander,

2002, p. 119),[4] leaving the languages barely used in high-status functions and especially neglected as written languages.

The 1996 Constitution of South Africa promotes the use of African languages in South African society thus

> Recognizing the historically diminished use and status of the indigenous languages of our people, the state must take practical and positive measures to elevate the status and advance the use of these languages. (p. 5)

Since 1997, the new Language in Education Policy has promoted an additive bilingualism approach to language learning, meaning that teaching is based on the MT of the students, and other languages are added to this, either as subjects or co-teaching mediums. More than a decade later, however, this policy has not yet been systematically implemented and the necessary materials have also not been created and published in African languages. As a result, most schools continue with the same educationally unhealthy brew of subtractive bilingual education that most African-language-speaking children experienced under apartheid. This approach offers children at best 3 years to learn in their MT, after which there is an abrupt switch to the use of English, irrespective of whether or not they understand the language well enough to do so. The situation thus continues to be one where only English- MT-speaking children (and some Afrikaans speakers) experience teaching and learning in their home language throughout their education. PRAESA has been one of the few organizations in South Africa which has dedicated itself over many years to researching, training trainers and teachers and creating appropriate reading materials for multilingual education and reading culture development (Bloch, 2005; Edwards, 2008). In doing so, it both advances and supports the process of language policy implementation.[5]

Given that PRAESA is based at the University of Cape Town, it is thus not surprising that the Western Cape Education Department (WCED), which governs all Cape Town public schools, was the first of nine regional education departments to begin its Language Transformation Plan in late 2007. MT-based bilingual education, that is, 6 years of learning through MT as well as the introduction of learning through another language, is being piloted in 16 schools. According to the WCED (2007) Language Transformation Plan, the need to transform was based on the following:

> All school-based systemic evaluation and testing at primary schools, as well as the analysis of performance by learners who are not being tested in their MT at Grade 12 level, plus the high drop-out rate, send a clear message that the system is not working as it should and, in some cases, not at all. We need to take a sharp look at the languages of learning and teaching which are being used in schools and accept that it is the responsibility of the WCED to point out very clearly the disadvantages of dropping the MT too early. (WCED, 2007, p. 2)

The Language Transformation Plan supports both the use of MT as language of learning and teaching till the end of Grade 6, and, where practicable, the development of communicative competence in all three languages of the Western Cape.

A first step is that all schools must develop a written School Language Policy that shows how MT-based bilingual education will be introduced. Then, the WCED supports schools by training school governing bodies, principals, and teachers on how to implement the policy and provides training for a pool of specialists who will help schools and communities with this process.

In the pages that follow, we describe the work that Guzula and Nkence are doing with Nelli, Lumka, Sibongile, and other teachers to help them gain understanding and acceptance of the value of MT education and begin to implement systematic MT-based teaching. Since January 2008, this has involved school visits, classroom observations, demonstration lessons and workshops. Two initial advocacy workshops have been followed by regular workshops on MT teaching and learning as well as on issues related to literacy and numeracy, such as creating print-rich environments, numeracy and lifeskills corners, getting children to read for enjoyment, establishing school libraries and planning the literacy half hour. The demonstration lessons allow teachers to observe alternative teaching methods and strategies and reflect on their observations in journals. In turn, Guzula and Nkence recorded the process in written journals in which they reflected on their experiences of the process.

Teachers, Community and Schools

Nelli and Lumka both teach at Sibulele Primary School[6] in Site B, a poor, working-class, informal settlement within one of the big sprawling townships[7] called Khayelitsha on the outskirts of Cape Town. Most of the residents in the area are Xhosa speakers who have migrated to Cape Town from the largely rural eastern Cape, seeking employment. When they arrive, many stay with relatives. Often homes become overcrowded and the newcomers build shacks from corrugated iron while they continue looking for work. If they are successful and their prospects appear stable, some start building brick homes. A few Sotho speakers also live in Khayelitsha, and they tend to speak Xhosa with native-like proficiency.

However, English and/or Afrikaans are the languages people need to master in order to have a chance of achieving economic well-being in Cape Town. Most of the Site B residents do not speak either of these languages when they arrive and they do not actually have any need to use English and Afrikaans in their communities. They only require these languages when they go into Cape Town to do business.

Sibulele Primary School takes children up to Grade 9 and has a total of 800 students. There are 28 children in each of the two Grade 1 classes, which means that numbers are relatively low compared to many schools. However, some classes in the intermediate and senior phases have up to 56 children. Until recently, the school followed a typical subtractive bilingual/early exit approach with teaching and assessment being carried out in Xhosa up to the end of Grade 3, after which English was used for all reading and writing tasks and assessment.

In an interview, Nelli explained to us that although she has had several years experience teaching intermediate phase students (Grades 4 to 7), this is the first time she has taught Grade 1 students. She qualified as a junior primary teacher many years ago, and had no in-service education until recently, when she was motivated by the changes in the curriculum to do an Advanced Certificate in Language and Literacy Education. She lives with her three grandchildren in Gugulethu Township, a more established, predominantly Xhosa-speaking area, which is a 30-minute taxi ride from Sibulele Primary School. Nelli said that her livingroom is full of children's books and some newspapers and that during her spare time she likes to read—mostly in English—because the magazines she likes are in English. She has not read any novels recently, though she has begun to read children's books to her class and at home to her grandchildren. Nelli tends to speak Xhosa at home with her grandchildren, though she sometimes speaks and reads in English with her oldest grandchild because he attends an English-medium 'coloured' school. She explained that she sent her oldest grandchild to an English-medium school because of her concern to give him a 'better' education, knowing that many boys drop out of school and engage in what she terms 'other' (negative) activities. As he was the only child she was looking after at the time, she could afford the fees of an English-medium school. But because she can only pay such fees for one child, her youngest grandchild attends the school where she teaches.

Lumka teaches science and mathematics in Grade 4 at Sibulele Primary School, and told us that she feels very positive about teaching these subjects in Xhosa this year. She is proud of the fact that she surprised her colleagues by electing from the beginning to use Xhosa for scientific terms such as 'gases, solids and liquids'. A qualified senior primary teacher, Lumka also holds a further Diploma in Education. She lives alone in a more formal settlement of Khayelitsha called Bongweni (often referred to as 'Brick Homes' by those staying in informal settlements), and it takes her 5 minutes to drive to school each morning. She told us that she likes to watch television and read magazines and local newspapers. Referring to a book which she read recently by Chinua Achebe called *Crooked Rib*, she added: 'I don't want to lie, I read in English.'

Sibongile is a qualified junior primary teacher, who teaches Grade 1 at Lotus Avenue Primary School. Until our intervention at this school, Xhosa- and Afrikaans-speaking children were taught in English; now, Lotus Avenue Primary has decided to change its policy from English-medium only to being a parallel Xhosa/Afrikaans/English-medium school. The school was built after 1994 and is situated in the culturally diverse community of Leiden in Delft, with both Afrikaans and Xhosa speakers living side by side. Like many Xhosa-speaking professionals, Sibongile lives in a predominantly Afrikaans-speaking suburb, Eerste River, with her husband, who works for the WCED, and her two sons, one 13 years old, and another, aged 2. The family speaks Xhosa most of the time at home, although she and her husband sometimes mix Xhosa and English.

Sibongile's husband drops her off and picks her up each day from school, which is a 20-minute drive from their home. Her older son finds his own way by bus to his school; he studies in Grade 6. His school enrolls mainly Xhosa-speaking students and follows the usual early exit bilingual model from Xhosa to English.

Sibongile told us why he had to change schools: 'His level required that I send him there. I first took him to a "coloured" school, but he struggled with Afrikaans and English. There was totally no Xhosa language at the school.' During her spare time, Sibongile now likes to make charts for her class and write songs and poems in Xhosa for her students on her computer. She says she loves reading, but that she only reads baby magazines: 'I like children. I also get lots of advice on raising children, child nutrition and stages of development.' She reads these in English as they are not available in Xhosa.

Shifts in Paradigms and Practices

Working with the teachers at Sibulele and Lotus Avenue Primary Schools has highlighted the fact that change is never easy and that all South African teachers have had more than their fair share of it since 1994—beginning with a complex and contradictory curriculum-change process. This involved the National Department of Education's uncritical embracing of an outcomes-based education system, entitled Curriculum 2005, which was implemented for the first time in 1998. There were many problems with implementation (Jansen, 1997), ranging from the inaccessible terminology to the impracticability of applying certain teaching methods in overcrowded classes. It was later revised into what is now known as the National Curriculum Statement. The curriculum was not all negative, though, as it included the introduction of constructivist, meaning-based teaching methods for literacy learning which, among other things, promote reading for enjoyment through a 'literacy half hour'. It is of great significance that opportunities now exist to counter the widespread narrow rote-learning, isolated skills-based methods used widely in postcolonial Africa to teach early literacy (Bloch, 2006). The reality for most children whose home lives are mainly carried out using oral language has been, and continues to be, that they get little or no chance at home to form insights related to reading and writing. First encounters with print tend to be at school. At last, these are starting to include story reading, writing activities and other purposeful literacy experiences.

Despite the inclusion of 'new' methods, which offer a 'balanced approach' to teaching reading and writing (WCED, 2006), thus far literacy assessments at regional, national and international levels indicate that many children still do not read or write at 'grade level' by the end of Grades 3 and 6 (WCED, 2008). One of the critical contributing factors to this is that language policy and curriculum changes have not been thought through or implemented together (Bloch, 2000, p. 62). Another is the influence of contested global ideological approaches, such as the 'back-to-basics' initiatives arising from Reading First and No Child Left Behind Acts in the United States and related high-stakes testing, which emphasize 'scientific', brain-based 'evidence'. This provides an escape route from the messy authenticity of holistic teaching methods for those at all levels of the education system, who are understandably confused by these contradictory pedagogical messages. Thus, at the same time as policy statements point to the value of meaning-based approaches (at the heart of which has to be a language you understand), the system is easy prey for programmes which emphasize the systematic teaching of 'synthetic phonics' in English (such as Teaching Handwriting Reading And Spelling Skills; THRASS, 2007) as well as the introduction of DIBELS[8]-like testing (Early Grade Reading Assessment, 2008). Such programmes, launched officially by government, tend to be accompanied by corporate funding and immediately attract many teachers who have not had much exposure to conceptions of literacy as being embedded in sociocultural practices. It is difficult for teachers to see how concentrating on factors that stimulate meaning-making, like reading for enjoyment and supporting the creation of print-rich environments, are conducive to learning how to read and write, let alone the implications of bi/multilingualism for literacy learning. Many teachers, therefore, feel relieved to be offered the use of familiar, behaviourist, isolated skills/phonics methods—usually for a short while in the MT—but in the knowledge that it is actually reading and writing in English that literacy teaching is *really* about. When this is coupled with widespread poverty-associated factors and HIV/AIDS issues that drain families' emotional, economic and intellectual resources—as well as the large numbers of children in poorly resourced classrooms—it is unsurprising that the hoped-for success stories of the new curriculum are not widespread and the addition of the Language Transformation Plan is seen as a burden. As our work progressed, it thus became clear to us that a lot of advocacy would be needed to allay fears and bring hope and support to the teachers.

Advocacy

Advocacy workshops are intended as an initial step to provide information to teachers that might help allay their fears about teaching in the MT. This fear is often expressed adamantly, but incorrectly, as a belief that African language education simply means Bantu education,[9] the intentions of which are summed up in the following statement:

> There is no place for the African in the European community above the level of certain forms of labour. It is of no avail for him [sic] to receive a training which has as its aim, absorption in the European *community*. (Verwoerd, 1953 as cited in Bloch, 2006, p. 19)

Workshops at Lotus Avenue Primary and Sibulele Primary School conducted by Guzula and Nkence revealed how teachers at both schools feel uneasy about using Xhosa as *the* teaching medium, even though many teachers said that the introduction of MT-based education is 'a beautiful idea'. Our many years of experience in PRAESA discussing language policy with teachers and teacher trainers across the country about these issues have inevitably given rise to the same interrelated feelings, misapprehensions and questions as the ones listed below.

Nelli and her colleagues captured the sense of frustration of most teachers at Sibulele Primary School about too much and too frequent curriculum-related change when they asked the following:

> How are we supposed to make changes, as we are pilot schools with an already heavy load of administration and are already overcrowded?

> What guarantee do we have that the Western Cape Education Department will deliver on its promise to support MT-based education?

Teachers were concerned that though their schools have begun the implementation process, the WCED has not provided sufficient or adequate learning programme materials and documents, in spite of their promises. For instance, the assessment standards for the curriculum that have been given to them in both languages differ significantly from one another, leaving teachers having to decide which to follow. If non-governmental organizations like PRAESA did not run research programmes, which provide materials and advice, the schools would not have much guidance or support at all.

Moreover, there has been little systematic support for choosing Xhosa textbooks to replace English ones and there is not much information provided about which Xhosa textbooks are now available. Sufficient textbooks and appropriate terminology for some subjects have not yet been developed, or even if they have, the teachers have not been informed. As the teachers noted,

> Where are the resources? The WCED must deliver materials and not expect teachers to teach, translate and be terminologists at the same time.

Teachers also expressed their fears that they might not know how to teach in Xhosa because, although it is their MT, they were trained as teachers in English:

> We have not been trained to teach in Xhosa, how is the department going to support us?

Teachers born in the Western Cape felt that they do not know enough Xhosa to teach through it, as their variety of the language is very different from standard written Xhosa. There are also a few Sotho-speaking teachers in the school, and it remains unclear how speakers of other African languages will be accommodated in the implementation process.

> How can we deal with the issue of different languages and language varieties in the classrooms?

> Some children speak languages other than Xhosa and we are not sure how to meet their needs.

Teachers were sceptical about the assertion that English is part of MT-based education and worried that it would be neglected if the focus was on Xhosa in the foundation phase. They thought that parents would also feel insecure about Xhosa continuing as a teaching medium in the intermediate phase, and thus take their children to other schools that offer teaching through English only. They asked,

> You talk about bilingual education, but doesn't MT-based bilingual education actually mean a 'Xhosa-only' education system?

Teachers themselves can understand the logic of MT teaching in the foundation phase, because the children do not know English yet, but the teachers worry about disadvantaging the children if they teach them in MT in the intermediate phase, not least because there are few or no materials in Xhosa for content subjects such as mathematics and science.

> How are we going to teach maths and science in Xhosa in the intermediate phase?

Teachers feel that if we want children to be able to answer matric exams (the final school-leaving exam) in English, we have to introduce English as soon as possible. This view reflects a common understanding that the best way for children to learn a new language is for them to learn it from the beginning. Related to this is the misunderstanding that continuing to use a home language in school hinders learning English because children's brains, like a container which is having too much liquid poured into it, become too full; thus, they get confused and cannot cope (Cummins, 2000). This view is expressed in the following question as a concern that information learned through the MT will not transfer to English:

> How are we to believe that school results have a correlation with the language used and will matric exam papers be in Xhosa?

Compounding their concerns, teachers noted the absence of School Management Teams (principal, deputy principals and heads of departments) as well as Department of Education officials in the advocacy workshops:

> Where is management? They are supposed to be part of the workshop. How will they support us if they are not here? You are here for us, but do they care?

Discussion

Guzula and Nkence's reaction to the teachers was to affirm all of their concerns and to inform them that some of the problems have solutions, whereas in the case of others work has begun to address the issues they raise, but sometimes a lack of communication prevents teachers from knowing that initiatives are underway. In summary, the following response was given:

- First, it is not accurate to describe MT-based bilingual education in 'all or nothing' terms—that is, as an 'either Xhosa or English' situation. It is a 'both Xhosa and English' scenario for good reason, as research shows that this is how we can offer the best opportunity for children to learn effectively, *and* learn English (e.g. in the South African context, see Bloch & Alexander, 2003). However, it is necessary for teachers to consider the available information for themselves and come to trust that this is possible, given that it takes time for results to show. Moreover, when teachers reflect on their classroom language use, they realize that although they say they teach in English, they perpetually switch to and from MT to bridge the 'learning gap', and they do so without textbooks in MT or any prior training in MT instruction (Plüddemann, Braam, October, & Wababa, 2004). Because this is the beginning of a process, teachers and parents will have to wait for the evidence that rather than educationally disadvantaging children, this will provide the best of both worlds. In fact, the current system does not allow Xhosa-speaking children to learn well in any language. When children learn through their MT, it does not mean that they will not learn English, but rather that they have to be taught English explicitly. This is similar to Afrikaans speakers who learn in Afrikaans throughout their schooling and learn English as a subject and who eventually become competent English speakers and get good jobs. Xhosa speakers too need opportunities to learn well in Xhosa so that the academic skills they learn can transfer from one language to the other.

- Second, the WCED is aware that they need textbooks and storybooks during this implementation process, and the issue of materials has begun to be addressed. The WCED is now collaborating with publishers and non-governmental organizations like PRAESA to translate textbooks into Xhosa in the different learning areas (subjects) and there are programmes to get storybooks into schools and to get children reading for enjoyment both in MT and English. For instance, a science dictionary is available in Xhosa and language dictionaries have also recently been published.

- Third, regarding the introduction of English as a second language, it is inadequate to only introduce it orally in Grade 3, when in Grade 4 the curriculum assumes a high level of literacy in English. If the intention is to offer bilingual education, biliteracy should be considered earlier on, if and when there is support for teachers. Regarding the place of other languages in school, teachers can explore strategies to welcome and use other languages in class, for instance, through songs and greetings and, where available, teachers should invite speakers of those languages to visit class to tell and read stories. Teachers also need to be trained as language specialists who understand the relevant theories of language learning and acquisition so that they know how to teach English properly.

Beginning to Apply the New Language Policy

Following advocacy meetings, a process of negotiation by teachers and the school-governing bodies[10] has resulted in draft language policies for each school. At Sibulele Primary, the new policy states that Xhosa will be used from Grades 1 to 6 as a language of teaching, learning and assessment. From Grades 7 to 9 the language of teaching, learning and assessment will be English. The policy does not state when English is to be introduced as an additional language but, from further discussions with the school, some teachers felt that it should be introduced from Grade 3 as an oral language. We suggested that biliteracy is possible if teachers know how to introduce and teach a new language and if the children are exposed to the second language, from as early as the reception year (a preschool year for 5- to 6-year-old children).

Both Nelli and Lumka were aware that the Language Transformation Plan requires them to teach in the MT. Although they did not know the details of their school language policy, because they had not read it, Nelli said, 'According to our knowledge, we know that children must be read to in their mother tongue, they must write and learn in their mother tongue.' This seemingly obvious statement is significant; for many teachers and parents across the continent, teaching literacy is assumed to mean teaching in English.

Although they were both happy with the policy, Nelli said she felt anxious about the pilot after the recent removal of the Minister of Education from his portfolio,[11] as he had been driving the Language Transformation Plan. She said she had spoken to her principal, as she was worried that the new minister might actually revert to English-only education. Her principal told her that she is equally worried, but assured her that the school will not change its language policy. Nelli also noticed that not everyone is as convinced as she is: 'I hear other people complaining and chatting that "so and so" teaches in Xhosa but that the children are writing in English. They say we will be failing the children if we allow them to write in Xhosa. That does not deter me.' She has seen that '… children are free in the classrooms. I don't think there's a child who fears talking in class now, although the children said it was difficult at first because of the lack of Xhosa teaching and learning material in the form of textbooks.'

One of the remarkably negative features of lessons in classrooms across Africa is that children rarely speak, as they are not allowed to do so, except to answer questions that the teacher has asked. Another is that lessons are dominated by choral chanting of the required phrases, sentences or other lesson material. Because these features involve both language medium *and* teaching method, there is always a marked improvement in the atmosphere of a classroom where children and teacher understand one another. 'The use of mother tongue helps us a lot,' said Lumka. 'We only teach English as a subject in the intermediate phase. Children now learn faster. Before you [PRAESA] came, I used to mix languages. We were supposed to teach in English but when we realized that children do not understand, we used Xhosa. It was a very long and tiring process because I was repeating lessons. When I taught in English, they would not really understand the concepts, but now when I teach in Xhosa, the children understand. They are actively involved even if they make mistakes. They are very confident. . . . They ask you surprising questions.' This comment alludes to another common and related feature of many classrooms—that many teachers tend to have very low expectations of children's potential and capabilities. When children use a language they understand, teachers realize that they are far more intelligent and competent than they had previously thought possible.

Lumka noted that because she has been teaching continuously in Xhosa it feels problematic to carry on teaching English as a subject in the intermediate phase. She even asked one of her colleagues to take over teaching English because she wants to focus on using Xhosa now: 'Honestly speaking, I teach in Xhosa now. I wish we could teach in Xhosa in Grade 7 as well. English confuses me now.'

In the foundation phase, teachers always used Xhosa for teaching and assessment. The difference is that they teach with more confidence now, knowing that what they are doing is both legitimate and pedagogically sound. It makes a huge difference that they do not have to 'get to English' quickly, and they are becoming more conscious about the way they use language. Previously, foundation-phase classrooms could display and use any mixture of print in English or Xhosa, but the assumption was that English was more important. English charts and teaching materials are generally commercially produced and thus looked very neat and well-kept, whereas those in Xhosa tended to be handmade by the teachers and looked less neat. Now handmade posters and charts in Xhosa are improving in quality.

In the intermediate phase, there have been significant changes in the language of teaching and assessment. All subjects are being taught in Xhosa, and study notes for children are written in Xhosa as well. This has been a bold step for Lumka, who has had to face opposition from others:

> The most interesting thing which happened recently is that the school welcomed student teachers from local universities. The students were told to teach in Xhosa and this came as a shock to them and their supervisor. The supervisor was reported to be very unhappy about us as we insisted on our mother-tongue policy.

New Language Policy at Lotus Avenue Primary

Lotus Avenue Primary has defined its draft school language policy objectives as being to promote multilingualism among children, teachers and non-teaching staff, to promote non-racism in the school and the community, to teach the three official languages of the Western Cape to learners and staff, to implement MT-based bilingual education from the reception year to Grade 6 and to make provision for it in Grade 7 in the future, depending on a needs analysis investigation. The policy does not explain how MT instruction will be supported, but it does say that English is to be introduced in Grade 1 in both Xhosa and Afrikaans parallel classes as a first additional language (informally through songs, games, simple instructions and basic greetings). This should gradually increase in Grade 2 and be formally assessed from Grade 3 onwards. It is ironic that English becomes the first additional language for both Afrikaans and Xhosa speakers who know and use each other's languages in the community. In other words, the policy does not offer any choice of first additional language.

Assessment from Grades 4 to 6 will still be in English for Xhosa MT speakers who are taught in Xhosa, while assessment matches the language of teaching for Afrikaans and English MT speakers. It is thus likely that students' results will suffer because of the mismatch between language of teaching and language of assessment. Moreover, this may continue to be an incentive for teachers to teach more

English and less Xhosa to prepare their students for the tests (Menken, 2008). The team who wrote the school's language policy attributes this mismatch between language of teaching and assessment in the Xhosa classes to the fact that there is a lack of print and textbooks in Xhosa and that assessment will only happen in Xhosa after they have consulted with the rest of the teachers and established common standards for assessment in all grades. English is currently used to teach Xhosa MT speakers in Grade 7 and, as there are no Xhosa-medium high schools, they want to prepare the students for English high schools.

Sibongile said that she is aware that her new school language policy requires children to learn in their MTs up to Grade 6, but she felt that it would be better if it was still only up to Grade 3. She is comfortable with the use of Xhosa in the foundation phase because it is the language the children speak, but in the inter-mediate phase, she would prefer children to be taught through English and Afrikaans, with Xhosa as a subject. Her concern was about integration, as the children are separated into language streams: 'I am saying this so that we can integrate the children, so that they live together like they do in the community.'

When asked if the use of English would not create the same problems for the Xhosa-speaking children as it had created for her son who she had to move back to a school in a Xhosa-speaking setting when he could not cope with English-medium instruction, Sibongile said that she had not thought about this consciously. She now found that relating the issue to her personal experience changed. She has been thinking about language at work. She realized that the 'English stream' consists of many Afrikaans- and Xhosa-speaking children who are struggling and are thus disadvantaged: 'I have a problem with the English classes. I would prefer it if there were Afrikaans and Xhosa classes only. These children will experience the problems that my son experienced.'

From Mother Tongue or English, to Mother Tongue and English

One of the pervasive assumptions underpinning our education system and the subtractive bilingualism base from which it gets delivered to African language-speaking children is that *somehow* children will be able to start learning through English at the beginning of Grade 4. Yet there is little attention paid to how English will be taught and learned, and many of the teachers themselves have a poor command of English and are thus ill-equipped as linguistic role models for English. The introduction of an intentional bilingual system thus offers a chance to think through and address how to teach English effectively.

At Sibulele Primary, there is a lack of clarity among the teachers about when English is supposed to be introduced in the new bilingual model or how it should be taught. The present situation is still that English is taught as a subject for the first time in Grade 3 by an intermediate-phase teacher. At Sibulele Primary, English has always been introduced orally only at the Grade 3 level, so Nelli does not read in English at all to the Grade 1 students. As she says about her Grade 1 class: 'I don't want to lie, I don't do English in my class. I think I will start by introducing rhymes and songs and labelling things, but I am not sure if I will be doing the right thing.' Although Nelli has many English books in her class, she has not read them in English to the children. Instead, she translates them into Xhosa as she reads.

Although the policy at Lotus Avenue Primary states that English has to be introduced in Grade 1, Sibongile has not yet begun this process as she did not know the details of the policy until recently. She feels that English should be introduced by using a lot of pictures and labels. For example, if she talks about dogs, she feels there should be a picture with the word *dog* on it. She calls this the translation method for second-language teaching, adding that she would not limit the children's use of their MT, but let them draw on it to help them to learn English.

Negotiation and Resistance: Early Literacy and Numeracy in the Classroom

Our observations provide further evidence that many teachers continue to follow narrow, skills-based teaching methods (Bloch, 1994). Although official policy promotes constructivism and a 'balanced approach' to literacy learning (WCED, 2006), the kind of displays and activities that are prevalent in both Sibongile and Nelli's Grade 1 classes imply that reading means reading from charts specifically designed to teach letters of the alphabet, letter–sound combinations and unrelated words. Language is broken down into small parts that get put together to form whole words from part to whole, simple to complex. This is illustrated by a glimpse at Nelli's charts and lesson below:

Chart 1	Chart 2
Usapho luka-M (*Family of M*)	Masifunde ngo-P (*Let's read about P*)
Ma, me, mi, mo, mu	Pa, pe, pi, po, pu
Mama (*mother*)	Ipapa (*porridge*)
makazi (*aunt*)	ipoloni (*polony*)
mamela (*listen*)	ipinki (*pink*)
amasi (*sour milk*)	ipolishi (*polish*)
umalume (*uncle*)	ipeyinti (*paint*)
amanzi (*water*)	ipilisi (*pills*)
	iparafini (*paraffin*)

The intended lesson sequence was, as the following example illustrates, for the children to read the letter first, build sounds by adding vowels and then say words to list all of the words that begin with the particular letter.

[Teacher points to individual children who take turns to lead the reading of charts.

Child leads the class in reading from the wall using a pointer and the whole class reads in unison]:

F
fa, fe, fi, fo, fu.
Faka (*put in*)
fola (*queue up*)
fota (*take a photograph*)
futha (*steam*)
funda (*read/learn*)

Xoli's Journal Notes (June 11, 2008)

After making suggestions related to teaching reading with real texts, and while the teachers waited for storybooks in Xhosa to be delivered,[12] we demonstrated how to prepare lessons using well-known rhymes and songs. We asked teachers to write some of these down to read with the children. Sibongile found this difficult because she felt strongly that typed-up charts and posters look better than hand-written ones, but Nelli's classroom walls now display rhyme and song posters that she changes every week. Because both schools have a literacy half-hour session, we have planned timetables with both teachers and children, with the children taking the lead on what they would like to do during the literacy half-hour session every morning. We have agreed on storytelling on Mondays, teachers reading aloud or doing shared reading[13] on Tuesdays, paired reading[14] on Wednesdays, silent or independent reading[15] on Thursdays and introducing new rhymes, songs, games and riddles on Fridays. These would then be read before the next reading sessions.

Though Sibongile is receptive to the idea of using MT for literacy, she resists teaching numeracy in Xhosa. A common perception among many teachers is that it is easier for children to learn 'their numbers' in English than in Xhosa and that Xhosa is not a language that can be used for mathematics. On one observed occasion, Sibongile was teaching the sequence of numbers and had written the following:

2, 3, ….
4, 5, ….
7, 8, ….
2, 4, ….
4, 6, ….

She pointed to the numbers 2 and 4, saying 'two, four …' and the children added the next number (6) in the sequence. They did all of this in English.

When asked why she taught mathematics in English, she responded: 'It is difficult for children to do numbers in Xhosa. At home they don't count in Xhosa, inye (one), zimbini (two). So now what must I write? Must I write "zine" for "four"? I'm not the only one who does this. Other teachers struggle to teach mathematics in Xhosa.' Because Sibongile is unaccustomed to using numbers in Xhosa, she found it hard to accept the validity of representing 'four' by 'zine'. She is correct that many teachers feel this way.

One of Sibongile's colleagues at Lotus Avenue Primary, who teaches Grade 4 in the intermediate phase, also struggles to teach mathematics in MT. After being accustomed to teaching in English, she was required to teach in the Xhosa parallel stream in Xhosa. We observed her using English mathematics textbooks, though she tried to talk in Xhosa to the children. However, her language emerged as code-mixing rather than the systematic use of one or the other language, when she asked the children to read the sum they were correcting in their books:

Teacher:	Uya kangaphi u*seven* ku*thirty*? (How many times does seven go into thirty?)
Learners:	Kayi*four* (four times)
Teacher:	Ewe kayi*four* kusale u*two* (Yes four times and the remainder is two). [Next question in English]
Learners read:	Divide six twenty by five (in English)

It will take some effort and time for teachers to stop using code-mixing as it has become common practice with many. The need to code-mix will only fade once all significant aspects of teaching are delivered as a matter of course in Xhosa.

Discussion

At the time of writing this chapter, although Xhosa is being used more systematically and classrooms are becoming more print-rich, with books in both languages, the teachers are in some ways still wary about our approach. Nelli, who is used to making sure that her students can sound out letters and sight words, has expressed the fear that because some children cannot yet point to the words they are reading in the rhymes, this might mean they are merely memorizing and might never learn words properly. She has also confessed that she is still not clear about what to do with writing, as she does not know how to begin. We have answered her concerns by suggesting that she can still use her trusted method with flashcards but ask children to match the words on the flashcards with those on the song or rhyme chart. With regards to writing, we have suggested letter, journal and message writing to encourage and motivate children to write for real and personally meaningful reasons (Bloch & Alexander, 2003; Hall, 1989).

We have also given demonstration lessons where we asked children to bring photographs of themselves which they wrote about and which we then made into a collage. Neither the teachers nor the children had done this before, and Sibongile commented how amazed she was at what the children can already write: 'They loved writing about themselves, which is something different from their normal routine' (Sibongile's journal entry, 15 July 2008).

Teachers find it difficult to appreciate the power and value of reading for enjoyment for learning (Krashen, 1993). Pleasure reading does not happen in most African classrooms (Bloch, 2006), including, for example, in Nelli's and Sibongile's classrooms, because they cannot see its significance for learning how to read in the early stages. Thus, they tend to resist reading aloud to the children because they regard it as unnecessary, particularly as it is not assessed: '…What I noticed after you read a story is that you did not assess children afterwards. There's nothing they write down that shows what they have read from the story. Now how do you make sure that you know what they have learnt?' (Sibongile's journal entry, 13 August 2008*).*

Neither the literacy teaching approach issues discussed previously nor the issue of which language to use for teaching numeracy are ones that will be resolved in a short space of time. They are part of an ongoing process to help teachers understand and reflect on their challenges. For instance, the fact that children tend to know numbers in English can be regarded positively in a bilingual system, as the teachers can now add to this knowledge by providing the English-equivalent of Xhosa words and helping the children distinguish between English and Xhosa.

Conclusion

In this chapter, we have contextualized and described the first 6 months of a 4-year development research project focused on language policy implementation. The teachers we are working with are beginning to think about how to shift their perceptions and practices under very difficult conditions. They are fascinated by their students' changing attitudes towards reading and writing, which has been instrumental in helping them reflect on their teaching methods. We, in turn, are thinking about ours. There are no quick-fix solutions to the language-related challenges that we face in classrooms across South Africa. Ten years ago, we wrote about the 'glimmers of hope educators feel when small but deeply significant steps are taken, which serve to inspire us all to carry on' (Bloch & Nkence, 2000, p. 30). In 2008, these words remain as apt as they were then.

Discussion Questions

1 This chapter mentions several different language policies that the three teachers must negotiate. List at least three of the policies mentioned, what they are and how they affect language instruction.

2 What is the significance of South Africa's 1997 Language in Education Policy for social justice and a more egalitarian country post-apartheid?

3 Imagine that a new policy was adopted in your school district requiring you to be a 'language implementation policy pioneer' like the teachers in this

chapter and teach in a language that you and your students knew but that had never been used before as a medium of instruction. What supports would you need to be successful? Which supports do the South African teachers in this chapter receive and which do they still need?

4   Literacy instruction is a topic addressed in several chapters of this book, including this one as well as Chapter 14 on Chilean language policy. In what ways is literacy instruction important for language learning?

Notes

1   In South Africa, this is defined as education which begins and continues with children's mother tongue, while another language (typically English) is gradually added to become a co-teaching medium.

2   Names of teachers and the schools where they work have been changed.

3   Under apartheid, the Group Areas Act was used to force people to live according to racial classifications—people were labelled as black, coloured, white or Indian. Schools too were segregated along racial lines in an unequal education system with 'white' (English- or Afrikaans-speaking) children attending better resourced schools than those for 'coloured' (Afrikaans- or English-speaking) or 'black' (African-language-speaking) children.

4   This means that the native speakers of the languages value their languages—but only within certain limits. They do not believe that these languages can ever be as powerful or have the same status as the hegemonic, ex-colonial languages like English or French.

5   Although based at the University of Cape Town, PRAESA is an independently funded organization. Because language is a deeply political and contentious issue in Africa, with many believing that a system with English as second language is the only way to 'overcome' multilingualism, it is difficult to get South African government funding or funding from the South African business community. We are thus a small organization, which has been in a position to take independent initiative and provide leadership in this domain.

6   Names of schools have been changed.

7   The term *township* is still used to refer to the suburbs where 'black' and 'coloured' people were forced to live under the Group Areas Act during the apartheid years.

8   Diagnostic Intervention of Basic Early Literacy Skills.

9   *Bantu education*, an inferior system of education aimed at keeping black people in menial positions in society was the term given to the schooling imposed on all children except those labelled *white* under apartheid.

10   These are the official management teams of schools made up of teachers, community members and parents.

11   Local politics in the Western Cape tends to be unstable, with positions of responsibility changing hands fairly frequently.

12   PRAESA donated storybooks in Xhosa and English to each of the two schools so that the teachers could create reading and writing corners in their Grade 1 classrooms.

13   In shared reading, the teacher and the children read together. A book may be read and re-read many times. At first the teacher does most of the reading but as the children get to know the story, they join in and 'share' the reading (Cunningham & Allington, 1999).

14   In paired reading, a child takes turns to read with and to another child or adult. They help each other read and talk about the story.

15   In silent or independent reading, children choose what and when to read on their own.

References

Alexander, N. (2002). Linguistic rights, language planning and democracy in post-apartheid South Africa. In S. J. Baker (Ed.), *Language policy: Lessons from Global Models* (p. 119). Monterey, CA: Monterey Institute of International Studies.

Bloch, C. (1994). *Report on the acquisition of literacy in young children in South Africa.* Unpublished report prepared by PRAESA on behalf of the Independent Development Trust.

Bloch, C. (2000). Don't expect a story: Young children's literacy learning in South Africa early years. *International Journal of Research and Development 120*, 57–67.

Bloch, C. (2005). Building bridges between oral and written language: Facilitating reading opportunities for children in Africa. In N. Alexander (Ed.), *Mother tongue based bilingual education in southern Africa: The dynamics of implementation* (pp. 69–82). Frankfurt Am Main-Cape Town: Multilingualism Network.

Bloch, C. (2006). *Theory and strategy of early literacy in contemporary Africa with special reference to South Africa.* Cape Town: PRAESA.

Bloch, C., & Alexander, N. (2003). Aluta continua: The relevance of the continua of biliteracy to South African multilingual schools. In N. Hornberger (Ed.), *Continua of biliteracy: An ecological framework for educational policy, research, and practice in multilingual settings* (pp. 91–121). Clevedon: Multilingual Matters.

Bloch, C., & Nkence, N. (2000). Glimmers of hope: Emergent writing and reading in a multilingual foundation phase classroom. *Proceedings of the teachers inservice project (TIP).* University of the Western Cape, 3rd Annual Colloquium 1998. Cape Town: University of the Western Cape.

Cummins, J. (2000). *Language, power and pedagogy: Bilingual children in the crossfire.* Clevedon, England: Multilingual Matters.

Cunningham, P., & Allington R. (1999). *Classrooms that work: They can all read and write* (2nd ed.). New York: Longman.

Early Grade Reading Assessment (EGRT). (2008). *Early grade reading assessment toolkit.* Research Triangle Institute Park, NC: Research Triangle Institute International. Retrieved March 30, 2009, from https://www.eddataglobal.org/documents/index.cfm?fuseaction=pubDetail&ID=149

Edwards, V. (2008). *The culture of reading: An evaluation of a key programme of PRAESA.* Cape Town: PRAESA.

Hall, N. (Ed.). (1989). *Writing with reason: The emergence of authorship in young children.* London: Hodder & Stoughton.

Jansen, J. (1997). *Curriculum 2005 and OBE language teachers' dream or nightmare?* Retrieved June 8, 2009, from http://www.geocities.com/Athens/Delphi/4368/c4obe.htm

Krashen, S. (1993). *The power of reading: Insights from the research.* Englewood: Libraries Unlimited.

Menken, K. (2008). *English learners left behind: Standardized testing as language policy.* Clevedon: Multilingual Matters.

Plüddemann, P., Braam, D., October, M., & Wababa, Z. (2004). *Dual medium and parallel medium schooling in the Western Cape: From default to design.* Cape Town: PRAESA.

Teaching Handwriting Reading And Spelling Skills (THRASS). (2007). *THRASS Absa TalkTogether literacy project moves forward with launch of second TalkTogether school.* Press release. Chester, UK: Author. Retrieved June 8, 2009, from http://www.kidzworld.co.za/thrass/thrass_absafundsthrassupdate.htm

Western Cape Education Department (WCED). (2006). *Literacy and numeracy strategy 2006–2016.* Western Cape: Author.

Western Cape Education Department. (2007). *Language transformation plan.* Western Cape: Author.

Western Cape Education Department. (2008). *Media Release, 1 November, 2008.* Retrieved November 1, 2008, from http://wced.wcape.gov.za/comms/press/2008/67_litnum.html

Enacting Language Policy through the Facilitator Model in a Monolingual Policy Context in the United States

Bonnie English and Manka M. Varghese

Introduction

The purpose of this chapter is to provide a description and analysis of a case study of two teachers, an English-as-a-second-language (ESL) teacher and a classroom teacher, working together in a facilitator model (which will be explained later in the chapter) within a restrictive district policy in Washington State. First, we provide background on the national, state, and district context, especially with regards to language policy. Then, we provide a description of the case study followed by a discussion of the collaboration between these two teachers in relation to how they negotiate their particular language policy context. This book provides a number of much-needed examples of teachers enacting language policies at the classroom level, an area within the study of language policy that has not been given enough attention. This chapter, in particular, contributes to this body of research not only by looking at the collaboration between two teachers as they negotiate a language policy but also in two other significant ways. The first way is by understanding how the negotiation of language policy at the classroom level must be examined through the staffing models that are shaped and often constrained by the broader language policy context; in this case, the state, districts, and schools (Creese, 2005). Moreover, the limited research that has been done on teachers negotiating and enacting language policy has mostly focused on teachers wrestling with how to add a layer of multilingualism to a monolingual policy (Varghese, 2008; Varghese & Stritikus, 2005). Therefore, the second significant contribution that this case study makes is by looking at how teachers wrestle with a monolingual policy and restrictive staffing model in their practice to different degrees.

Background

It is well known that the United States does not have an official language policy. However, in effect, English has functioned as the official language existing alongside pockets of linguistic diversity that have waxed and waned since the 1600s. Overall, the attitudes toward the existence, promotion, and repression of linguistic diversity in the country have been shifting over the centuries. A number of scholars have linked these shifts to debates over immigration, national origin, national unity and racial purity (for more information and analysis about the historical evolution of language policy in the United States, see Crawford, 1999; Hornberger, 2005; Wiley & Wright, 2004).

In the wake of the Civil Rights Act, President Lyndon Johnson signed into law Title VII, The Bilingual Education Act (BEA) in 1968 to channel federal funds to both economically and linguistically disadvantaged students in schools. The BEA did not recommend a particular language policy or instructional approach but rather provided funds for programs for these students as well as teacher training. The BEA, as stated by August and Hakuta (1997, p. 16), has sought to provide "meaningful and equitable access for English-language learners to the curriculum, rather than serving as an instrument of language policy for the nation through the development of their native languages." In a similar fashion, the major court case that has provided the legal mandate for providing special services to children who speak a language other than English—*Lau v. Nichols* (1974)—has also not resulted in a specific instructional or programmatic recommendation, which would have provided a possible language education policy.

Many would agree that since the relatively tolerant policies of the 1960s, there has been a gradual shift toward a monolingual environment in the country (Menken, 2008; Wiley & Wright, 2004). This has been underscored by a general shift toward the funding and support through the BEA of programs that support English-only instruction (compared to those that support native-language instruction) through various administrations as well as a national English-only movement and various states' English-only policies, most notably Proposition 227 in California and Proposition 203 in Arizona (passed in the past decade).

Most recently, at the federal level, the passage of No Child Left Behind (NCLB), which reauthorized the Elementary and Secondary Education Act in 2002, removed the term bilingual education from federal legislation and programs. The Language Instruction for Limited English-Proficient and Immigrant Students (Title III of the NCLB) replaced Title VII, the BEA. At the same time, one of the intended outcomes of this new legislation has been an increased accountability of districts and schools toward the educational progress of these students, as all students must now be assessed and tested. It is also important to keep in mind that Title III does not prohibit native-language instruction, although it pays particular emphasis, especially through its funding, on programs and instruction that focus on learning English.

As noted in the previous paragraph, states have taken different approaches toward their own language policies with an increasing number of states choosing more restrictive and monolingual policies, such as those instituted in California and Arizona, among others. The case of Washington in this context has been an interesting one in which to investigate the growth, instruction, achievement, and policy context for English language learners (ELLs). This is because it is one of the states that has experienced the largest growth of this student population in the past decade with 10% to 15% of the school-age population currently being desig nated as ELL (Kindler, 2002). Federal funding goes through the state office, which in turn supports instructional services in school districts enrolling eligible students. In addition, the default program in the state is one using native-language instruction, which the state refers to as a bilingual program. It is important to note that native-language instruction is not prohibited in Washington State, and on paper it is actually encouraged. In actual practice, however, the number of programs that use native-language instruction is small. ESL programs are supported by the state guidelines where it is also stated that when the use of native-language instruction is not "practical," ESL programs are allowed to serve the needs of ELLs. The guidelines do not provide many specifics of types of programs that districts and schools should implement.

This section provides important background to the national and state language policy in which the two teachers examined in this case study work in Eastlake District.[1] It shows how Eastlake District exists in the following layered context: (a) a national shift toward an exclusive focus on learning English and increased accountability for the achievement of ELLs, and (b) a state that allows (and in name, encourages) native-language instruction, but where most programs focus on learning English and do not use native-language instruction.

The Case Study

Eastlake: District Context

Eastlake School District is located near a major metropolitan area in Washington State. The district's boundaries encompass a span of urban and suburban neighborhoods with more than 15,000 students. Eastlake has 16 elementary schools, 7 middle schools, and 6 high schools. Eastlake is a nationally distinguished district with five of its high schools selected for *Newsweek Magazine*'s list of top 200 high schools in America.

Eastlake has a linguistically diverse student population speaking more than 20 different languages, and the largest immigrant populations are from Asian countries. The three most common languages among ELL students are Korean, Japanese, and Chinese. Many immigrant families come to the Eastlake area with contracts to work as engineers or software developers for a large corporation with headquarters there. The district's total student population is approximately 57% White, 25% Asian, 8% Hispanic, and 10% other. Eastlake is a relatively affluent school district, with less than 18% of students qualifying for free or reduced lunch.

Eastlake's Language Policy: A Focus on English and Structures of Support

Eastlake's official language policy states: "All ELLs will learn at high levels and all staff will share in that responsibility." Similar to many districts across Washington State, Eastlake's policy focuses on learning English without the use of the native language. Eastlake has two structures to support the implementation of their language policy. The first structure is a newcomer program. Students who enter Eastlake schools with very little exposure to English attend a half-day newcomer program for intensive English oral-language development. Newcomer students spend the other half of their day in a mainstream classroom learning math, social studies, and science with their grade-level peers. The newcomer program is a temporary support for students, removed when students demonstrate intermediate fluency in spoken English. The newcomer program supports the district's official language policy sharing responsibility among staff members for educating ELLs and rapidly transitioning them into mainstream education.

The second structure of support for ELLs in Eastlake is the facilitator model. This model is designed to support all ELLs not in the newcomer program and includes students who have tested out of the newcomer program and/or who enter Eastlake schools with some English fluency. The facilitator model is an inclusion model, designed to help ELLs succeed in the mainstream classroom. Rather than providing support directly to students, the policy aims at improving classroom teachers' instruction through facilitation. The official description of the facilitator model states:

> The ESL Facilitator works together with the classroom teacher, and principals, to serve students at the Intermediate level of English proficiency in the mainstream classroom. Supporting Intermediate level English Language Learners is a collaborative process in order to meet the academic needs of each student. The ESL Facilitator models how to scaffold and provide accommodations for the ELLs working within the context of the Eastlake School District curriculum. The ESL Facilitator, and the classroom teacher, closely observe the Advanced level ELL, but may not work directly with the student. Ongoing conversations and observations allow both teachers to support the students when needed. (ESL Facilitator Document, revised 2007)

Eastlake's facilitator model is essentially an inclusion model with ongoing support and professional development available to classroom teachers. Classroom teachers are responsible for all instruction of ELLs. There is no required experience or specialization for classroom teachers in working with ELLs. It is assumed that the linguistic needs of students will simply be addressed through what De Jong and Harper (2005) critically term "good teaching" strategies for all students, in this case ones that the classroom teacher learns from the facilitator.

In theory, the facilitator model supports the district's language policy by sharing the knowledge and expertise of ESL teachers with the entire teaching staff. ESL facilitators are certificated teachers with specialized knowledge of ESL methods.[2] Many facilitators have prior experience as ESL teachers. As the label "facilitator" indicates, ESL facilitators shift away from their role of teaching students to a new role of facilitating teacher learning and thereby providing professional development. As the case study highlights, in practice, the staffing of facilitators limits the actual capacity for sharing of knowledge and expertise.

ESL facilitators are assigned to schools on the basis of the number of students qualified for ESL services. Across the Eastlake District, only four elementary schools have one or two full-time facilitators. The majority of facilitators are spread across two school sites. Twelve of the elementary schools in the district have half-time facilitators attempting to cover every classroom with an ELL. Facilitators typically worked with 10 to 20 teachers at each school. The facilitator model expects that facilitators "provide support to the general education teacher and link all planning and teaching to the Eastlake district curriculum. The ESL teacher works directly with the classroom teacher. . . ." The intention, as we discuss in the next section, is to build instructional capacity, with limited resources, across the entire staff for effectively teaching ELLs.

The Philosophy of Eastlake's Facilitator Model

Responding to their multilingual population with discourses of equality and integration, Eastlake School District adheres to a facilitator model that focuses on immersion in mainstream classrooms. The facilitator model, adopted in 2003, intends to increase the capacity of mainstream classroom teachers, seeing language development as something that is easily integrated into the curriculum. ESL is deemed to be a set of strategies or accommodations and not considered an area of expertise in and of itself. The work of Gibbons (2002) is cited by district administrators and used in professional development as the foundation for this model. The district administrators point to Gibbon's claim that the mainstream curriculum is the best language-learning environment.

In interviews with district administrators, two prominent philosophies emerge as rationale for the facilitator model. District administrators emphasize equality and integration as principles on which the facilitator model rested. The facilitator model promises systematic services that are consistent for all students, supported by a discourse of "equal access." One ESL Administrator explains it the following way:

> And our belief system was we needed to provide a system that worked for every child. If there's one Urdu-speaking child in our district, we need to provide the same level of service that we do for the majority of our non-English-speakers. (interview, January 15, 2008)

The emphasis on equal access validates the district's adoption of the facilitator model. Consequently, funds and attention are directed away from first-language services. There is no feasible way to ensure that all ESL students will receive primary language support; therefore, it is seen as unfair for any student to receive this support. One significant consequence of the new policy is a change in personnel. Multiple, bilingual, para-professional positions have been eliminated and replaced with a part-time, certificated, monolingual ESL specialist. The knowledge and expertise of a certified ESL teacher fits within the equal-access discourse for the administration, whereas the primary language support offered by the bilingual para-professionals does not.

For instance, in Eastlake School District there is a Spanish Immersion Program[3] at one school, but its intention is not to support students whose first language was Spanish. Rather, the school was established to provide language diversity and enrichment for native English-speaking students. The ESL director clearly delineates the Spanish Immersion Program from bilingual education:

By the way, it was one of the points of conflict with the *State Director of Bilingual Programs* is when he was teaching a bilingual class . . . he and *a local university professor* both wanted to know why couldn't we set up a school for Hispanics in this district. I said, "You mean a segregated school for just ESL Hispanics?" and *the university professor* said, "Well, you've done it at Dos Lagos." "No, we have not done it in Dos Lagos. There is one Hispanic in Dos Lagos. We have a Spanish Immersion School in Dos Lagos, but it's not a school—center for Hispanic kids." (interview, February 14, 2008)

In this quote, the ESL director equates bilingual education that provides first-language support with segregation. The Spanish Immersion Program at Dos Lagos is not designed to support or even include Spanish-speaking students. In fact, Dos Lagos has the lowest percentage of ELLs of any school in the district. The lack of primary language support in Eastlake is justified by the district through discourses of equality (all students receiving the same type of support) and integration (primary-language support would lead to segregation).

In the next section, we examine the facilitator model in two school contexts. The two schools share one ESL facilitator: Amy Allen. The two schools are typical of the 12 elementary schools in the district that have half-time facilitators. We offer a descriptive narrative of how Amy interprets and enacts the facilitator model within the two school contexts, one less successfully (at Birchfield) and one more successfully (at Cedar Valley). We provide an example of the more successful enactment at Cedar Valley through an analysis of the collaborative partnership between Amy Allen and Carolina Cross.

Eastlake Language Policy Enacted at Birchfield and Cedar Valley

Amy Allen is an ESL facilitator in Eastlake School District and splits her time between Birchfield and Cedar Valley elementary schools. Birchfield Elementary has more than 500 students in grades K-5. About 26% of Birchfield's population is Asian, nearly 60% is white, and 15% of the student population qualify for free or reduced lunch, a common measure for socioeconomic status. Over the course of the year, there are 60 students at Birchfield who qualify for ELL services. Only eight of these students attend the newcomer program and are not on Amy's caseload. ELL students at Birchfield are spread across all 23 classrooms.

Amy's second school, Cedar Valley, is a larger school with 600 students. More than 50% of the school's population is Asian. Cedar Valley is a gorgeous school located in a prestigious neighborhood. Less than 5% of the student population qualify for free and reduced lunch. Over the course of the year, there are 60 students at Cedar Valley who qualify for ELL services. Ten of these students attend the newcomer program. ELL students at Cedar Valley are spread across all 29 classrooms.

Across the two school sites, Amy Allen has a case load of over 100 students and 50 teachers. In alignment with district policy, Amy attempts to work collaboratively with teachers and provide them with resources and support to improve their daily instruction. Amy offers teachers a variety of resources such as team teaching, collaborative lesson planning, modeling instructional strategies, providing visual resources, recording books on tape, and suggesting additional scaffolds[4] teachers could implement to make their instructional content accessible to ELLs.

With such an overwhelming caseload, Amy has to decide how to allocate her time. She bases her priorities on the students with the greatest language needs. She sets aside time to work with them in class every week, usually for about an hour or so. These in-class sessions usually involve scaffolding whatever assignment the rest of the class was doing. To support teachers' daily instruction, Amy also posts lessons, supplemental materials, and resources on a shared curriculum website, but sees very little evidence of these materials being used.

Despite the facilitator model's promises of collaboration and ongoing support, Amy's caseload limits the amount of time she can earnestly collaborate with teachers. This creates great frustration for both Amy and the teachers at both schools. Classroom teachers complain that Amy does not give them enough time. Some tell her that they see her so infrequently that they really do not feel like it is worthwhile. Amy expresses her frustration to Bonnie, wanting to say to teachers: "Do you want to see my schedule! I have so many teachers to see and I give you all the time I've got" (fieldnotes, January 12, 2008).

Halfway through the year, Amy redesigned her schedule in response to teachers' demands to see her more often. She blocked out 20- to 30-minute periods to go into each classroom every week to work with students. Teachers did see Amy more often, but the types of services Amy was able to provide changed. Amy's new schedule does not support or include collaborative sessions, as she works almost exclusively with students, usually leaving a note for teachers about what she does with suggested follow-up. Amy spends most of her time in classrooms sitting next to students while the teacher gives direct instruction or provides scaffolding for whole-class assignments. In negotiating the demands of the teachers at her two schools with the expectations of the facilitator model, the collaborative intention of the policy is lost.

After 2 years as a facilitator, Amy is frustrated with how little change she has seen in classroom instruction. She laments that her lack of administrative power means that she cannot actually enforce any of the recommendations that she gives to teachers. Without any authority to bring about instructional changes, Eastlake's facilitator model creates a "sink or swim" environment for intermediate and advanced ELL students and fails to provide the intended supports for language learning. Many teachers "opt out" of providing any language support to students. A number of teachers turn Amy away at the door, telling her not to enter. One district administrator's response to teachers' opting out is, "What I say to my staff is, 'Don't go for the ones that you're having to hit your head against the door to get in. Find the open door'" (interview, January 15, 2008). The students in the classrooms with closed doors are effectively denied the services that they are legally entitled to receive.

After her weekly visits to certain classrooms, Amy vents her frustration about the ELL students she sees drowning in the mainstream classroom. Despite Amy's multiple attempts to offer resources and strategies, many classroom teachers do not open their doors, and those who do are not accommodating the needs of ELLs in ways that are apparent to Amy.

Eastlake's facilitator model intends to streamline and standardize ESL services across the district. In these two schools, the enacted model has the opposite effect. Each classroom teacher interprets and implements the facilitator model differently, employing a range of attempts to support ELL students, which rely primarily on their (lack of) personal knowledge and expertise in appropriate ESL pedagogy.

In the next section, by contrast, we provide a case study of one teacher who stands out for her transformation of the district's policy and advocacy for the ELLs in her classroom.

Teacher History

Carolina Cross is a second-grade teacher with 5 years of teaching experience at Cedar Valley (where Amy is a half-time ESL facilitator). Carolina taught for 3 years in another district before coming to Eastlake. During her teaching credential program, Carolina did not take classes focusing on ESL, and she did not subsequently receive much formal professional development on teaching ELLs. Carolina attributes her strong commitment to ELLs to two aspects of her personal life: her parents and her previous teaching experience. Carolina mentions her parents during one interview as a motivating factor for advocating for ELLs:

> But I think my background also helps me to empathize with these kids because my parents were from the Philippines—they spoke English but I mean they still—have an accent, they still don't conjugate verbs correctly, you know, and yeah, since I don't, I want people to look at them like they're normal and so that's how I feel about my kids. (interview, June 4, 2004)

Carolina's personal experience seeing her parents being treated as not "normal" drives her commitment to ensure her students will not suffer the same discrimination. Before coming to Cedar Valley, Carolina taught in a district about 50 miles south of Eastlake. At her previous school, Carolina developed an understanding of working with ELLs through a close relationship with the ESL specialist there. In interviews, Carolina often refers to her past teaching experience as an ideal system of support for ELLs:

> Okay. I think, like through my perspective, 'cause I came from a different school, where I saw the ESL, our ESL model or whatever from the district really work. And I think it's really failed here. I mean it's, it's failing—we've even told the School Board it's failing, like at our meetings. (interview, June 4, 2008)

When we press Carolina to explain what really worked in her old district, she elaborates:

> There was a lot of collaboration—actually as I'm cleaning out my stuff, I looked in my special ed and ESL box . . . the ESL teacher who was also our

special ed teacher, sat down with every teacher and you filled out—and it was different the way we do it here. But you filled out the goals at the beginning. . . . Like I remember coming in as a first-year teacher and my very first meeting was with [the ESL and Special Education teachers]. They sat down with me and said, "Here are your kids in your classroom," and they came to me telling me who these kids are, why they're in special ed, why they're getting ESL, it was never me. And I go, "Okay, great. What can I do?" So it was completely reversed. (interview, June 4, 2008)

At her previous school, Carolina's students received targeted support 3 to 5 times a week from the ESL specialist. The constant communication between teachers and specialists helped Carolina learn how to support students in the classroom. The responsibility for educating ELLs was shared by the classroom teacher and the ESL specialist. When Carolina came to Cedar Valley and saw that her students were not receiving any targeted language support, she realized that something was missing.

In her interpretation and transformation of Eastlake's facilitator model, Carolina draws on her personal experiences. As the daughter of immigrant parents, Carolina wants to protect her ELLs from the prejudice her parents had experienced. She thinks the best way to do this is through targeted instruction, resembling her previous teaching experience. In her classroom instruction and her interactions with Amy, the ESL facilitator, Carolina acts as a change agent.

Into Action: Advocacy and Personal Commitment

In contrast to the support, collaboration, and communication in her old district, Carolina finds Eastlake's facilitator model inadequate. Carolina responds to the perceived inadequacies by advocating for ELLs. At the beginning of the study, Carolina had one ELL: Sam. In April, Tomoku, another ELL, joined her class. Carolina has committed herself to providing the best education to these two boys. She advocates for her students in three ways, which we will illustrate with examples. First, she frequently seeks advice from the facilitator and commits herself to improving her own instruction. Second, she creates alternative structures to provide the targeted language instruction she feels her students need. Third, she actively works to change the facilitator model at the school and district level.

Teacher Learning

At the beginning of the school year, Carolina approached Amy to help her use revising and editing checklists as a strategy for teaching writing. Carolina had one student (Sam) in her class who qualified for ESL support, and a few other students who no longer qualified for services, but needed some extra language support. Amy suggested that they coteach the lesson, meaning that they teach the lesson together. The two met and looked over the materials Carolina typically used for teaching editing and revising. The two teachers divided the responsibilities for the lesson. Amy offered to modify the checklist to make it more accessible for ELLs. Carolina was responsible for writing a brief paragraph with numerous errors that could be corrected using the checklist.

During instruction, Carolina and Amy modeled using the checklist for the students, explaining how it would help them revise their writing. When it came time for independent practice, Carolina and Amy both circled the classroom, having students explain the different items on the checklist and show how they were using them. Carolina had a chance to go over the whole checklist with Sam one more time, answering his questions and providing extra scaffolding while Amy monitored the rest of the class.

Carolina raves about coteaching with Amy:

> But I think it's so, like that's where I learned the most from Amy is when she was teaching with me, then I can see how she's working with the ESL kids and what she does and I think that's so valuable. (interview, March 4, 2008)

Carolina has also managed to persuade other teachers in her grade level to coteach the same lessons with Amy. When we ask Carolina what specifically she learned from these coteaching lessons, she states the following:

> I've actually learned to be a lot harder with my ESL kids. Like even in a whole group setting like calling them out and really helping them figure out what words are—Amy has taught me that. As opposed to like not calling them 'cause not wanting them to feel embarrassed. (interview, March 4, 2008)

In fact, Carolina approaches Amy for advice and support more than any other teacher on either staff. Unlike many teachers at the two schools, Carolina has a strong foundational understanding of what support for ELLs could look like based on her previous teaching experiences. She eagerly seeks to recreate that for her students at Cedar Valley by creating alternative structures to ensure her ELLs receive the specialized, targeted instruction she values.

Alternative Structures

Every lesson in Carolina's class involves differentiated instruction specifically for Sam. She explains to us how Sam is at the center of her lesson planning process:

> I guess a lot of lessons I'm just super explicit. And I write and highlight things for Sam so he understands. It just makes my job easier too because then his hand's in the air a couple of times. So if I prep everything. Like anything I give them, like worksheets, I'll make sure to read through it just in case if I think Sam won't know. Then I'll highlight, write it out. Things like that. . . . And so when I'm reading things I actually am looking through how would Sam see this? What would be difficult for him? I would say that's a good way of kind of summing up how I look at the lessons. Or anything I play on the Smart

Board. Making it visual. How is this easier? If Sam can understand it then everybody else can. (interview, April 6, 2008)

Carolina's response to the lack of support for ELLs in Eastlake's facilitator model has been to transform her whole teaching approach to focus on what is best for her one ELL. She has taken on ESL support as her own personal responsibility, creating structures and procedures that focus on language development for Sam.

To sustain this type of intensive support for Sam, Carolina also draws upon external resources to create alternative structures in her classroom. When Bonnie, the first author, came for the first observation in Carolina's classroom, Carolina's parent volunteer did not arrive to help during the literacy hour. Carolina explained that she usually spent the literacy block working one on one with Sam while the other students rotate between working with the parent volunteer and working independently. She asked if Bonnie would work with Sam so that she could work with the other students. For the next few weeks when Bonnie came in, Carolina had different books or projects for Bonnie to work on with Sam.

Carolina assumes the responsibility for her ELLs and provides Sam with the amount of support she deems appropriate. However, with this much attention to one student, the other students in her second-grade classroom are often left to work independently or with a parent volunteer. She explains:

> I'm lucky because I've set, I think the expectations are pretty high in the class that the rest of the 24 kids they could actually sit there for a good 45 minutes and be quiet, do their work. You know. And so that allows me to work one-on-one with Sam. (interview, June 4, 2008)

The amount of time and energy Carolina dedicates to Sam, and later Tomoku, is truly impressive. Carolina recognizes that her students are not going to receive any support or services unless she does it all herself. While Carolina's alternative structure is ambitious, it is clearly not best educational practice. The mainstream students in Carolina's class are receiving less attention and support than they deserve. In addition, Carolina's limited specialization in or knowledge of ESL does not make her the best person to provide targeted instruction to Sam. Carolina's self-determination and advocacy are also apparent in her efforts to change Eastlake's facilitator model, as the next section makes clear.

Advocating beyond the Classroom

Carolina's personal responsibility to her ELL students means not only working within her classroom but also ensuring the system changes to support these students and teachers like herself. Carolina has joined together with her grade-level team to resist Amy's suggestion to group all of the ELL students into one classroom. Carolina is adamant that this is the wrong direction to take:

> And so they wanted—and Amy's point was too it would be easier for her since she is split between classes to come in to a classroom, serve all the kids

in that one classroom. Well, when you come in sometimes once a week, not even an hour of the day, and then the rest of the week the teacher is left with five ESL kids. I mean that's tough. I think it should be spread out. So that happened. So now at second grade I know upstairs (there's a classroom with more ELLs) Amy's only been in there once. (interview, March 4, 2008)

Carolina's concern for ELLs and the effects of the facilitator model extends beyond her own classroom. She saw that one of her colleagues had been given a larger number of ELLs, and this colleague was receiving less support than Carolina. Eastlake's facilitator model depends completely on the classroom teacher to provide accommodations, scaffolding, and language development. The facilitator's time is so scarce that the teachers do not feel that it is a reliable form of service. At the same time, Carolina perceives that putting all of the ELLs in one classroom would create an inequitable learning environment.

During the year of this study, the school board investigated the district's ESL facilitator model. Carolina went to an open school board meeting and advocated for a change in policy. She said,

I think, like through my perspective, 'cause I came from a different school, where I saw our ESL model or whatever from the district really work. And I think it's really failed here. I mean it's, it's failing—we've even told the School Board it's failing, like at our meetings. (interview, March 4, 2008)

Carolina again relies on her previous experience to advocate for her students. Carolina plans to go into an administrative preparation program the next year. She explains that as an administrator she will keep ELL students at the center of her vision.

And I think just always keeping in mind like, when I am a vice principal or principal some day that I don't ever want to lose sight of what matters and it's really about the kids and the teachers. I feel like that doesn't happen in this district . . . across the school you could sit there and listen to the teachers and they're saying they're not getting serviced, they're not, we're not getting any help . . . I hope when I am a vice principal or principal that I could have a school where somehow I could work with the staff so that we do have something that does work for our kids. (interview, June 4, 2008)

Carolina's commitment to "doing something that works" for her kids is enacted in multiple ways as she interprets and transforms Eastlake's facilitator mode. Within and outside the classroom, Carolina pushes against the facilitator model because she finds that it provides so little support to teachers or students. In her classroom, Carolina creates alternative structures that allow her time to deliver specialized, targeted support to her ELLs. Outside the classroom, Carolina brings her concerns to the school administrators and the school board. Carolina's previous experience teaching in a school with an ESL program "that worked" and her understanding of the difficulty of learning a second language are the cornerstones of her interpretation of Eastlake's policy.

Discussion

What makes this case study particularly important to consider is that it highlights how the negotiation of language policy has to be considered within a particular staffing model, an issue that has been brought up by Creese (2005) in the British context. It also shows that the success of a particular language policy in how it serves students who need additional linguistic and academic support cannot fall on a particular teacher or a collaboration between two teachers (as in the case of Amy and Carolina), but rather must be addressed systemically. Moreover, this particular staffing model, the facilitator model, is one that is being pushed in the state of Washington and in many parts of the country. This model is built on several assumptions: first that ESL is a set of strategies that mainstream classroom teachers can use, and second, that ELL students will learn best if they are not pulled out of their classroom, an approach advocated by a number of scholars (Echevarria, Vogt, & Short, 2000; Gibbons, 2002). It is very similar to the idea of mainstreaming that Creese (2005) discusses in her work on teacher collaboration in the United Kingdom. However, at the same time, this model also coexists with two other realities—that the district basically has a monolingual language policy and that limited resources have been put into this staffing model.

Eastlake School District's policy and program for ELLs focuses exclusively on teaching these students English without any native-language support. This approach, as explained earlier, is very similar to most of the other programs in the state, although the state's suggested default program for ELLs entails the use of native-language instruction. The discourse of the ESL administrator in Eastlake with regards to not using native-language instruction is similar to some of the explanations used in popular media and culture in the United States, that any form of native-language instruction would be a disservice for the ELLs as it would mean not paying sufficient attention to English. Moreover, the administrator we interviewed explained that it would be inequitable to provide some students native-language support and not others, as doing so could possibly even create a segregated learning environment.

At the same time, there is an increased emphasis on accountability and responsibility for the achievement of ELLs, nationally and locally. What seems almost contradictory with this is the lack of resources that have been put into this model. In addition, the facilitator model devalues ESL as a specialization, positioning it as a set of strategies mainstream teachers can easily integrate. It is clear, therefore, that due to these issues the facilitator model as it stands in Eastlake is overall not very successful.

Even though language policy has to be addressed systemically, the wide disparities across the nation about how policies for ELLs are interpreted and put into practice (Rumberger & Gándara, 2004) make it critical to understand the circumstances when such instances are successful. As pointed out in other studies that have looked at the interpretation and negotiation of language policy at the classroom level, the particular backgrounds of the teachers is crucial (Varghese, 2008; Varghese & Stritikus, 2005). In these studies, it has been pointed out that teachers of color who have themselves been marginalized in their own childhoods, like Carolina, are more likely to make substantive efforts to make a difference for the ELLs in their classroom. Another crucial aspect that comes out in these studies related to the background of the teachers is their professional experience (Varghese, 2008; Varghese & Stritikus, 2005). Carolina has her own previous teaching experience in another district where she was able to experience firsthand a successful system of support for ELLs. Moreover, these previous experiences enable her to try to make a difference inside and outside the classroom. In being an advocate for her ELLs, it is also important to notice that Carolina at no point mentions the use of students' native language. Her advocacy for ELLs is in the context of the current English-only policy. Finally, we must also acknowledge that Carolina's school, Cedar Valley, has more resources and Carolina had only two ELLs in her classroom, so that she has been more able to provide individualized attention to these two students.

Conclusion

This case study underscores that systemwide successful language policy can only occur when there are enough resources (financial, staffing, professional development) that are put into serving ELLs. Moreover, there has to be thoughtful planning done around how teachers can work together on these issues. The case study of Amy and Carolina shows that there can be successful collaborations at the individual level but that these rely on individual teachers (their backgrounds, classroom environments, and support) to make these positive changes. Even with successful collaboration, the ESL teacher was permitted only limited access to the ELLs being educated through this model. ELLs are, therefore, limited by their classroom teacher's lack of ESL expertise.

Three questions must finally be raised about the assumptions and consequences of the facilitator model. Can a classroom teacher, untrained in ESL, successfully provide educational opportunities to ELLs in the mainstream classroom? What resources would be necessary for the facilitator model to work? To what extent can a monolingual policy with no native-language support ultimately work?

Discussion Questions

1   What language policy would you put into practice in your own classroom?

    a   Reflect on your own background and experiences. To what extent can you connect these to the language policy you would put into practice?

    b   What else might determine the language policy you put into practice?

2   Imagine you are a classroom or ESL teacher at a school board meeting for Eastlake School District. What would you say to the administrators at Eastlake?

3   To what extent can you consider a monolingual policy with no native-language support to be successful?

4   Initiate collaboration with either a classroom teacher or an ESL teacher to improve the instruction for the ELLs in your classroom and document the process.

5   Find out what explicit or implicit language policies exist in your district or school and how they were developed. Identify ways you can make policies more additive in your own classroom and put these changes into practice. Document the process.

6   Initiate a professional development group in your own school of other teachers who are interested and committed to ELLs. Reflect on what the goals and actions of this professional development group should be. Document the process.

Notes

1   Pseudonyms are used throughout this chapter for the name of the school district, schools and the teachers.

2   In Washington State, teachers may earn an ESL endorsement as a supplement to their K-8 teaching credential. There is no teaching certificate specifically for ESL.

3   Spanish Immersion is a program designed for American, monolingual English speakers to become fluent in Spanish. The program is primarily taught in Spanish. Students attend the program from grades K-5.

4   Scaffolds are help a teacher can provide that will enable a learner to accomplish a task he or she would not have been able to accomplish independently (Gibbons, 2002).

References

August, D., & Hakuta, K. (Eds.). (1997). *Improving schooling for language minority students: A research agenda.* Washington, DC: National Academy Press.

Crawford, J. (1999). *Bilingual education: History, politics, theory, and practice* (4th ed.). Los Angeles, CA: Bilingual Education Services.

Creese, A. (2005). *Teacher collaboration and talk in multilingual classrooms.* Clevedon, Avon: Multilingual Matters.

De Jong, E., & Harper, C. (2005). Preparing mainstream teachers for English language learners: Is being a good teacher good enough? *Teacher Education Quarterly, 32*(2), 101–124.

Echevarria, J., Vogt, M., & Short, D. J. (2000). *Making content comprehensible for English language learners: The SIOP model.* Boston, MA: Allyn & Bacon.

Gibbons, P. (2002). *Scaffolding language, scaffolding learning: Teaching second language learners in the mainstream classroom.* Portsmouth, NH: Heinemann.

Hornberger, N. H. (2005). Nichols to NCLB: Local and global perspectives on U.S. language education policy. *Working Papers in Educational Linguistics, 20*(2), 1–17.

Kindler, A. (2002). *Survey of the States' limited English proficient students and available educational programs and services: 1999–2000 summary report.* Washington, DC: National Clearinghouse for English Language Acquisition and Language Instruction Educational Programs.

Lau v. Nichols, 414 U.S. 563 (1974).

Menken, K. (2008). *English learners left behind: Standardized testing as language policy.* Clevedon, Avon: Multilingual Matters.

Rumberger, R. W., & Gándara, P. (2004). Seeking equity in the education of California's English learners. *Teachers College Record, 106,* 2032–2056.

Varghese, M. (2008). Using cultural models to unravel how bilingual teachers enact language policies. *Language and Education, 21*(8), 289–306, 73–87.

Varghese, M., & Stritikus, T. (2005). "Nadie me dijó [Nobody told me]": Language policy negotiation and implications for teacher education. *Journal of Teacher Education, 56*(1), 73–87.

Wiley, T. G., & Wright, W. E. (2004). Against the undertow: Language-minority education policy and politics in the "Age of Accountability." *Educational Policy, 18*(1), 142–168.

Chapter 8

Between Intended and Enacted Curricula

Three Teachers and a Mandated Curricular Reform in Mainland China

Yuefeng Zhang and Guangwei Hu

Curricular Reform and the Task-Based Language Teaching Initiative

Since mainland China adopted the twin policy of opening up and reform and launched its modernization agenda in the late 1970s, the country has experienced rapid economic progress and has become an increasingly active player in the global economic and political arenas. In support of China's peaceful rise and sustainable development, its educational system has witnessed an unprecedented level of reform effort over the past quarter of a century (for some of the nationwide change initiatives, see Chinese Communist Party Central Committee & State Council, 1999; Ministry of Education, 1998; State Council, 2001). A deluge of top-down reform initiatives directed at various components of the educational system—curriculum development, assessment of schooling, instructional practice, learning materials, educational management, teacher education, status and conditions of teachers' work, to name a few—has been instigated as an integral part of China's drive for modernization and national development (Hu, 2005a, 2005b).

English language teaching at the different levels of the Chinese educational system has been at the forefront of many recent educational reforms and language policy initiatives (Hu, 2005b). By and large, the language policies and reform endeavors have been driven by two related forces, among others. One driving force is the widespread acceptance of a modernization discourse on the importance of English for China and its citizenry that links national proficiency in English to China's modernization. This prevalent discourse assumes that English has "a multitude of economic, commercial, technological, political, social, cultural, and educational roles" (Hu, 2008, p. 202) to play in China's national development. The other driving force is a persistent and growing dissatisfaction with the quality of English language teaching among policymakers and other stakeholders (Hu, 2005c). It is widely assumed that the crux of the problem is the entrenched use of traditional teaching methodologies. These two driving forces, together with other factors, have led to a top-down flux of curricular and pedagogical reforms aimed at increasing English language provision and improving the effectiveness of English language teaching in the school system.

One recent reform initiative is the top-down promotion of communicative language teaching that started in the early 1990s in response to growing criticisms of the low quality of English provision (Hu, 2005c). Communicative language teaching is a popular language teaching approach of Western origins that valorizes meaning negotiation and construction in the classroom, language learning through using the target language to communicate, and authentic and meaningful communication as the goal of classroom activities (Richards & Rodgers, 2001). Although the pedagogical approach has been advocated to develop communicative competence rather than linguistic competence in language learners, available research (Cortazzi & Jin, 1996; Hu, 2005c) indicates that like similar efforts in other contexts (see Canagarajah, 1999; Holliday, 1994), the top-down effort has failed to effect fundamental changes to classroom instruction. A major cause underlying this failure is the "globalization from above" approach to educational reform that disregards contextual influences on pedagogical practices, the local meaningfulness (or lack thereof) of imported practices, and the (potential) clash of such practices with the local cultural ecology (Canagarajah, 2005a, 2005b; Kumaravadivelu, 2006). This, however, is not the whole story of communicative language teaching in China. An updated version of communicative language teaching—task-based language teaching—has been prescribed as the desired pedagogy by the current national English curriculum for primary and secondary education, *English Language Curriculum Standards* (Ministry of Education, 2001). This chapter focuses on three teachers' responses to the task-based language teaching initiative.

Task-based language teaching "seeks to reconcile methodology with current theories of second language acquisition" (Richards & Rodgers, 2001, p. 151) and centers on the use of tasks as the core unit of curricular planning and classroom instruction. Zhang (2005, pp. 11–14) summarizes the main characteristics of a task: (a) a task is communication oriented, (b) its performance involves cognitive processes, (c) it is contextualized and authentic, (d) it is primarily meaning focused, and (e) its completion normally leads to a nonlinguistic product (e.g., a route drawn on a map). A task differs from a purely form-focused activity, also called "exercise" (Ellis, 2003; Tong, Adamson, & Che, 2000). Tong (2005) distinguished three forms of task-based language teaching. A strong form takes tasks as the only unit of language teaching, in which students acquire the target language by performing tasks in contextualized, meaning-focused communication (Ellis, 2003). A medium form involves tasks as the main activity, supplemented with some form-focused, teacher-controlled activity. A weak form treats tasks as opportunity for learners to practice more freely the language items that they have learned in a teacher-controlled way. In this weak form, tasks are only supplementary activities undertaken before or after the form-focused instruction (Ellis, 2003).

The task-based language teaching initiative in China has been promoted in a top-down, centrally controlled manner. Although the late 1990s saw some decentralization of educational decision making in China (Hu, 2005a), curriculum planning has largely resided with the central educational authorities. In general, curricular reform in the centralized educational system has followed a top-down model. In this model of educational change, the central government initiates new curricular visions and goals, usually through its Ministry of Education (Deng, in press). Under the latter's close supervision, these visions and goals are then translated into curricular guidelines or frameworks and expressed in new instructional materials, assessment revision, revamping of teacher education, and so on. These initiatives are expected to steer what is taught and learned in classrooms. That is, teachers are required to implement the externally and centrally developed curriculum and learning materials faithfully (Snyder, Bolin, & Zumwalt, 1992). Such a top-down model of educational change has been adopted to implement the task-based language teaching initiative. The initiative was launched in the autumn of 2001 through the centrally issued *English Language Curriculum Standards*. The new curriculum was first tried out and implemented in 38 national experimental districts throughout the country. It was then implemented in provincial experimental districts in the autumn of 2002, reaching 10% to 15% of the entire student population. In 2004, its implementation expanded to 2,576 cities/counties and 65% to 70% of students across the country (Li, 2003). The nationwide implementation of the curriculum initiative was supposed to be achieved by 2007 (Liu, 2004).

In a review of recent teaching reform programs of different countries, including those of China, Calderhead (2001, p. 794) noted that "Surprisingly, in the formulation of reforms, little attention has been given to understanding the processes of teaching and learning as they occur in the classrooms and to the factors that influence and support the quality and effectiveness of those experiences." "Reform efforts," he pointed out, "have often been based on quite simple and probably quite inappropriate notions of how teaching and learning interact and of how schools and teachers produce the effects that they do." This chapter represents our effort to address the problem by examining how task-based language teaching was interpreted, negotiated, and enacted by three Chinese teachers in their primary English classrooms. The remainder of the chapter is organized into five sections. A discussion of the theoretical work that informs our study is followed by a description of our methodological design. Next, we outline the intended curriculum before we zoom in on the three teachers' enactment of task-based language teaching. We conclude the chapter with a discussion of factors impacting on the teachers' curricular enactment and the implications of our study for language education policymaking in China and elsewhere.

Levels of Curriculum Making and the Enactment Perspective

In recent years, curriculum researchers have moved away from a fidelity perspective on curriculum planning and implementation that stresses teachers' faithful implementation of a curricular change as intended by curriculum specialists to a more differentiated view of curriculum making as a multiplicity of processes operating at different levels. In this study, we draw on theoretical work that conceptualizes curriculum making at multiple levels. We find a 3-level framework of curriculum processes (Deng, in press; Doyle, 1992a, 1992b) particularly useful in informing our examination of curricular change. These three levels are as follows: the institutional, the programmatic, and the classroom.

Institutional curriculum making is at the interaction between society, culture, and schooling, linking education to social and cultural systems. It is an ideological as well as an educational undertaking, "capturing aspects of the educational ideals and expectations that exist within a society and representing the forms and procedures of schooling as responses to these ideals and expectations" (Doyle, 1992a, p. 70). The institutional curriculum that has motivated the task-based language teaching initiative in China is manifested in the central government's educational policy statements such as Chinese Communist Party Central Committee and State Council (1999; also State Council, 2001). These policy statements frame education as the foundation for national revitalization and modernization and typify effective schooling as an active, interactive, meaningful, and transformative process whereby students' problem-solving skills, creativity, and independent thinking are cultivated.

Programmatic curriculum making "bridges the gap between the abstract curriculum and the classroom" (Doyle, 1992a, p. 71) by translating the ideal institutional curriculum "that defines the essential character, that is, the experiences and outcomes, of a school or school system" (Doyle, 1992b, p. 487) into operational frameworks or instruments for use in curriculum events. In the words of Westbury (2008, p. 49), curriculum making at this level "seeks to precipitate societal and cultural symbols and narratives into workable organizational frameworks for the delivery of schooling." The product of programmatic curriculum making takes the form of formal curriculum documents and materials, known as intended/resourced curriculum, which spell out content standards, instructional frameworks, assessment criteria, and criteria for materials development and adoption (Deng, in press). For the task-based language teaching initiative, the intended or programmatic curriculum consists of the *English Language Curriculum Standards* (Ministry of Education, 2001) and the officially approved textbooks.

Classroom curriculum making is comprised of processes of interpretation and construction that transform the institutional and programmatic curricula into curriculum events in a particular classroom. The product of curriculum making at this level is a classroom curriculum, or an enacted curriculum, which consists of educative experiences for the students. The enacted curriculum is "an evolving construction resulting from the interaction of teacher and students" (Doyle, 1992a, p. 72). It is powerfully shaped by local factors in and outside of the classroom: the teacher's personal practical knowledge; students' experiences, interests, and capacities; shared meanings and perspectives between teacher and student; school culture and expectations; and parents' aspirations, to name only a few. It is the locally produced and jointly constructed curriculum in the classroom and factors affecting its construction that we focus on in our study of the three teachers' responses to the task-based language teaching initiative promoted in the programmatic curriculum embodied by the *English Language Curriculum Standards* (Ministry of Education, 2001).

The three-level curriculum-making framework outlined previously allows us to take what has come to be known as "the enactment perspective" in our research on the Chinese teachers' transformation and representation of a curricular reform initiative in their classrooms. Though it has been acknowledged in the general curriculum literature for some time (Snyder et al., 1992), the enactment perspective has only recently received considerable attention in second-/foreign-language curriculum research (Graves, 2008). It focuses on "how curriculum is shaped through the evolving constructs of teachers and students" (Snyder et al., 1992, p. 404). Thus, curriculum is viewed from the enactment perspective as educative experiences jointly created by teacher and student in a situated process of reconstruction that is sensitive and responsive to the local realities in and out of the classroom.

It should be clear from the discussion above that the enactment perspective connects well with the overarching question that this volume aims to address collectively. It rejects the assumption that curriculum knowledge resides only in external experts. Although it does not rule out externally developed curricula, it views such a curriculum as "a resource for teachers who create curriculum as they engage in the ongoing process of teaching and learning in the classroom" (Snyder et al., 1992, p. 429). In other words, it recognizes that institutional and programmatic curricula must be enacted to become teaching and learning experiences (Graves, 2008; Hargreaves & Evans, 1997). Genuine curriculum change, viewed from this perspective, is an ongoing process of growth for both teachers and students. Clearly, the enactment perspective acknowledges the central, crucial, and fundamental roles that teachers play in effective curriculum making (Fullan, 2001; Kelly, 2004; Stenhouse, 1975).

Research Questions and Research Design

In keeping with the enactment perspective, this study examines how the three primary school English teachers in Shenzhen—a social, cultural, and economic hub of Southern China—negotiated and represented the officially promoted task-based curriculum in their classroom practice.[1] It attempts to answer two research questions: (1) How did the three teachers interpret, negotiate, and enact the task-based language teaching innovation in their classrooms? (2) What are the factors shaping their interpretation and construction of the task-based language teaching innovation?

To address the research questions, we adopted a case study research design that made use of naturalistic observations to study the focal teachers' behaviors in classrooms and that employed interviews to uncover teacher beliefs and cognition. In addition, we conducted document analysis to identify institutional and

Table 8.1 Personal Data of the Focal Teachers at the Time of the Study

Name	Age	School	No. of lessons per week	No. of classes	Work experience (years)
Fanny	23	District level	12	3	1.5
Gavin	29	City level	16	4	7
Helen	34	Province level	7	1	14

programmatic curriculum intentions. By means of purposeful sampling, we chose to focus on three primary English teachers in Shenzhen. These teachers were selected through purposive sampling from 112 primary school English language teachers in Shenzhen who participated in a questionnaire survey on teachers' understanding of task-based language teaching (Zhang, 2005). In the questionnaire, the three teachers claimed to have used task-based language teaching and volunteered for the study.[2] They differed in teaching experience and other work-related respects, including types of school and school districts where they were teaching.[3] As summarized in Table 8.1, Fanny was a female teacher with one and a half years' teaching experience.[4] She taught one Grade 3 class (i.e., children 9–10 years old) and two Grade 4 classes (i.e., children 10–11 years old). Gavin was a male teacher with 7 years of teaching experience. He taught one Grade 3 class and three Grade 4 classes. Helen was a female teacher with 14 years of teaching experience. She taught only one Grade 3 class but also worked as a student counselor in her school. One Grade 3 class of each teacher was observed from March to May 2004 to guarantee the comparability of the collected data. For each teacher, 10 consecutive lessons were observed. The observations focused on the three teachers' task-based language teaching practices. The types of activities used in the teaching were identified and timed. Pre- and post-lessons interviews with teachers were conducted to follow up on some emergent issues in their teaching practices.

Official documents concerning the curriculum innovation were acquired from the Internet or the local education authorities in Shenzhen. These official curriculum documents were analyzed to decode how the curriculum makers conceived of task-based language teaching and intended it to be implemented in classrooms. Handouts from curriculum workshops/seminars for teachers and textbooks in use were also analyzed to determine how the teacher trainers viewed and disseminated task-based language teaching in teachers' training activities and how the textbook writers represented it in textbook resources. Two teacher trainers from local education bureaus were also interviewed to ascertain the main measures of the task-based language teaching initiative being undertaken in the districts under study. School leaders in the three schools were approached informally to find out how they responded to task-based language teaching and influenced the enactment of task-based language teaching by the three teachers.

The Intended Task-Based Language Teaching Innovation

To examine the complex relationship between the intended and the enacted curriculum, we present the intended curriculum before we focus on the teachers' enactment. As pointed out earlier, the official intention regarding the curriculum innovation is expressed in the *English Language Curriculum Standards* (Ministry of Education, 2001). According to the programmatic curriculum, traditional teaching methods "over-emphasize grammar and vocabulary knowledge, neglect the development of students' practical language competence" (Ministry of Education, 2001, p. 1) and cannot meet the perceived need for communicative competence in English arising from socioeconomic developments in China.[5] Thus, the *English Language Curriculum Standards* turns to task-based language teaching, an internationally popular language teaching approach that emphasizes communicative use of the target language and active participation by learners, and advocates what appears to be a medium form of the pedagogical approach (Tong, 2005).The programmatic curriculum recommends (Ministry of Education, 2001):

> Teachers should teach according to the general objectives and contents described in the curriculum. They should creatively design activities that are close to students' real life to attract them and motivate them to participate. Students accomplish their learning tasks by thinking, investigating, discussing, exchanging and cooperating. (p. 29)

In addition, the programmatic curriculum lays down six general principles that teachers are expected to follow when they design task-based activities:

1   The activities have definite and achievable purposes.
2   The activities start from students' life experiences and interests and contain authentic content and processes.
3   The activities are beneficial to students for them to learn English and cultivate language skills, so that their practical abilities to use the language can be improved.
4   The activities promote the integration and connection of English with other subjects to contribute to students' whole-person development, including the ability to think and imagine, aesthetic interest and experience of arts, and spirit of cooperation and creation.
5   The activities enable students to obtain, exchange, and use information; communicate with others in English; and develop the ability to solve practical problems in English.
6   The activities are not limited to classroom teaching and extend to learning and life outside of classrooms. (Ministry of Education, 2001, p. 29)

The principles implicitly characterize tasks as purposeful, authentic, life related, holistic, process oriented, and communication oriented (Zhang, 2005) and thus echo some of the task features discussed in the international task-based language teaching literature (Ellis, 2003).

A look at the officially recommended textbooks is in order because textbooks, as pointed out by Apple (2008, p. 26), constitute "the most usual way in which curricula are planned and made available [to teachers] in most nations." Among the textbooks officially recommended by the educational authorities in Shenzhen for the task-based language teaching innovation, two series were popular at the time of study: *New Welcome to English*, published by Longman (Hong Kong) and *Primary English for China*, modeled on the former series and written collaboratively by Longman (Hong Kong) and the Shenzhen Teaching Research Institute. Book Six of *Primary English for China*, which was used by both Fanny and Gavin at the time of the study, was illustrative of the two series. It contained eight thematic units and two units of review (Units 5 and 10). Each of the eight thematic units was organized into three parts: the pretask part that consisted of presentation of vocabulary, structure pattern practice, story presentation, comprehension checking, letters, and sounds; the task part that contained a task or an activity; and the posttask part that included songs, chants, or rhymes. Five out of the eight tasks were surveys. Although its organization appeared to be task based, a major part of the textbook was devoted to vocabulary items, letters and sounds, sentence patterns, and dialogues. Apart from the small numbers of tasks included in the textbook series, there were very few task-based language teaching resources for teachers to use in their teaching. Although these textbooks claimed to be task based and included some tasks, more often than not they focused mainly on pretask language items and adopted a weak form of task-based language teaching (see Tong, 2005).

The Enacted Task-Based Language Teaching Innovation

Having presented the intended curriculum, we focus in this section on the most critical phase for curricular change to take place in school contexts, that is, how teachers enact the intended change in their teaching (Doyle, 1992a; Snyder et al., 1992). We attempt to show how our three focal teachers—Fanny, Gavin, and Helen—interpreted and constructed task-based language teaching in their classroom practices, paying attention to the factors shaping their local constructions of the curriculum innovation.

Fanny's Enactment of the Task-Based Language Teaching Innovation

Fanny encountered the *English Language Curriculum Standards* in her final year of preservice training in 2001. Because she was too busy with her graduation project, she did not have much time to study the document carefully or read other sources to find out more about task-based language teaching. Nor was she exposed to this pedagogical approach in her preservice training. By and large, her lecturers adopted a traditional, form-focused, teacher-centered, knowledge-oriented approach to language teaching. In spite of her lack of professional training in task-based language teaching, Fanny said in an interview that she did not need to learn to improve her classroom teaching through the pedagogical approach because she graduated from college after its launch, expressing the belief that her preservice training at college had prepared her adequately for the innovation. In any case, there was little in-service task-based language teaching training available for her after she started teaching in her current school. Her understanding of the pedagogical approach was based on her interpretation of *renwu* as meaning "assignments" or "objectives."[6] Therefore, she believed that she used task-based language teaching in every lesson by setting objectives and giving learning assignments to her students.

Partly due to the form-focused and knowledge-transmitting approach that Fanny experienced as a student and preservice teacher, the learning objectives and assignments that she set for her students involved mastery of mainly vocabulary items, sentence structures, and grammar items. She believed that such linguistic forms and contents were the foundation of communication in English. As she explained,

> I pay much attention to grammar teaching. Basic knowledge such as vocabulary and grammar need to be emphasized. It is necessary to imprint the basic rules on the students' memory.

Her perception of what task-based language teaching should be about was supported by the form-focused midterm and term test papers mandated by the local education bureau. Consequently, the most frequent instructional activities Fanny used in class were didactic instruction in grammar rules, sentence pattern drilling, drilling of dialogues, reading aloud, and doing form-focused exercises—all activities with a strong focus on linguistic accuracy rather than use of language in communication. She spent most of the class time (four 40-minute periods a week) drilling her students in target linguistic forms and taught much grammar in a deductive way. Her preference for deductive grammar instruction was based on her perception that "it is impossible for me to induct the [grammar] rules together with the students."

There was no sign of conscious use of tasks (i.e., as understood in task-based language teaching) in Fanny's lessons. The only tasks that she used were occasional adaptations of the survey tasks found in the textbook, in order to provide her students with some variations of practice activities aimed to help them memorize linguistic items. For example, Book Six of *Primary English for China*—the textbook Fanny used—had a group task that required students to conduct a survey of favorite sports in groups and report their results to the whole class. Fanny changed the task format and simplified the suggested procedures by asking each student to walk around the classroom and interview 10 other students to find out their favorite sports and then report the findings to the whole class. The postlesson interview revealed that she had chosen this activity to make her students practice the target vocabulary items, that is, the names of sports. It also emerged that she was not aware that this activity was actually a task.

As an inexperienced teacher, she encountered quite a few challenges in her classroom teaching. She lacked the experience of dealing with a whole textbook, as she had only been taught how to teach a single lesson in her preservice program. She had difficulty in maintaining discipline with 49 students in her classroom. For most of the time, she had to struggle alone to solve the problems she encountered, as there was little collegial support from other teachers in the English department. Perceiving learning as a receptive, passive process, she spent much time regulating students' discipline and tried to gain control over the students' learning process. Furthermore, her limited English ability prevented her from communicating fluently with her students in authentic and natural English. She used Chinese to translate her instructions when students did not understand her in English. Overall, her teaching was mainly teacher dominant, form focused, and grammar based, exhibiting sporadic features of a weak form of task-based language teaching.

Gavin's Enactment of the Task-Based Language Teaching Innovation

In spite of the advocacy of task-based language teaching in the *English Language Curriculum Standards*, the dominant pedagogical approach in Gavin's school, a reputable city-level school, was a traditional, teacher-fronted, drilling-based one, rather than a task-based one. Gavin first encountered the Chinese terms for tasks and task-based language teaching in an in-service training seminar given by a university professor in his school and later noted them in the new curriculum document. At the beginning he was quite enthusiastic about this new teaching approach, considering it an opportunity for professional development and for exploring effective instruction. Led by his initial interest and enthusiasm, he read about task-based language teaching and wrote an article about this pedagogical approach in 2003 when Mr. Fan, one of the vice-principals, asked him to write about his pedagogy for the school magazine. In the article, Gavin described ways in which games, songs, and other activities encouraging student participation could be used with a task-based language teaching orientation. The article demonstrated Gavin's incipient understanding of some features and principles of a strong form of task-based language teaching. When Mr. Fan read the article, he was quite impressed, in particular, by the label *renwu xing jiaoxuefa* (task-based language teaching) and praised Gavin for his creativity. However, when he found out that *renwu xing jiaoxuefa* was the pedagogical approach advocated by the *English Language Curriculum Standards*, he was displeased and forcefully asked Gavin to think of his own name for the pedagogy. When approached by one of us about this incident, Mr. Fan explained his rationale as follows:

> Teachers can write excellent [pedagogical] articles only when they creatively use their own terms, which should be distinctive and have never been used. Even if you copy the content from books, you should at least change the terms into your own to make them your own. If you don't change the ingredients, you should at least change the soup.

This rationale was based on a recently institutionalized system of professional promotion whereby promising pedagogical pioneers would be identified and

Table 8.2 Gavin's Data-Recording Grid for a Survey on Doing Housework

Name	Set the table	Sweep the floor	Wash the dishes	Water the plants	Clean my room	Make my bed
Jeff	always	never				

provided with an official platform to share and promulgate their own innovative ideas.

Discouraged by Mr. Fan's negative response, Gavin was not as enthusiastic with task-based language teaching as before and regarded further work on it as neither creative nor facilitative of the development of his unique teaching style. He began to see tasks in less positive light:

> The term "task" is too rigid. It sounds like a term used in the army. When an officer assigns a task to you, you must fulfill it. When it's used between teachers and students, it's quite inappropriate and dehumanizing. We'd better use terms such as activities, situations, or games.

Gavin's interpretation of task-based language teaching differed considerably from the standard interpretation in the literature. Gavin's understanding of the pedagogical approach was largely shaped by his textbook, Book Six of *Primary English for China*, which mainly included survey tasks. Gavin defined tasks as activities or surveys, and task-based language teaching as an activity approach: "a task in Chinese means there's an activity to complete, and to do a task is to organize an activity for children to participate in."

Gavin used only a few tasks in the 10 lessons observed. One task that Gavin used consciously was doing a survey on the frequency of doing housework. There were three steps suggested in the textbook: asking questions, taking down information, and reaching a consensus on the basis of the survey results. However, Gavin asked his students to complete only the first two steps. He instructed them to walk around, interview their peers, and write down the information in Table 8.2. The last step of pooling the survey data and identifying the most helpful student, the part of the task that would involve communicative use of language in problem solving, was skipped to save time. Gavin used the task mainly to provide the students with freer practice in the scripted dialogues taught earlier, rather than to engage them in purposeful communication.

Apart from occasional use of communicative tasks such as surveys and riddles, Gavin's teaching was essentially teacher dominated, form focused, and drill centered.

Some of the most often used instructional activities in Gavin's lessons were deductive teaching of grammar items, reciting dialogues, doing grammar exercises, reading aloud, and making sentences with given words. Such a pedagogical approach was derived from, among other things, his own form-focused, memorization-based English-learning experience; his beliefs about the nature of language learning; his perceptions of the students' low proficiency in English; and the form-focused test papers mandated by the local education bureau. He believed that the students would need to build a solid linguistic foundation before they could communicate well in the target language. To him, this linguistic foundation consisted of vocabulary and sentences found in the textbook. Consequently, he frequently asked his students to copy words and sentences from the textbook and memorize dialogues or passages there. In addition, he often translated target English vocabulary items and sentences into Chinese in his lessons. For example, when he taught some adverbs of frequency, he asked the students to repeat after him in chorus:

"Always," "Always" *shi zongshi* [Chinese equivalent for "is always"]

"Usually," "Usually" *shi tongchang* [Chinese equivalent for "is usually"]

"Sometimes," "Sometimes" *shi youshi* [Chinese equivalent for "is sometimes"]

"Never," "Never" *shi congbu* [Chinese equivalent for "is 'never'"].

These practices, he believed, would be more effective than task-based language teaching alternatives in making his students acquire the linguistic foundation and do well because they would help them "improve their memory of the content" and "cope with the tests."

Helen's Enactment of the Task-Based Language Teaching Innovation

Helen was an experienced teacher and student counselor in a prestigious province-level school. She was introduced to task-based language teaching mainly through her personal communication with a teacher trainer in her district when she helped with some district-level in-service training programs. She understood the curriculum innovation as embracing more student-centered, life-related education. Influenced by the teacher trainer's interpretation of the curriculum innovation, she identified task-based language teaching as problem-based teaching and believed that

[E]very problem emerging in the lesson can be a task. Problems can come from the students themselves. Every student will meet with different problems in class. So we can choose the problems which most of the students meet with or are interested in, and guide them to solve the problems.

This was a narrow interpretation of task-based language teaching. Although problem-based teaching and task-based language teaching share some epistemological and pedagogical assumptions, the former focuses on a smaller set of learning processes, as compared with the wide variety of learning processes accommodated by the latter (Ellis, 2003). Helen was aware of her limited understanding of task-based language teaching and lamented the rather limited in-service training support of the pedagogy in her district.

Helen was attracted to task-based language teaching mainly because it resonated with her own pedagogical philosophy. She believed in the value of student-centered, life-related, and interactively oriented teaching. To her, the paramount goal of primary schooling was to enable children to enjoy their school life and to develop healthily in both physical and mental terms. Her empathetic personality and work as a student counselor contributed to her understanding of primary students' characteristics, needs, and interests. She respected students' different paces of learning and set different learning objectives for different students in her class based on their learning needs. Tasks, as she saw them, could be related to students' life experience and designed to stimulate students' interest. Thus, tasks could not only provide students with opportunity to communicate in English but also cater to their learning needs and boost their confidence in learning English. Helen's learner-centered approach and experimentation with innovative pedagogical practices were greatly valued and supported by her principal.

Helen had to design most of the tasks that she used in her teaching because her textbook—*New Welcome to English* (Book 3)—did not include many tasks. Because it was time consuming both to design tasks and to use them in class, she did not use them in every lesson. She also admitted that she did not make a deliberate effort to use tasks (i.e., to use tasks for the sake of using tasks) but included them naturally (i.e., where they fitted her scheme of work). Five types of tasks were observed in the 10 lessons observed: group discussion, communicative dialogue making, guessing game, survey, and picture description. The last task type was her favorite. She frequently asked her students to talk about pictures, first individually and then cooperatively in groups. She encouraged the students not only to talk about the pictures but also to relate them to their lives and express their personal feelings. For example, in a lesson based on Unit 6 of the textbook, Helen organized her students into groups of five or six and asked each group to make up a story about a picture. Each group member had to contribute a sentence to their group's story. The groups then took turns to read out their stories to the whole class. To illustrate, some groups' stories about a picture with the cue words of "wet" and "stay inside" are reproduced here:

Group 1:   The weather is wet. Why it's wet? Because it's raining. What is the boy doing? He's playing inside.

Group 2:   It is spring. It's wet. Where is the boy staying? The boy is staying inside. He is unhappy.

Group 3:   Today it is a raining day. So it is wet. The boy is staying in home. He cannot go out. The boy is sad.

In this way, the task allowed the students to make meaningful and purposeful use of what they learned to communicate in the target language.

Helen's frequent use of tasks in her teaching was facilitated by several factors. She had a relatively small class of 39 students to work with, which made small group activities and her support of such activities more manageable than would be the case with Fanny's and Gavin's large classes. There was also a generous allocation of curriculum time for English (seven 40-minute periods per week) in her school, which put less pressure on Helen to cover the prescribed curricular content. Her good command of English enabled her to expose her students to natural, meaning-focused communication in English. Although her pedagogy did not fully embrace the task-based innovation, her practice reflected many characteristics of medium- and strong-form task-based language teaching. To a large extent, Helen's case demonstrated that the development of an understanding of students may act as the key trigger of teachers' professional development in other areas, including knowledge of pedagogy, knowledge of self, knowledge of subject matter, and knowledge of curriculum.

Conclusion

This study investigated how three primary school English teachers in mainland China interpreted, negotiated, and represented the recent task-based language teaching innovation in their classroom practice. Although it was recommended in the national curriculum as the new, desired pedagogy of English language teaching to meet the demands of globalization, there was only limited information about the innovation in the programmatic curriculum and little concerted effort to adopt the pedagogical approach at the school level. Also, there was no effective accountability system at the school level. As a result, it was up to individual teachers to decide whether to adopt the task-based language teaching innovation. An array of factors relating to the focal teachers, their working environments, and task-based language teaching per se—for example, the teachers' beliefs about language teaching, their understanding (or lack thereof) of the intended curriculum, their perceptions of the students' learning needs, prevalent instructional practices found in their teaching contexts, availability of resources, support (or lack thereof) for the adoption of the innovation—interacted with each other, which influenced their interpretation and construction of the pedagogical approach in their classrooms. In this regard, our study supports Adamson and Davison's (2003) position that the local enactment of educational change is a complex and context-bound process shaped by the interaction of all levels of stakeholders and by complicated contextual factors (also see Carless, 1998; Kennedy, 1988; Markee, 1997; Zhang, 2007; Zhang & Adamson, 2007). Like the Sri Lankan teachers described by Canagarajah (1999), our teachers translated officially and externally sanctioned pedagogical practices to suit their existing beliefs, perceived objectives of English instruction, and recognized needs of the students in their classrooms.

From the perspective of enactment of curricular innovations, several implications can be drawn from our study for curriculum policymaking in China and elsewhere. First, given the crucial role played by schools in pushing curriculum change (see Goodlad, 1979), it is imperative to channel infrastructural resources into the building and enhancing of schools' capacities to promote curriculum innovations (see Fullan, 2001). Second, as "the indispensable agents of educational change" (Hargreaves & Evans, 1997, p. 3), teachers' professional development deserves much more attention than is currently given. In this study, both the preservice and the in-service programs provided the focal teachers with only limited training related to the pedagogical innovation and were jointly responsible for their limited understanding of the innovation. Without a solid understanding of the aims and goals of a given curriculum, teachers tend to adopt practices that either can be easily incorporated or are compatible with their existing pedagogical practices. Third, in view of the powerful effect of apprenticeship of teaching, teacher educators need to gear their own pedagogical practices to promoting change and demonstrating through their own teaching how a curriculum innovation can be enacted in actual teaching. Fourth, a more positive and supportive working environment should be created to facilitate teachers' enactment of curriculum change in their classroom teaching. This entails that incompatible assessment criteria and practices such as the mandated form-focused test papers should be replaced with those aligned with the promoted curriculum change. This also entails that more curriculum resources should be made available to teachers in the form of required textbooks and other learning materials. In addition, this entails cultivating and nurturing a culture of collegial collaboration that enables teachers to draw on their distributed expertise and support each other in their construction of learning-rich educative experiences for their students.

Up to this point, our focus has been on curriculum-making at different levels and factors that impinge on curricular enactment. We have said little about whether task-based language teaching is appropriate for Chinese classrooms and effective in improving the quality of English instruction. Nor have we given explicit attention to the epistemology underlying the centrally driven reform initiatives that involve the importing of pedagogical practices of foreign origins to solve localized educational problems. By way of conclusion, we offer a brief critique of the pedagogical approach per se and the epistemological perspective giving rise to its promotion in the national curriculum. As pointed out earlier, task-based language teaching is a pedagogical approach that originated in Western educational contexts and that embodies a "learning group ideal" (Holliday, 1994, p. 54) and communication norms rooted in a particular social psychology. Like its predecessor—communicative language teaching—some of its central tenets and valued practices lack contextual appropriateness and local meaningfulness, whereas others may clash with the Chinese culture of learning (Hu, 2005c).[7] Communicative language teaching has largely failed to produce fundamental changes to classroom practices. There is little reason to expect task-based language teaching to fare much better. Such a prospect necessitates a critical examination of the perspective adopted by the Chinese policymakers in promoting task-based language teaching in a centrally driven and top-down manner. We argue that the perspective taken is a technological one based on an autonomous assumption about the existence of universal knowledge and "the 'best method' that ensures successful learning" (Canagarajah, 2005a, p. xxviii). Such a perspective assumes that an innovation or initiative that is effective and appropriate in one social and cultural context also works well in a different one. In other words, a strategy successful in one educational context is expected to "lead in a neat, deterministic manner to a predictable set of learning outcomes" (Tudor, 2001, p. 9) in another. Thus, the technological perspective disregards contextual diversity and overlooks its impact on educational practices; it promotes "notions of global homogeneity" (Canagarajah, 2005a, p. xiii) and advocates reductive practices. Given the multitude and complexity of localized developments in postmodern social, cultural, and economic life, this technological perspective is bound to be unproductive.

We concur with Canagarajah (2005a, p. xiv) that there is a need for a reorientation in policymaking and "a shift in our practice of knowledge-making." This reorientation should reject reductive policy efforts that consist simply in applying, translating, or contextualizing universal knowledge to the local. It should recognize the valid contributions to pedagogical practice that local knowledge is capable of making and enable us to construct contextually relevant knowledge. This calls for, again in the words of Canagarajah (2005b, p. 14), "a deconstructive and reconstructive project" that ensures a clear grounding in the local and an ongoing engagement with productive knowledge by "deconstructing dominant and established knowledge to understand its local shaping" and "reconstructing local knowledge for contemporary needs."

Discussion Questions

1   In his widely acclaimed *The New Meaning of Educational Change*, Fullan (2001, p. 39) points out that educational change in practice is multidimensional:

> There are at least three components or dimensions at stake in implementing any new program or policy: (1) the possible use of new or revised materials (instructional resources such as curriculum materials or technologies), (2) the possible use of new teaching approaches (i.e., new teaching strategies or activities), and (3) the possible alteration of beliefs (e.g., pedagogical assumptions and theories underlying particular new policies or programs).

At which of these dimensions did the three focal teachers change in relation to the task-based language teaching initiative? Which of the changes, in your opinion, would have more fundamental effects? Which would have more superficial effects? Why?

2   In their influential review of research on curriculum implementation, Snyder et al. (1992, p. 427) identified three different perspectives that "operate from different underlying assumptions about curriculum knowledge, knowledge change, and the role of teachers." There is the fidelity perspective that assumes that curriculum knowledge resides primarily out of the classroom with curriculum specialists and is created for teachers to consume and implement in the ways intended by the specialists. From this perspective, curriculum change is "a rational, systematic, linear change process" (p. 429) whose

management can be improved by a growing knowledge of the factors facilitating and inhibiting the smooth operation of the system. A second perspective, known as mutual adaptation, shares with the fidelity perspective the assumption about the external origin of curriculum knowledge but recognizes that a curriculum is never really implemented as intended. This perspective sees the need for teachers to adapt an externally developed curriculum to the local context without losing its integrity. Unlike the fidelity perspective, "change is viewed as a more unpredictable, less linear process with a more active 'consumer' at the end of process" (p. 429). It is further assumed that an intimate knowledge of the change process is necessary to explain what happens to the curriculum. Finally, there is the enactment perspective as discussed in the section of the chapter entitled "Levels of Curriculum Making and the Enactment Perspective."

If a fidelity or mutual adaptation perspective is taken to study the task-based language teaching initiative, what research questions are likely to be addressed? How may such research help us understand curriculum change? What purposes will such research serve? How may they differ from those served by research adopting the enactment perspective?

Notes

1 Shenzhen is a city in southern China's Guangdong province, situated immediately north of Hong Kong. Shenzhen became China's first Special Economic Zone right after the opening and reform policy was initiated in the late 1970s. Since 1991, the English language has been taught from grade one in Shenzhen's primary schools. This has made Shenzhen one of the leading cities in English language teaching in mainland China.

2 We do not claim that these three teachers were representative of all primary school English teachers in China, given the great diversity of education development across the country and the small sample of participants we worked with in our case study. However, since the three teachers worked in Shenzhen, where the national curriculum reform was most vigorously disseminated, their responses to task-based language teaching may provide some valuable insights.

3 According to their basic facilities and quality of teaching, the Ministry of Education ranks public schools into province-level schools, city-level schools, district-level schools, ordinary schools and weak/poor schools. Province-level schools are elitist schools that are supposed to offer better quality teaching and can get more funding from the government.

4 The chapter uses pseudonyms for all the informants to keep their identity confidential and to protect their privacy.

5 All quotations from the Chinese curriculum documents and interview data collected for this study were translated by one of the authors.

6 The *English Language Curriculum Standards*, written in Chinese, translates "task" as *renwu* and "task-based language teaching" as *renwu xing jiaoxuefa*. Although the Chinese polysemous term *renwu* appears 20 times in the text of the *English Language Curriculum Standards*, only 10 of these incidences have to do with tasks in task-based language teaching; the other 10 occurrences of the term denote either "assignment" or "teaching objective." As a result, the meaning of *renwu* in the *English Language Curriculum Standards* can be a source of confusion to teachers. This problem is exacerbated by a lack

of any explicit definition of 'task' or task-based language teaching in the curriculum document.

7 The Confucian philosophy regards learning as accumulation of knowledge and the reading of authoritative books, and stresses maintaining hierarchical but harmonious teacher-student relations. According to the philosophy, a good teacher is to be a model for students to follow, pass on authoritative knowledge, and teach the correct way of learning. Such expectations favor and support a teacher-dominated, knowledge-transmitting, and grammar-based pedagogy in ELT.

References

Adamson, B., & Davison, C. (2003). Innovation in English language teaching in Hong Kong primary schools: One step forward, two steps sideways? *Prospect, 18*(1), 27–41.

Apple, M. W. (2008). Curriculum planning: Content, form, and the politics of accountability. In F. M. Connelly, M. F. He, & J. Phillion (Eds.), *The Sage handbook of curriculum and instruction* (pp. 25–44). Thousand Oaks, CA: Sage.

Calderhead, J. (2001). International experiences of teaching reform. In V. Richardson (Ed.), *Handbook of research on teaching* (4th ed., pp. 777–800). Washington, DC: American Educational Research Association.

Canagarajah, A. S. (1999). *Resisting linguistic imperialism in English teaching.* Oxford, UK: Oxford University Press.

Canagarajah, A. S. (2005a). Introduction. In A. S. Canagarajah (Ed.), *Reclaiming the local in language policy and practice* (pp. xiii–xxx). Mahwah, NJ: Lawrence Erlbaum.

Canagarajah, A. S. (2005b). Reconstructing local knowledge, reconfiguring language studies. In A. S. Canagarajah (Ed.), *Reclaiming the local in language policy and practice* (pp. 3–24). Mahwah, NJ: Lawrence Erlbaum.

Carless, D. (1998). A case study of curriculum implementation in Hong Kong. *System, 26,* 353–368.

Chinese Communist Party Central Committee & State Council. (1999). *Zhonggong zhongyang guowuyuan guanyu shenhua jiaoyu gaige quanmian tuijin suzhi jiaoyu de jueding* [Decision on deepening educational reform and promoting quality education]. Beijing: Author.

Cortazzi, M., & Jin, L. (1996). English teaching and learning in China. *Language Teaching, 29,* 61–80.

Deng, Z. Y. (in press). Curriculum planning and systems change. In B. McGaw, E. Baker, & P. Peterson (Eds.), *International encyclopedia of education* (3rd ed.). Oxford, UK: Elsevier.

Doyle, W. (1992a). Constructing curriculum in the classroom. In F. K. Oser, A. Dick, & J.-L. Patry (Eds.), *Effective and responsible teaching: The new synthesis* (pp. 66–79). San Francisco, CA: Jossey-Bass.

Doyle, W. (1992b). Curriculum and pedagogy. In P. W. Jackson (Ed.), *Handbook of research on curriculum* (pp. 486–516). New York: Macmillan.

Ellis, R. (2003). *Task-based language learning and teaching.* Oxford, UK: Oxford University Press.

Fullan, M. (2001). *The new meaning of educational change* (3rd ed.). New York: Teachers College Press.

Goodlad, J. I. (1979). The scope of the curriculum field. In J. I. Goodlad & Associates (Eds.), *Curriculum inquiry: The study of curriculum practice* (pp.17–41). New York: McGraw-Hill.

Graves, K. (2008). The language curriculum: A social contextual perspective. *Language Teaching, 41,* 147–181.

Hargreaves, A., & Evans, R. (1997). Teachers and educational reform. In A. Hargreaves & R. Evans (Eds.), *Beyond educational reform: Bringing teachers back in* (pp. 1–18). Buckingham, UK: Open University Press.

Holliday, A. (1994). *Appropriate methodology and social context.* Cambridge, UK: Cambridge University Press.

Hu, G. W. (2005a). English language education in China: Policies, progress, and problems. *Language Policy, 4*, 5–24.

Hu, G. W. (2005b). Professional development of secondary EFL teachers: Lessons from China. *Teachers College Record, 107*, 654–705.

Hu, G. W. (2005c). Contextual influences on instructional practices: A Chinese case for an ecological approach to ELT. *TESOL Quarterly, 39*, 635–660.

Hu, G. W. (2008). The misleading academic discourse on Chinese-English bilingual education in China. *Review of Educational Research, 78*, 195–231.

Kelly, A. V. (2004). *The curriculum: Theory and practice* (5th ed.). Thousand Oaks, CA: Sage.

Kennedy, C. (1988). Evaluation of the management of change in ELT projects. *Applied Linguistics, 9*, 329–342.

Kumaravadivelu, B. (2006). *Understanding language teaching: From method to postmethod.* Mahwah, NJ: Lawrence Erlbaum.

Li, J. (2003). *Xin kecheng shiyan tuiguang paichu shijianbiao* [Schedule for implementing the new curriculum]. Retrieved May 19, 2003, from http://www.ncct.gov.cn/jsp/detail/detail.jsp?detailID=631

Liu, Z. (2004). *The curriculum innovation in basic education faces the dilemma of "wearing new shoes and walking on the old road."* Retrieved February 2, 2005, from http://www.yblxx.com/ detail.asp?n_id=753

Markee, N. (1997). *Managing curricular innovation.* Cambridge, UK: Cambridge University Press.

Ministry of Education. (1998). *Mianxiang ershiyi shiji jiaoyu zhenxing xingdong jihua* [21st century-oriented action plan for revitalizing education]. Beijing: Author.

Ministry of Education. (2001). *Quanrizhi yiwu jiaoyu putong gaoji zhongxue yingyu kecheng biaozhun (shiyangao)* [English language curriculum standards for full-time compulsory education and senior secondary schools (trial version)]. Beijing: Beijing Normal University Press.

Richards, J. C., & Rodgers, T. S. (2001). *Approaches and methods in language teaching* (2nd ed.). Cambridge, UK: Cambridge University Press.

Snyder, J., Bolin, F., & Zumwalt, K. (1992). Curriculum implementation. In P. W. Jackson (Ed.), *Handbook of research on curriculum* (pp. 402–435). New York: Macmillan.

State Council. (2001). *Guowuyuan guanyu jichu jiaoyu gaige yu fazhan de jueding* [State Council's decision on reforming and developing basic education]. Beijing: Author.

Stenhouse, L. (1975). *An introduction to curriculum research and development.* London: Heinemann.

Tong, A. S. (2005). *Task-based learning in English language in Hong Kong secondary schools.* Unpublished doctoral dissertation, University of Hong Kong, Hong Kong.

Tong, A. S., Adamson, B., & Che, M. M. (2000). Tasks in English language and Chinese language. In B. Adamson, T. Kwan, & K. Chan (Eds.), *Changing the curriculum: The impact of reform on primary schooling in Hong Kong* (pp. 145–173). Hong Kong: Hong Kong University Press.

Tudor, I. (2001). *The dynamics of the language classroom.* Cambridge, UK: Cambridge University Press.

Westbury, I. (2008). Making curricula: Why do states make curricula, and how? In F. M. Connelly, M. F. He, & J. Phillion (Eds.), *The Sage handbook of curriculum and instruction* (pp. 45–65). Thousand Oaks, CA: Sage.

Zhang, Y. (2005). *The implementation of the task-based approach in primary school English language teaching in mainland China*. Unpublished doctoral thesis, University of Hong Kong, Hong Kong.

Zhang, Y. (2007). TBLT-innovation in primary school English language teaching in Mainland China. In K. Van den Branden, K. Van Gorp, & M. Verhelst (Eds.), *Tasks in Action: Task-based language education from a classroom-based perspective* (pp. 68–91). Cambridge, UK: Cambridge Scholars Publishing.

Zhang, Y., & Adamson, B. (2007). Implementing language policy: Lessons from primary school English. In A. W. Feng (Ed.), *Bilingual education in China* (pp. 166–181). Clevedon, UK: Multilingual Matters.

Educators' Negotiation of Language Education Policies Influenced by Situation/ Context/Community (Social)

Chapter 9

Māori Language Policy and Practice in New Zealand Schools

Community Challenges and Community Solutions

Mere Berryman, Ted Glynn, Paul Woller, and Mate Reweti

Introduction

This chapter discusses Māori-medium education in New Zealand and the policies and curriculum that reconnect Māori language and culture to a worldview that is Māori. In so doing, teachers, families, and communities, contribute to pedagogy that is both culturally appropriate and culturally responsive and thus more likely to facilitate change for both schools and their communities. In the future, practices such as these could lead the way to better inform and modify Māori language policies, curriculum, and pedagogies in mainstream schools for Māori students in English-medium settings.

Historical Background

The indigenous Māori language in Aotearoa/New Zealand has survived near extinction after a history of repressive colonization that threatened not only the language but the unique identity of the Māori population and their culture (Durie, 1998). Education, within this context, failed to address any aspirations of the ethnic minority and instead was seen by colonial governments as the means of assimilating Māori students into the lower levels of European culture and society (Berryman, 2008; Bishop & Glynn, 1999). However, the adaptation and adjustment by Māori society to the impacts of colonization has shown an amazing resilience, confounding the predictions, and perhaps the wishful thinking, of late 19th-century European commentators.

Following a low point of approximately 42,000 in 1896, the Māori population began a slow but steady increase (King, 2003). It is from this point at the beginning of the 20th century that the resurgence of Māori language and culture can be charted, as Māori battled to survive their drastically changed circumstances and struggled to reassert their identity as Māori, within an increasingly English-speaking, European-dominated society. Today, there remains only a very few (rural) tribal regions where Māori is spoken among all generations on a daily basis, within local communities. Māori continue to struggle to achieve the degree of autonomy and independence promised within the Treaty of Waitangi, signed in 1840 between Māori and representatives of the British Crown, but which is even now vigorously contested by the State.

Kaupapa Māori

The imminent loss of the Māori language in New Zealand (Benton, 1983) and the ongoing loss of cultural aspirations, contributed toward a strong grassroots movement of resistance to colonization by Māori that became known as *Kaupapa Māori* (Bishop, 2005; Smith, 1999). In the early 1980s, Kaupapa Māori led to the establishment of Kōhanga Reo (Māori language preschools). The formative foundation provided by the Kōhanga Reo movement and the ongoing desire to revitalize Māori language and to save it from extinction was exerted through a range of protest and legal actions that saw a Waitangi Tribunal claim (1985) confirm the Māori language as a taonga (precious possession) of the indigenous population and, therefore, entitled to full protection by the government under the terms of the Treaty of Waitangi. This, in turn, empowered an increasing number of people to both learn in and teach through the medium of the Māori language (Smith, 1999). Families of Kōhanga Reo graduates started the demand for Māori-medium education (teaching the entire national curriculum through the medium of the Māori language) into primary schooling, and thus the revitalization and retention of the Māori language at a tribal, subtribal, family level, and subsequently, at every level of education provided by the state. Kōhanga Reo and Kura Kaupapa Māori (schools designed by Māori for Māori to uphold and represent authentic Māori values and beliefs) provided the reemergence of social and pedagogical structures for learning, based on pedagogical values and practices from traditional Māori society. For example, Te Aho Matua, the set of traditional cultural principles that have become the foundation of most Kura Kaupapa Māori, is seen as an important representation of ancestral knowledge used to guide and inform contemporary practices. To this end, the Ministry of Education's shift in policy direction (Ministry of Education, 1998) enabled Māori language to be taught as the center of the learning process and as the medium for delivery of the entire curriculum rather than as merely a separate subject within the curriculum. The development of Kura Kaupapa Māori and rumaki (mainstream Māori immersion) classrooms or schools, focused on two important objectives. These objectives are the promotion of higher levels of achievement for Māori students and the revitalization and maintenance of the Māori language (Education Review Office, 1995). One of the basic tenets of the Māori-medium education movement was to afford self-determination to Māori learners and their families, over what constitutes an appropriate model of education, including the language medium of that education.

In 2008, approximately 15.6% of all Māori students accessed some form of Māori-medium education within the compulsory education sector, either bilingually or Māori language alone. The demand to access learning opportunities in Māori is expected to continue to grow.

Some of the Challenges

The long-term effects of language loss through language-suppressive public education policies and practices continue to be felt with many Māori parents and community members who are only limited second-language speakers of their own language or who are unable to speak their language at all. As a result, many contemporary Māori parents and family members do not have sufficient understanding of the language or the customary cultural practices to provide their children with meaningful and authentic contexts in which the day-to-day use of the language outside of schools can be encouraged and fostered.

In order to better understand the present Māori-medium situation it is crucial to also acknowledge that relative to English-medium education, Māori medium is still in its infancy (Bishop, Berryman, Glynn, & Richardson, 2000; Rau, Whiu, Thomson, Glynn, & Milroy, 2001). Much of the theory and practice regarding effective policy, curriculum, and pedagogy for Māori-medium education is still being identified. Though there is undoubtedly a genuine desire among Māori communities to learn and teach in Māori medium, in order to ensure effective practice and high educational outcomes, there is also a degree of tentativeness as these teachers and school communities work to identify what effective practice might look like and how it is best disseminated.

Issues facing Māori-medium education continue to be complex and interrelated. However, critical discussion of these issues focuses on the dearth of research and information on effective practice in Māori-medium pedagogy and assessment (Education Review Office, 2008; Ministry of Education, 2002), rather than focusing on what schools, teachers, and communities can and are doing in order to bring about change.

National Language Policies

Māori language education is one of four focus areas of the current national Māori Education Strategy, Ka Hikitia: Managing for Success Māori Education Strategy 2008–2012 (Ministry of Education, 2008). This strategy clearly outlines the important place of the Māori language and culture within Māori immersion settings and in all areas of education:

> Kōhanga reo, kura kaupapa, wharekura [secondary] and wānanga [tertiary] involve much more than immersion in Māori language. These Māori language providers operate within a specific cultural framework and iwitanga [tribal context]. They play a key role in realising community aspirations and dynamically continuing and regenerating tikanga [traditional cultural practices], mātauranga [knowledge] and te reo Māori [the Māori language]. (Ministry of Education, 2008, p. 26)

The emphasis on the language as "the essence of culture" and "the vehicle through which Māori culture, spirituality and thought are expressed" (Ministry of Education, 2007, p. 38) illustrates the inseparability of language and culture and the continued grassroots, political influence of Māori communities on Māori language policy over the past 25 years.

Thus, although no official national Māori language policy as such has been formulated, a range of strategies have been implemented at a governmental level that give official recognition to the language and promote its protection, revitalization and use. These include the passing of the Māori Language Act (1987) that confirmed the Māori language as one of the official languages of New Zealand and the establishment of Te Taura Whiri i te Reo Māori, the Māori Language Commission. There is also a cross-government Māori Language Strategy developed and implemented by Te Puni Kōkiri (2003), the Ministry of Māori Development, to monitor government efforts at sectoral, intersectoral, and at a national level, to revitalize and "secure the future" (p. 29) of the Māori language. This Māori Language Strategy has been supported in the education sector by other education-specific strategies including Te Reo Matatini: Māori Medium Literacy Strategy (Ministry of Education, 2007), Ka Hikitia: the Māori Education Strategy (Ministry of Education, 2008), and Te Marautanga o Aotearoa (The Māori Medium Curriculum; Ministry of Education, 2008). All of these documents acknowledge Māori values, knowledge, heritage, and culture and the importance they hold for the well-being and development of Māori communities.

Although government agencies have played a key role in formulating and installing these strategies within governmental systems, this has only happened as a result of the ongoing action from Māori communities to ensure the survival of their unique tribal and subtribal identities that make up their Māori cultural identity (Harrison & Papa, 2005). These strategies have also been developed alongside a national movement in New Zealand toward schools becoming self-governing. This movement, known as Tomorrows Schools (Education Act, 1989), provided the context for schools to interpret national strategies and curriculum by developing their own learning policies at the school level. Through this process, the policies and the practices of Māori medium, by and large are able to be repositioned away from mainstream control and returned to the Māori communities in which these education settings are located. These policies and practices are reconnecting Māori education to the patterns of life that extend from pre-European contact, which are inherent in the beliefs, narratives, and logic that form a Māori *worldview*. This view of the world is patterned on traditional experiences, belief systems, and ways of thinking that form the central system or "conceptions of reality to which members of a culture assent and from which stems their values system. The worldview lies at the heart of the culture, touching, interacting with and strongly influencing every aspect of the culture" (Marsden & Henare, 1992, p. 3). Walker (1978) further suggested that the messages or cultural imperatives within traditional Māori stories, when properly understood, provide clear knowledge and understanding about how to face the future. Bruner's (1996) analysis of culture also links to the importance of understanding traditional stories, proposing that the way the human mind has developed and works is linked to "a way of life where 'reality' is represented by a symbolism shared by members of a cultural community in which a technical-social way of life is both organised and construed in terms of that symbolism" (Bruner, 1996, p. 3). In turn, this shared symbolism is "conserved, elaborated and passed on to succeeding generations who, by virtue of this transmission, continue to maintain the culture's identity and way of life" (Bruner, 1996, p. 3).

Māori literacy genre such as whakataukī (traditional adage or wise sayings) and whakatauākī (traditional adage or wise saying that can be attributed to a particular speaker) are more than just an analogy or likeness between things; they are creative metaphors that can be used as a means of understanding and making sense of one's own experiences (Heshusius, 1996). The metaphors and pedagogies that a culture employs are in turn connected to the relationships and interactions that develop and form within learning contexts (Bishop, 1996; Heshusius, 1996). For example, many Māori-medium curriculum policies at a school level are developed around whakataukī/whakatauākī that not only embed policies in a worldview that is Māori but also in the very communities that they relate to and seek to serve. Thus, a Māori worldview and the metaphors and understandings that flow from this source provide a powerful context for responding to contemporary challenges around language learning and provide contexts for solutions, revitalization, and growth (Berryman, 2008; Walker, 1978).

Responsive to and Appropriate for the Community

Māori language immersion settings and the teachers who work within them belong to the communities within which they are located and reflect the desires and aspirations of those communities. In practice this means that not only do teachers impart their knowledge of the language through teaching curriculum topics alone but also the people, tribal histories, and cultural practices of the communities in which they work are powerful contributors to the curriculum and pedagogy.

The relationship of Māori communities to their schools and the role that teachers play in those relationships are expressed in the following narrative, gathered using a series of in-depth, semistructured, face-to-face interviews with a school principal who also had a dual teaching role. This narrative emerged from a study that set out to learn from Māori-medium teachers who had been identified by their home communities as "effective" (Bishop, Berryman, & Richardson, 2001). This teaching principal, one of eight classroom practitioners who provided similar narratives, spoke in great detail about the crucial place of whānau (family, familial, and/or metaphoric) in directing classroom practice and subsequently about the ethos and well-being of the entire school community.

Teaching Principal: When ERO [Education Review Office] came to do a visit the first thing we said to them was we believed that we were a whānau [extended family] driven school so that's what they set out to discover. Is that true? Do we walk that talk or not and gladly they thought we did, so that was a relief.

. . . every whānau has elected to send their child to kura and when we have a pōwhiri [formal welcome] for those new entrants we are actually receiving their whānau as well, its not just the child that we're getting it's the whānau.

She acknowledges the connections to communities being able to determine their own educational choices for their children. Although this has reemerged as a result of Kaupapa Māori and Tomorrows Schools, in traditional Māori society this would have been standard practice.

> Teaching Principal: They've elected not to just go with the flow of the mainstream. They want a different path for their child so I think that's a great place to start and whatever people's criticisms of Tomorrows Schools, the part that interests me is the ability for parents to have the power to make real choices about what and how their tamariki [children] learn and the ways in which they learn, we're still able to keep that real whānau base. Everybody knows everybody else and half are related to everybody else. . . . We can all meet together in one room and talk about those issues face to face.

She also acknowledges the importance of family being able to contribute to the pedagogy within this school model and then contrasts it to a mainstream school model that she understands is more likely to be imposed from the principal down.

> Teaching Principal: I guess its like a triangle inverted, in mainstream its very much the principal at the top of the triangle and then teachers acting on children, whereas I guess I see the model more as, perhaps not even child centered, but whānau centered so that really the idea is that kura becomes a one-stop shop [and] that in the future we'd like to see kōhanga on site.

She recognized that while there were reciprocal roles and responsibilities, in order for the school to be responsive to the community, community participation must be determined by the community rather than by the school. She identified that one of the ways to ensure this outcome was by school staff working alongside well-known and respected people from the community. In the next extract she refers to the kaiwhakahaere (school administrator) as such a person.

> Teaching Principal: So that everybody's got the chance to be supported and learn, whānau development is really important, like sorting out what wānanga [sites of learning] we want to have through the year, where whānau can learn, and what things they want to learn. It's a really important part of our strategic plan for the year. I work cooperatively a lot with our kaiwhakahaere.

The kaiwhakahaere had come from the community with many skills and longstanding commitment to the school.

> our kaiwhakahaere is very skilled socially, very skilled in terms of organization, and computer skills and so forth and was one of the people who started the kura and has served as chairperson, so it made good sense to have her working alongside me.

Participation by elders or kaumātua was seen as another way to ensure positive community and parent participation at all levels.

> Teaching Principal: Some of our tamariki [children] don't have [the] experience of having their kaumātua [elders] around them so it's really essential having older people in our kura, its really important. Because I guess it's filling that role that doesn't always happen at home.

By being culturally responsive in her role, by listening and taking the lead from the community she was then able to make effective connections to the curriculum.

> Teaching Principal: To have that whānau input then I can easily link in with the curriculum, I can find all sorts of things in the curriculum to make those connections.

Responsive to and Appropriate for the Culture

She also identified that successful participation, for students and whānau alike, was more likely to occur when they are able to stand tall in their own cultural identity within all aspects of the school. To achieve this level of participation, the school needed to ensure that the images, icons, metaphors, and pedagogical practices were culturally appropriate.

> Teaching Principal: Some of that [weaving] was from the children but I'd like to have an awful lot more because I'm always saying to our whānau, what's the difference? What is it that makes our kura a kura kaupapa Māori? That's what we want to see happening, that kind of mahi [activity], and it should be really different from what's happening in mainstream, it shouldn't just be a brown version of mainstream ... like having an organic garden, and we've got some big plans for that wetland area, we want to plant that out in different sorts of flax, so we can have it as a resource base for weavers to come and use. They want tamariki doing those traditional kinds of things. Working with the land, learning about looking after the animals, is just as important as the reading, writing, arithmetic stuff, and that takes a while to work out and there's lots of important questions, because we are a young kura, it's about [establishing] our identity, what kawa [cultural protocols] we follow; they are questions really for the adults to talk about and to work out and for me to follow their lead.

Shared Vision

This teaching principal talked about effective participation resulting in shared visions using the metaphor of having everyone on board the same waka (canoe).

She spoke of the positive changes and reciprocal learning that can occur with effective whānau participation.

Teaching Principal: The positive changes, having whānau have a really good understanding of what's happening and being able to express it. When they [Education Review Office] came I was tremendously proud because that night the whānau sat down at the table and every one of them stood to express why kura was important and I thought this is great because everybody was able to articulate a vision and it was a shared vision and so that was the exciting part for me. We are all on the same waka even though we've got different skills and that's actually the strength because it's not about me having to have all the knowledge, all the answers. We've got different abilities and different strengths and we can play to those.

She warned, however, of her concern that whānau must not be manipulated. Rather, they should be making their own decisions. In order for the people, the processes, and the practices to be culturally safe, she identified the crucial element of tikanga (traditional cultural practices) that must be adhered to at all stages and the essential role that elders have in this process.

Teaching Principal: Sometimes I have to be really careful, there's plusses and minuses because sometimes I've got something that I personally would like to see happen and I feel sometimes like I'm engineering it so the whānau wants it to happen. Sometimes I am, but I have to be wary of that too and make sure that whānau have real valid opportunities to participate and make changes and so, sometimes there's things that might not sit particularly comfortably with me, but I guess it's about not feeling the need to be a jack of all trades. For example when it comes to tikanga [cultural practices], then I'm always going to defer to our kaumātua and our kuia [female elder] is always right even when she's wrong because she's our kuia. And so we just go along with it, if she says do it, we all do it and it's a part of that walking the talk that the tamariki see the adults follow that as well.

Implications for Classroom Practice

Within the culturally responsive and culturally appropriate contexts where the community is able to actively initiate and contribute to the planning and pedagogy of their school, students too are likely to be seen as active initiators of their own learning. They may themselves be encouraged to take the initiative when engaging in learning activities. From a Māori worldview, Pere (1982) uses the term *ako* to describe the learning that occurs when there is a balance of power between the roles of teacher and learner. Ako incorporates teaching and learning as reciprocal activities where learning is interactive and where knowledge is constructed between teachers and learners.

Another learning principle demonstrated in this narrative was that of modeling, whereby elders and others from the community who had particular expertise were able to contribute to the pedagogy in the school. The role of the less experienced in this modeling process was to watch, learn, think, and reflect in preparation for the time when it would be their turn to contribute to the learning of others. In sociocultural contexts such as this, learning often requires little explicit instruction or direction from the teacher. For example, very young children soon learn and maintain the rhythm and movement needed to participate in a cultural action song from watching older siblings perform, and typically, this occurs long before they become part of the group themselves.

Rogoff (1990) has interpreted this form of learning as *guided participation* to highlight one of the important ways in which children learn as they take part in and are guided by the practices of their own communities. Just as this community was able to initiate conversations with the school and was seen to be part of the school community, their children may "also often initiate conversations with adults or with other children that help them learn" (Rogoff, 2003, p. 283). Through the process of guided participation, more skilled and interactive learning partners such as teachers, family members, and peers can serve both as guides and collaborators. Children, together with collaborators who mediate their learning, are able to draw on their own cultural resources and experiences to construct learning and make more sense of their world. One important way in which children achieve this level of understanding and skill is by participating in contexts where there is regular and sustained interaction with more skilled individuals around *genuinely shared* activities. Genuinely shared activities are those that are meaningful and purposeful for both the less skilled and the more skilled participants.

Responsive Social Contexts for Learning

Through genuinely shared activities, as were discussed by the teaching principal above, learning interactions can have reciprocal benefits for both participants, so that the more skilled participant can be both a guide and a collaborator. Regular interactions around these shared activities lead to children developing and refining their knowledge and skills within specific domains, such as language learning. The knowledge and skills acquired through these activities are also those that provide generic process knowledge about how to exercise a measure of autonomy in learning. Regular participation in these activities affirms and extends the interdependent positive social relationships between learning partners. These important interactive and social contexts for learning have been identified as responsive social contexts (Glynn, Wearmouth, & Berryman, 2006).

From a Western/European worldview, this type of *social* and *interactive* context is only more recently being seen as fundamental to the development of individual cognition and language learning. Traditionally, English language acquisition was understood as a unified individual achievement that opened the way to the development of cognitive and intellectual skills. Hence, traditional Western pedagogy, as experienced in many mainstream language-learning classrooms, focused on learners as individuals. However, this may have come at the cost of understanding the learner as a member of different social and cultural communities of practice. From a sociocultural perspective, then, when engaging in any classroom language or literacy activity, children and teachers bring to that activity not only their own prior experience and understanding of that activity but also the experience and understanding they have shared with others in their own families and other communities of practice. For example, prior to Māori-medium education, many Māori children in New Zealand might have entered English language-learning contexts already competent and as literate performers of tribal chants, action songs, and customary forms of greeting, as well as being able to recite genealogy and oral history. However, their success in the classroom language-learning context may well have depended upon whether or not that language knowledge and lived experiences could safely be brought into classroom and affirmed and legitimated through language interactions with their teacher and peers (Bishop & Berryman, 2006). In New Zealand, Māori-medium education is providing a legitimate site for these activities to be validated in the classrooms once more.

The following four characteristics of responsive social contexts resonate with a Māori worldview (Glynn, Wearmouth, & Berryman, 2006). Each characteristic is described, then separate research studies that the writers have each been involved with, are used to briefly exemplify how each characteristic has been effectively applied in Māori-medium classrooms to facilitate active engagement with Māori language assessment or literacy learning.

1   Learner Initiations in Responsive Social Contexts

Whether the context is one of infants learning to speak their first language or of students learning to speak a second language or of students learning to read or write, if learners are to have agency over their own learning, they must be able to initiate interactions with others, around learning activities, and not simply respond to adult or peer directions and questions.

Many classroom language-learning tasks and tests are not genuinely shared activities. They provide the student with little opportunity to *initiate*, but only to *respond* to directions and questions from someone else. These questions may or may not respond to a student's understandings of the learning tasks. They leave little or no room for a *conversation* about the learning activity, in which the student might have some degree of control over what is said. Responsive teachers might set out some interesting language materials and activities and then wait until the student has selected an activity and has begun work. Then, rather than asking questions, this teacher might show their interest by moving close and waiting for the student to initiate some statement or comment. The teacher would then respond to that initiation in a conversational manner.

In a responsive language-learning relationship, students not only learn the language but also how to use language to obtain particular information or to access materials and activities, and they also learn a powerful general strategy for engaging and maintaining language interactions with others.

In response to teacher requests, the concept of responsive language-learning relationships was used in this study (Berryman, Togo, & Woller, 2007) to develop three oral language assessments that more effectively discriminate the Māori language competencies of students entering Māori-medium education at age 5.

The recognition of students' own prior experiences or "cultural toolkit" (Bruner, 1996) and the importance of the contextualized *social* interactions between the assessor and the child have been a significant part of the development process. The assessments use a series of carefully constructed tasks with the assessor attending and responding to the student's engagement with the tasks, providing consistent cues and support to keep the student engaged, but, at the same time, not preempting or supplying the correct answers.

The content of all three assessments relies heavily on the use of pictures or other items to stimulate language responses. Therefore, items incorporated in the assessments were chosen on the basis of their perceived relevancy to Māori students, with the intention that students would then be able to draw on their prior knowledge and experiences in their responses. The assessments involve the student choosing the items and to a certain extent, being able to direct which items to talk about, and the content of the discussion. The cultural validity of the assessments is indicated by students having some ownership of the process in that they have choice and agency (a degree of control) over what they talk about. Students are able to bring themselves, their language, cultural identity, and particular expertise to bear on the assessment tasks. Methods used to assess reliability and validity (i.e., internal consistency, test retest, content of the measure, and response processes) also demonstrated that these assessments have measurement reliability and validity.

Teachers who participated in the trial of these assessments commented that they were easy to use and practical and could also be understood by family members who were not fluent speakers but who had sufficient proficiency in Māori language to understand the required tasks. Importantly, these teachers believed that the results from the assessments not only indicated the level and depth of children's Māori language proficiency for summative purposes but could also provide important information for formative purposes.

2   Shared Activities between Less Skilled and More Skilled Learners

Responsive social contexts should provide opportunities for learners to engage in shared activities with more skilled performers, with whom they have positive social relationships. The notion of shared activity implies that the learning activities or tasks are functional, enjoyable, and familiar experiences for both the less skilled and the more skilled participants in the language interactions. A relaxed conversation can be an enjoyable shared task in that control over the topics and direction of the speech are shared by both participants because both are positioned to gather some information about what the other person knows and thinks.

Regular and extended conversations around genuinely shared tasks affirm and strengthen the relationship between participants. In contrast, language interactions in which an adult continually asks *leading* questions, which minimize the opportunity for the student to initiate, are not genuinely shared tasks. Similarly it is not a shared task when teachers *test* students by asking a set of questions, especially when students are well aware that the teacher already knows the answers. Such a strategy is highly unlikely to lead to engaging and interesting conversations.

TATA is a Māori language resource that provides opportunities for learners to engage with a trained person in shared, oral-language activities (Berryman & Rau, 2003). TATA focuses on developing phonological awareness while simultaneously increasing students' oral language so that students are able to progress more successfully to reading and writing. Students participate in one-to-one tutoring sessions with a person who is a fluent Māori language speaker. Sessions last for 10 to 15 minutes and take place at least 3 times a week. During each session, a range of exercises are used to promote oral language and also assist students to identify and manipulate the sounds in some of the words they are using and to connect some of these sounds to letter shapes. These exercises utilize a large range of small toys from which the student is able to choose items as the basis for his or her talk.

In this next study, a mainstream teacher in a bilingual unit used TATA to accelerate and consolidate the Māori language of her mainly 5-year-old new entrants. With community support, this teacher implemented TATA and within a relatively short period of time (27 to 66 sessions), students' phonological knowledge improved along with their confidence and ability to speak in Māori. This teacher shares how the students had enjoyed participating in TATA:

> All children responded positively to the program and displayed a keenness to attend. The boys became competitive and showed curiosity as to how others were achieving and endeavored to do better than their peers. The variety of activities that are incorporated in the set days of TATA activities [from the TATA manual] kept the children's focus and maintained their attention span.

The pre- to post-test gains of participating students were not only statistically significant but they were also of substantial effect size (Berryman & Woller, 2008).

3   Reciprocity and Mutual Influence

Responsive social contexts are also characterized by reciprocity and mutual influence. Each party in a learning interaction has an impact on the other and modifies the learning and behavior of the other. Studies showing reciprocal learning gains for tutors and tutees also commonly report that these gains are accompanied by positive social and cultural outcomes, in terms of forming new stronger relationships and cultural understandings.

Rīpene Āwhina ki te Pānui Pukapuka (RĀPP), a tape-assisted reading resource for students learning to read in Māori, provides opportunities for students to self-manage (initiate, monitor, and record) their own reading progress within and across a range of reading texts. RĀPP also provides specific activities for adults to engage in and support their children's learning to read in Māori, either at school or at home. Māori language stories were read onto tapes by fluent native speakers, including elders. In addition, two comprehension activities accompany each book and tape. These resources were trialed by teachers in Māori language immersion units in two mainstream schools (Berryman & Woller, 2007). The results of this study demonstrated statistically significant increases in the difficulty levels of books students could read successfully, and students maintained comprehension rates on the more difficult texts. Teachers from each of the two schools in this study viewed the RĀPP resource as a means to increase students' reading mileage while also developing their reading comprehension. An additional benefit was reported in the positive interactions between school and home when students took the program and resources home. A participating teacher discusses the benefits of using RĀPP with her students:

> Those tamariki who were on this [RĀPP] have got their comprehension about print; they know where to start, they know where to go. They have got their letters and their word attack skills, and I think the main thing that RĀPP will work on is broadening their vocabulary and their understanding.

> I liked the monitoring book that the tamariki [children] could use to self-assess themselves when they were ready to kōrero [talk] to an adult. I also liked the cloze activities. I liked the resource itself, everything being there to use. It's really straight forward and I can see the benefits. I liked the interaction with home, the kids were good, and everything came back.

4   Amount and Type of Feedback

A fourth characteristic of responsive social learning contexts is the nature and quality of feedback received for learning by both participants. For example, under-achievement in written language in some classroom settings may be in part a function of feedback that is excessively delayed, excessively negative, and contingent mainly on errors in surface features and language structures. It is not uncommon for students to receive only this type of feedback, and no feedback at all on the content or message they are writing. Continued exposure to this feedback regime is likely to result in students writing less in order to minimize the risk of negative feedback from attempting to incorporate new words and language structures.

A socially responsive context for writing in Māori was trialed by using responsive written feedback (Glynn, Berryman, O'Brien, & Bishop, 2000). This strategy involves responding in writing to the messages conveyed within the piece of student writing but not focusing on structure, error correction, or evaluative comments. In this study students from one school, who were more fluent in Māori language, wrote regular, weekly, brief, and personalized responses to students (with less language fluency) who were writing to them from another school. The responders were encouraged to respond to what they were able to understand of the messages in their student's stories rather than respond to errors in spelling or language structure.

Both groups of students gained considerable benefit from participating in the responsive written feedback program. They increased their correct writing rate per minute and received higher ratings for both audience impact and Māori language quality. These ratings were provided by an independent reader who was a fluent speaker of Māori, but naive as to the writers of specific text samples, and to the order (early or late) of these samples within the program. Comments from the participating teachers indicated that responsive writing had made a positive difference to their students' attitude toward writing. All students liked not having to rewrite or reformat their original story. Their writing was accepted just the way it was. They also appreciated that the waiting time between writing and responsive feedback was short (turnaround within the week) and that the responses were regular. Because someone was going to read what they had written, writing for these students became an authentic task with high credibility. The kaiārahi i te reo (in-class language expert) from the school of the more fluent writers indicated that responsive written feedback had made a positive contribution to their Māori language writing program. She observed: (translated from Māori)

> I am a kaiārahi i te reo, my job is to provide the language so that the language will not be lost. This process is different from how I have been teaching the language, and now that I have seen their writing I can tell that it's been very good.

When asked about any benefits she had noticed for students she replied:

> I could see that they were comfortable to sit and talk, it is easy for them to express themselves, their writing is good, and that is what is good to me.

Conclusion

In Aotearoa/New Zealand long-term intergenerational effects of language loss continue to be felt by the indigenous Māori people. Strong grassroots initiatives have driven the movement toward Māori language revitalization, with many Māori parents and families wanting language learning opportunities for their children which they themselves did not have. Utilizing culturally appropriate and culturally responsive pedagogies, as discussed in this chapter, can shift teachers a long way from the model of tight instructional control evident in many mainstream language-learning settings. In handing over a much greater share of control to the learner, teachers would be following a responsive, interactive role, rather than a directive or managerial role. However, they would be, as were the teachers in this chapter, well on the way toward establishing their classrooms as effective language-learning communities.

Establishing positive learning communities in classrooms where policies and pedagogies are socially and culturally responsive and centered around students' shared life experiences is critical if target languages such as Māori are to be revitalized. While the Māori language may currently lack the power and dominant status of the language of government and wider society, the contributions of teachers, students, and communities is critical to understanding how the Māori language can be affirmed and legitimized in classrooms and thus also contribute to change within communities and wider society.

Discussion Questions

1 Discuss the Māori language revitalization movement in Aotearoa/New Zealand.
2 What aspects of this movement differ from and apply to other language revitalization examples that you are aware of?
3 In this chapter, whānau (extended family) were central to policy and practice. Explain both the benefits and challenges of this stance.
4 How might schools and teachers respond to the different views of whānau when establishing a safe but challenging place to learn and grow?
5 From your reading of the chapter, and any other sources, define "responsive social contexts for learning."
6 How did the principal exemplify "responsive social contexts for learning" in her school?

References

Benton, R. (1983). *NZCER Maori language survey: Notes on the purposes and methodology of the sociolinguistic survey of language use in Māori households and communities.* Wellington: New Zealand Council of Educational Research.

Berryman, M. (2008). *Repositioning within indigenous discourses of transformation and self-determination.* Unpublished Doctoral of Philosophy Thesis, University of Waikato, Hamilton.

Berryman, M., & Rau, C. (2003). *TATA—Te Tāutu Reta: Making connections between spoken language, letter sounds and letter shapes.* Wellington: Ministry of Education.

Berryman, M., Togo, T., & Woller, P. (2007, November). Poipoia te reo kia penapena: Nurture the language. Paper presented at the Language, Education and Diversity Conference, University of Waikato, Hamilton.

Berryman, M., & Woller, P. (2007). RĀPP: Tape-assisted reading to support students' reading in Māori in two bilingual schools. *SET Research Information for Teachers, 2,* 19–23.

Berryman, M., & Woller, P. (2008). TATA: A phonological awareness resource to assist five year olds prepare for reading in Māori. Paper presented at the New Zealand Association for Research in Education Conference, Massey University, Palmerston North, New Zealand.

Bishop, R. (1996). *Collaborative research stories whakawhanaungatanga.* Palmerston North, New Zealand: Dunmore Press.

Bishop, R. (2005). Freeing ourselves from neo-colonial domination in research: A kaupapa Māori approach to creating knowledge. In N. Denzin & Y. Lincoln (Eds.), *Handbook of qualitative research* (3rd ed., pp. 109–138). Thousand Oaks, CA: Sage.

Bishop, R., & Berryman, M. (2006). *Culture speaks: Cultural relationships and classroom learning.* Wellington, New Zealand: Huia Publishers.

Bishop, R., Berryman, M., Glynn, T., & Richardson, C. (2000). *Diagnostic assessment tools in Māori medium education: Stock take and preliminary evaluation. Final report to the Ministry of Education.* Wellington: Ministry of Education.

Bishop, R., Berryman, M., & Richardson, C. (2001). *Te Toi Huarewa: Effective teaching and learning strategies, and effective teaching materials for improving the reading and writing in te reo Māori of students aged five to nine in Māori medium education. Final report to the Ministry of Education.* Wellington: Ministry of Education.

Bishop, R., & Glynn, T. (1999). *Culture counts: Changing power relations in education.* Palmerston North, New Zealand: Dunmore Press Ltd.

Bruner, J. (1996). *The culture of education.* Cambridge, Massachusetts: Harvard University Press.

Durie, M. (1998). *Te mana, te kawanatanga: The politics of Māori self-determination.* Auckland: Oxford University Press.

Education Act. (1989). Retrieved November 13, 2008, from http://www.legislation.govt.nz/act/public/1989/0080/latest/DLM175959.html

Education Review Office. (1995). *Kura Kaupapa Māori* [Māori Language Schools]. Wellington: Education Review Office.

Education Review Office. (2008). *An evaluation of the quality of Māori language teaching in secondary schools: Manukau.* Wellington: Education Review Office.

Glynn, T., Berryman, M., O'Brien, K., & Bishop, R. (2000). Responsive written feedback on students' writing in a Māori language revitalisation context. Paper presented to Language Revitalisation Symposium: Xornadas de Lingua e Literatura Galegas, Centro Ramón Piñeiro: Ramon Pineiro Center for Humanities Research, Santiago di Compostella, Galicia, Spain.

Glynn, T., Wearmouth, J., & Berryman, M. (2006). *Supporting students with literacy difficulties: A Responsive approach.* Maidenhead: Open University Press / McGraw-Hill Education.

Harrison, B., & Papa, R. (2005). The development of an indigenous knowledge program in a New Zealand Māori—Language immersion school. *Anthropology and Education Quarterly, 36*(1), 57–72.

Heshusius, L. (1996). Modes of consciousness and the self in learning disabilities research. Considering past and present. In K. Kim Reid, W. P. Hresko, & H. Lee Swanson (Eds.), *Cognitive approaches to learning disabilities* (pp. 617–651). Austin, TX: PRO-ED.

King, M. (2003). *The penguin history of New Zealand.* Auckland: Penguin Books.

Māori Language Act. (1987). Retrieved November 13, 2008, from http://www.legislation.govt.nz/act/public/1987/0176/latest/DLM124116.html?search=ts_all%40act_Maori+language&sr=1

Marsden, M., & Henare, T. (1992). *Kaitiakitanga: A definitive introduction to the holistic world view of the Māori.* Wellington: Ministry of the Environment.

Ministry of Education. (1998). *Education statistics of New Zealand 1997. Data management unit.* Wellington: Ministry of Education.

Ministry of Education. (2002). *Monitoring the achievement of Māori students: In New Zealand Schools Ngā Kura o Aotearoa 2001. A report to the Minister of Education on the compulsory schools sector in NZ 2001* (also known as the Schools Sector report 2001). Wellington: Ministry of Education.

Ministry of Education. (2007). *Te Reo Matatini: Māori medium literacy strategy.* Wellington: Ministry of Education.

Ministry of Education. (2008). *Ka Hikitia: Managing for success Māori education strategy.* Wellington: Group Māori, Ministry of Education.

Pere, R. (1982). *Ako: Concepts and learning in the Māori tradition* (Working Paper No.17). Hamilton: University of Waikato.

Rau, C., Whiu, I., Thomson, Glynn, T., & Milroy (2001). A description of success in reading and writing for five-year-old Māori medium students. Unpublished report to the Ministry of Education, Wellington, New Zealand.

Rogoff, B. (1990). *Apprenticeship in thinking: Cognitive development in social context.* New York: Oxford University Press.

Rogoff, B. (2003). *The cultural nature of human development.* Oxford: Oxford University Press.

Smith, L. (1999). *Decolonizing methodologies research and indigenous peoples.* Dunedin: Zed Books Ltd, University of Otago Press.

Te Puni Kōkiri [Ministry of Māori Development]. (2003). *Te Rautaki Reo Māori* [The Māori language strategy].Wellington: Te Puni Kōkiri.

Walker, R. (1978). The relevance of Māori myth and tradition. In M. King (Ed.), *Tihei mauri ora* [The breath of life] *aspects of Maoritanga* [Māori culture] (pp.19–32). New Zealand: Methuen Publications.

Chapter 10

(Re)Constructing Language Policy in a Shi'i School in Lebanon

Zeena Zakharia

Introduction

Language and sociopolitical struggle are intimately intertwined. This chapter explores the central role of teachers in (re)constructing language policies in schools, as they interpret and negotiate top-down national and school-based "official" policies, and ultimately implement their own, based, in part, on personal language beliefs, and in response to realities "on the ground"—that is, their students' interpretations, negotiations, and needs, during periods of political instability, economic uncertainty, and postwar reconstruction. The chapter explores language policy as a complex social practice with political and socioeconomic dimensions and considers these dimensions in relation to the basic need for human security.

Focusing on the language practices at one Shi'i school in Beirut's Southern Suburb after the 2006 summer war between Hizbullah and Israel, the chapter draws on ethnographic data to illustrate how teachers and students, together, negotiate and (re)construct language policy through a critical and participatory learning process, in order to create safe spaces for language development, political expression, and critical engagement of contemporary social concerns.

The chapter gives attention to teachers as central policy actors. Specifically, it explores how language teachers negotiate between the demands and pressures of external standards in education and students' academic and social needs during periods of acute sociopolitical crisis and repeated school disruption. I suggest *reconstruction* as an analogy to capture how teachers strip foreign languages of their colonial associations, isolating them from their origin, and then through a generative pedagogical process, reconstruct the languages as local by integrating real-world and community-centered concerns into language teaching. At the same time, the social and pedagogical practice of reconstruction makes it possible for teachers to engage students in meeting government-mandated educational standards while giving due attention to students' needs. I argue that community-centered reconstruction of State language policy is effective for historically marginalized communities, particularly those directly affected by conflict. Reconstruction as a policy process contributes to the success of this particular school's foreign language programs for students who come from largely monolingual neighborhoods and who have little if any contact outside of the school with the languages they are learning.

In the section that follows, I provide a brief historical overview of national language policy in education to situate contemporary bilingual education within a broader history of colonial and missionary schooling, contestation over language status, and social struggle. I introduce the larger sociopolitical context in which the Shi'i school was immersed during the period of study and under which language learning was taking place. I then discuss the research methods and conceptual approach employed to pay attention to the "ideological and implementational spaces" carved out by the school to allow for rich engagement in language study (Hornberger & Johnson, 2007). I examine the general language policies and practices of the school in relation to national language policy in education. Based on extensive observational and interview data, I then provide illustrative classroom examples to demonstrate how French and Arabic teachers reconstruct language policy in their classrooms. Finally, based on components of this pedagogy, I provide a framework for working with youth during acute conflict. I conclude by explaining the importance of such reconstructive pedagogy for language learning in postcolonial and postwar contexts, during periods of insecurity, particularly for historically marginalized communities.

National Language Policy in Education: From Colonial and Missionary Roots to Contemporary Bilingual Practice

Bilingual education in Lebanon may be traced at least as far back as the early-1800s when Lebanon was part of the Ottoman Empire (Shaaban & Ghaith, 1999). The appearance of various Christian schools, founded by European and American colonial and missionary sponsors with competing interests in the region, established a pattern of bilingual schooling at this time. Arabic and the language of the mission—French, English, German, and Russian—became the languages of instruction. Each religious community tended to have a colonial or missionary sponsor through which they actively sought access to schooling. Largely in response to the success of Christian missionary schools, the Ottoman authority opened schools modeled on the French-Catholic exemplar, but with Islamic features and Turkish and Arabic as the media of instruction (Fortna, 2002). Thus, while the Catholics and Maronites tended to be schooled largely in French, the Sunni Muslim, Greek Orthodox, and Druze elites were schooled in English (Frayha, 2004). Turkish and Arabic were learned by Muslims more generally. In this way, foreign languages spread through educational institutions along religious lines, establishing a tradition of bilingual schooling. In addition, a number of Christian and Sunni Muslim schools were established by local individuals and groups by the late 19th century, following the same model. The Shi'i Muslims, however, had no major part in the educational movement of the period (Abouchedid & Nasser, 2000).

With the decline of Ottoman rule, Lebanon came under the authority of the French Mandate from 1920 to 1943. During this time, French became the official language of the State alongside Arabic. The institution of a national system of education and examination based on the French lycée promoted French as the language of the educated elite (Frayha, 2004; Shaaban & Ghaith, 1999).

In 1943, Lebanon gained independence from France, and Arabic was reinstated as the sole official language with supporting government-initiated curricular reforms to strengthen its position. The Arabic language was seen as critical to Arab unity and identity (Suleiman, 1994). However, the civil war between 1975 and 1990 deteriorated the government's authority over education. A burgeoning private school business promoted foreign languages, diminishing the symbolic value of Arabic for national unity. Among the French-speaking Lebanese, 75% were Christians by the 1990s (Abou, Kasparian, & Haddad, 1996).

Post-civil war constitutional amendments in 1990 established a government-mandated national curriculum with basic principles to promote an Arab national identity, balanced by openness to other cultures. The corresponding bilingual national curriculum and examination system was launched in 1997. The system involves a dual language structure, in which Arabic and either French or English are required for all public and private school students starting from the elementary grades. In addition, a third language is required starting in Grade 7 (National Center for Educational Research and Development; NCERD, 1995). The tripartite language policy thus promotes Arabic as the common denominator for all students and places French and English on equal footing as foreign languages.

The Shi'i School in Sociopolitical Context

Shi'i Muslims in Lebanon comprise one of 18 officially recognized religious sects and have been generally marginalized, both politically and economically, for most of the nation-state's history (Deeb, 2006). The material and educational development of the Shi'a began later than for other religious groups, due in part to colonial and missionary projects that largely ignored them. Under Sunni Ottoman rule, the Shi'a, who had resided in parts of modern-day Lebanon since the 9th century, were often persecuted. The confessional political system established at Lebanon's independence in 1943 ensured their underrepresentation in government and later in postindependence development through the institutionalization of sectarianism as a means of accessing resources. Unequal development eventually contributed to their mobilization into various political parties in the 1960s and 1970s and later into sectarian political movements (Deeb, 2006).

The Shi'i school at the focus of this chapter was opened in 1997 by a charitable organization and currently enrolls over 2,500 Shi'i students, including girls (Grades K–12) and boys (Grades K–9) in gender-segregated classrooms. It runs both Arabic–English and Arabic–French bilingual programs of the Lebanese national curriculum, as well as biweekly religion classes and daily morning prayers, much like the Christian missionary school model prevalent among private schools in Lebanon. As a university preparatory program, the school primes students for the terminal national examination—the Lebanese Baccalaureate—at the end of Grade 12, as well as the Scholastic Achievement Test (SAT) for students seeking entry into American universities in Lebanon or abroad. Students and teachers are, with few exceptions, Shi'i, and as students told me in interviews and surveys, and teachers confirmed, they come from essentially monolingual Arabic-speaking neighborhoods in Lebanon and from varied socioeconomic backgrounds.

Shi'i Muslims in Lebanon are often referred to as a "community"; however, I use this term with caution as it masks the diversity therein. Such designations give prominence to difference based on presumed sectarian affiliation and oriental accounts of primordial associations, rather than paying due attention to the significant role that the political economy plays in the process of differentiation. Furthermore, the designation of "community" also implies inaccurate generalizations about their political affiliation to Hizbullah, a political party that represents the opposition movement in the U.S.- and French-backed government. Though many of the teachers and students at the Shi'i school at the focus of this chapter did express affiliation to Hizbullah's political party or its social and charitable associations, others had no stated relationship, even though they sympathized with the opposition movement, were actively engaged in opposition politics, and admired its leader Hassan Nasrallah.

The period of research was one of great upheaval in Lebanon. Between 2005 and 2007, the Lebanese witnessed the withdrawal of Syrian occupation; a war between Hizbullah and Israel; internal sectarian violence; multiple political assassinations; civilian terror targeting; protests, sit-ins, and riots; a second war between the Lebanese army and an al-Qaeda-inspired insurgent militia; and a power vacuum amidst conflict over power and representation between progovernment and opposition parties. During the July 2006 war with Israel, more than 350 schools were damaged or demolished in 34 days (Shehab, 2006). These schools were disproportionately Shi'i educational institutions. Other schools across the country sheltered displaced families. The summer was followed by a series of politically motivated assassinations, roadside bombs, and other violent events that resulted in daily disruptions to schooling during the course of the study. For students and teachers at the Shi'i school, this was a particularly poignant period as many students or their larger families had lost their homes during the July 2006 war and were living in temporary housing. In addition, some students had lost their parents, and many expressed in interviews and informal conversations their fears of resumed hostilities.

This sociopolitical context is important because it provides the larger context for classroom activity in which students and teachers were engaged in teaching and learning, and which cannot be divorced from the larger arena of social, political, and economic uncertainty. Students and teachers articulated a sense of insecurity, which created an impetus to learn foreign languages at the same time that it created a pull toward Arabic, couched in notions of patriotism during turbulent times (Zakharia, 2009). Thus, youth at the Shi'i school and elsewhere expressed both a strong connection to the Arabic language and strong multilingual ideology.

This observation is supported by cross-school survey data involving 1,000 secondary school youth (Zakharia, 2009). Students talked about disparities in bilingual practices, the bilingual qualities of their school, and their personal bilingual proficiency in relation to insecurity about the future and social injustice. These narratives centered on (a) political instability in Lebanon and the region; (b) access to higher education and employment opportunities, as forms of superseding instability; and (c) linguistic discrimination (Zakharia, 2009). Thus, students widely expressed the importance of learning foreign languages in terms of human security and as a means of reducing social disparities. They related the knowledge of multiple languages to a good education and a way of securing a future.

Methods and Conceptual Approach

The research presented in this chapter draws on a larger study comprising 21 months of fieldwork between 2005 and 2007 at 10 religious and secular Lebanese secondary schools in the Greater Beirut region. The study entailed a multilayered approach in line with Hornberger and Johnson's (2007) conceptualization of ethnographic research as slicing through the layers of the language policy and practice onion to connect micro- and macro-processes in education. This chapter draws mainly on the ethnographic research conducted at the Shi'i focal school to understand the ideological and implementational spaces created by teachers and students for learning multiple languages.

I focus on the Shi'i school for this discussion because it was effective in its delivery of multilingual education to students from monolingual neighborhoods and communities. It also schooled a segment of the population most directly affected by the July 2006 war and the ensuing political conflicts. Furthermore, it provides insight into an opposition movement, and therefore, spaces for oppositional discourse within State-determined educational mandates. In contrast with other schools in Lebanon, the Shi'i school demonstrated a well-articulated language policy, which not only outlines expectations regarding French and English language practices for teachers and students but also includes other school personnel and measures for Arabic language use and development, specifically regarding the use of *fuṣḥā* and *'āmiyya*.[1]

This chapter makes particular use of qualitative data from daily participant observation of Arabic and French classes, library activities, and other extracurricular undertakings, such as performances, lectures, and exhibits at the school over a 6-month period. In addition, data are drawn from interviews with teachers and administrators, an examination of school documents, and an audit of the visual and auditory presence of languages at the school to understand school language policies in practice.

The chapter takes a sociocultural and sociopolitical approach to understanding teachers as change agents in language policy and practice. Such perspectives assume that "social relationships and political realities are at the heart of teaching and learning. That is, learning emerges from the social, cultural, and political spaces in which it takes place, and through interactions and relationships that occur between learners and teachers" (Nieto, 2002, p. 5).

The study assumes an artificial discursive distinction between policy and practice, as policy is seen to be generated through practice and practice is seen to be a form of unstated policy in which individuals and groups "engage in situated behaviors that are both constrained and enabled by existing structures, but which allow the person to exercise agency in the emerging situation" (Sutton & Levinson, 2001, p. 3). Languages serve as sites of ideological contestation, particularly in postcolonial contexts and situations of sociopolitical struggle (Suleiman, 2004). "Official" policy mandates, such as those of the national curriculum, government examination system, and school administration, claim authority over managing top-down policies, delivering an "operating manual for everyday conduct" (Sutton & Levinson, 2001, p. 2). However, teachers create ideological and implementational spaces (Hornberger & Johnson, 2007) in which language policies are negotiated and reformulated from new and preexisting elements. This process of reformulation or (re)construction is at the focus of this chapter. As Lin and Martin (2005) point out, understanding new phenomena and people's desires to learn former colonial languages in diverse postcolonial contexts requires a break from the binary logic of imperialism–resistance analyses. Languages are appropriated by policy actors to serve a variety of intentions and purposes "whether it be the acquiring of socially-upward identity, or the creation of a bilingual space for critical explorations of self and society" (p. 5).

Creating Ideological and Implementational Spaces for Language Policy at a Shi'i School in Lebanon

The bilingual educational system in Lebanon is a vestige of missionary and colonial enterprises in the region. While centralized at the level of the national curriculum and examination system, educational practices are largely decentralized at the level of the schools, of which the vast majority is private.[2] Thus, all schools in Lebanon, whether public, private, or parochial, implement the government-mandated national curriculum and language-in-education policy framework and prepare students for government examinations in two languages at Grades 9 and 12. Less than 40% of secondary school students are enrolled in Arabic-English-medium programs, as compared with more than 60% enrolled in Arabic–French programs (CRDP, 2005).

According to the national language policy in education, from Grade 1 an equal number of hours is assigned to the two major languages (Arabic and either French or English) as language and literature education.[3] From Grade 7, the dual-language structure of schooling assigns equal weight to the two languages of instruction in terms of the number of teaching hours per subject in each language of instruction. The humanities and social sciences are taught in Arabic, and mathematics and sciences are taught in the first foreign language (French for some students and English for others). In addition, the second foreign language (French or English) is taught as a subject and is given lesser weight, with the general aim of achieving basic interpersonal communication skills.

Schools are actively involved in complex and multifaceted day-to-day language policies enacted by an array of actors. Students and teachers are keenly aware of these unwritten and sometimes unspoken codes of conduct regarding language use. Observations of classroom, library, and extracurricular activities; meetings; administrative procedures; and hallway and playground interactions; as well as the visual and auditory presence of languages within schools reveal how richly schools are infused with stated and unstated, or tacit, language policies and their hidden messages regarding language status. With a centralized curriculum, but decentralized schooling practices, the Lebanese national language-in-education policy, therefore, sees much variation in how it is implemented across religious and secular schools and school networks and within varied socioeconomic, demographic, and language–schooling contexts in Lebanon.

The Shi'i school's language policy outlines expectations regarding Arabic, French, and English language practices for teachers, students, and other school personnel. Because Arabic ʿāmiyya is the prevalent language variety or mother tongue, used at home and in everyday communication in students' neighborhoods, its development is not specified. Rather, school policy consciously permits students to speak in ʿāmiyya with each other, but encourages them to practice their other languages in communication with teachers. Aspects of the school language policy related to Arabic and French, and some of its underlying premises, as relayed by the head of the secondary section and supported by teacher interviews, may be summarized as follows:

- Languages are highly valued and the school is committed to developing Arabic fushā, French, and English.
- Languages require special attention because students do not have sufficient exposure and practice in using foreign languages and fushā outside the school.
- Languages should be promoted not just for instrumental purposes but also for aesthetic purposes and for the development of the whole person.
- Foreign languages are to be further developed through their use in the teaching and learning of sciences and mathematics subjects. Fushā to be further developed through its use in the teaching and learning of humanities and social science subjects. Thus, subject learning should serve the goal of language development by complementing language study.
- Each teacher, administrator, and other school personnel who have contact with students, such as the supervisors, librarians, nurse, and counselors, selects a primary language of communication (French, English, or fushā) and is expected to be consistent in its use inside and outside the classroom.
- Arabic fushā, French, and English are to be developed for the purposes of public speaking.
- Fushā, English, and French are to be used in all school performances, including the end-of-year show (unless a play requires ʿāmiyya as part of its script).
- The development of languages requires the consistent efforts of an entire team of educators.

According to the secondary school head, a measure of success in promoting foreign languages will be when students begin to communicate with each other using

English and French in the playground. "That is my dream," she told me (interview, June 12, 2007). Communicating in foreign languages is central to the image of a modern, educated person. In the largely monolingual neighborhood of the school, this would be seen as a particular victory, particularly as languages are seen to be avenues for reversing socioeconomic disparities.

During my time at the Shi'i school, I observed the implementation of these policies and principles in classrooms, hallways, and extracurricular activities. In explaining their approach, the Shi'i administrators and teachers linked the teaching of languages to the development of an educated person, a student immersed in research and lifelong learning. As Ms. Maryam,[4] the academic coordinator for the Arabic language told me, "A language teacher must be passionate about her subject and have a personal connection with the language herself. She must be ongoing in her own learning in order to inspire student lifelong engagement" (interview, in Arabic, May 3, 2007). This attitude permeated the hallways, which were lined with student research and group work in different languages—a neural synapse drawn and labeled in French, a research project on the history and types of Arabic language dictionaries, concept mapping of works of English literature, interviews in French of Lebanese women in professional fields, and research in Arabic on the lives of martyrs. On any given day, the bulletin boards exhibited such works alongside signs to mark events and celebrations, such as Resistance and Liberation Day, or calls to get involved in school activities, such as fundraising for community service projects: "Go East, Go West! Our popcorn is the best!" At the top of each work, bulletin board, or chalkboard were the words, "In the name of God the beneficent and merciful" or the shorter version "In His Name" in one of the three languages. In addition, the school published student works in Arabic, French, and English in their literary magazines and book projects. The growing 10,000-volume library was also organized and functioned to promote inquiry in a number of languages, by placing all nonfiction and reference texts on a particular topic together, regardless of the language of publication, rather than dividing the library into three language arenas. In the playground, colorful posters reminded students to practice their *fuṣḥā* and highlighted grammatical rules. In addition, student performances showcased their achievements and proficiency in the three languages. Thus, the school promoted a strong visual presence of the three languages on campus.

The auditory presence, however, lagged, despite a well-articulated language policy. Like the majority of the schools in the larger study, teachers communicated with each other in *'āmiyya*, as did students in the hallways and recreational areas. Thus, language teachers expressed concern over how effectively they could develop student language skills given the limited language contact.

(Re)Constructing Language Policy during Periods of Sociopolitical Conflict

The study revealed that teachers negotiate a number of top-down policies in their classrooms, including various aspects of the national curriculum, such as content of topics, order of topics, and pedagogical strategies for language acquisition. In addition, teachers negotiated school policies regarding the use of languages in their classrooms. For example, teachers allowed for the use of '*āmiyya* during designated group work in French classes in order to encourage participation and critical thinking. At the same time, teachers negotiated the broader sociopolitical context that provoked oppositional discourses about former colonial and missionary languages in the classroom, while paradoxically intensifying a need for these languages to supersede the economic, social, and personal insecurities created by conflicts in the region.

In what follows, I focus on the practices of four language teachers who, in departing from the content of the national curriculum, negotiate between the demands of external standards and students' academic and social needs during acute conflict. I describe several illustrative lessons and then turn to a discussion of the teachers' pedagogical strategies, offering additional examples from other classes. Taken together, the exemplars demonstrate how teachers reconstruct language policy through a critical and participatory, community-centered learning process in order to create safe spaces for language development, political expression, and engagement of contemporary social concerns. In doing so, they effectively meet and surpass external standards for language proficiency. I draw on the lessons to outline a framework for reconstructing language policy in the classroom and argue that this is a particularly effective strategy for language development in postcolonial and postwar contexts.

Ms. Amna: "We Construct a Relationship between the Student and the Language in Daily Life"

When I arrive 5 minutes before the start of class, students are already on task with the teacher, even though it is not yet 7:30 a.m. and students from other classes are still roaming the hallways, making their way to first period. The teacher greets me with "bonjour." . . . The students stand and greet me in unison with "bonne journée." On the board, under the words "En Son Nom" [In His Name] it reads:

En employant des phrases simples et des phrases complexes, racontez en 3 lignes ce qui se passe à Tripoli.--10'

The teacher says in French, "Don't write your opinions—just what you think is happening in Tripoli." They quickly review the structure of simple and complex sentences together, and then students work silently on their texts. There are 19 students in the class, seated in rows at paired desks. ... The students work individually. They learn "Tripoli" and ask what the word for "army" is in French. They want to ask other questions, but [Ms. Amna] says, no questions, and encourages them to think on their own. (fieldnotes, May 29, 2007)

In this lesson, students were given 10 minutes to write three lines to tell what is happening in Tripoli in simple and complex sentences. At the time of the lesson, fierce fighting was taking place between an al Qaeda-inspired militant group, Fatah al Islam, and the Lebanese army in a Palestinian refugee camp and its surroundings in the city of Tripoli (*Trablus*, in Arabic), north of Beirut. The outbreak of violence was sudden and created a national crisis, as civilians found themselves in the midst of cross-fire and activities by international relief organizations and the media were unable to access victims, deliver services, or accurately report on what was happening to the people inside the camp.

When the 10 minutes allocated for writing individual accounts were over, Ms. Amna asked each student to contribute a new word from his paper to generate a class vocabulary list on the board.

> One student asks [in French, except where indicated by italics], "How do you say, *mukhayyam* [refugee camp]?" The teacher responds by asking, "What do you call the place where children play, or where scouts meet and sleep?" . . . Eventually, one student suggests "camp" and she corrects his pronunciation. (fieldnotes, May 29, 2007)

During the vocabulary discussion, students drew on their knowledge of Arabic and English to decode word meanings or to identify French word equivalents. The teacher facilitated without offering definitions, but through word associations. For example, one student contributed the word "missile" to the vocabulary list. Ms. Amna checked the class for understanding, citing the common local names for three types of missiles with which the students were personally familiar. The class then moved to other words and put up a long list of vocabulary words, which included the following among them:

> guerre—massacre—le movement de "Fatah al Islam"—les soldats libanais [war—massacre—the Fatah al Islam movement—Lebanese soldiers]

The teacher added, "les civils—les habitants du camp (Palestiniens)" [civilians— the inhabitants of the camp (Palestinians)]. Students copied down the vocabulary list generated by the class into their notebooks.

In the next segment of the lesson, they engaged in writing a paragraph on the events in Tripoli together as a class:

> They begin by discussing the events orally in French. Ms. Amna asks for someone to offer a sentence. Three hands shoot up. A boy begins the discussion by expressing anti-Lebanese army sentiment, because the army, in his opinion is [in French] "weak and unable to protect anyone." He is also referencing the inability of the army to defend civilians against Israel. What ensues is an animated discussion. The other students protest. Various students raise arguments in defense of the Lebanese army—[in French] "They are trying to defend the country and they would defend any of us from this terrorist movement [Fatah al Islam], but they are weak." Another says [in French], "They [the army] are afraid," showing compassion for the individuals who constitute the

army ranks. Another student argues [in French] that: "The army is protecting us from a civil war." (fieldnotes, May 29, 2007)

The discussion is generated by the students and facilitated by the teacher, who encourages them to respond to each other and not to her. They discuss the role of journalists and voice a common concern: "We don't want terrorists breeding here [in Lebanon]." At this point, the initial speaker who expressed anti-army sentiment says (in French), "If [the Lebanese army] knew how to do their job, they would just go in [to the camp] and kill everyone." Ms. Amna now intervenes in the discussion to direct it (in French):

"Kill civilians? Who's with this idea?" she asks the class. They vote by a show of hands. Only three students raise their hands in support. [Ms. Amna] throws her hand over her mouth to indicate surprise and disapproval. "You are with killing people like this?" she asks one of the students. "*Alors, [the three students who raised their hands] sont les pirates de la classe. Ils aiment tuer les gens*,"[5] shaking her head. Now the class formulates a paragraph together on the board generated from the discussion. (fieldnotes, May 29, 2007)

In composing each sentence of the paragraph together, they discuss elements of the sentence, including vocabulary, grammatical rules, and structural features. They also discuss the grammatical function of each word in the sentence. The paragraph proceeds as follows:

Le dimanche passé, à Tripoli, l'armée libanaise était en train d'accomplir son travail, tout près du camp "Nahr-al-Bared," un movement terroriste qui se nomait "Fatah-el-Islam" l'attaquait et tuait trente-trois soldats. . . . [Last Sunday in Tripoli, the Lebanese army was working near the refugee camp "Nahr-al-Bared," when a terrorist movement called "Fatah-el-Islam" attacked them and killed thirty-three soldiers ...] (fieldnotes, May 29, 2007)

Throughout the lesson, students appear to be engaged in learning, by repeatedly raising their hands or calling out responses and comments excitedly, with the exception of one boy who remains quiet throughout. The class functions entirely in French, except for a handful of word associations. By the end of the lesson students appear to be completely engrossed in deconstructing the parts of speech.
According to Ms. Amna (in Arabic):

I try to promote French usage by having students discuss issues relevant to their daily lives, and political and current events in French. For example, I have them discuss what's happening with Iran's nuclear power, or in Palestine.... I also asked students to write on the issue of landmines in the South after the July War. By using French to discuss these issues we construct a relationship between the student and the language in daily life. We build relevance, which is the key to encouraging usage and for the foreign language to begin to take a life of its own. . . . I want students to be able to relay their thoughts and concerns in French. (interview, May 10, 2007)

The "life of its own" that Ms. Amna refers to is a postcolonial life—one relevant to student experience. Lessons with other groups of students over the research period included generative discussions on love, male–female relationships, grief and loss, rights and obligations, and francophone literature from different contexts in Africa and the Arab world. Ms. Amna also engaged French as a "vehicle for trauma intervention" (interview, in Arabic, May 10, 2007). Citing the following example, she explained (in Arabic) how French is used to encourage critical reflection, dissipate trauma, and engage topics relevant to students' everyday concerns—issues that go beyond French language textbooks, regardless of whether they are published in Lebanon or in France:

> At the beginning of the [2006–2007 academic] year, for example, I worked on a writing project with students about the July War. The students were deeply hurt by the images of Israeli children writing messages to them on Israeli rockets [which were then fired into their villages] during the summer. So we asked students to compose a letter [in French] in response, addressed to the Israeli children in these images.
>
> At first we let them free-write whatever they wanted or needed to say. After the free-write, we examined the letters, which, as you can imagine, were even more terrible, as a first reaction. We then engaged students in a conversation about their responses. We discussed how Islam and Judaism are above this and do not allow for this kind of response.... We cannot allow ourselves to be dragged down [by our circumstances], but rather, we must rise above, as our religions dictate.
>
> We then had students rewrite their letters. Most students changed their responses entirely—they were more reflective, thoughtful. (Ms. Amna, interview, May 10, 2007)

As Ms. Amna illustrates, conflict necessitates bringing social concerns into the language classroom. Conversely, such pedagogical strategies help to promote language learning. I will return to a discussion of these strategies later.

Ms. Sara: "The Language Gains Value from Its Relevance to Their Lives"

Ms. Sara taught French as a first foreign language to students in the Arabic–French program and French as a second foreign language to students in the Arabic–English program. She explained to me that, although the school generally frowned upon the use of Arabic 'amiyya in the French classroom, she found it necessary to do so in order to engage students in the Arabic–English program who study French as a second foreign language: "At this stage [Grade 10], their knowledge of the language lags behind their intellectual ability. They only have two periods per week. I have to let them use Arabic to engage them in learning French" (interview, in Arabic, May 29, 2007). In my observation of these lessons, I noted the frequent use of Arabic (italicized below):

Ms. Sara: Est-ce que vous avez peur de ce qui ce passe maintenant au Liban? *Are you afraid of what's happening in Lebanon right now?* Qui a peur?

She asks them to raise their hands if they are worried. They want to answer in English and Arabic, but she says, "non" and encourages them to explain in French. A student offers: "Oui, j'ai peur parce qu'il y a des terroristes" . . . Students translate the responses to each other into Arabic.

Ms. Sara: Si la guerre éclate, est-ce que tu veux voyager? Qui veut?

A student responds in Arabic that she wants to leave for a vacation only; she would not leave if there were a crisis in the country.

Ms. Sara: Pourquoi tu veux rester? (fieldnotes, May 29, 2007)

In this discussion, Ms. Sara engages Grade 10 girls in a conversation about their anxieties regarding the unfolding violence and whether they would want to leave the country if the violence erupted into war again. In her view, such discussion is more appropriate to their intellectual maturity. The discussion is also relevant to their lives, and as such, is more likely to evoke engagement in language learning than the government-approved textbook, even though it means using Arabic to support the discussion.

According to Ms. Sara,

Students in the [Arabic–English] program question the value of French; it is understandable when English is the global language and they are studying sciences in English. Even the [students in the Arabic–French program] are not certain of the value of French. The language gains value from its relevance to their lives. (interview, in Arabic, June 6, 2007)

In a Grade 10 French class where girls are learning French as a first foreign language, she demonstrates how relevance is made possible:

After a review of grammar, students take turns to present projects they have been working on. [Ms. Sara] tells them [in French]: "[This class] worked the hardest to prepare, and I am very proud of you and to have you as my students."

A student introduces a presentation in French, asking why youth face problems. What obstacles do they face? Can they play the role of adults? Another student starts the film they have prepared. It is a film written, performed, and directed by a group of students in the class. It depicts problems faced by youth. The characters are four girls living in one room. Each embodies a

problem of youth as they attempt to imitate adults. . . . A discussion in French
follows. . . .

The next group film is a mini-documentary. The students interview everyday
people on the street downtown (in Arabic): "What is the impact of politics on
your life?" One girl responds, "It's better to live without politics and just focus
on your studies" . . . (fieldnotes, June 13, 2007)

Through these well-researched presentations, students in Ms. Sara's class employ
French to engage in social and political youth concerns. All of the projects involve
interviewing adults and/or youths in order to survey opinions of interest and relevance to students' lives. Ms. Sara thus negotiates language policies related to content in the Arabic–French class and related to content and Arabic use in the
Arabic–English class in order to "give value" to the language through its relevance
and intellectual appropriateness.

Ms. Maryam: "They Are Connected to the Language because of Religion, but We Want Them to Be Connected for Intellectual Pursuits Too"

Ms. Maryam has taught Arabic for many years. According to her, the government
curriculum has a negative impact on the learning of Arabic *fuṣḥā* because it is
lacking in content and the teacher has to supplement the government textbooks
substantially. She is concerned that students be able to think critically and discuss
issues in Arabic *fuṣḥā*, rather than recite it. However, given that *fuṣḥā* is no one's
home language and that many subject teachers present material in Arabic *ʿāmiyya*
instead of *fuṣḥā*, the Arabic classroom becomes a critical site where this language
development must takes place. Thus, she conducts her classes entirely in *fuṣḥā*.
Students too respond entirely in *fuṣḥā*. However, in undertaking group work, they
occasionally consult with each other in *ʿāmiyya* before proceeding in *fuṣḥā*. I
observed a class in which students engaged in a discussion of Lebanese-American
writer and artist Khalil Gibran who wrote during an era of "serious discrimination against African-Americans and his poetry reflects his observations of their
suffering" (Ms. Maryam, in Arabic, fieldnotes, May 7, 2007).

> The teacher relates the main ideas to a particular verse of the Qur'an. The
> students recognize the connection and acknowledge it by reciting the verse.
> . . . Students are assigned to take the main ideas from one of Gibran's poems
> and to write a skit that discusses them. They are to take a pair of dialectical
> terms—black/white, Arab/West, rich/ poor—and place them in conversation,
> making use of their personal points of view and integrating them with those
> of the poet. They are told that they can disagree with the author. They work
> in groups of four to develop their ideas. (fieldnotes, May 7, 2007)

Thus, students in Ms. Maryam's class engage *fuṣḥā* in critical and creative thinking, while demonstrating that they are also adept with the more traditional modes

of Qur'anic recitation. Ms. Maryam thereby challenges the policy norms of memorization and recitation for *fushā* while negotiating with students the instances in which *'āmiyya* might be allowed.

Ms. Heba: "The Aim Is to Choose Books with Depth from Which to Step Off into a Discussion about Causes and Social Concerns"

Ms. Heba's student-led book talks in the library include texts translated into *fushā* from other languages and texts published originally in Arabic. "The point is to have students debate ideas stemming from a work of literature. At the same time, the discussion encourages reading in Arabic" (Ms. Heba, interview, in Arabic, June 2, 2007).

> The [Grade 11] girls file in for Arabic class in the library. They are accompanied by [Ms. Heba] and the librarian. They sit around tables at the back of the library—about 7 to a table. A student introduces the author in *fushā*. "Abdel Rahman Munif was a Communist," she says, "when proclaiming Communist beliefs was illegal in the Arab world. He was imprisoned for his beliefs." . . . The librarian clarifies that the legality of Communism was never questioned in Lebanon, only in other parts of the Arab world. Students now ask questions of the student presenter and she answers confidently. The discussion proceeds in *fushā*. The girls all appear to be focused on the student presenter. (fieldnotes, June 2, 2007)

During this book talk, students and teachers engaged in a conversation about political imprisonment in the Arab world and the significance of freedom of ideas to the well-being of civil society. Students were told that the author was a leftist who was against the one-party rule of Arab regimes. Among the points of contention among the students was how the author was coerced, and accepted, to sign a paper rescinding his beliefs in order to end his suffering. The conversation then shifted to human rights issues for prisoners in the Arab world, more generally, and the importance of intellectual freedom.

> Ms. Heba [in Arabic]: You cannot jail people just for their ideas. We are free to have our political beliefs. . . . We have to understand that just as we have our beliefs and ideas and opinions, others have theirs and we must accept their right to have them and voice them. And from an Islamic point of view too—to accept the Other and the Other's point of view. We cannot dream of a real civil society otherwise. (fieldnotes, June 2, 2007)

During this complex critique of Arab states and their human rights violations, students engaged animatedly in *fushā* about the principles of democracy in nondemocratic states. In doing so, they reflected on the constraints that have been placed on their own beliefs and how to ensure the rights of others. One student in particular had difficulty with the idea that she must accept those who do not share her beliefs, saying, "I can't accept this." She was invited to speak with the teacher and the librarian further after class.

Pedagogical Strategies and Policy Reconstruction

Having offered a handful of concrete illustrations of language classroom practices, I now turn to a discussion of the teachers' pedagogical strategies and policy reconstruction process in three components: (1) the topic or subject content of instruction, (2) the pedagogy, and (3) the language development goals.

The four teachers at the focus of this chapter integrated pressing social concerns into their pedagogical practices to address fears, while engaging students in constructive learning activities, motivating achievement, and providing a safe arena for discussing social and political realities and injustices. The topic of Ms. Amna's Grade 7 lesson, for example, was the violence at the forefront of everyone's minds at that time, and students needed an outlet to talk about their anxieties. In addition, other language teachers worked with students on topics related to social injustice, such as the abuse of prisoners in the Arab world, and slavery and apartheid. Two schoolwide topics for French classes addressed women in the Arab world and women at work and at home. Students conducted research on Palestinian and Iraqi women to understand how their lives have undergone change due to sustained conflict. These topics, or subject content of instruction, departed from the content of the national curriculum by focusing on a community-centered learning process. Using issues relevant to the daily realities of students, French and Arabic *fuṣḥā* were also made relevant through their development as modes of communication about personal and social concerns.

Among their pedagogical strategies, teachers integrated these topics into lessons with planned language objectives, rather than separating the classroom from the outside world. In Ms. Amna's lesson, for example, words were first generated by students, and then sentences, followed by a discussion that engaged students' insecurities productively into a critical discussion of current violence. A paragraph was then generated from the sentences, bearing in mind grammatical and other rules learned in previous lessons. Like other teachers, the process was participatory, allowing for students to explore their ideas openly. Thus, the teachers affirmed students' concerns and drew on their knowledge and experience to develop the text for the lesson, rather than providing a prescribed text.

The teachers varied the teaching format from class to class (group work, dialogue, focus group interviews, etc.); however, four common pedagogical strategies emerged from observation. First, the lessons were participatory and placed student engagement as a central strategy. Second, the lessons were generative and constructive, drawing on students' knowledge to develop text. Third, the lessons validated or affirmed student concerns. And finally, the lessons were critical, challenging power structures or the status quo through student inquiry into social concerns.

The teachers integrated various language development goals into their lessons in the areas of oral and written competence, including argumentation, written expression, vocabulary building, grammar and usage, and so on. In doing so, they set high standards for language learning in their classrooms as the national curriculum was employed only to set the minimum benchmarks for language development.

The effect of the pedagogical process, ultimately, was to reconstruct national language policy in the classroom. First, the topic of instruction and the critical, participatory, generative, and affirming teaching strategies served to strip the French language of its colonial associations as students engaged in critical contemporary concerns, rather than discussing what they might do on a visit to France, ordering in a café overlooking the Eiffel Tower—a journey that few would ever make. Such content serves to idealize French culture and to present it as monolithic, rather than engaging students in the reality of its ethnic, religious, and linguistic diversity, for example. Rather than focusing on French in France, the teachers employed French to discuss Lebanese, Arab, religious/moral, and ethical concerns, and thus to critique the vestiges of colonialism. The effect is "nativizing" or "localizing" the French language, thus helping to break it from a colonial/sectarian history of inequity and social injustice and appropriating it for the spread of Islamic and modern values. The meanings associated with learning French are, therefore, changed to reflect community-centered values.

Similarly, Arabic *fuṣḥā* is stripped of its traditional baggage by using it to engage students in intellectual and personal explorations. By giving *fuṣḥā* contemporary relevance beyond religion, teachers separate the language from commonplace associations with stagnation. Rather, language learning is promoted through critical dialogue in *fuṣḥā*.

Finally, in meeting (or surpassing) national curricular standards or language development goals, the Arabic and French teachers in this study became agents in the reformulation of national language policy in the classroom. Language policy was thus reconstructed from preexisting elements (the curriculum) and new elements generated in the classroom in collaboration with students. In this way, national language policy was reconstructed within a school community with allegiances to the government opposition movement.

Conclusion

Language policy is no *fait accompli*. It is contested, negotiated, and reconstructed in the classroom to deal with contemporary social, political, and economic conditions that are rooted in a history of sociopolitical struggle. Language policy in education is, therefore, context specific and elaborated by school actors, such as teachers, as they participate in policy production through their classroom practices. This chapter illustrates how teachers responded to the policy mandates of a national curriculum, exam system, and school codes of conduct, on the one hand, while exercising autonomy over classroom policy to meet students' needs during periods of sociopolitical crisis. By integrating real-world social concerns into language teaching, teachers created safe spaces for language development and academic and social engagement during turbulent times.

Critical, participatory, and reconstructive pedagogy is particularly effective in working with marginalized communities (because it explores power), in post-colonial contexts (because of the disassociation with colonial language–power asymmetries), and in postwar contexts (because it integrates the pressing concerns of students). Furthermore, the policy maintains high standards to meet national curricula and examinations such that all students have the opportunity to go to university. It is in the ideological and implementational spaces that we find teachers as policy actors, effecting change in their communities. It is important to note, however, that the teachers at the focus of this inquiry were also supported by school policy, which gave high status to the Arabic language as *lingua sacra* and *lingua franca*, as well as French for intellectual and social extension. As such, the reconstruction process was facilitated by policy processes at other layers of the policy onion.

Discussion Questions

1 Conduct a visual and auditory survey of languages at a school with which you are familiar. How visually present are various languages? Include bulletin boards, written communications with parents and teachers, school websites, library books, signs, and so on in your visual audit. Where do you hear different languages in the school? Consider which language(s) is/are used in the classroom, hallways, assembly, playground, and staff room, between students, between students and teachers, between teachers, and between administrators and students/teachers. What hidden message(s) is/are conveyed to students, teachers, and parents by the visual and auditory presence of languages? What are the benefits/disadvantages of the functional allocation of languages in a school?

2 Think about a time when there was a crisis in your life, community, or in the news. What opportunities were provided for you to discuss your concerns about the crisis in class? How did that affect your engagement in learning? What are the advantages of integrating discussion of "real-world" crises into pedagogical strategies? Brainstorm some of the ways that this can be achieved in a language classroom.

3 Research the sociopolitical history of a language spoken by students at your school. Why is it important to understand the contemporary sociopolitical context and history of the language(s) of instruction at your school in relation to students' home languages?

4 How can teachers negotiate between the pressures of curricular demands and real-world crises that cause disruptions to schooling?

5 If feeling "safe" is important to academic engagement, what does it mean for classroom policy and practice?

6 How can/do students succeed in learning a language, even when their family and community do not speak it, or when their only exposure to the language is at school?

7 How might students be engaged in social justice issues through the language curriculum?

Notes

1 *Fuṣḥā* is the term used to refer to classical Arabic and Modern Standard Arabic (MSA), both of which have written forms and are considered "high-status" varieties. *Fuṣḥa* is nobody's mother tongue. Its history is linked to the spread of Islam, Islamic educational structures, and other historical circumstances. MSA is the contemporary standardized form of *fuṣḥā*, used across the Arab world and internationally, and spoken during formal occasions and in the media. It is the language variety employed in all contemporary written text. *'āmiyya* is the locally spoken vernacular or colloquial form of Arabic that varies from area to area within and across nations. The spoken dialects diverge in form increasingly with greater geographic distances, but are generally mutually intelligible.
2 Almost 65% of Lebanese students are currently enrolled in private schools (CRDP, 2007).
3 Though most public schools choose to teach all subjects, other than French and English language classes, in Arabic during the elementary years, legislation in 1994 provided latitude in determining the appropriate language medium, whether Arabic or a foreign language or both, for subject instruction in Grades 1 to 6 in public and private schools alike. Pressured in part by parents requesting an increase in foreign language teaching, based on a perception that it will improve examination results, many private schools have increased foreign language teaching in the elementary grades (personal communication, 2006). Some private schools strive for a 50–50 instructional time model from Grade 1; others provide greater instructional time to the first foreign language. Still others also introduce the second foreign language in the elementary grades.
4 All names are pseudonyms.
5 The teacher demonstrates her disapproval by telling the three students that they have hijacked the class (*pirates*) with their ideas.

References

Abou, S., Kasparian, C., & Haddad, K. (1996). *Anatomie de la francophonie libanaise* [Anatomy of the Lebanese francophonie]. Beirut: Université St-Joseph; Montreal: AUPELF-UREF.

Abouchedid, K., & Nasser, R. (2000). The state of history teaching in private-run confessional schools in Lebanon: Implications for national integration. *Mediterranean Journal of Educational Studies, 5*(2), 57–82.

CRDP. (2005, 2007). *Al nashra al ihsa'iyya.* [Statistics bulletin]. Beirut: Ministry of Education Centre de Recherche et de Développement Pédagogiques. Retrieved August 15, 2008, from http://www.crdp.org/crdp/Arabic/ar-statistics/a_statisticpublication.asp [In Arabic]

Deeb, L. (2006). *An enchanted modern: Gender and public piety in Shi'i Lebanon.* Princeton, NJ: Princeton University Press.

Fortna, B. C. (2002). *Imperial classroom: Islam, the state, and education in the late Ottoman Empire.* Oxford, UK: Oxford University Press.

Frayha, N. (2004). Developing curriculum as a means to bridging national divisions in Lebanon. In S. Tawil & A. Harley (Eds.), *Education, conflict, and social cohesion* (pp. 159–205). Geneva: UNESCO International Bureau of Education.

Hornberger, N. H., & Johnson, D. C. (2007). Slicing the onion ethnographically: Layers and spaces in multilingual language education policy and practice. *TESOL Quarterly, 41*(3), 509–532.

Lin, A. M. Y., & Martin P. W. (Eds.). (2005). *Decolonisation, globalization: Language-in-education policy and practice.* Clevedon, Avon: Multilingual Matters.

National Center for Educational Research and Development (NCERD). (1995). *New framework for education in Lebanon*. Beirut: NCERD.

Nieto, S. (2002). *Language, culture, and teaching: Critical perspectives for a new century*. Mahwah, NJ: Lawrence Erlbaum.

Shaaban, K., & Ghaith, G. (1999). Lebanon's language-in-education policies: From bilingualism to trilingualism. *Language Problems & Language Planning, 23*(1), 1–16.

Shehab, S. (2006, October 16). 350 schools completely destroyed or damaged because of the aggression: Lebanon commends the support of the UAE as it confronts the challenges of the new academic year. *Al Bayan*. Retrieved December 4, 2006, from http://www.albayan. ae/servlet/Satellite?c=Article&cid=1158495929288&pagename=Albayan%2FArticle% 2FFullDetail [In Arabic]

Suleiman, Y. (1994). Nationalism and the Arabic language: An historical overview. In Y. Suleiman (Ed.), *Arabic sociolinguistics* (pp. 3–24). Richmond, Surrey: Curzon Press.

Suleiman, Y. (2004). *A war of words: Language and conflict in the Middle East*. Cambridge, UK: Cambridge University Press.

Sutton, M., & Levinson, B. A. U. (Eds). (2001). *Policy as practice: Toward a comparative sociocultural analysis of educational policy*. Westport, CT: Ablex Publishing.

Zakharia, Z. (2009). Language-in-education policies in contemporary Lebanon: Youth perspectives. In O. Abi-Mershed (Ed.), *Trajectories of education in the Arab World: Legacies and challenges*. New York & London: Routledge.

Chapter 11

Cases of Language Policy Resistance in Israel's Centralized Educational System

Elana Shohamy

Introduction

Locating cases of "bottom-up" language policies in centralized educational systems poses a special challenge. After all, the basic premise of such policies is that they are uniform and homogenous and expected to be implemented and imposed nationally across the whole educational system. This approach is even more intensive as central policies are often accompanied by a set of overt and covert mechanisms (e.g., tests, curricula, textbooks) meant to *ensure* that the national policies are introduced to the system and indeed practiced (Shohamy, 2006). One wonders, therefore, whether it is at all possible in such strict conditions to resist these policies and to locate instances of grassroots resistance when language educational policies are so comprehensive, closed, and restrictive. Yet, as will be shown in this chapter, even in centralized and strict educational systems such as the one in Israel, pockets of resistance can be found either in "noncompliance" or through various initiatives presenting innovative language policies. Along with that, a question that is often raised with regards to language educational policies (and any educational policies) is whether policies that are manifested in policy documents in the forms of laws or other official statements are in fact *meant* to be implemented, or if they only serve bureaucrats as ideological statements and evidence of action and intentions without serious concern for their actual feasibility or meaningful implementation. How else can one explain the phenomenon whereby many educational policies are not followed and their implementation is not studied? Is it the case that language *practices* are in fact more powerful than any stated and declared policies? Alternatively, is it the case that policies are often not very realistic so that "on-the-ground" practices have energies of their own, so that regardless of any top-down statements, bottom-up *de facto* policies are practiced in relation to feasibilities and realities and, therefore, often do not comply with written policies that are imposed from top-down? This chapter will examine the nature of this relationship between top-down language educational policies via various types of policy documents, and bottom-up forces, referring to the responses and/or initiatives of those who are engaged in the process of policymaking. This process will be examined within the context of Israel, where the first uniform national educational language policy was introduced in 1996 (see Spolsky & Shohamy, 1999, for a detailed description of the policy).

I begin the chapter by pointing at the complexity of the relationship between the two forces mentioned above, namely, top-down and bottom-up and argue for complexity of the act of policymaking which involves multiple stakeholders beyond governments and schools, all engaged in some way or another in the act of policymaking and practice. This process is far more complex than the association often attributed to the process as two opposing linear forces. Examples of stakeholders include teachers, test makers, principals, textbook writers and publishers, testing agencies, parents, school board members, and researchers. Stakeholders include students as well, as it is often in their power to comply or resist policies as manifested in learning. All these stakeholders need to be viewed as "policymakers" who are deeply engaged in the act of creating and reacting to educational policies. "*Real*" language policymaking is a synthesis of these forces as they are all deeply engaged in explicit or implicit interpretations and negotiations of the policies in very complex ways. There is a need, therefore, for a deeper understanding of the process through which language policies are made and their outcomes generated.

It is also worth noting that due to the dynamism of actual policymaking, which often stands in sharp contrast to declared language policy documents, it is still the case that new *de facto* language policies constantly emerge from these different stakeholders in spite of the strict, centralized, and declared language educational policies. This is also due to the fact that policies cannot be limited to certain agents and stakeholders, but must be contextualized within a broader sociopolitical and economic ecology. Thus, even the most explicit policies that are accompanied by a set of restrictive mechanisms may not lead to *de facto* policies in linear ways as major contextual factors play important roles, often in unpredictable ways, in the generation and creation of *de facto* policies. Consequently, various language policies are practiced and carried out while overlooking or even ignoring the declared ones, given specific contextual conditions.

I will now turn to three cases within the language educational policy of Israel in order to illustrate the claims above. As noted, the existence of formally declared policies is by no means a guarantee that they are being implemented; rather, as the cases demonstrate, practices have "a life of their own" so that certain *de facto* policies do take place even without any mention of these practices in the declared policies. It is these types of policies that are often driven by contextual factors that go beyond the thinking and the planning of the policymakers. They change over time and subsequently defy and even resist them. In each of these cases, I will illustrate the role of local initiatives that are situated within social, economic, and political contexts. These cases provide insight as to the need to interpret language educational policies within broader contexts—global, national, regional, and local—in given points in time, driven by sociopolitical and economic factors.

Israel: Language and Policymaking

Israel presents a case that demonstrates that language policies are not created in a vacuum; rather, they are products of multiple social, political, economic, global, ethnic, religious, and educational ideologies. Israel is a state founded on the basis of a strong ideology of creating a homeland for dispersed people so that they could exercise cultural and religious self-rule. Yet it is the nature of ideologies that when they meet reality and practice they tend to require adaptations and changes to the very context in which they are implemented. So was the situation in the early days of the Zionist ideology, which was implemented in Palestine at the beginning of the 20th century, meeting realities of Jewish immigrants coming from a large number of countries with diverse linguistic and cultural backgrounds. While the revival of the Hebrew language was not part of mainstream Zionist ideology in its early days, it soon became one of its central symbols. Specifically this meant that Hebrew, a dormant vernacular at the time for most Jews in the world, had soon been adopted as a major symbol of national identity aimed at the creation of a common language and as a strong device for the creation of a collective and cohesive society and identity. This meant that all immigrants arriving in Palestine, using a vast number of territorial languages and/or a variety of Jewish languages such as Yiddish, Ladino, or Jewish Arabic, were "forced" to learn Hebrew and use it both in public and in the private domains of the family and home. For children in schools, Hebrew was introduced as the only language of instruction for all school subjects. The explicit and implicit policy also implied the downgrading of all home languages used by immigrants that went through a process of marginalization and, in many cases, total disappearance as Hebrew was constructed as the only language representing and symbolizing Zionist ideology (Shohamy, 2008a). Other languages used by non-Jews, such as Arabic, used by Arabs living in Palestine, and English, used as a government language especially by British officials in Palestine, were considered official languages only until 1948 when the British Mandate was terminated. When the state of Israel was declared, the official status of English was dropped while Hebrew and Arabic remained as the only official languages of the newly founded state. In terms of educational policy, this meant that Arabic was the medium of instruction in Arab schools and Hebrew served that role in Jewish schools. English, a language that was marginalized in the first decade right after the end of the British mandate, regained its prestige (although not official status) during the 1960s with its growing status and role as an international and global language, making it a compulsory language in all schools, officially beginning in 4th or 5th grades.

As vast migration to Israel (exclusively Jewish) from various parts of the world continued, so did the implementation of the ideology of one language-one nation. This meant that all new immigrants were expected to acquire Hebrew, the hegemonic and powerful language, and it remained the only medium of instruction in Jewish schools. This subtractive policy continued and still continues nowadays, leading to the disappearance of immigrant languages. Following the classic immigration patterns, first-generation immigrants adopted Hebrew to various degrees, whereas their children became monolingual in Hebrew. Arabs continued to use Arabic (Modern Standard Arabic [MSA]) in Arab schools as the language of instruction, and a variety of spoken dialects, mostly Palestinian, were used at home and in the community. Arabs learn Hebrew in schools as an additional language from an early age (second or third grades), mostly out of necessity, given its hegemonic role in Israeli society; English is also taught in Arab schools from an early age, usually from fourth grade and up until the end of high school. Though some efforts were made for Jews to learn Arabic, perceived by all to be "an important language to know," these efforts did not succeed as only a small number of Hebrew speakers acquired acceptable levels of proficiency in the language. This accounts for the current situation, where most Jewish Hebrew speakers have mastery in Hebrew and English, learned in schools as well as widely used in multiple domains of life. On the other hand, most Arabs are trilingual in Arabic (both in the spoken dialect in MSA), Hebrew, and English to varied proficiency levels, learned in school from an early age. As to the many languages of immigrants, these basically continue to disappear, although some small pockets of language vitality do exist (Shohamy, 2008b; Spolsky & Shohamy, 1999).

The Language Education Policy

It is within this linguistic reality that the 1996 language policy was created and introduced into Israeli schools by the Ministry of Education (1996) and published as a special document (Shohamy, 2003; Spolsky & Shohamy, 1999). The document was in fact the first educational language policy ever introduced into the Israeli educational system that addressed all languages together, as in previous years policies addressed specific languages separately, namely, English, Arabic or Hebrew. The 1996 policy introduced a *comprehensive* policy incorporating all languages taught in the educational system. In the policy document, a distinction was made between Jewish and Arab school systems; in each of the systems students were required to learn the same three languages, but in a different order, plus a number of optional languages (e.g., heritage, community, and world). The policy stated that for Jews the three compulsory languages would be as follows: Hebrew, as the medium of instruction in schools, Arabic (or French in some rare cases) and English. For the Arabic community, the order was Arabic (MSA) as language of instruction in schools, Hebrew, and English. The policy also stressed the need to maintain home languages and expand the linguistic repertoire of the country, mostly for Jewish immigrant languages; it was also declared in the policy document that steps should be taken to prevent further loss of the variety of immigrant languages that had previously been lost as part of Zionist ideology and the subtractive policy related to the revival of Hebrew.

It is important to note, as happens in other contexts, that the new language education policy was somewhat different than the national language policy regarding to the official languages. While the national policy includes both Arabic and Hebrew as official languages, the educational policy includes English as well, in fact in a more central place as it plays a principal role in both Hebrew and Arabic language education policies in schools due to its status as an international language. This priority given to English is related to the special relationship between Israel and the United States, and the current status of English as a *lingua franca* for Jews worldwide. English is, therefore, a compulsory language taught from an early age through secondary school, and even at universities where it is used as the main language for reading academic texts.

Language Education Policies: A Critical View

The policy just described needs to be understood in critical ways, especially given how it emerged; this understanding is necessary in order to better examine the bottom-up initiatives currently taking place. Though the 1996 policy stressed a number of central issues such as the promotion and encouragement of multilingualism, the learning of Arabic by Hebrew speakers, and the need to maintain immigrant languages, there is no reference as to the level of proficiency learners are required to obtain and the specific methods for policy implementation. It does not specify levels of achievement in different languages, how often heritage and/or community languages should be taught, the degree to which languages should be maintained, whether students should learn academic content in any of these languages, or the degree to which the "plus" component is to be implemented. Furthermore, the policy totally ignores all the stakeholders who are responsible for implementing it such as teachers, curriculum writers, testers, and testing policymakers. Whereas the policy was introduced in 1996 in a special document published by the director general at the time, no follow-up study has ever taken place to examine its actual implementation (Shohamy, 2008b).

One wonders, therefore, whether the policy served mostly as a declaration of intentions and lip service to mulitilingualism, rather than as a meaningful document. At the time, criticism was raised as to the methods of crafting the document: the top-down approach; the lack of representation of constituencies, especially teachers who are eventually responsible for carrying out the policy; or citizens, such that their language wishes and aspirations were not addressed. It was also noted that the policy addressed only schools at the K-12 level and ignored higher education; that it failed to take into account the rich research available on second language learning, such as the length of time it takes to learn languages; and that immigrants receive only limited time and/or accommodations before they must be tested in a language they have not yet mastered. A call was made also for the need to focus on the mechanisms used in educational systems as part of language policy, such as tests. The reality is that policies need to be interpreted in light of covert mechanisms used to impose them, such as the entrance exams to the university that are administered in Hebrew, especially for Arab students who are using Arabic as a medium of instruction in elementary and secondary schools; the language of the exams thus are in contradiction to the declared policy.

Still, in spite of the centralized language policy, one can identify a number of examples that illustrate how bottom-up resistance is taking place "on the ground."

Three Cases of Resistance

Teaching Spoken Arabic in Jewish Schools

Arabic is an official language in Israel, used as a primary language among the 20% of Arabs who live in Israel, and it is the language used in the neighboring countries, most of which are in the midst of political conflicts. Arabic is also a heritage language for a large number of Israeli Jews, who immigrated to Israel from Arabic-speaking countries. There is consensus in Israel that the learning of Arabic by Hebrew speakers is important, yet for different reasons; these vary from "it is important to know the language of the enemy" as is the case of those learning Arabic for military and "security" purposes, to a need to be integrated in the Middle East and/or to bridge the political conflict. Yet, despite efforts on the part of the Ministry of Education to promote the teaching of Arabic as a second language in Jewish schools by making it a compulsory subject for 3 years (Grades 7 to 9), as stated in the 1996 language education policy described above, the teaching of Arabic to Hebrew speakers is extremely problematic (Donitsa-Schmidt, Inbar, & Shohamy, 2004). Issues include negative attitudes and stereotypes toward Arabic and its speakers by Jewish students and their parents, accompanied by low motivation and resistance to studying it (Ben-Rafael & Brosh, 1991; Kraemer, 1993). It is, therefore, not surprising that only low levels of proficiency are attained, with barely 2% of those starting to learn Arabic choosing to continue their Arabic studies in the higher grades of secondary school. Although Arabic is considered a mandatory language for a period of 3 years, French can be chosen to replace it, as per the policy. Still, 60% of Jewish students choose to study Arabic as a mandatory language for 3 years in Grades 7 through 9.

Indeed, a number of research studies have shown that adult Jews express negative attitudes toward and little appreciation for the Arabic language, Arab culture, and Arabic speakers (Bar-Tal, 1996; Shohamy & Donitsa-Schmidt, 1998). Furthermore, given that attitudes develop early in childhood, like all aspects of the development of cognition and affect, it follows that even young children develop negative or positive attitudes toward other languages and their speakers as a result of their socialization process (Aboud, 1994). Research conducted in Israel shows that Israeli Jewish children and adolescents were found to harbor negative perceptions, stereotypes, and prejudices toward Arabs (Bar-Tal, 1996). An additional factor relevant to the study of language-learning motivation and attitudes is the status of the language and its speakers. Changing attitudes and increasing motivation to study the language seems to be more difficult in cases where the language studied is of low prestige and spoken by a minority group (Shohamy & Donitsa-Schmidt, 1998).

Thus, despite the fact that both languages are official, it is Hebrew that has been the national language since the establishment of Israel in 1948, easily and rapidly dominating Arabic, the other official language. The hegemony of Hebrew is evident in all aspects of daily life and is legitimized through the various social institutions, including the educational system. Hebrew is the language used in the Knesset (Parliament), the courts, and the government as well as academic institutions, electronic media, business and finance, and most published books and newspapers—significantly marginalizing Arabic. The asymmetry between the two languages, as noted above, is perpetuated in the K-12 educational system. In addition, Hebrew acts as a gatekeeper to all institutions of higher education in Israel, where Hebrew is the language of instruction.

One of the main arguments brought forth to explain the difficulties encountered in the teaching of Arabic as a second language to Hebrew speakers, in addition to the complex sociopolitical situation described above, is that the language variety taught in all schools is that of MSA and not a spoken variety of Arabic. There are several distinct varieties of Arabic, with a major distinction between the literary or written form and the spoken dialects. The literary forms are comprised of classical Arabic and MSA, the latter which has evolved from the classical form through extensive terminological innovations and is presently used in newspapers, radio, and modern literature. Both literary forms are under the strict control of grammarians and language academies and are not restricted regionally or nationally. By contrast, the different vernaculars spoken in the Arabic world are made up of local dialects, are open to local variation, and show constant change under the pressures of vernacular usage (Ferguson, 1959). The modern literary Arabic, MSA, is dominated by the structure of the classical language in both morphology and syntax, but differs greatly from the spoken form. Of the two forms, the lexicon of the spoken language is much more innovative whereas that of the written standard language is much more conservative (Blau, 1981). It is the dialect used for daily communication to which children are first exposed in their immediate surroundings, whereas MSA is utilized in more formal settings and introduced later in the school context.

The great difference between MSA and the various spoken dialects poses an acute dilemma for those who teach Arabic as a second or foreign language (Ryding, 1991). Over the years, there has been much debate in Israel over whether to teach the spoken form or MSA as a second language, or, if both varieties are taught, which variety to start with and at what level. Currently, it is MSA that is taught from Grades 7 through 9 for pedagogical and political reasons (Brosh, 1988).

At the same time, one frequently hears from teachers and pupils that MSA is not a useful language for the creation of personal communication given that it is not a spoken dialect, whereas the spoken language, though less prestigious, is used in everyday life. Teachers, therefore, feel that the lack of ability to speak is a major obstacle and a demotivating factor in the language learning process and may result in the discontinuation of studies (Spolsky & Shohamy, 1999). In addition, a study that investigated the effects of teaching spoken Arabic to Hebrew speakers aged 15 who subsequently studied MSA showed that the teaching of the spoken variety does not harm the acquisition of MSA and can often even enhance it (Naiman, 1999).

Given the above, a number of attempts have been made, in a number of cities in Israel to improve student attitudes and motivation by introducing a policy of teaching the spoken form of Arabic before the literary one, with the goal being to make the language more meaningful and functional for the learners. Furthermore, a decision was made, given that attitudes are established at an early age, to begin teaching the spoken Palestinian dialect as early as in Grade 4 instead of Grade 7.

In the late 1990s this project included 4,000 Hebrew-speaking students from 38 Jewish elementary schools, comprising 65% of all Jewish elementary schools in the Tel Aviv area. Schools were chosen at random for inclusion in the project by the Tel Aviv municipality based on available resources at the time. Located in different neighborhoods of the city, the schools reflected its heterogeneity. They included students of lower and higher socioeconomic status, students of Middle Eastern origin as well as students from other countries of origin, secular and religious students, schools with large percentages of newly arrived immigrants, and schools with few immigrants. It should also be noted that Tel Aviv, which is Israel's largest city and located in the center of the country, has 350,000 residents out of whom 330,000 are Jews and 20,000 are Arabs. This bottom-up policy was supported by the municipality of Tel Aviv, but had strong opposition from the Ministry of Education and the Arab inspectorate, which continues to discourage the learning of spoken Arabic and does not recognize it as a legitimate variety. Therefore, only local initiatives have been promoting this variety from a very early age.

In a study by Inbar, Donitsa-Schmidt, and Shohamy (2000), it was shown that the learning of the spoken dialect in fact promotes positive attitudes toward Arabs, their culture, and people. Specifically, the study investigated whether teaching spoken Arabic rather than MSA and lowering the starting age of instruction in Israeli schools affect students' attitudes. The findings reveal that students who studies spoken Arabic (the experimental group), as opposed to those who did not (control group), reported holding more positive attitudes toward the Arabic language, its culture, and speakers and claimed to be more motivated to study the language. Students who studied the language rated Arabic higher in terms of its importance and attributed more pragmatic benefits to knowledge of the language than those who did not study it. These students also mentioned with higher frequency than the control group the contribution of knowledge of Arabic to peace between Israel and its Arab neighbors, and accentuated to a lesser degree the role of the language for military and espionage purposes. The students' attitudes toward the language and culture were found to be a significant predictor of their desire to continue studying Arabic and prioritized the spoken variety over MSA at a young age. Based on this research, it seems vital to include the spoken variety as a major component of the curricula.

Yet these results did not convince the Ministry of Education to change its policy, as their view of Arabic is not as a language of communication, but more as a language that is part of the political conflict. Though some pockets of teaching the spoken Palestinian dialect of Arabic do exist, as described above in the case of Tel Aviv, these are very limited. However, one initiative brought forward by the Ministry of Education and some nongovernmental organizations (NGOs) in Israel is the teaching of Arabic by native speakers, something that is rare in the Israeli scene. The main rationale behind it is that there is a need for closer interaction between Arabs and Jews in the educational system. This initiative is accompanied by the development of new teaching materials that emphasize a "communicative" intermediate variety of Arabic, which is a mixture of the spoken and written languages, and is currently gaining momentum (Dubiner, 2008). This initiative by the Avraham Foundation and Merhavim Foundation to introduce the teaching of the intermediate variety of Arabic by native speakers is currently being studied to examine its effect both on achievement as well as on improved attitudes. It should be noted that though these programs began as local initiatives, they do get some support from the Ministry of Education once they are in operation; even so, many of these programs do suffer from lack of funds and legitimacy, in spite of strongly motivated students and parents. The basic assumption underlying these programs is that the learning of Arabic could play a pivotal role in bridging political conflicts and reducing ethnic tensions. Yet the Ministry of Education still insists that the teaching of MSA is the only viable policy.

Arabic–Hebrew Bilingual Schools

Another case of bottom-up policy which is also embedded within the political conflict of Israel and uses language in order to bridge that conflict is the establishment of three bilingual Hebrew–Arabic schools (Bekerman, 2005). These schools are privately funded by various organizations in Israel and abroad and get no support from the Ministry of Education.

The first school opened in 1997, and since then two other schools opened (Bekerman, 2005). Both Arabic- and Hebrew-speaking students participate, learn together and attempt to acquire each other's languages. There is ample research about these schools, a unique phenomenon in the Israeli educational context, as well as conferences; meetings; and the establishment of an organization called 'Yad B'Yad. It clearly offers a case of successful bottom-up initiatives supported by private financial sources and not by the Ministry of Education, which has been going on for more than 10 years. National conferences address the difficulties of running these schools, the problems of selecting the appropriate bilingual teaching methods, and the difficulties of overcoming a tense ethnic situation in order for the schools to deal with these issues successfully. This is the most significant policy which can be termed "bottom-up" in the past decade within the Israeli language-learning scene, and it has profound goals: The schools aim to bridge the divides, repair inequalities, redistribute language powers, promote achievement, improve attitudes, increase acceptance, and fight stereotypes.

According to Bekerman (2005), the idea of creating bilingual-bicultural Palestinian–Jewish coeducation is, in and of itself, a daring enterprise. The school established in 1997 sought to foster egalitarian Palestinian–Jewish cooperation in education, primarily through the development of such institutions. In 1998, two more schools were established, following similar principles. During the 2000–2001 school year, the school in the Upper Galilee was comprised of three classes, from Grade 1 to Grade 3. A total 41 Palestinian children from cities and villages in the vicinity of the school and 35 Jewish children living in nearby settlements attended. The school uses the standard curriculum of the state's nonreligious school system, the only difference being that both Hebrew and Arabic are used as languages of instruction, and employs a strong additive bilingual approach in that it emphasizes symmetry between both languages in all aspects of instruction. Two homeroom teachers, a Palestinian and a Jew, jointly lead all classes.

The central goal of the Center for Bilingual Education in Israel (CBE), as expressed in its official public relations publication, is to develop a new educational scheme for Jewish–Palestinian schools that integrates children, parents, and the rest of the community jointly with governmental institutions (local education authorities) in building a cooperative framework structured on the basis of equality and mutual respect. The CBE document posits that bilingual study of Hebrew and Arabic can be instrumental in deepening each group's understanding of the other and mentions that bilingual education is an empowering pedagogy that helps increase the self-esteem of minority students.

Clearly, such initiatives need to be incorporated into a new national language policy that builds on these experiments taking place in the field and adopts them as part of the official policies. In contested areas like Israel, schools like these can be instrumental for purposes that extend far beyond just language. There is an effort to stimulate educators, parents, and policymakers into thinking about how to develop dual-language programs on a wider scale to address the particular contextual challenges that, when left unaccounted for, can prejudice their bilingual educational efforts.

Teaching English in Grade 1 by Homeroom Teachers

The third and last initiative reported here pertains to the teaching of English at a younger age than what is specified in the 1996 educational language policy document. The high status of English resulting from its role as an international language and global *lingua franca* led to major pressures on behalf of parents to start teaching English at an earlier age. Though the 1996 policy document recognizes the special significance and centrality of knowledge of English as a world language, it stipulates that the learning of English should begin not earlier than Grade 4; in fact, there is strong resistance on the part of policymakers at the Ministry of Education and the English inspectorate to begin learning English at an earlier age, a view often supported by a number of experts in the field.

At the same time, there is strong and intensive pressure by parents, communities, students, and schools to begin teaching English at an earlier age. This pressure led to a trend whereby 90% of schools allocate private and personal funds to carry out programs that start English earlier, even as early as kindergarten. These programs are generally financed by the schools themselves, by municipalities, by the parents, or at times by diverting funding from other programs of the school for this purpose. Thus, though the issue of teaching English to young learners has been a controversial one for a while, it ceased being a *controversial* issue, as schools simply enforce their own policies and openly defy the Ministry of Education policy and the English inspectorate. Schools create their own *de facto* policies, and the ministry acknowledges their existence but still continues to resist them by refusing to allocate financial support. In fact, there are no official teacher training courses or programs that provide professional preparation for teaching young learners. At the same time, there are ample materials and textbooks produced for teaching young learners. Whether this new *de facto* policy is successful or effective is still an open question, as no meaningful research has yet been conducted to examine it; however, regardless of such results, given the status of English and the understanding that it is critical for further success and learning, the demand will always be there.

Not surprisingly, given that early English instruction is an undeclared, *de facto* policy that is widely being implemented in Israeli schools today and that no mechanisms to professionalize teachers for such programs actually exist, there is a major shortage of professional English teachers. Consequently, some municipalities employ homeroom teachers as English teachers for Grade 1 students. The program was very controversial, as it was initiated by the municipality of a major city in Israel, in opposition to the Ministry of Education policy not only in terms of early teaching but also in terms of employing nonprofessional English teachers. The homeroom teachers received some training and the programs were carried out in a number of schools in several towns and eventually received some recognition from the Ministry of Education and even the English inspectorate, who recognized their existence and initiated a call for research to examine the success of the programs; at the same time, there was strong opposition to the programs by the English language teacher's union.

In 2004, I was approached by the Ministry of Education with a request to carry out a research study to examine the effectiveness of the teaching of English by homeroom teachers versus by professional English teachers, to compare their effectiveness. The research study was conducted in 2004 (in collaboration with Ofra Inbar—see Inbar-Lourie & Shohamy, 2009; Shohamy & Inbar, 2006) and examined the effects of homeroom teachers teaching English in the first grade. The focus of the study was a comparison of the effectiveness of two teacher models implemented for teaching English to young (6- to 7-year-olds) students: The first model comprised expert English as a foreign language (EFL) teachers who exclusively teach English, whereas the second model involved homeroom or generalist teachers who taught English to their first-grade students along with the other subject areas, such as literacy, mathematics, and science (Shohamy & Inbar, 2006).

Teaching and learning in these two models were compared on a number of parameters: the students' achievements, attitudes, self-assessment, and the teaching methods employed. The assessment tools comprised of a listening comprehension test and an individual oral test. The findings of the study revealed that students studying with the EFL teachers scored significantly higher on the listening comprehension test than those studying with homeroom teachers (86.46 vs. 81.39, $p < .05$). On the oral test, only small differences were found in the word recognition section in favor of students who learned with the EFL teachers.

We concluded that the results need to be interpreted with reference to the other research findings obtained in the study, specifically the data gathered via classroom observations. Each of the teachers who participated in the research (10 teachers from 7 schools) was observed teaching English in the first-grade classroom. Teachers were observed for the duration of two or three lessons, with each lesson lasting about 45 minutes, and observations focused on the class activities and materials used, the classroom interactions, and the language used by both teachers and students (English vs. the students' first language, Hebrew). This observation data revealed differences between the two teaching models: Though the expert EFL teachers taught English as a subject in a way that was detached from other school subjects studied in first grade (e.g., following a "language-focused" teaching approach), the homeroom teachers anchored and integrated their teaching within the knowledge of content areas (e.g., native-language literacy, arithmetic, science, arts and crafts, and music). In doing so, the homeroom teachers followed the notions of "the embedding model" as described by Johnstone (2000). In one instance, for example, a homeroom teacher insisted on teaching the beginning EFL learners how to ask "WH-" questions in English despite their relatively low proficiency in the language. In the interview that followed, she explained that she decided to work on WH- questions since the children were concurrently studying how to form questions in their native language, Hebrew, in two other subject areas: native-language literacy and mathematics. The homeroom teacher felt that presenting an overriding conceptual understanding of what it means to ask such questions in a number of content areas contributed toward establishing and solidifying this concept in the children's cognition.

Our view then is that the aforementioned conventional language-focused assessment tools that we developed for this research project did not pick up on the very unique teaching and learning experiences and rich interactions that took place in the classroom where content and English were embedded. Our claim, therefore, is that the results obtained via usage of the conventional types of listening and speaking tests represent a very narrow dimension of knowledge gained by the language learners, specifically when teaching was conducted by the homeroom teachers.

The demands for English led to a very vibrant controversy with regards to the ideal age to begin teaching English and the specific methods that should be used; issues also surrounded the extent to which English language policy should be carried out based on "popular demand" by parents. Clearly, in this case as well, though the 1996 language education policy stipulated the importance of English, debates and conflicts persist over the type of English that needs to be taught, by whom, at what age, and for what purposes, given the current issues surrounding the language and its role in the next decades as well as the effectiveness of content-based language instruction (Graddol, 2006).

Conclusions

In a centralized society like Israel's, there are very few bottom-up language policy initiatives, as most policies are dictated by central governments that lock the system within a set of mechanisms that create little room for resistance. Yet criticism was raised in this chapter regarding the way top-down language education policy was introduced in Israel, specifically for overlooking the representation of constituents (e.g., teachers, experts, language users), even though they are the ones expected to carry out the policy. Especially lacking is any connection between the statements made in the policy and research on the likelihood of the policy's success, given that it is detached from research on second-language education. Through three examples accompanied by research, one on the teaching of spoken Arabic, another on bilingual Arabic–Hebrew schools, and the last one on the teaching of English to young learners by homeroom teachers, it was shown how when the conditions are right, there are spaces for initiatives to fill the gaps that the official policy left open. Each of these bottom-up initiatives represents a new direction motivated by relevant and current issues, including social, economic, and political needs—the teaching of spoken Arabic to bring together groups in conflict, the establishment of bilingual schools to help create closer coexistence between Arab and Jews, and the teaching of English to young learners to strengthen linguistic capacity in a language that is considered by many a key to success. The views of experts in all three of these situations is not significant for explaining the demand, but rather for offering alternatives to existing and traditional views on the role of language in politics and society. One main conclusion of these bottom-up policies is the need to divert the creation of policies to a negotiated process of policymaking. Language policies need to be negotiated by incorporating a variety of factors, such as the wishes of constituents within political contexts as well as empirical studies that provide evidence of the effectiveness of policy implementation and the extent to which the priorities set in the language policies are realistic.

Central educational systems such as Israel's need to be more open and *encourage* bottom-up initiatives to allow new ideas, new creations, and new policies that are not always in-line with *national* ideologies. The idea of a nation-state imposing identical ideologies on its entire population through its policies does not hold in this day and age, especially within a domain such as Israel with its rich multilingual environment and history. Instead, there is a need for grassroots voices to engender more creative and responsive policies, and these should be encouraged and adopted. The surrender of people to national policy of one hegemonic language that is reinforced by central funds to create a homogenous society, serves only to limit the rich linguistic repertoire that already exists and the diverse aspirations of people. It is only fitting that teachers, who play a most important role in this process, should be encouraged to cultivate such initiatives and given training and knowledge in language education policy. I would claim that an important component of any language education policy document is the need to incorporate teachers and school systems to develop and initiate policies that are appropriate in their own contexts, defying the notion of one national policy for all. It is the role of the Ministry of Education or the schools themselves to evaluate the success of these policies in implementation, but they are essential for the continued interaction and negotiations between policies and practices. Bekerman (2005) commented in the case of bilingual schools:

> Language is not necessarily the only way through which to organize the world, or the only path to a socially just and multicultural society. Moreover, educational institutions need not be the first (nor the only as they usually are)

places in which to achieve linguistic rights and even when chosen for that purpose, they should be viewed in the wider national/political and communal/cultural contexts in which they come to function, paying special attention not to fall back into the reification of unitary groups. . . . We will do well to remember that in the end it is concrete political/structural changes that help bring an end to human suffering. (Bekerman, 2005, p. 17)

This seems to apply not only to top-down national initiatives but also to those, like the ones discussed here, which work in the opposite direction. What need to be addressed are the deeply entrenched paradigmatic perspectives that support the nation-state ideology and its traditional monoculturalism and monolingualism. Bekerman (2005), therefore, doubts whether bilingual educational initiatives, even the best intentioned of them, will achieve the dream of an equality that allows for and acknowledges sociocultural differences as affirmed in multicultural, bilingual discourse, as language is not the only path to a socially just and multicultural society. Moreover, schools need to be viewed within the wider national/political and communal/cultural contexts in which they come to function even with regard to bottom-up initiatives.

Discussion Questions

1   Shohamy mentions the 1996 Language in Education Policy in Israel. Describe the policy and discuss whether you think that on paper it opens spaces in schools for multilingualism or restricts those spaces.
2   This chapter offers three instances of bottom-up resistance to the 1996 policy. Discuss each one and the ways that each promotes or curtails the development of bilingualism. In addition, how do these programs promote language rights, representation, and equality?
3   Visit or research a school with a bilingual education program in your country. In what ways are its goals similar or different from the goals of the Hebrew–Arabic programs described in this chapter? Do you think that bilingual programs can change students' attitudes toward people who are different from them?
4   How can we conduct a study that will examine the quality and implementation of a particular language policy? Similarly, what is the evidence that practitioners would need to collect in order to convince authorities to "accept"/ implement bottom-up policies?

References

Aboud, F. (1994). *Children and prejudice.* Cambridge, MA: Blackwell.
Bar-Tal, D. (1996). Development of social categories and stereotypes in early childhood: The case of "The Arab" concept formation stereotype and attitudes by Jewish children in Israel. *International Journal of Intercultural Relations, 20*(3/4), 341–370.
Bekerman, Z. (2005). Complex contexts and ideologies: Bilingual education in conflict-ridden areas. *Journal of Language, Identity, and Education, 4*(1), 1–20.

Ben-Rafael, E., & Brosh, H. (1991). A sociological study of second language diffusion: The obstacles to Arabic teaching in the Israeli school. *Language Problems and Language Planning, 15,* 1–24.

Blau, J. (1981). *The renaissance of modern Hebrew and modern standard Arabic: Parallels and differences in the revival of two Semitic languages.* Berkeley, CA: University of California Press.

Brosh, H. (1988). *The effect of learning Arabic in elementary school on achievement in literary Arabic in the 7th grade.* Unpublished doctoral dissertation, Tel Aviv University, Israel.

Donitsa-Schmidt, S., Inbar, O., & Shohamy, E. (2004). The effects of teaching spoken Arabic on students' attitudes and motivation in Israel. *Modern Language Journal, 88*(ii), 217–228.

Dubiner, D. (2008). *The impact of incipient trilinguality on the linguistic and socio-affective development of elementary school children in Israel.* Unpublished doctoral dissertation, Carnegie Mellon University, Pittsburgh.

Ferguson, C. A. (1959). Diglossia. *Word, 15,* 325–340.

Graddol, D. (2006). *English next.* Manchester: The British Council. Retrieved July 6, 2009, from www.britishcouncil.org/learning-research-english-next.pdf

Inbar, O., Donitsa-Schmidt, S., & Shohamy, E. (2000). Students' motivation as a function of language learning: The teaching of Arabic in Israel. In Z. Dornyei & R. Schmidt (Eds.), *Motivation and second language acquisition* (pp. 297–311). Honolulu, HI: University of Hawaii, Second Language Teaching & Curriculum Center.

Inbar-Lourie, O., & Shohamy, E. (2009). Assessing young language learners: What is the construct? In M. Nikolv (Ed.), *Contextualizing the age factor: Issues in early foreign language learning* (pp. 83–96). Berlin: Mouton de Gruyter.

Johnstone, R. (2000) Context-sensitive assessment of modern languages in primary (elementary) and early secondary education: Scotland and the European experience. *Language Testing 17*(2), 123–143.

Kraemer, R. (1993). Social psychological factors related to the study of Arabic among Israeli high school students. *Studies in Second Language Acquisition, 15,* 83–105.

Ministry of Education. (1996). *Policy for language education in Israel.* Jerusalem, Israel: Office of the Director-General, Ministry of Education, and Culture.

Naiman, I. (1999). *The effect of studying spoken Arabic on achievements in literary Arabic.* Unpublished master's thesis, Tel Aviv University, Israel.

Ryding, K. (1991). Proficiency despite diglossia: A new approach for Arabic. *Modern Language Journal, 75,* 212–218.

Shohamy, E. (2003). The issue: Implications of language education policies for language study in schools and universities. Perspective, *Modern Language Journal, 88*(ii), 277–286.

Shohamy, E. (2006). *Language policy: Hidden agendas and new approaches.* London: Routledge.

Shohamy, E. (2008a). At what cost? Methods of language revival and protection: Examples from Hebrew. In K. King, N. Schilling-Estes, L. Fogle, J. Lou Jia, & B. Soukup (Eds.), *Sustaining linguistic diversity: Endangered and minority languages and language varieties* (pp. 205–218). Washington, DC: Georgetown University Press.

Shohamy, E. (2008b). Language policies and language realities in Israel: A critical review. In A. Stavans & I. Kupferberg (Eds.), *Studies in language and language education. Essays in honor of Elite Olshtain* (p. 479). Jerusalem: Hebrew University, Magnes Press.

Shohamy, E., & Donitsa-Schmidt, S. (1998). *Jews vs. Arabs: Language attitudes and stereotypes.* Tel Aviv, Israel: Tel Aviv University, Tami Steinmetz Center for Peace Research.

Shohamy, E., & Inbar, O. (2006). *The teaching of EFL in the first grade: EFL teachers versus homeroom teachers.* Jerusalem: The Israeli Ministry of Education, The Pedagogical Secretariat (in Hebrew).

Spolsky, B., & Shohamy, E. (1999). *The languages of Israel: Policy, ideology and practice.* Clevedon, Avon: Multilingual Matters.

Chapter 12

Traversing the Linguistic Quicksand in Ethiopia

Michael Daniel Ambatchew

Introduction

In the current trend of globalization, common policies are being prescribed by global powers as a panacea for the ills of developing countries. One example of this is the education programmes being implemented in numerous African countries. Parents, teachers, students and education bureaus many times accept these policies, and at other times they go about their lives in ways that suit them, disregarding the policy.

This chapter reviews some of the practices in implementing the ambitious and inclusive 1994 language education policy in Ethiopia, which allows for every language in the country to become a medium of instruction. Findings presented in this chapter are based on existing literature, evidence the researcher has gathered over decades as a student, teacher and researcher in Ethiopia, as well as interviews and observations in several primary schools conducted for this chapter.

General Background

Reviewing the Historical and Socio-Political Background to Ethiopia's Language Policy

Ethiopia is located in the horn of Africa and is bound on the northeast by Eritrea and Djibouti, on the east and southeast by Somalia, on the south by Kenya and on the west by Sudan. It covers an area of 1,104,304 km² and has diversified geographical and linguistic landscapes. Ethiopia is a federal democratic republic composed of 11 national regional states; Tigray, Afar, Amhara, Oromia, Somalia, Benishangul–Gumuz; Southern Nations Nationalities and Peoples Region; and Gambella, Harari, Addis Ababa and Dire Dawa. The last three are city-states. Ethiopia presents a mosaic of nationalities, speaking many languages, which are divided into four groups—three of them tracing a common ancestry to a parent language called proto-Afroasiatic. From this language sprang not only the languages spoken in Ethiopia but also a number of languages spoken in the northern half of Africa and in south-western Asia. The three language groups of the proto-Afroasiatic family spoken in Ethiopia are known as Cushitic, Omotic and Semitic. Whereas Cushitic and Omotic are the most ancient languages, Semitic is the most recent. A fourth group of languages belongs to an independent family known as Nilo-Saharan. The Semitic branch in northern Ethiopia leads to several languages including Amharic, the official language of the country (Sissay, 2005). Amharic has enjoyed the position of national language for centuries. The introduction of Amharic to unify Ethiopia was started by Emperor Tewodros II (1855–1868).

Ethiopia has 75 identified tribes (Institute for the Study of Ethiopian Nationalities, 1985) and over 80 different languages with 4 of the 5 Afro-Asiatic languages spoken in the country. According to Ferguson (1972), Ethiopia has five major languages (Amharic, English, Tigrinya, Oromignya/Afaan Oromo and Somali), thirteen minor languages (Afar, Anyuak, Beja, Chaha Gurage, Derasa, Gumuz, Hadiya, Janjero, Kefa, Kembeata, Sidamo, Tigre and Wellamo/Welaiyta) and three special languages (Ge'ez, Italian and Arabic). Ferguson (1972) did not cover the remaining languages because of the lack of sufficient data at the time. To date, no exhaustive study of the Ethiopian languages has been made, yet the minor languages are getting to be more widely known, one of which is thought to have as few as 250 speakers. Moreover, with more languages being introduced now as media of instruction and languages of local administration, the profile of languages is changing rapidly.

Ethiopia currently has an extremely explicit and comprehensive language education policy, which on paper allows for and encourages all 80 or so languages to be used as media of instruction in primary school. It thereby gives a legal framework for the UN International Convention on the Rights of the Child, which was ratified by all countries in the world except Somalia and the United States in the early 1990s, and the convention declared that all children should get primary education in their mother tongue. An overview of the socio-political context and historical background of the country is helpful to understand how such a liberal policy came into place.

The traditional education system of education in the 19th century was in Ge'ez and Amharic. The first modern school in 1908 concentrated on teaching French, English and Arabic at the expense of other subjects, as these three languages had gained dominance due to colonialism and international trade. During the Italian colonial occupation (1936–1941), vernaculars were used as media of instruction with the ultimate goal of disuniting the country. Afterwards, Emperor Haile-Selassie (1941–1974) vigorously tried to implement modern education. Sissay (2005, p. 30) describes the condition of education saying:

> After the 1941 victory [of the Italian colonizers], during the reconstruction period, the Ministry of Education and Fine Arts was among the first to be formed and provided education to more than 20,000 students in government schools alone by 1944. In the following two decades great achievements were scored in the education field as there were also mission, private, community and church schools starting to appear apart from government schools. By 1969 there were 2,114 elementary and secondary schools with 14,500 teachers that provided education for more that 683,500 students.

The need to reunify the country led Emperor Haile-Selassie to change the medium of instruction to Amharic in government schools in the 1940s. However, several schools continued to use other media of instruction including English, French and Italian. Although these schools were primarily intended to cater for expatriate communities, Ethiopians were also allowed to learn in these schools.

The socialist government (1974–1990) recognized 'the language rights of other ethnolinguistic groups (termed nationalities) and the utilization of some of these languages for literacy and post-literacy education' (McNab, 1990, p. 66). However, the government did not introduce these languages immediately as media of instruction, probably wary of the negative consequences of using languages that had not been adequately developed as media of instruction.

With the abrupt end of the Cold War at the end of the 1980s, both the socialist government in power and the opposing guerrillas following Albanian communism found themselves grasping for viable ideological alternatives. The socialist government switched to a 'mixed market' economy and ideology. In 1991 the socialists were ousted and democratic rule was imposed. Having dunked their Albanian communist ideology in history's dustbin, they were willing to embrace a most forward-looking and idealistic language education policy. The government allowed instruction in different languages before even adopting the official language policy in 1994, which allows for every language in the country to become a medium of instruction.

Various scholars question whether this action was based on academic or political imperatives. Alemu and Tekleselassie (2006, p. 161) say:

> The current instructional language policy in Ethiopia is dictated by the ruling party in line with its political ideology rather than being based in genuine attention to student learning and, ultimately, in national economic advancement.

On the other hand, Bloor and Tamrat (1996, p. 330) comment: 'Considered in terms of sentimental as opposed to instrumental interests, at least, the new policy can be viewed as a marked improvement on the Amharic linguistic hegemony of the past.'

The present government restricted Ethiopians from registering their children in international medium schools, stating absolute belief in the United Nations Educational, Scientific and Cultural Organization (UNESCO) declaration of 1954 that mother-tongue education was the best. Very little language planning was done prior to introducing the other languages as media of instruction. Basic preparation such as graphization, standardization and modernization of several of the languages has only recently begun (Siebert, 2002). Departing from the common government line of claiming unconditional success in all its activities, the National Director of Curriculum and Instruction has admitted to having little or no literary stock in the new media of instruction (Alemu & Tekleselassie, 2006). This is how Ethiopia has ended up with one of the most advanced language policies on paper, but with questionable practices on the ground.

Language Education Policy

As mentioned, in the 1950s UNESCO declared that the best language to teach a child to read was the mother tongue. Dutcher (2003, p. 11) concurs:

We all know that most children who begin their education in their mother tongue make a better start, demonstrate increased self-confidence and continue to perform better than those who start school in a new language.

Commenting on the Ethiopian language policy, Heugh, Benson, Bogale and Yohannes (2007, p. 7) declare; '... the current MoE [Medium of education] policy of 8 years of mother-tongue medium school is one of the best on the continent and promotes sound educational practice.' However, very few people have cared to read the caveat in the UNESCO declaration, which says, 'provided the languages are equal'. In an ever-globalizing world, it is indisputable that some languages are more equal than others. Printed materials, trained teachers, satellite television and contact with numerous cultures and people, all tend to render languages anything but equal. Even Dutcher (2003) conceded that the promise of mother-tongue education is rendered ineffective if there is a lack of support material, poor teacher training and inadequate language development.

Although mother-tongue education is ideologically noble, for it treats all human beings as equal, other considerations need to be taken into account. There are practical realities when educating a child in a language spoken by a few thousand people, in the absence of teaching materials or trained teachers. Therefore, an ever-increasing cry for multilingual education is now being heard on the African continent and elsewhere. Without ever denouncing monolingual mother-tongue education in an endangered language, UNESCO has gracefully changed its aims to 'promote multilingualism through its educational and cultural programmes to protect the world's oral and intangible heritage' (UNESCO, 2008, p. 2). This is perhaps a reflection of the unequal power relations of the North and South, where countries aiming at dominating the world see it as imperative that everybody speaks their language, despite the fact that multilingualism and diversity is the reality on the ground.

There is spatial multilingualism in Ethiopia, meaning that children who live in a certain area are not necessarily speakers of the local dominant language, which may be spoken by only one of the ethnic groups. So, selecting the dominant language as a medium of instruction does not ensure that all the children in the classroom in which that language is being used actually speak it.

Many policies in Ethiopia state certain things in black and white, but are then subsequently modified by internal directives, which can run directly counter to the original policy. A number of variations are often found from region to region in Ethiopia, as well as within regions, caused by implementation differences on the ground. For instance, in some regions the local language is only used as the medium of instruction for 4 years, whereas it is used for 6 or 8 years in others. In fact, a common line of defence by government officials when questioned about the appropriateness of policies is to say that the policy is perfect, but the implementation is marred. Following the disputed elections in 2005, some regional states changed the medium of instruction from local languages to English at the second cycle of primary education, reflecting even the administration's doubt of the value of being educated in an Ethiopian language.

But it is the classroom teacher and the classroom context that makes the difference between success and failure. Marsh (2006, p. 31) states, 'Regardless of what language our educational policymakers decide, it is the social microcosm of the classroom which reflects the success or failures of any nation's citizens in the future.' For example, in schools in a district in the Southern Nations and Nationalities Region, some schools are seen as doing well in national examinations, and others do poorly, despite having the same medium of instruction and teaching materials (Link Community Development, 2008). Obviously, factors such as whether or not parents send their children to school, how teachers are trained and what materials are available, all influence the learning process. Alemu and Tekleselassie (2006) point out that the government failed to consult grassroots-level professionals and parents in drawing up the Ethiopian language policy. This has obviously forced these stakeholders to express their views in other ways, such as stopping sending their children to school, or sending them to regions that offer their preferred medium of instruction.

The rest of this chapter reviews how two sets of actors—teachers and parents—negotiate both the Ethiopian state language policy and that of local schools, which sometimes differs.

Teachers' Ways of Adapting Policy

It is the teachers in the classroom who have to negotiate and/or recreate the language education policy. Because of the multilingualism in Addis Ababa, as elsewhere in the country, it is very rare to find a monolingual group of students and a monolingual teacher. Therefore, quite a lot of code-switching takes place when the teacher is capable of speaking more than one language and knows the mother tongue of some of the students. This has been previously observed (Ambatchew, 1996) and has been confirmed in more recent observations (Heugh et al., 2007). The rest of this section looks at how teachers adapt the medium of instruction by engaging in code-switching. García (2009) has called the responsible use of code-switching to educate, 'translanguaging'. The first two examples that follow are about using translanguaging successfully as a bilingual pedagogy (to facilitate students' understandings and for terminology). But the last two examples (to facilitate teachers' expression and for comfort) are about the spontaneous use of code-switching in classrooms. It is interesting to note that this spontaneous use of code-switching takes place especially when the lesson is being carried out through the medium of English, which teachers themselves have not mastered adequately. The fact that there is instruction in English points to the tension between the state's language education policy, which requires the use of the children's mother tongues, and schools' language education policies, which continue to respond to parents and communities.

Code-Switching to Facilitate Students' Understanding

Many times students who are not speakers of the language of the class would not understand the meaning. In such cases, multilingual teachers would then say it in that students' mother tongue, and look for the beaming smile of understanding on the student's face.

In one particular class observed in Addis Ababa, a teacher had a teaching assistant who spoke the language of the student, and she requested the assistant to translate her instruction for the student. Interestingly, in one private school, teachers teaching through Amharic code-switched into English for the sake of Ethiopian children who had returned to live in the country after living abroad. Regardless of who the children were, teachers were interested in educating them and code-switched responsibly to do so.

Code-Switching for Terminology

In some of the classes observed in Addis Ababa for the purposes of this study, the teachers struggled with new terminology that had been coined. Especially in subjects like science and maths, many teachers would say a word in Amharic and then repeat it in English. What was interesting was that at times, the English terms would actually be more familiar to the teachers themselves rather than to the students, for whom the term in both languages would be equally alien. A Science teacher says: '*Yehay demkida yebalal. Demkida Artery. Dem kelib yemiwesd.*' The teacher repeats the word for 'artery' in English to clarify her point. Similarly, during my observations I heard teachers repeat in English words like 'factor', and 'decimal point'. Although these terms have been coined in local languages, they remain unfamiliar to the teachers and the students as they are seldom used outside the classroom. Again, the teacher code-switches to ensure that the meaning of the lesson is understood by the students.

Code-Switching to Facilitate Teachers' Expression

On the other hand, there are times when teachers code-switch simply because they are weak in the medium of instruction in which they teach. This type of code-switching may lead to poor learning. It was especially prevalent among those required to teach in English in private English-medium schools. Those teachers teaching in English only were observed to make minimal utterances that lacked life, humour and spontaneity.

But sometimes the same could be said of teachers teaching in their mother tongue. Some of these languages had never been taught before in school. Although fluent and able to use their mother tongues in the community, these teachers struggled to teach through this medium and relied on code-switching to communicate with the students.

Code-Switching for Comfort

Another type of spontaneous code-switching observed was the teacher teaching the subject in one language and then switching to another when talking to the teaching assistant or scolding and advising students. This was seen most frequently while teaching English or French rather than Amharic. For example, one teacher teaching through the medium of English said to the students: 'We cut paper with scissors.' But then, she turned to the assistant and said in Amharic, '*Ebakish mekes akebign*' [Please pass me the scissors].

Parents' Ways of Circumventing Policy

Beyond the Words

In Africa in general, and in Ethiopia in particular, leading politicians pay lip service to mother-tongue education. However, in most cases their children are sent to schools where English or French are the sole media of instruction. Ironically, both the present prime minister and the former socialist president sent some of their children to the same French-medium school, where some of the previous Emperor's grandchildren were also educated. This is a good indicator that regardless of the huge changes in the policies of language of education over the past three regimes, not much change has taken place in the rulers' attitudes to where and how a good education for their children can be obtained. Obviously, the politicians want to have their children possess universal currency for social and economic advancement, but do the general public aim for any less for their own children? About 85% of college students in Ethiopia desire their children to be educated in English (Ambatchew, 1999). This is so despite the fact that the mastery of English is probably unattainable for the majority of African students (Alexander, 2000).

The adaptation and implementation of the language policy in Addis Ababa city-state is no exception to the general situation in Ethiopia, though Addis Ababa may be seen as more privileged in regards to access to materials, manpower and modern means of communication. The examples that follow are evidence of what parents do in order to ensure that their children are educated in English or Amharic.

Turning a Blind Eye

According to the national language education policy, schools must use the language selected for administration as the medium of instruction. Therefore, as Amharic is the official language in the city-state of Addis Ababa, schools are not allowed to use other languages. Recently, Addis has been reinstated as the capital of the Oromiya Region and a few schools are being considered to use Afaan Oromo as the medium of instruction. Moreover, a few international community schools are allowed to have different media of instruction, such as English, but Ethiopians are denied access to these schools. Nevertheless, private schools using English as a medium of instruction are becoming a common sight. Billboards even have 'English medium of communication' written under the school's name.

It appears that such private schools using English as medium of instruction have connections to the education ministry and thus to the inspectors of schools.

A teacher in one English-medium school visited for the purpose of this research narrates how in one occasion the director was pre-informed of a supposedly surprise visit and informed the teachers to teach in Amharic for the day. The supervisors came to inspect and entered one lower primary class. The teacher pointed to the colour blue and asked in Amharic, 'What colour is this?' The whole class roared out 'Blue!' in English. The flustered teacher replied, 'Yes blue is *semayyawi* in Amharic.'

The writer of this article personally went to the Addis Ababa Regional Education Bureau and informed an official that he wanted to enrol a child in an English-medium school. The official immediately rattled off a list of a dozen or so schools. The author then said that he wanted to open an English-medium school and the same official replied that it was against the law. When asked how come the schools named were above the law, the official glibly said that the schools taught English well, but did not teach in English. Taking it further, the author went to the Head of the Bureau's office and asked for an appointment to discuss the issue of medium of instruction. The secretary informed him that the Head was always busy and in meetings, so if the author could leave his call card she would get back to him. He did and has never got a return call.

Changing Nationality and Being an Exception

The author also paid a visit to an international community school, to inquire about admission regulations. The director responded that for some years now most international schools have been forbidden to accept Ethiopians.

When the school principal was told that the school was filled with quite a few Ethiopian children speaking Amharic, he replied that these were children whose mothers had gone abroad and delivered there. Consequently, the children had foreign passports and were eligible for admissions. Some of the students were older and were born before the prohibition of Ethiopians in these schools, and so were allowed to continue. Moreover, there were 'special cases' of children, who got exceptional permission to study in an international school. Parents could apply to the Ministry of Education and get special permission. Consequently, the children of Ethiopian diplomats or other Ethiopians who had lived abroad could gain admission to English-medium schools.

The director confided that some Ethiopians simply went abroad for a vacation and got special permission, whereas others seemed to have connections and got permission without leaving the country. Apart from the discrepancies in implementation, the general directive is enacted as meaning that a child who moves from another region to Addis Ababa is forced to learn in Amharic, but one who moves from abroad can learn in an international language.

Hiring Private Tutors and Going to Evening Classes

Frustrated by their children's lack of language proficiency as well as by their poor mastery of the other subjects, many parents are now hiring private tutors.

Teachers are also taking advantage of this to supplement their meagre wages. The sight of banners advertising home-to-home tutorial services has now become common. A comparatively well-paid teacher in a private school confided that he made more than his regular salary giving private tutorials to children.

Ethiopian athletes who suddenly find themselves propelled into the international arena knowing hardly a word of English are also hiring private language tutors. Many athletes are now finding themselves faced by a foreign journalist after breaking a world record and being unable to communicate. Therefore, a few language centres are even offering courses called 'English for Athletes'.

Moreover, due to globalization, many business people are finding that they have to deal with foreign exporters and are hurrying to English classes. Although Alexander (2000) says it is an anomaly to have a nuclear scientist who does not speak English, in Addis it is very common to find successful businessmen parking their luxury cars outside expensive language centres to learn English.

Moving to Sunnier Skies

As explained previously, a territorial principle is used in the selection of the medium of instruction; that is, the dominant language of a certain region or area is selected as the medium of instruction. Thus, parents have found ways to move to areas that use their preferred medium of instruction. Hoben (1994) states that in several regions, parents withdrew their children from the schools with new mother tongues as media of instruction, leading to the plummeting of enrolment rates. Some families have migrated to Addis to ensure that their children can learn in Amharic, and others have sent their children to live with relatives in Addis. A lecturer confided that she is raising her brother's children because the medium of instruction in the region where they were living had changed. The father wanted to move with his children to Addis so that the children could continue their education in a language to which they were accustomed, but he could not find work in Addis. This obviously raises serious issues as to whether it is in the best interest of the child to live with her or his parent and learn in an unfamiliar medium or live away from her or his parents and learn in a familiar medium.

Ethiopian parents whose children were going to an international school with English as the medium of instruction once went to complain to a Minister of Education about a hike in the school fees. She advised them to send their children to Amharic-medium schools. A disgruntled parent remarked that although she was advising this, the minister had sent her own children to England.

Recommendations

Although the current Ethiopian language policy is often said to be perfect, it is obviously far from it. Steps are being taken by teachers and parents to open up new spaces in the language policy, as administrators themselves have started to revise it.

Multilingual Media of Instruction

A first step worth looking into is allowing individual schools to select their own medium of instruction, as well as two or more media of instruction, according to their students' ability, parents' wants and the availability of trained staff and teaching materials. This could produce interesting results in that though initially many parents may opt for English instruction, later on how much the students actually learn may sway preferences. For instance, private schools like St. Joseph and Nazareth that teach in Amharic are chosen over others that do not do so well in educating their students through English as their medium of instruction. Besides, monolingual media of instruction are not the only choice; recent research tends to show that students who study in bilingual programmes tend to understand more and attain better grades than students in monolingual schools (García, 2009). It has previously been noted that students in Ethiopia showed 'surprising multilingual ability' (Ambatchew, 1996, p. 6) and it would be a shame not to build upon this resource.

The government cannot have a one-size-fits-all policy. Heugh et al. (2007, p. 104) state, 'Countries with top-down decision making often attempt to implement one single educational language policy for all, with little regard for differences in terms of language attitudes and use, exposure to national and/or official languages, goals of schooling and so on.' Therefore, in line with its decentralization policy, the Ethiopian government should give schools a freer hand to select multiple media of instruction. A new phase of the education sector programme is to begin with the central aim being to improve the quality of education. This programme has promised to give individual schools block grants of money, instead of the money being controlled at a central level. Hopefully, this might give schools greater flexibility to experiment with which mix of languages aid their students' learning the most (Ambatchew & Prew, 2009).

Better Trained Teachers

If teachers are not educated properly, they cannot teach effectively, even in their mother tongue. Currently, teachers are at times trained in another language and then expected to teach in their mother tongue. Teachers have to be seriously educated, especially primary teachers, as this is where the basis of education is laid.

Teachers who have to teach in another language, like English, ought to be given intensive courses in the language and prove their competence in it by passing standard examinations. If not, education efforts are doomed to fail, and meaningless memorization of phrases is what is achieved at best. Postponing the teaching of a foreign language until students have developed literacy and other skills and then introducing them to the foreign language with a highly skilled teacher for a shorter period may produce better effects than having them grope in the darkness with a poorly trained teacher who has not mastered the language through which instruction is meant to occur.

Adequate Language and Materials Preparation and Production

As pointed out over a decade ago,

> As long as the ultimate aim is to give the students a sound education, the decision to use some of these languages as media of instruction may have to be revised in favour of making them subject languages for the time being. (Ambatchew, 1994, p. 9)

Unfortunately, the reverse planning which took place after the elections in 2005, whereby the local language was quickly replaced by English as a medium of instruction, has indicated that if a people are not convinced that their language is adequate to convey the necessary information to their children, they will oppose it sooner or later. Therefore, serious efforts must be made to standardize the languages and develop them to a stage where they facilitate rather than hinder knowledge acquisition.

Not only must the basic preparation such as graphization, standardization and modernization of the media of instruction be undertaken seriously, but also an abundance of materials must be produced at various levels, including the pre-literate level. It has been previously noted that one teacher had never seen a single book outside of the classroom texts in a local language he used as a medium of instruction (Ambatchew, 1996). Students start developing their emerging literacy skills even before coming to school, so unless a rich environment of books, posters, television and radio programmes is created in the medium or media of instruction, the students are doomed to failure. Consequently, much more must be done to produce a print-rich environment than simply producing the main course textbook in the class.

Awareness Creation

The sudden reversal of the language policy after the 2005 elections in some regions, as well as the sending of government officials' children to the French- and English-medium school and the placing of 'special children' in foreign-medium schools, all show that there is no consensus on the benefits of mother-tongue instruction. In their recent assessment of the Ethiopian educational system and media of instruction, Heugh et al. (2007, p. 106) note:

> At nearly all levels of the education system as well as the general public expressed to us their belief that English MOI [Medium of Instruction] helps students learn English and, further, that the earlier English becomes MOI, the more successful students will be in school, in examinations and in life.

It is important to investigate the advantages and disadvantages of using different and multiple media of instruction. Teachers and parents must be made aware of the dynamic nature of language policy education and of the advantages of multilingual education.

Conclusion

Undoubtedly, Ethiopians are grappling with the right language education policy; however, a perfect decision has not been reached. With globalization, the future of Ethiopia depends upon how we educate the children. Therefore, serious efforts must be made to ensure that the present language policy is indeed leading to improved learning and has been accepted by all stakeholders. If not, sincere measures must be taken to overcome the obstacles and reassure all stakeholders, especially students, teachers and parents that improvements are and will continue to be made.

Discussion Questions

1   Who should ultimately have the power to decide in what language a student should be instructed?
2   What are the pros and cons of having multilingual teachers?
3   How do you feel minority language speakers should be integrated into a classroom?
4   If you moved abroad, would you opt for your child to be educated in the dominant language of that country?
5   If financial constraints stop you from using all the languages in a country as media of instruction, how would you go about selecting which ones should be used?
6   How would you deal with linguistic decisions that could be pragmatic but politically incorrect?

References

Alemu, S. D, & Tekleselassie, A. A. (2006). Instructional language policy in Ethiopia: Motivated by politics or the educational needs of children? *Planning and Changing, 3*(3 & 4), 151–168.

Alexander, N. (2000). English unattainable but unassailable: The Dilemma of language of education in South Africa. *PRAESA occasional papers* (No. 3). Cape Town: PRAESA/ University of Cape Town.

Ambatchew, M. D. (1994). Possible implications of Ethiopia's new language policy for primary school education. Presented at the Panafrican Colloquium: Educational Innovation in Post-Colonial Africa, Cape Town.

Ambatchew, M. D. (1996). Mother tongue, national language or international language? The case of Ethiopia. Presented at the Seminar on Language Education in Africa, Cape Town.

Ambatchew, M. D. (1999). English in Ethiopian education. Presented at the Oxford International Conference on Education and Development, Oxford.

Ambatchew, M. D., & Prew, M. (2009, February). Good governance and educational reform. Organisation for social science research in Eastern and Southern Africa. *Bulletin, VI*(I), 41–55.

Bloor, T., & Tamrat, W. (1996). Issues in Ethiopian language policy and education. *Multilingual and Multicultural Education, 17*(5), 321–338.

Dutcher, N. (2003). *Promise and perils of mother tongue education.* Washington, DC: Center for Applied Linguistics.

Ferguson, C. A. (1972). *The role of Arabic in Ethiopia, Sociolinguistics.* New York: Penguin.

García, O. (2009). *Bilingual education in the 21st century: A global perspective.* Malden, MA & Oxford: Wiley/Blackwell.

Heugh, K., Benson, C., Bogale, B., & Yohannes, M. A. G. (2007). Study on medium of instruction in primary schools in Ethiopia. Addis Ababa, Ethiopia: Commissioned by the Ministry of Education.

Hoben, S. J. (1994). The Language of education in Ethiopia: Empowerment or imposition? In H. G. Marcus & G. Hudons (Eds.), *New trends in Ethiopian studies* (pp. 182–197). Lawrenceville, NJ: The Red Sea Press Inc.

Institute for the Study of Ethiopian Nationalities. (1985). *Achir YeEthiopia Bihereseboch Mawekia* [An Overview of Ethiopian Nationalities]. Addis Ababa, Ethiopia: Author.

Link Community Development. (2008). *Termly report for Ethiopia.* Mimeo.

Marsh, D. (2006). *English as medium of instruction in the new global linguistic order: Global characteristics, local consequences.* Jyväskylä: University of Jyväskylä.

McNab, C. (1990). Language policy and language practice: Implementing multilingual literacy in Ethiopia. *African Studies Review, 33*(3), 65–82.

Siebert, R. (2002). *Recent developments regarding education policy and languages in North Omo administrative region* (Electronic Survey Reports 2002–058). Ethiopia: Summer Institute of Linguistics International.

Sissay, G. E. (2005). *Foundations in Ethiopia.* Unpublished masters thesis, The University of Bologna, UNIBO.

UNESCO. (2008). *International mother language day.* Retrieved May 7, 2009, from http://www.portal.unesco.org

Chapter 13

Language Policy in Education and Classroom Practices in India

Is the Teacher a Cog in the Policy Wheel?

Ajit Mohanty, Minati Panda, and Rashim Pal

Introduction

Though linguistic diversity is seriously threatened today, linguistic minorities and speakers of marginalized and dominated languages are also asserting their identities. This trend is quite evident in South Asian countries, which are also characterized by the dominant presence of English. Though politically indigenous languages have been given rhetorical support to symbolize national identities, English has established itself as the language of power often benefiting from internal conflicts between competing linguistic assertions.

In spite of widespread multilingualism, South Asian societies are characterized by a typically hierarchical relationship between languages that can be seen as a double divide between English at the top of the three-tiered hierarchy, the mass language(s) of the majority at the middle rungs, and the marginalized indigenous and minority languages—often stigmatized as dialects—at the bottom (Mohanty, 2008a). The chasm between policy and practice with respect to the place of languages and minority mother tongues leads to educational failure and capability deprivation of the minority linguistic groups (Mohanty, 2008b). The English–vernacular divide is severally negotiated and contested in these societies (Ramanathan, 2005).

This chapter focuses on the various modes of such negotiation and resistance in Indian classrooms—the processes by which the ground-level contextual realities of linguistic diversity, embedded in the macrostructure of hierarchical power relationship between languages, are negotiated by the teachers and the field-level functionaries in the school system in direct contact with immediate issues and problems. The context of the classrooms and school-level transactions are analyzed through a brief discussion of the language education policy in India to show that some explicit policy provisions have largely remained unimplemented and have failed to substantially influence what actually happens in Indian classrooms. Weaknesses in the processes of implementation and governance of policies have resulted in a wide range of actual practices in the classrooms where multilingual diversity seems to have yielded to chaos. Under such conditions, teachers and field-level educational administrators have a difficult task in negotiating between the prescribed curricular and pedagogic practices and the real challenges they face in their classrooms. What actually gets transacted in the classrooms is often borne out of the ground-level contextual appreciation of the problems of individual children from linguistically diverse backgrounds. The teacher is not just another cog in the policy wheel; she is an active problem solver trying to deal with children's classroom learning in her own framework and understanding of the reality.

Multilingualism, Language Education Policy, and Inequality

In the 1991 Census Survey of India, more than 10,000 mother tongues were named. These were classified into 3,372 mother tongues out of which 1,576 were listed and the remaining 1,796 were grouped under the "other" category. The mother tongues are variously classified into 300 to 400 languages. Out of these, 22 are recognized as official languages listed in the VIIIth schedule of the Constitution of India. In addition, English is recognized as an associate official language. India ranks fourth in the world in terms of the number of languages (Skutnabb-Kangas, 2000). However, the uniqueness of Indian multilingualism goes beyond the presence of many languages in different spheres of social life of the masses.

The psychosocial dimensions of the patterns of language and communication are characterized by several special features (see Mohanty, 1991, 1994, 2006). Dynamics of the relationship between languages and their users, the organization of the languages in the Indian society, and their complex manifestations in the daily lives of the common people make the ethos of language use in India quite distinct from the dominant monolingual societies. With most people and communities using multiple languages in various domains of routine communication, multilingualism is widespread and languages tend to be maintained in situations of mutual contact. A high degree of maintenance of languages is possible because of the fluidity of perceived boundaries between languages, smooth and complementary functional allocation of languages into different domains of use, multiplicity of linguistic identities, and early multilingual socialization (Mohanty, Panda, & Mishra, 1999). With such characteristic features, multilingualism and maintenance of mother tongues remain a positive force for the individuals and communities clearly associated with cognitive and social benefits (Mohanty, 1994, 2003).

Despite such positive features of multilingualism and the maintenance norms, many Indian languages are endangered and most of them happen to be tribal languages.[1] For example, in 1971 Orissa was one of the most linguistically diverse states in India with 50 languages, including 38 tribal languages. Now, official documents of the Government of Orissa show the number of tribal languages in the state to be 22. Many languages coexist and are maintained in the Indian multilingual mosaic and, at the same time, many are also victims of discrimination, social and political neglect, and various forms of deprivation. There is a wide gap between the statuses of languages; though some are privileged with access to power and resources, others are marginalized and disadvantaged and, therefore,

Indian multilingualism has been described as a "multilingualism of the unequals" (Mohanty, 2004).

Linguistic discrimination and inequalities in India are formally rooted in the statutory and political processes of governance. With constitutional recognition to only 22 of the languages as official, most of the Indian languages are effectively kept out of the major domains of power. There is also specific official recognition of languages for many other public purposes, such as for promotion of culture and literature, and for use in limited spheres of governance. Such recognition is a reflection of the political power of the linguistic groups. The Constitutional amendment of 2003 conferring official language status to Bodo and Santali was possible due to the assertive language maintenance movements by the two tribal language communities. Other weak voices for similar recognition are ignored in the dynamics of power and politics. Despite statutory provisions for their preservation and development, minority and indigenous languages suffer from pervasive discrimination and neglect in all spheres of governance; tribal and other linguistic minorities are deprived of their voices and equality of opportunity for democratic participation. Yet another major basis of institutionalized inequality is the exclusion of most of the Indian languages, except those with an official status, from the system of schooling and formal education.

Languages in Indian Education: Policy and Practice

There is an explicit constitutional provision that the state and the local authorities shall endeavor to "provide adequate facilities for instruction in the mother tongue at primary stage of education to children belonging to minority groups" (Article 350A, Constitution of India, 1950). This provision remains unimplemented and till today there is no explicit policy with respect to languages in education or with respect to the protection and development of minority languages. The three-language formula proposed in 1957, and modified thereafter, recommended use of a regional language or mother tongue, Hindi, and/or English and an additional modern Indian language in all schools (see Mohanty, 2006, 2008a). However, because of a lack of clear distinction between mother tongue and regional language and ambiguities with respect to the relative places of Hindi and English, the three-language formula and subsequent policy formulations "have mostly remained political and ideological statements far removed from the actual practices, which were quite diverse" (Mohanty, 2006, p. 275). In fact, despite the rhetoric about the mother tongues and Indian languages, English has replaced Hindi as a compulsory second-language subject in most of the schools in India; in the majority of states, it is taught from Grade 1 in regional-language- or vernacular-medium government schools. Furthermore, widespread preference for English-medium education (mostly private schools) has relegated Hindi and other major regional and constitutional languages to lesser positions in education (Kurien, 2004). The recent National Curricular Framework (National Council of Educational Research and Training [NCERT], 2005) makes a strong plea for mother-tongue education, but the ground-level impact of this framework is conspicuously absent; mother tongues continue to be ignored for children's early education and schooling.

At present only 41 languages are used in schools either as the medium of instruction or as school subjects. The number of languages taught as school subjects actually declined from 81 in 1970 to 67, 58, 44, and 41, respectively, in 1976, 1978, 1990, and 1998 (Mohanty, 2006). The number of languages used as the medium of instruction has also declined. Between the years 1990 and 1998, the number of languages used as medium of instruction declined from 43 to 33 in primary grades (1 to 5); 31 to 25 in upper primary grades (6 and 7); 22 to 21 in secondary grades (8 to 10); and 20 to 18 in higher secondary grades (11 and 12). Thus, education in mother tongue is available only for children from a limited set of major languages, and the mismatch between home and school languages and neglect of mother tongues in schooling impose on the tribal (as well as other minority) children a subtractive language-learning experience that leads to high push-out rates and educational failure (Mohanty, 2008b). The negative consequences of such mismatch have been documented in several Indian studies (e.g., Jhingran, 2005; Mohanty, 1994, 2000, 2008b).

It should be noted that in the quasifederal structure of governance in the Indian union, education is a concurrent subject, which means that both the federal and the state governments exercise some control over education and the national recommendations are not binding on the states. This has added further to the chaos with respect to actual language education practices. The three-language formula, for example, is variously interpreted in different states leading to very different combinations of languages in school curricula. There are, however, broad common practices across the states: The state government schools use the major state language as the language of teaching for all children with few exceptions, and English is placed as a major language subject in government schools early in primary grades (from Grade 1 in most of the states). Besides, a rapidly increasing number of private schools all over the country are English-medium schools, where the language of teaching from the beginning of schooling is English. Mohanty (2006, 2008a) has discussed the various nominal forms of multilingual education in India in which mother tongues and other languages are variously placed in the formal school curriculum, and it is not uncommon for classroom activities to be informally transacted in different languages, particularly when the officially prescribed language of teaching is not the home language for some or most of the students. It is quite evident that the ground-level realities with respect to positioning of languages in Indian education are quite diverse, far removed from what is suggested as a policy framework in major statutory and policy documents, and appear to be chaotic and muddled in their confusing variety. With the growing significance of English and the rising demand for English-medium private schools predicated on the popular myth of English-medium superiority, the language situation in the Indian classrooms has become quite fluid. Mohanty (2006) has discussed the social implications of English-medium schooling in India questioning the popular myth of the English-medium superiority, but what happens at the ground level is far removed from the academic discourse on the role of English. As Shohamy (2006) points out, propagation of such myths about language influences *de facto* policies.

Negotiating the Double Divide

In essence, the local educational practices in India remain quite heterogeneous and unorganized and reflect the social macrostructure of the double divide referred to earlier. The Indian educational scenario is affected, on one hand, by the English–regional majority language divide or what Ramanathan (2005) calls the English–Vernacular divide and, on the other, by the Vernacular–Minority[2]/ Indigenous Language divide (which will be called Vernacular–Other divide, here-after). This double divide yields to a hierarchical pecking order in which English relegates Hindi and other major languages to positions of lesser significance and power, as the state majority languages push other languages out of education and major domains of use. The double divide is, however, variously resisted, contested, and negotiated in the society through individual and collective identity strategies. The divergent identity processes have contributed to the rising demand for English and English-medium schooling and to the progressive domain shrinkage of other languages in favor of English and, at the same time, have led to many instances of movement for the removal of English (and Hindi, in parts of the country). The processes of linguistic convergence and divergence in relation to English have led to disparate trends of *Anglicization* and *Sanskritization* of Indian languages.

The hierarchical relation of languages has affected the identity strategies of the speakers of dominated and indigenous languages (Mohanty, 2007b). In some cases, collective identity strategies have led to language movements, assertive maintenance, and revitalization of languages (such as Bodo and Santali). In others, individual identity strategies have resulted in passive acceptance of the dominance of major languages (Mohanty, 2007b), which is evident from the endorsement of the major languages for education and domains of economic sig-nificance and the indigenous language for in-group identity. Such identity strate-gies are also reflected in instances of linguistic identity without language (e.g., Oriya monolingual Konds with Kui[3] linguistic identity) and language without identity (e.g., the upper class English-educated Bhojpuri speakers who do not identify with Bhojpuri[4]). Often the use of indigenous and vernacular languages is associated with shame leading to denial of proficiency in these languages. Thus, there are complex social psychological reactions through which such hierarchical linguistic structure and the double divide are variously negotiated in the Indian society (Mohanty, 1991, 2007b). Ramanathan (2005) discusses several such processes of appropriation, nativization, and hybridization of English in the con-text of the English–vernacular divide in India. She focuses on the pedagogic prac-tices through which the English–vernacular divide is negotiated in college education in Gujarat in different types of Gujarati/Vernacular-medium and English-medium institutions. Ramanathan (2005) analyzes the divergent cultural models of English literacy transacted in schools using Gujarati or English as a medium (K-12) and relates them to the processes of contestation and negotiation of the English–vernacular divide.

This chapter has a focus on how the more complex double divide (English–vernacular and vernacular–Other) is variously addressed in the early school years (mostly primary grades, that is, Grades 1–5) by the teachers and the school-level educational administrators/managers (including school Headmasters/Principals and school supervisors/inspectors). Our observations are drawn from over three decades of work with schools and school teachers in tribal areas in Orissa, India, and from an ongoing study of an English-medium charity school in Delhi for children from lower class and lower middle-class families. We will discuss the school and classroom practices with respect to the teaching of English and then focus on teaching in vernacular-medium schools in tribal areas.

Negotiating Language Barriers in the Classroom

School Practices in Teaching English

English is taught in all schools in India beginning with early primary grades to children whose mother tongue is not English. However, there are gross differences in the nature of schools and in how English is placed in the school program. In private schools English is the formal language of teaching, and in government schools it is taught as a language subject only. In terms of the quality (and cost) of schools and the social strata they cater to, English-medium schools in India are quite heterogeneous (Mohanty, 2006). Apart from the very exclusive residential schools (such as the Doon School) where the cost of schooling in the primary grades is as high as 1,000,000 Indian Rupees (approximately US$20,000) per year, other English-medium schools can be broadly categorized as high-cost schools for the privileged social class (cost ranging from 100,000 to 300,000 Indian Rupees per year for nonresidential programs) and low-cost English-medium schools for the less privileged social class (cost from 5,000 to less than 20,000 Indian Rupees per year) with few exceptions.

Though all schools purport to promote Indian values and knowledge of Indian culture and traditions, the elite and upper class schools are distinctly Westernized in school practices and classroom teaching. The students are not allowed to use any language other than English in school premises, all classroom transactions are in English, and the physical culture of schools is Anglicized. In contrast, the low-cost English-medium schools for the lower social strata go for cosmetic Anglicization insisting on Western school uniform (usually with a tie and shoes) and behavioral routines (such as saying daily school prayers in English, greetings with "good morning," etc.). However, the classroom language transactions are much more nativized and hybridized—languages other than English are freely used even in teaching English.

As part of our ongoing study of different teaching and learning strategies in negotiating the English language as the formal medium of instruction in average-quality English-medium schools, we have some nonparticipant-observation-based information from Grades 4 and 5 in an English-medium charity school in Delhi run by a private trust with some government support. Children in this school are from middle or lower middle socioeconomic strata and the parents of most of the students do not have a high school education. All teachers, irrespective of the subjects they teach in the school, including English language teachers, said that they used "mostly Hindi in the class to make the students understand the subject matter," although they were aware that the formal medium of instruction in the school was English. Typically, the teacher would say something in English, mostly reciting or reading from a textbook, and quickly proceed to translate the text or elaborate the main theme in Hindi, often freely mixing the main content words in English with Hindi. The teachers justified this transgression of the school norm by referring to students' noncomprehension of English. One teacher explained the need to combine English with Hindi in the following words:

> Whenever we use only English in the class, after sometime, the students sit with blank faces with no participation or interaction waiting for the bell to ring for next period. However, if the same concept is explained by using Hindi, students not only look curious and alert but they also participate and interact more actively in the classroom. They give more input, raise doubts, ask questions, and gain some knowledge and understanding of the main ideas.

The teaching in this school mostly focuses on learning of the main content and memorization of the information that the teachers cover in the class. This is also the case with English language teachers who read a sentence or two from the English language textbook and then proceed to translate/elaborate in a code-mixed Hindi–English variety. The main information or content words are usually repeated in English, sometimes after a single translation in Hindi. It seems the requirement of the formal medium of instruction (and the language in which the students are to write their answers) weighs heavily in structuring the nature of code-mixing because the content knowledge or the main information is usually given in English words embedded into Hindi elaboration. The teachers also engage the students in drilling routines in which they ask a question and provide the model short one-sentence answer in English (with the key word in a high-pitched voice) that the students repeat in chorus. Thus, the teachers consider transaction of content information central to the lesson as more primary than the language of instruction.

In our Delhi English-medium school the teachers refer to the students' requirement to memorize the correct answers so that they can perform well in the examinations in which they are to write in English. As one of the teachers in this school said,

> We have to get the children to repeat the correct answer several times in the classroom so that they remember how to write an answer correctly in English. They do not study much in their homes. They cannot write correctly in English even if they understand. Their parents cannot teach them. So we have to do this in the classroom.

Interestingly, the consideration of limited English proficiency of students also affects the assessment practices in the school. An unwritten norm in the school is to set examination questions for the monthly class tests in a manner that minimizes writing of elaborate answers. The examination questions usually include many multiple-choice items requiring little writing and some direct questions mostly from the ones drilled in the classroom. Teachers justify this assessment strategy by saying that students' understanding of the concepts is more important than their ability to write in English, and it is necessary for them to do well in the early grades so that they can develop some confidence and motivation to perform better in higher grades. The school also does not have much ability to develop English-speaking skills. Outside the classroom, students freely speak in their own variety of Hindi. Few students occasionally participate in English debate/public-speaking competitions organized by other institutions, sometimes seeking help from the teachers or from others to write down and memorize their speeches.

The school program and classroom transactions in this school are found to be mostly focused on textbooks; teaching–learning practices are directed at learning and rote memorization of the main information content from the textbooks. With emphasis on structured examinations and lack of availability of other books particularly in the government schools, there is a general "textbook culture" in Indian schools (Kumar, 1987). This is also the case with the low-cost English-medium schools for the less privileged class. In these schools, as in the government schools, the textbook culture prevails also because parents cannot afford books for their children outside the prescribed texts. The English-medium schools generally choose among different textbooks available for specific grade levels covering the prescribed grade-level curriculum, and the parents buy the chosen ones from the market (or, quite often, from the schools). The quality of textbooks across schools is quite divergent and so is its cost. Usually the low-cost English-medium schools opt for textbooks of indifferent quality, which usually cost less. In the English-medium school that we observed, the textbooks are generally cheaper with poor quality paper, printing, illustrations, and fewer pages, compared to the ones used in other schools catering to the upper class. We examined the Science textbooks for Grades 4 and 5 in the school and found that the books are of lower quality than the one used in other English-medium schools in Delhi. The main focus in the books is on introducing the required concepts as per the prescribed government syllabus without much elaboration and additional information. There is also minimal focus on activities for stimulating students' interest and curiosity. Also, the exercises given at the end of each chapter were found to be simple and direct, requiring short textual answers and leaving little space for creative and nonstandard answers. A teacher described the school textbooks as "very easy books." Most of the teachers in the school are aware of the overall quality of the books, but justify their use; they believe that their students cannot cope with books of "higher standard" because of their poor socioeconomic background and low levels of education of the parents. One teacher admitted:

> In good quality English medium schools, teachers cover the basic concepts and leave the rest to the students and their parents who work with them to

develop better understanding. In science books there are project work for students. The parents help the children with the project work and explain it to them. The parents of our children are not educated. So they cannot help them with English books. We have to accept that.

The school system and the teachers recognize the need to scaffold the learning experience of their students in their mutual efforts to circumvent the English–vernacular divide. The divide, however, is more complex than a language divide; it is deeply rooted in the social macrostructure within which languages, schools, and social classes are themselves embedded. The power of English in instilling learning aspirations among students (to be empowered through it) is the cause, as well as consequence, of social class differences in the Indian society. At one level, the English language teaching and learning practices are informed by the vernacular as Ramanathan (2005, p. 87) points out:

> Medium of instruction, then, is only one social cog indexing very different social worlds, with divergent ways of producing and consuming knowledge. While the degree to which the Vernacular is embedded is relative, being more heightened in some contexts than in others, the fact remains that the Vernacular informs ELTL [English language teaching and learning] realities in a range of local ways in multilingual contexts that are not necessarily apparent in Anglophone countries.

At another level, the relationship between English and vernacular is itself socially constructed. Therefore, the manner and the processes through which this relationship is mediated are sensitive to the various other contextual conditions ("local ways"), including the social class background of the learners. The meaning and implications of the English–vernacular divide are quite different across different levels of social class. Differences are rooted in early socialization processes with different levels of material, and social and parental support for English in different social strata. In fact, it can be said that children from the privileged classes and those from the less privileged ones are already located in different sides of the English–vernacular divide by the time they enter formal schools—the former on the other side of the divide already with the early advantages of a home environment in which English is amply supported and the latter still trying to scale the divide because English is alien to their early experiences. The schools and teachers of this latter group have a difficult task in devising strategies for their students to negotiate the divide. The pedagogic practices in the English-medium schools for the less privileged are to be appreciated from the problem-solving perspective that the schools and teachers assume in recognition of resources and limitation of the students.

Teaching English to Tribal Children

The pedagogic challenges in English language teaching and learning in the case of students from the less privileged social classes discussed so far are difficult, but, at least, there is just the English–vernacular divide to negotiate, with some purpose and willingness to circumvent the divide. But the challenges are extremely formidable for children and their teachers who have to simultaneously negotiate the English–vernacular divide as well as the vernacular–Other divide and who find themselves struggling unwittingly with a foreign language like English twice removed from their social reality. The tribal children in India, who come to schools with an indigenous tribal language as their mother tongue and with very limited or no proficiency in the dominant language of school teaching, are taught English as a third language early in primary grades—from Grade 1 or 2, in most cases. The following discussion is based on our interactions with the teachers and observations of classroom transactions in Grades 4 and 5 in a number of Oriya-medium government schools, with a majority of Kui-mother-tongue Kond children in Kandhamal District and Saora-mother-tongue (Saora tribe) children in Gajapati District of Orissa (India). Our reflections here are partly based on over two decades of study till 2002. Then English was taught to these children from Grade 4 as in the rest of the government schools (now it is taught from Grade 3 in all Oriya-medium government schools in Orissa).

The Kond and Saora children with Kui and Saora mother tongues, respectively, come to schools with very limited proficiency in Oriya, which is the language of teaching for all government schools in Orissa. The mismatch between their home language and school language leads to large-scale push out (more than 50% of the tribal children entering Grade 1 are out of school by Grade 5) and educational failure (see Mohanty, 2008b, for a discussion of the language barrier for these children). Those who manage to reach Grade 4 have acquired some (generally below grade level) proficiency in Oriya. At Grade 4, English is introduced as a language subject. It should be pointed out that the English language has negligible presence in the tribal areas with occasional road and commercial signs written in English and almost no use of the language in the media or other forms of local communication. Therefore, the children have very little contact with English. The teachers have low competence in English, although they had English as a language subject through their high school (Grades 10–12). Most of the children are first-generation learners and their parents have no knowledge of English. Thus, it is not surprising that English is taught in the classrooms in the tribal areas of Kadhamal and Gajapati Districts in Oriya, sometimes mixed with Kui or Saora for greater clarity. Like the Delhi school discussed earlier, the teachers read from the text—a single word or a sentence at a time—and immediately translate the same and elaborate in simple Oriya occasionally using Kui/Saora (only when the teacher knows Kui/Saora). Children are engaged by the teacher in a lot of choral practices seeking to have the children memorize English alphabets and numbers in sequence, some words in English taken from the state government English textbook for the grade level and sometimes routine conversational exchanges (e.g., "My name is Baruna; my father's name is Dhani," etc.). The teachers ask the students to copy from the blackboard—initially single alphabets traced repeatedly while the alphabet names are spoken aloud, and then some words. In effect, the teaching practices in these schools are directed at symbolic efforts to meet the curricular requirement for English, without any serious attempt at teaching and learning of a foreign language.

It is generally accepted that not much can actually be achieved, as not much is expected. The official system also supports this lack of any substantive English learning for tribal children. Assessments are very loosely done and officially, even if a student may fail in English, he or she is considered suitable to move up to the next higher grade. The teachers, headmasters, and local school administrators as well as the parents and community members agree that there is not much to be expected from the teaching of English to the tribal children, not at least in the primary grades. A teacher in a residential school (Ashram School) for tribal children in a remote rural area near Phiringia in Kandhamal district (which was then called Phulbani district) says:

> Sir, these children do not even understand Oriya. What English will they understand? We somehow manage by using sometimes Kui and sometimes Oriya. Luckily they are not failed if they fail in English.

Pedagogues of English in Orissa, who have contributed to designing the school curriculum and English textbooks, often blame the teachers for giving up too soon and not doing enough to follow the desired teaching methods. Perhaps one can argue that, given the right kind of teaching–learning support, English is achievable for these children. But it should be noted that optimal teaching–learning conditions remain elusive in the kind of ground-level reality of the abject limited resource conditions of these schools for tribal children—insufficient number of teachers in almost every school (a single teacher teaching two to three grades at a time is quite common), lack of training in language teaching methodology, and generally impoverished conditions of schools—to point to only some of the factors contributing to poor quality.

School Practices in Teaching (Vernacular) Language to Linguistic Minority Children

In 1979, when a major research project of the first author on bilingualism among the Konds started in Phulbani (now Kandhamal) district, the system of school education projected a very dismal picture particularly for the Kui-speaking Kond children in parts of the district. Oriya, the majority language in the state of Orissa, was the medium of teaching; almost all the teachers were from nontribal communities and hardly knew any Kui.[5] The Kui-speaking children had some but limited and inadequate exposure to Oriya. The teachers, both nontribal and tribal, complained of the tribal children's problem of noncomprehension due to very limited proficiency in Oriya, the language of teaching, and most of them believed in the limited learning potential of the tribal children. This was also equally true of other tribal children in Orissa, including the Saora children in Gajapati. Following is a typical statement often heard from the teachers in the area, narrated by an Oriya nontribal teacher in Baida Ashram School (residential school for tribal children) in Phulbani district:

> these Adivasi (tribal) children cannot learn. They do not even understand what we tell them in the classroom. Most of them do not know Oriya at all. Anyway, we are here to do our duty and we try our best to teach them.

The attitude of the teachers in the area has changed considerably during the past three decades. There seems to be a better understanding and appreciation of the issues in the education of tribal children, perhaps due to the cumulative effects of several government programs and a greater level of awareness among the teachers. Appointment of a larger number of teachers from the tribal communities has also contributed to this positive development.

Greater participation of tribal teachers in the processes of planning teaching strategies at the school level and also sometimes at the level of policy formulation has brought appreciable changes in school practices. The teachers who speak the tribal mother tongues seem to have a better appreciation of this difficulty for the tribal children; they themselves have somehow made it through the system of education in a major language, which was not their mother tongue. Mohanty (2007a) in his introduction to the Asian edition of *Bilingualism or NOT* (Skutnabb-Kangas, 1984) has cited the story of a Halvi-speaking tribal teacher who had dropped out of the Hindi classroom he did not understand as a child. He later became a teacher and was present among many other tribal teachers in a multilingual education workshop in 2006 in Raipur, Chhattisgarh. As the workshop was trying to persuade the participants for mother-tongue-based multilingual education for tribal children, many teachers pulled out various teaching–learning materials prepared by them in tribal languages for use in their classrooms. The materials were mostly handwritten (some with pictures and illustrations) and some were also printed (at teacher's own cost); they included stories, songs, number rhymes, and many other innovative materials that they had created. These teachers appreciated the tribal children's difficulty in negotiating the language divide between Hindi, the language of teaching, and the mother tongues, and they did not need the workshop to convince them that early education in and for strengthening the mother tongue is an effective strategy to get around the vernacular–Other divide. Even without any official policy or sanction for use of the tribal mother tongues and, of course, without any formal exposure to the principles of multilingual education, they improvised their teaching because of personal experience, as pupils and teachers, in negotiating the vernacular–Other divide.

Caught in the gulf between policy and practice, between what is prescribed by others and what is required for the children, teachers do innovate and find some solutions, even if not always the best ones. Such solutions and strategies address the immediate issues and problems that they face and, often, defy the more general policy positions. In December 2006, the first author, Mohanty, visited a primary-grade classroom in a school (Bhaliapani U.P. School) in Kandhamal district in preparation for a project on multilingual education in some tribal schools in

Orissa. The class teacher surprised him by recalling his name from a Kui language primary-level textbook *(Badu Endina* printed in Oriya script) that was developed for the government of Orissa in the year 2000 by some teachers working with his (Mohanty's) guidance. The text was printed in 2001 but it was never used or circulated because the government policy of introducing tribal mother tongue in primary grades had changed by then.[6] When Mohanty wondered how the teacher could know about the Kui book, because he was not a part of the team of teachers who worked on the book project, the teacher pulled the book from one of the children in the classroom and showed it to him. In fact the books were there with every single child in the classroom. The books looked much worn out and overused. It turned out that some of the teachers in the school felt that introducing the Kui-speaking children to literacy through this book in their language, printed in Oriya script, would be an effective strategy. Four years earlier, they had managed with some influence in the government office to get some copies of the printed text that were lying in the office store without any use. The copies of the book, which the teachers had managed to smuggle out, had since then changed hands from one to the next batch of students in the school. The prescribed Oriya language book of the government (which is given free to each tribal child) was being taught formally in the school, but the Kui book was also used to prop up the emergent literacy initiative in Oriya.

Interestingly, teachers in some schools in Gajapati district in Orissa also used a similar book *(Yerai Yerai)* in Saora language (developed earlier by a team including the second author of this chapter under the same government program). In both these contexts, teachers were conscious of the formidable language divide for the tribal children in forced submersion programs of schooling and had found some way of dealing with it in their own ways. In these instances, the teachers in the two areas in Orissa may have chanced upon an available resource to support their initiatives, but even otherwise, they do engage in routine classroom practices that show their constant resistance to the language divide deeply rooted in weak, covert policies and official recommendations. Instances of classroom improvisation in negotiating the language divide are not uncommon.

We will briefly look at some general classroom practices in the context of tribal children's education in the forced submersion programs. Again, the observations are drawn from the Oriya-medium schools in Kandhamal and Gajapati Districts in Orissa (India), particularly those with a large proportion of tribal language (Kui/Saora) mother-tongue children. At one level, the classroom transactions in the Oriya-medium government schools for the Kui/Saora-speaking tribal children resemble the ones in the Delhi English-medium school we have described earlier. Oriya and Kui/Saora are mixed as freely in these schools in Kandhamal/Gajapati Districts as English and Hindi in the Delhi school, and in both the contexts the main content words are taken from the target language, Oriya in Kandhamal/Gajapati and English in Delhi, embedded in translation, simplification, and elaboration in the pupils' mother tongue. A common strategy seems to trigger the classroom practices in all these settings: use the pupils' developed language to prop up comprehension in the target language. However, unlike the school in

Delhi, those in the tribal schools in Orissa are linguistically diverse. Children vary in the degree of exposure to and proficiency in Oriya and occasionally, depending on the specific location of a school, there may be some Oriya mother-tongue children in the class also. Adding to the diversity, proficiency in the tribal language of the area varies from one teacher to another. Tribal teachers with Kui/Saora mother tongue are proficient in both the languages. Their strategy is to optimally use the tribal language, as well as Oriya, depending on the composition of the classroom and also the specific pupil(s) being addressed. The hybrid variety of code-mixed language, however, pivoted around the main content word(s) in the school's target language, Oriya. For explanation and elaboration, Kui/Saora and simple Oriya are used sometimes in a simultaneous translation mode (same meaning expressed in two languages one after the other) and sometimes in parallel forms (some ideas in the tribal language followed by others in Oriya). Such concurrent use is more common when the linguistic composition of the classrooms is diverse. Teachers seem to be aware of an emergent bilingual child's relative proficiency in Oriya and Kui/Saora at any point in time. They would ask questions in Kui/Saora or in Oriya depending on their own assessment of a child's proficiency. Often the children also engage in "translanguaging" (García, 2009), drawing from their mother tongue and school language and code-mixing for effective communication in the classroom with a bilingual teacher and with other children who know both the languages. Thus, though both Oriya and tribal language are used in classroom transactions, the bilingual tribal teachers contextually modulate the nature of the bilingual code-mixed and code-switched communication. Quite often, when the teachers feel that some concept is not clearly communicated through expressions in one language, they draw on a more commonly occurring expression from another language. Thus, it can be said that translanguaging classroom practices are often used strategically for effective communication.

How does the nontribal Oriya monolingual teacher negotiate the classroom linguistic diversity? As we have observed, most teachers have limited proficiency in Kui/Saora language, and therefore, cannot engage in bilingual transactions like their tribal counterparts. They usually explain and elaborate classroom concepts using a simple local variety of Oriya and engaging the pupils in a lot of choral repetitions of the focal information. Often, these teachers "collaborate," with some proficient bilingual tribal pupils in classroom transactions inviting them to fill in on behalf of the teacher. The bilingual child in such cases proceeds to "teach" repeating after the teacher and offering some clarification in Kui/Saora for the benefit of the other Kui/Saora-speaking children who fail to understand the teacher. The following is an example of such collaborative teaching in a Grade 2 classroom in Biragada U.P. School in Kandhamal:

Teacher (T):   (asking a question to Student 1) *barasha pani keunthu ase re?*
              "Tell me, where does rain water come from?"
Student 1(S1): akasha ru.
              "From the sky"

T: *akasha ru na baadala ru, re?*
            "From the sky or from the cloud, tell me?"
S1:   (remains silent)
T: *akasha ru na <u>baadala</u> ru?*
            "From the sky or from the cloud?" (With emphasis on the word for cloud)
S1:   *baadala ru.*
            "From the cloud"
T: *akasha aau baadal bhitare kana tafaata janichhu kire?*
            "Do you know the difference between sky and cloud?"
S1:   (looks confused)
T: (turning to S2, a Kui–Oriya bilingual child) *tora bhai ku tikie bujhei de re.*
            "Explain (it) to your brother (classmate)"
S2:   (proceeds to explain in Kui, using Kui words for sky and cloud)
T: (To S1) *bujhilu re?*
            "did you understand?"
S1:   (nods his head)
T: *achha*
            "Good"

Sometimes, teachers ask the students from a higher grade to explain some concepts to younger ones. Such collaborative practices are used for the tribal, as well as Oriya language, depending on which child needs further clarification. Calling upon the students from higher grades has become a common classroom practice in tribal areas of Orissa, as very often multiple grades share the same classroom with a single teacher. In multigrade classrooms students do engage in a lot of cross-linguistic communication between older and younger students and such mutual helping is encouraged so that the single teacher would have time and space to attend to children from another grade in the same room.

The classroom practices in the Oriya-medium schools for the tribal children are noticeably multilingual and multicultural. Teachers as well as students draw from different languages (and cultures) and from the multilingual resources in the classroom (in the form of the presence of students with different levels of proficiency in one or the other language). Communicative practices in such contexts involve effective use of nativized, hybridized, and translanguage varieties, and sometimes simplified registers of the target language to support students' learning. Often a teacher also draws from the tribal mother tongues or the familiar language and also from children's familiar cultural experiences and everyday concepts to develop understanding of classroom concepts. For example, in Seranga Ashram School (residential school) for the Saora tribal children in Gajapati District, the mathematics teacher in Grade 1 introduced the universal number system, which the school follows by referring first to Saora number words followed by the Oriya symbol for the corresponding number. The correspondence between a number word and the quantity was established initially by using Saora number words that the children were already familiar with. The teacher showed a flash card with the picture of one mango on one side and its symbol in Oriya on the other and read it as *aboy* (the word for number one in Saora). He followed a similar practice for all other numbers up to 10. He used the Saora words to teach the relationship between the quantity and the symbols. Each time the number corresponding to the number of items in the picture is uttered in the class (by the teacher or students), the teacher would show the reverse side of the flash card to show the number symbol (in Oriya). One excerpt from the classroom observation is presented here:

T (Teacher):	(showing the picture side of the flash card) *Keteta amba achhi?* "How many mangos are there?"
S (Student) 1:	*Aboy* "One"
T:	(the teacher did not mention the Oriya name for one, that is, *eka*, but went on to show the flash card for three) *Ethire keteta amba achhi kahila?* "How many mangoes are there?"
S2:	*Yagi* "Three" (in Saora)
T:	(showing another flash card with the picture of five mangoes) *Ethire keteta achhi kahila?* "Say, how many are there in this card?"
Ss:	(children started counting in Saora) *Unji* "Five" (in Saora, in chorus).

(The teacher then proceeds to show the flash cards for the other numbers from 1 to 10)

In the next three to four sessions, the teacher drew on the blackboard a number of items and asked the students to write the corresponding Oriya number symbol on their slates. This method was used to introduce writing of all numbers from 1 to 10. After nearly 10 sessions, the teacher introduced Oriya words for the numbers. The Saora number words were used in initial sessions to introduce Oriya number words. The teacher discouraged the children from using Saora number words once he introduced the Oriya number words. In three of the subsequent seven sessions (which were observed) the teacher told the children "Say only Oriya numbers; if you use Saora words in the class, you will never learn Oriya numbers." The teacher used children's familiarity with the Saora counting and their cultural experiences to support learning of the Oriya numbers and symbols. Evidently, the teacher used the principles of bridging in these sessions.

In the absence of any agency in the formulation and implementation of language policies, and systematic training in second language or third/foreign language teaching pedagogy, the teachers are left, at best, to themselves to do something meaningful that can qualify as formal teaching–learning activities in their views. This has led to development of numerous highly individualized pedagogic practices, which do not explicitly contest, but negotiate between the desirable and what is feasible in such a context (Panda, 2006). As many of the teachers in tribal area schools are not from tribal communities, they have very little familiarity with the children's language and culture. The requisite cognitive processes in these classrooms, therefore, have to be necessarily distributed among teacher, tribal students, and the cultural artifacts. As was noted in the earlier discussions of classroom processes, the more successful nontribal teachers take advantage of the classroom diversity and children's cultural knowledge to coordinate the classroom activities and create conditions for peer learning and collaborative learning. With the help of peers and the students from senior grades, these teachers develop the transactional processes. Some of these interventions by teachers are Vygotskyan in some sense, though they may sometimes fail to create a zone of proximal development for the children (Panda, 2004, 2006). This is primarily because of the lack of formal training or understanding to organize and scaffold children's learning. The classroom practices like the ones we have discussed earlier do help the teachers communicate and transact in the classrooms under difficult circumstances, particularly with children from the lower social strata and indigenous communities. But they remain minimalist in teaching quality partly because the teachers have not been trained for effective multilingual and multicultural education and also partly because their agency has never been explicitly acknowledged.

At a formal level (and top-down practice), the schools for the tribal children are monolingual in the major language of the state. But in actual practice, classrooms are clearly, if not systematically, multilingual. From the top-down perspective, the classroom practices of the teachers can be seen as subversive. When this is pointed out to the teachers, their views are different. Many teachers defend the linguistic (and cultural) hybridity of the classrooms as inevitable and necessary in the real-life local context. For them, this "improvisation" facilitates learning in the medium of instruction and they do not see anything wrong with this practice. In other words, ground-level classroom practices are directed at effective negotiation of the vernacular–Other language divide. Unfortunately, the language education policy fails to take note of the language divide for development of structured pedagogy for effective classroom learning in multilingual contexts. The monolingual policy in a multilingual social context fails to acknowledge the necessary links between children's home language and the formal language of teaching. The classroom diversity entails hybridity as necessary for effective communication and learning. As García, Skutnabb-Kangas, and Torres-Guzmán (2006, p. 37) suggest,

> The hybridity that emerges from the multilingual students and parents "in between" or "borderland" experiences must be brought out into the open and acknowledged as different and important worldviews, and as an important pedagogical tool.

It seems the teachers' classroom practices in the schools of Kandhamal and Gajapati Districts do point to a variety of pedagogical tools contextually relevant and necessary for effective negotiation of the vernacular–Other divide.

Conclusion: Is the Teacher Just Another Cog in the Policy Wheel?

García et al. (2006, p. 25) point to "the tension between state imposed homogenization and real life multilingualism" as an issue that affects the future of multilingual schooling. At one level, the seminal statutory discourse concerning language policy in Indian education is clearly pluralistic in its promises for multilingual schooling. But as one enters the actual state practices the paradox is glaring; what is handed-down as the model for actual practices is superficially multilingual, at best. Languages do get into school curricula, mostly as language subjects and not as media of classroom teaching. The nominal forms of multilingual education fail to take note of the real-life multilingualism and classroom linguistic diversity. The homogenizing impact of the gap between the ideological policy discourse and school-level implementation is visible through two major state practices: (1) English has clearly emerged as the major language in schools both as a language of teaching and as a language subject, and (2) the dominated minority and indigenous *other* languages have been almost completely neglected in schools contributing to educational failure for a large segment of the Indian population.

The state practices have perpetuated the societal double divide, one, between English and vernacular languages, and the other, between the vernaculars and *other* languages. In the classroom reality of linguistic diversity and real-life multilingualism, the teachers negotiate the gap between what is handed over to them as state-prescribed teaching objectives with respect to languages and what they experience and confront in the classrooms. Our discussion of the classroom practices in teaching of English as an official medium of instruction (as in the Delhi English-medium school for the children from the lower social class) and as a school subject (in the vernacular-medium schools in Orissa for the tribal children) and of Oriya in submersion programs of vernacular-medium schools in Orissa shows that the teachers are not uncritical bystanders passively acquiescent of the state practice; in their own ways, they resist and contest the state policy or rather, in the Indian context, its absence and injustice by default. It is quite clear that the agency of the teachers in the classrooms makes them the final arbiter of the language education policy and its implementation. They confront the challenges of the societal language divide and state policy by improvising and creating their own space in the chain of policy and implementation. These strategies of improvisations and negotiation may not always stand the critical pedagogic scrutiny, but they do show the resistance of the teachers and their willingness to have a creative space in their classrooms. The actual classroom strategies and practices of the teachers do expose the weaknesses and ruptures in the policy wheel; they show that what is handed down to them as state policy is unjust, inadequate, and cannot be implemented, given the classroom realities that they confront. Taking note and responding to the teachers' agency is a key issue for language policy in Indian education.

Discussion Questions

1   What do Mohanty, Panda, and Pal mean by the English–vernacular divide and the vernacular–Other divide? How do these two different situations affect language education policy in India?

2   This chapter points to a three-tiered hierarchy of languages in India, with English at the top, the regional majority language or vernacular in the middle, and indigenous languages at the bottom. Are all languages completely equal in your context, or are some more powerful than others? If all languages are not equal, which is typically the case, draw a diagram showing a hierarchy of languages in your context from "top" to "bottom." How does such a hierarchy affect language education policy in your context?

3   What are the challenges and opportunities presented by English-medium schools in India? How do teachers negotiate the classroom situation?

4   Describe the challenges of educating tribal children in India. What does official policy say about their education? What happens in practice? Give specific examples from Mohanty's paper.

5   In your country/local context, in what ways does the English language serve as a gateway and/or barrier to opportunities? Is it important to know English in order to succeed in school? In what ways are students who do not speak English disadvantaged, if at all?

6   In your context, do teachers ever use more than one language in instruction (if you are unsure of local practices, go visit several schools—particularly those including culturally and linguistically diverse students)? Do students use more than one language when they are learning? If the answer is "yes" to either of these questions, how are the different languages used and for what purposes? For example, is the language spoken by the children used to clarify directions or for discipline, or instead for deeper instructional aims such as biliteracy development? Are there clear boundaries between languages or is language use more fluid?

Notes

1   The Indigenous or aboriginal communities in India are officially called "tribes" (*div si*) and are listed as "scheduled tribes" which are identified on the basis of "distinct culture and language," "geographical isolation," "primitive traits," "economic backwardness," and "limited contact with the outgroups" and also, sometimes, on political considerations. The Anthropological Survey of India, in its *People of India* project, has identified 635 tribal communities of which 573 are so far officially notified as Scheduled Tribes. Here the term "tribe" (rather than "Indigenous peoples") is used specifically in the Indian context in its formal/official and neutral sense.

2   It should be noted that no language is a national majority language in India. Speakers of Hindi, which is the largest linguistic group, constitute 38.93% of the national population.

3 Kui is the indigenous language of the Kond tribe in Kandhamal District of Orissa. In parts of the district there has been a shift of Kui in favor of Oriya, the state dominant language. The Oriya monolingual Konds in these parts of Kandhamal still identify with Kui language calling themselves "Kui people."

4 Upper class Bhojpuri speakers often assume a superordinate identity as Hindi speakers.

5 There was an incentive package (financial bonus and salary increase) for all teachers (and other government officials) to learn and clear an examination in the tribal languages including Kui. Many teachers successfully cleared the test but hardly maintained any proficiency in Kui and, hence, were unable to engage even in routine conversation in Kui with their pupils. The system still continues with somewhat better effect in recent years partly because of the influence of larger number of teacher colleagues from the Kond community now appointed in most of the schools in the district.

6 Multilingual education, called MLE, was again introduced by the Government of Orissa in the year 2007.

References

García, O. (2009). Education, multilingualism and translanguaging in the 21st century. In A. Mohanty, M. Panda, R. Phillipson, & T. Skutnabb-Kangas (Eds.), *Multilingual education for social justice: Globalising the local* (pp. 128–145). New Delhi: Orient Blackswan.

García, O., Skutnabb-Kangas, T., & Torres-Guzmán, M. (2006). Weaving spaces and (de)constructing ways for multilingual schools: The actual and the imagined. In O. García, T. Skutnabb-Kangas, & M. Torres-Guzmán (Eds.), *Imagining multilingual schools: Languages in education and glocalization* (pp. 3–47). Clevedon, Avon: Multilingual Matters.

Jhingran, D. (2005). *Language disadvantage: The learning challenge in primary education.* Delhi: APH Publishers.

Kumar, K. (1987). Origins of India's "textbook culture". *Occasional Papers on History and Society, XLVII*, 1–32.

Kurien, J. (2004, April 30). The English juggernaut: Regional medium schools in crisis. *The Times of India*, New Delhi.

Mohanty, A. K. (1991). Social psychological aspects of languages in contact in multilingual societies. In G. Misra (Ed.), *Applied social psychology in India* (pp. 54–66). New Delhi: Sage.

Mohanty, A. K. (1994). *Bilingualism in a multilingual society: Psycho-social and pedagogical implications.* Mysore: Central Institute of Indian Languages.

Mohanty, A. K. (2000). Perpetuating inequality: The disadvantage of language, minority mother tongues and related issues. In A. K. Mohanty & G. Misra (Eds.), *Psychology of poverty and disadvantage* (pp. 104–117). New Delhi: Concept.

Mohanty, A. K. (2003). Multilingualism and multiculturalism: The context of psycholinguistic research in India. In U. Vindhya (Ed.), *Psychology in India: Intersecting crossroads* (pp. 35–53). New Delhi: Concept.

Mohanty, A. K. (2004, July 13–15). Multilingualism of the unequals: The "killer language" and anti-predatory strategies of minority mother tongues. Keynote address, International Conference on Multilingualism, South African Applied Linguistics Association, University of the North, South Africa, July 13–15, 2004.

Mohanty, A. K. (2006). Multilingualism of the unequals and predicaments of education in India: Mother tongue or other tongue? In O. García, T. Skutnabb-Kangas, & M. Torres-Guzmán (Eds.), *Imagining multilingual schools: Languages in education and glocalization* (pp. 262–283). Clevedon, Avon: Multilingual Matters.

Mohanty, A. K. (2007a). Introduction to this edition. In T. Skutnabb-Kangas (Ed.), *Bilingualism or Not: The education of minorities* (pp. xvii–xxvi). New Delhi: Orient Longman.

Mohanty, A. K. (2007b). Multilingual socialization and negotiation of identities in contact between multilingual adults and communities: Social psychological processes. Plenary Talk, The Fifth International Conference on Third Language Acquisition and Multilingualism, University of Stirling, Scotland.

Mohanty, A. K. (2008a). Multilingual education in India. In J. Cummins & N. H. Hornberger (Eds.), *Encyclopedia of language and education* (Vol. 5, 2nd ed.). *Bilingual education* (pp. 165–174). New York: Springer.

Mohanty, A. K. (2008b). Perpetuating inequality: Language disadvantage and capability deprivation of tribal mother tongue speakers in India. In W. Harbert (Ed.), *Language and poverty* (pp. 102–124). Clevedon, Avon: Multilingual Matters.

Mohanty, A. K., Panda, S., & Mishra, B. (1999). Language socialization in a multilingual society. In T. S. Saraswathi (Ed.), *Culture, socialization and human development* (pp. 125–144). New Delhi: Sage.

National Council of Educational Research and Training (NCERT). (2005). *National Curriculum Framework 2005*. New Delhi: Author.

Panda, M. (2004). Culture and mathematics: A case study of Saoras. In K. Chanana (Ed.), *Transformative links between higher education and basic education: Mapping the field* (pp. 119–132). New Delhi: Sage.

Panda, M. (2006). Mathematics and tribal education. *Economic and Political Weekly, XLI*(2), 14–26.

Ramanathan, V. (2005). *The English-Vernacular divide: Postcolonial language politics and practice*. Clevedon, Avon: Multilingual Matters.

Shohamy, E. (2006). *Language policy: Hidden agendas and new approaches*. London: Routledge.

Skutnabb-Kangas, T. (1984). *Bilingualism or Not: The education of minorities*. Clevedon, Avon: Multilingual Matters.

Skutnabb-Kangas, T. (2000). *Linguistic genocide in education—or worldwide diversity and human rights?* Mahwah, NJ: Lawrence Erlbaum.

Chapter 14

Chilean Literacy Education Policies and Classroom Implementation

Viviana Galdames and Rosa Gaete

> "Reading and writing are important at school because they are important outside of it, and not the other way around."
>
> (Emilia Ferreiro)

Introduction

Chilean education was severely interrupted during the 17 years of dictatorship. After the return to democracy in 1990, the new government developed educational policies that especially targeted the teaching of Spanish language and literacy. These policies targeted thousands of schools located in poor areas.

Chilean literacy teaching has always followed traditional methodologies for reading and writing focused on a syllabic approach, wherein children start out reading syllables: "*ma-me-mi-mo-mu*," and so on. In fact, Chilean educators are responsible for the first popular reading *cartilla* [primer or first reader] in Latin America. Similarly, in 1884, the Chilean Claudio Matte published his *Silabario Ojo*. And, the *Silabario Hispanoamericano,* from which most children in Latin America have learned to read and write since 1948, was authored by a Chilean named Adrian Dufflocq Galdames. These reading primers focused on the decoding of syllables, equating learning to read with learning to decode syllables.

Reacting to the poor results of Chilean students in the area of language and literacy, educational policies since the return to democracy have focused on how to change this traditional methodology. This chapter focuses on one such transformative literacy teaching policy mandated by the Chilean Ministry of Education. First we describe the policy itself and then detail the professional development program that was carried out to help with policy implementation. Through a series of interviews with teachers involved in the professional development program, we examine how teachers are far from passive in their transformation of literacy practices in Chile. Teachers never fully adopt the policies and practices, but by interpreting them through their own experiences and beliefs, transform them. The chapter makes the point that teachers are never just passive participants and that their classrooms become laboratories for experimentation and transformation of policy.

Transformative Language and Literacy Policy: The Content

Traditional Chilean reading and writing pedagogy has failed to produce competent readers and writers. At the national level, 40% of students do not achieve the expected learning level in language or communication after completing the first cycle of primary school.

In 2004, Chile's Ministry of Education initiated a policy to support the transformation of literacy pedagogy by focusing on strengthening continuous teacher education in language, literacy, and mathematics (*LEM: Lectura, Escritura y Matemáticas*). For the reading and writing component, the policy named the following principles:

- The ability to participate in today's society—in its social, educational, cultural, and political dimensions—depends to a large extent on the functional development that citizens attain in written language. A lack of command of this communicative mode results in discrimination and sociocultural marginalization and makes it impossible to access important sources of information and knowledge.

- Knowing how to read and write involves more than just the technical execution of reading and writing. The concept of "literacy" emphasizes reflection, critical thinking, and holistic communication, inclusive of oral language (Cassany, 2006; Ferreiro, 2001).

- The balanced approach to teaching literacy has been shown to be most effective in developing quality literacy skills in all children, particularly those whose environment is characterized by an oral culture rather than a written one (Alliende & Condemarín, 2002; Chauveau, 2000, 2001; Condemarín, Galdames, & Medina, 2004; Linuesa & Domínguez, 1999; Pressley, 1999; Snow, Griffin, & Burns, 2000; Tompkins, 2001; Walqui & Galdames, 2005). The balanced approach includes both constructive ways of using literacy, alongside some structured literacy skills such as decoding.

- Children growing up in a context with a rich functional presence of written language, either at home or in their extended cultural environment, start school with preconceived notions about reading. These are powerful facilitators for the systematic process of developing literacy (Ferreiro, 1992; Freire, 1988). On the contrary, most children who live in rural areas, in marginalized urban contexts, or in indigenous rural communities, enter school without having constructed these notions. As a result, it is the responsibility of the school system and of teachers to develop in them an awareness of the functions of written language and of the multiple objectives that people have when they read and write.

- Regardless of the cultural differences derived from contact with a literate environment, all children can learn to be efficient readers of the world from very early on. This concept of "reading the world" (Freire, 1988) refers to the ability of children to interpret and understand their surroundings. For instance, they can anticipate events based on certain signs that they have learned to decipher through their family experience: "If my mother shuts the door brusquely, she may be tense and in a bad mood after work"; "If she puts on my wool cap and wraps me up to keep me warm, she will certainly take me for a walk"; "If the wind blows from a given direction, it will rain in a few hours," etc.

- Methods based solely on the learning of letters, syllables, or isolated words do not make use of students' prior knowledge or the comprehension potential which children bring when they enter school.
- Children must learn to read with whole texts and, therefore, discover meaning via several strategies, similar to the ones they use to "read the world": anticipating, interpreting, asking questions, and so on. In the context of that effort to understand a meaningful text, children should also be taught to identify syllables and letters and to decode words and sentences in a contextualized manner.
- All children, including the poor, have learning capabilities and possibilities.

A balanced literacy approach was identified as the best pedagogy for achieving the principles outlined above. In a balanced literacy approach, the emphasis is not only on teaching isolated reading (phonological awareness and decoding) and writing skills (orthography, calligraphy, syntax), but also on having students construct meaning of what they read and write. To do so, the teachers embark on the following.

- Provide children with complete (rather then abridged) texts that are meaningful for them and related to their cultures, experiences, and interests. The texts are also linked to different functions of language, so children read stories, letters, poems, recipes, news, posters, and so on. After contact with interesting and meaningful texts, children experience the need to make the code of written language their own, in order to facilitate the construction of meaning. In this way, phonological awareness and decoding skills develop in contexts that endow them with meaning and functionality.
- Focus on helping students develop different metacognitive reading strategies according to the type of text, its level of complexity, and the purpose for reading.
- Develop strategies for different moments in the act of reading—before, during, and after reading a text with students; and, develop strategies for the stages of the writing process—planning, first draft, revision, and rewriting.
- Emphasize oral communication, as well as reading and writing. Oral communication, which was disregarded for years, is given an important academic role.
- Create flexible interactional spaces within the classroom by employing different work modalities: in groups, partner work, individual work, in front of the whiteboard, in a circle, and so on.

The Professional Development Component

The key component of the LEM (Lectura, Escritura y Matemáticas) policy, and its accompanying balanced literacy approach, has been an innovative teacher professional development model that serves to familiarize the teachers with the organizing principles of literacy instruction and the methodology of balanced literacy. It addresses both theory and practice. The study workshops are based on concrete lessons, experiences, and material that may be used in the classroom, direct assistance by a teacher with more expertise, and implementation of didactic units. These didactic units cover the curriculum requirements in terms of the development of reading and writing.

The innovative teacher professional development model centers on having a consulting teacher work with teachers outside of classrooms for sustained support. Because continuous teacher education requires an adequate articulation between theory and practice, much of teacher learning can only be achieved through modeling and feedback on practice. Consulting teachers are selected because they are good teachers and come from a similar school. Because conceptions of literacy and the balanced literacy approach promoted in Chilean educational policy are new to the country's teachers, consulting teachers also need support. They are involved in biweekly workshops led by a team of language and literacy specialists from the university.[1]

Consulting teachers also led study workshops—spaces for reflection, reading, discussion, and practicing strategies to teach literacy in non-traditional and transformative ways. Consulting teachers devote part of the 20 hours per week of their contract to directing these study workshops in three public schools of a given municipality and spend the rest of their time visiting the teachers in their classrooms to model methods or to observe what the teachers do. Once the visit is complete, a pedagogical conversation or dialogue between the consulting teacher and the schoolteacher takes place. This dialogue is based on observational guidelines that contain a series of criteria about teacher work. After this process ends, the consulting teachers develop feedback workshops based on their observations, in which they create a space for joint reflection with all participants, focusing on the weakest aspects of the teaching and the progress observed.

The consulting teacher, a peer with greater experience who works in and out of classrooms, has turned out to be the most important aspect of this professional development plan. One of the teachers explained how the consulting teacher's practical experience and ability to model was most helpful[2]:

> The consulting teacher does not teach us; she works with us at school as if we were having a conversation, and we can ask her about theoretical concepts that we do not understand. She also gives us examples that are useful because they are activities she puts into practice, and that shows.

The fact that the consulting teacher was a peer was also important because the teachers felt supported by one of their own, instead of by university specialists. One of them said: "With this consulting teacher we have more confidence to tell her that we do not get something, because she understands us and explains using simple words."

The professional development program for consulting teachers and other teachers is based on a set of modules especially designed for the program, called the "LEM Language Didactic Units." These consist of two work notebooks—a study booklet for schoolteachers, which includes two weeks of lesson planning following the balanced approach, and a booklet for each student, which includes activities that he or she must complete.

Impact of Professional Development: Beliefs and Discourse, Adaptations, and Resistance

The balanced literacy policy, and its accompanying professional development program, has had some successes, although it has also faced resistance, as well as teachers' adaptations. Two aspects of literacy teaching in Chile have changed somewhat through the professional development plan—a change in belief systems and a transformation of teacher discourse. Chilean teachers often felt that students with impoverished backgrounds had little to contribute to schooling, but through the professional development program, teachers started to believe in the strengths of the students' homes. For example, one second-grade teacher said: "Now that I have changed my methodology and my students express themselves and participate more in my lessons, I realize that they know many things they have learned outside of school, and I had no idea of that."

Changes were especially evident in how educators spoke about the children and their own teaching practices. Not only did they express the strength of the students' homes but they also acquired technical vocabulary that little by little led to changes in practice. Terms such as "balanced literacy," "scaffolding," "functions of language," and "types of texts" were often heard in the teachers' dialogue.

The professional development also had an impact on student learning. In 2006, the Ministry of Education commissioned the Universidad Católica de Chile to conduct a study about the impact of the LEM principles, the balanced literacy approach, and the professional development component. About 60% of students studying in schools following the LEM principles and involved in the balanced literacy approach with the corresponding professional development tested on grade level in Spanish literacy. Only 54% of students in schools that were not involved in the program achieved the same level of Spanish literacy proficiency. This suggests that the LEM program was moving in the right direction, and this has influenced the sustained implementation of this policy for literacy development to this day.

As we said before, historically, the teaching of initial reading in Chile has been characterized by methods based on decoding, generally through primers focused on syllables, as Spanish is a phonetic language. It is for this reason that first- and second-grade teachers were found to be the most resistant to adopting a balanced literacy approach in their teaching. The belief that reading equals decoding is deeply seated in the discourse and pedagogical practice of these teachers. The broader idea of balanced literacy, which focuses not only on decoding but also on reading comprehension, is typically not accepted by teachers of the lower elementary grades; they resist a form of teaching that is not focused on the code and traditionally have deferred reading comprehension for more advanced stages.

Beyond the earlier grades, resistance is often expressed in terms of conflict between studying language as a system, instead of as an instrument of knowledge building. Specifically, many of the teachers want to include aspects of traditional grammar and were not convinced that children would acquire use of standard language without grammatical exercises.

Although there has not been full implementation, one can discern features and elements taken from the balanced literacy approach in the teachers' practices. For example, teachers now use clear and precise scaffolding, which is provided in the didactic units that were developed by the program.

Teachers' Voices: Appropriating and Contesting Balanced Literacy

To evaluate the impact of the policy initiatives thus far, we interviewed nine educators currently working in Chilean classrooms through individual, semistructured interviews, as well as through focus groups. The purpose of the interviews and focus groups was to determine their strategies for teaching literacy, particularly during the first years of elementary school, and the impact of the government policy. In addition, we wanted to know about the teachers' understandings of the balanced approach and the new literacy curriculum. The interviews were conducted between July and September 2008.

The teachers have diverse educational histories and professional backgrounds. Four teachers worked in a private school that followed the Freinet approach.[3] There were also three teachers who worked in public schools of different municipalities, where a traditional approach was followed. Another teacher worked in a partly state-funded private school, specifically for poor children. A teacher specializing in intercultural bilingual education was also interviewed, who is in charge of the implementation of these programs in a region where there is a high percentage of Mapuche Indigenous children.

The teachers' prior training was also very diverse. One of the teachers interviewed had just finished her university training and was working for the first time. Three teachers had completed their studies while already working as primary school teachers. All of the participants had worked in the first year of primary school, teaching children to read and write.

Appropriating Practices

The interviews with the teachers reveal that they have understood the principles of balanced literacy and use it well, although not consistently or thoroughly. Rather than imitating blindly, teachers borrow appropriately. Even so, the impact on pedagogical practices, and especially on their discourse, has been great. One teacher tells us how she understands the changes in her pedagogy:

> [W]hat happens is that the natural method allows the children to use their own experiences to learn to read and write. . . . For instance they start reading

their own texts or the texts of others. One is not pushy concerning orthography or the size of their handwriting, for instance, because when they are just learning to write one must try not to clip their wings by telling them: "You must write it this way or another." They should have the will to express. I never taught them . . . the letters, I never taught them the alphabet. In second grade, when I need to do certain things, which I always discuss with the other teacher, I photocopy the alphabet for them to know how to write the lower and upper case letters, hand it to each of them, and some children use it but others don't.

Most teachers have accepted the notion that reading must be, first and foremost, a pleasing experience, in which children can feel competent. For example, one teacher tells us:

Of course, if we show reading as a punishment, as a tedious responsibility, everything becomes much more difficult. I mean, if my classroom is full of children who find reading a bore and consider it a punishment . . . "the teacher is going to punish us, let's pay attention because otherwise we'll have to read," it will be much harder to get their attention, to make them want to practice, to have silent reading that is actually silent reading, and not a mere contemplation of letters. Since we can't monitor every child in very large classes, then the only thing that gives me peace of mind is knowing that they are somehow interested in reading.

All the teachers we interviewed are especially pleased with the diversity of the reading material that is available now and the use that the children make of the didactics unit that were prepared by the program. Approximately 90% of the teachers interviewed think that they employ the balanced literacy approach, and they have learned to speak as if they do, even if the practices themselves show numerous divergences. One teacher tells us:

Before the LEM plan, I taught with the syllable book in first grade and that worked with some children, but many weren't able to read anything by the end of the year. Since my school became part of the LEM plan, I teach differently. Now the children have short texts from the beginning, and so I teach the letters and syllables little by little. The kids are happier, although I still have some things to learn, and still some children are not able to read by the end of the year, but they are only a few now.

The impact of the professional development and the program has been broadly felt among the teachers. One of them explains to us how she has been able to implement the balanced literacy approach and what the change has meant to her:

Before I taught reading in first grade . . . mostly with the skills model I did so without knowing what reading was; I combined it, but it was all separate. This goes here, this other moment goes here, that goes there. Using LEM and realizing that what you do, or what you have been doing systematically, year by year, all that could be taken, combined, and the rest could be derived from a central axis, so that's what it meant. . . . I think the experience with the teachers is very enriching.

It is interesting to note that teachers are pleased with the balanced literacy program because the material that they are given is highly organized and was elaborated and organized in the official curriculum:

[B]ecause they organize everything for you, for instance, I used to check the Plans and Programs . . . . and showed [a colleague] how we worked. Look: the objectives, then come the contents, learning activities, indicators, generic activities, suggested activities. So it's like the Bible and I showed [her] my book, everything, and there are corrections because we exchanged them and she has passages underlined, and so do I, and it's all full of writing, because I told [her]—I read the observations, I read the whole grounding because it's really important for me, because that way one can learn. So, they give it to you organized, and one has to take it, and there are certain objectives for the first semester. And to achieve some things now we have the progress map, which tells me I have to teach this and that in first and second grade, children have to reach this level; so it has all the objectives, and if I skip one it's because there was a little gap, a little hole, see? So, one has to check all the time.

Teachers show understanding of the difference between traditional literacy methodology and the balanced approach. Speaking of the differences in the teaching of writing, one teacher tells us:

[P]rograms have the aspect of creativity deeply ingrained, the idea of creation, the idea that you must understand that writing is not just to copy and transcribe, but to write a text. In my generation, . . . if you could write well on the board you were writing perfectly, and the important thing was calligraphy, not whether you were able to write a coherent sentence. In that aspect . . . it's very, very different from what I was taught. I also believe that it's good for me to remember that, because learning to read and write wasn't very pleasant for me, so that keeps me from returning to the old methods. I remember how unhappy they made me.

Balancing Practices

Despite the fact that the discourse and some practices have changed, it is also clear that teachers have not given up on their traditional teaching methods entirely. Rather than import the balanced approach in its entirety, they borrow only features that they feel are complementary to their belief system and methodological convictions. In fact, they point out that they "balance" their teaching practices. The teachers have come to accept and believe that the traditional teaching of decoding skills in isolation is boring and uninteresting for children. Yet they implement cautiously, without giving up practices with which they are comfortable.

For instance, the private school teacher comments that she has not given up on worksheets. However, alongside the worksheets, she uses "the natural method, which is what people suggest today, the use of messages of free text." She adds that she always employs Freinet practices to teach literacy alongside with traditional practices:

> So I use a combination: natural method, the method advanced by Freinet, see? But I do completely traditional things as well. A percentage [of children] learned to read with the natural methods, of course! But I also used a syllable book. I mean, there were some who didn't . . ., I had the syllable book in the classroom and some parents bought it for their children, then they learned, maybe with the two systems: the global and the syllabic one.

The second-grade teacher also explained how she mixes elements of both a balanced literacy approach and a traditional decoding-only approach:

> When I teach in a more guided way, it is more syllabic: letter A, letter B, letter C. But I employed all the available methods, a lot of tongue twisters, a lot of poetry, texts, even if they didn't know all of the letters well.

Most teachers have learned to modify their balanced literacy programs for students with diverse needs, especially poor children or those who start school with low levels of literacy. One teacher explains how she does it:

> For instance, there were kids who had trouble seeing the organization of texts, they didn't know how to name one part, they didn't know in which direction to read, really basic things like those. . . . I also had to review with the students who had made the least progress [who didn't know] the letters: identifying letters, identifying syllables, doing lots of activities to develop phonological awareness, and to foster their love for reading, make them like enjoy writing again, checking lots of the texts they write. Last year I had a very talented girl, she was able to write . . . a two-page long story, in an excellent hand, and with two spelling mistakes, impressive. Also to foster the interest of the most advanced students . . . give them research work. In second grade most of them were at least able to decode; I think two of them weren't; then the idea was to make it more fluent, and I believe also to erase the trauma of reading. In fact, when we started with the reading plan, my colleague and I tried to find texts that were . . . very readable, I mean, the idea was not to . . . make them read eighty pages, no, but to give them really basic books with many pictures and to let them feel they were able to read a book, to make it more of a game. . . . We also balanced it; I would like to make the process more natural, but what

has worked for us is a sort of schedule: Joint reading on Monday. So every Monday, no matter what, the class starts with Joint Reading. On Tuesday, we have Language Arts too, so no matter what, the class starts with half an hour or 45 minutes of worksheets to develop skills, and we start combining things. On Friday, we promote reading; . . . I introduce a text to them, tell them the tale, they dress up as the characters, and take the book home for the weekend and bring it on Monday, and they tell us what they read, that sort of thing. And so we start integrating things. It's funny but it is a sort of gradual integration as we combine everything; we begin with many small things, because it works, and at least it's more acceptable for the school.

Despite the efforts of the policy to transform literacy practices by developing appropriate teaching material and supporting the teachers in the classroom, it is clear that these teachers still innovate in ways that may differ from the balanced literacy approach as prescribed by the policy. One teacher explains to us:

> I regarded the program as my Bible: I went and organized the contents, planned my lessons, but I also followed the suggestions closely. And, based on the suggestions I made innovations, because I wanted to leave my hallmark, so, what did I do? I took the program, asked questions, asked colleagues with years of experience. So that was it, I mean, I combined the program, my experience, and that of others, to start developing my work.

All teachers interviewed express some conceptual ambivalence. From the perspective of the balanced approach, both processes—construction of meaning and decoding—are inseparable parts, which cannot be developed as individual components. However, the literacy teaching methods employed over the years, with their emphasis on decoding, have not enabled teachers to see this clearly. Teachers understand the principles of LEM, but have not yet found an adequate way of operationalizing it at all times. The pervasiveness of the belief in decoding is rampant, and teachers are not willing to abandon it. A teacher tells us: "One has to decode to be able to read, because if you don't decode you will not learn anything, that's the thing . . ."

Some teachers flatly reject the balanced approach, focusing instead on structured language activities. For some teachers it is not a matter of methodological belief, but of teaching style. One tells us:

> [T]his free system wouldn't, it wouldn't work for me. For me as a teacher, because basically I would get too messy. On the other hand, with a more structured thing, you find your place, I mean, you know what strategy you will use later.

On the whole, it seems that teachers have not entirely integrated the elements of balanced literacy practices, and instead use different practices linearly. The balanced approach includes both constructive ways of using literacy, alongside some structured literacy skills such as decoding, used synthetically. But the practice of these teachers continues to separate the two, setting them up as competing approaches, instead of as one integrated approach. Nevertheless, balanced literacy is now part of the discourse of the teachers, and changes in beliefs about literacy are evident, along with practices.

Different Children, Different Practices

Teachers who believe that reading is a process of construction of meaning, often return to skills-based beliefs when faced with poor children or those unable to learn to decode with more holistic methods. A teacher explains:

> Then we had our first lesson, before school started, because there were some very traditional teachers who said: "No, not me, because children will not learn with your natural method, we have to use the syllable book." Well, and, of course! We had our great lesson. Sixty percent of the children in first grade learned to read with the global method and generic methods . . . and 30% did not. Then those who favor the syllable book said: "See?" [at this point, the teacher expresses that they took the children who did not learn to read and gave them the syllable book] . . . so then we learned that we must use all the necessary systems, because children are not all alike and certain methods are easier for some of them but not for others.

This is the same viewpoint expressed by the teacher who described how she abandoned the balanced approach. Speaking about a holistic method that they experimented with, she says:

> [It] didn't work well at all, no. The most talented students learned . . . .. Five children in each class were excellent and happy and the others weren't. So, last year, when they started to see the problems with this process, teachers began teaching explicit skills . . . to balance things a little. This year the holistic thing was completely discarded, because it wasted a lot of time, and now we are using a more skills-based mode than what the funding institution proposes. But another teacher and I, my partner, we still balance it a bit, the school has a very clear point of view, which we follow, but they are also very open if we introduce different ways to teach reading.

There is a pervasive notion that poor children cannot benefit from balanced reading approaches and that there are skills that must be taught explicitly to them. The second-grade teacher complained that basic skills had not been taught in the first grade and said:

> Right, [students started the second grade] without knowing how to write, without knowledge of calligraphy notebooks, without respecting baselines, without spatial orientation in the use of paper, because many of them worked with worksheets only, nothing but worksheets, so they didn't know how to use the notebook. They didn't know where to write headings; if they ran out

of space in their notebook and had to cut the sentence, they moved to the next page. They didn't know they had to continue below. Everyday things like these, which in the end make you waste a lot of time, I mean, having to draw a grid on the board, teaching them that a number goes in a square and not in the middle of the page, those details make one waste a lot of time.

A factor that works against the full implementation of a balanced literacy approach is that in 2008 the Ministry of Education recommended that children from impoverished areas should learn to read through decoding strategies. This policy stands in opposition with the LEM principles and forces schools that educate poor children to focus on decoding skills as a condition to obtain supplementary funding for literacy development. Thus, there are two competing policies when it comes to teaching literacy to children from poor communities—one that establishes balanced literacy as the best way to promote literacy for all students, and another one that establishes traditional reading strategies focused on decoding as the best for poor children. The teachers have also been caught in the middle of these competing government policies. This lack of clarity in policy further enables the teachers to interpret and adapt the policy, as they encounter different situations.

Another instance of this lack of clarity in literacy instruction involves present efforts to establish bilingual intercultural education programs in Chile. The interview with the Mapuche supervisor reveals that the literacy reform has focused on the creation of textbooks in Spanish with Indigenous and non-Indigenous cultural content to teach Mapuche children (who are native speakers of Spanish) to read. Before, teachers from these mostly rural schools employed decoding-based reading education methods that included the use of *cartillas*, that is, primers based on syllabic approaches. Although most students were Indigenous, there was no inclusion of Indigenous cultural content. The textbooks created for bilingual intercultural education reflect a balanced literacy approach. They teach decoding skills, but always in connection with Mapuche stories and legends. Teachers are happy with this change, and they say that now children learn more quickly and are very pleased with these texts that show pictures of their houses, crops, games, and so on. Besides, the texts use Mapudungun (the language of the Mapuches) vocabulary. Teachers say that this has enabled them to learn a little of their students' language and culture as well.

The Mapuche supervisor we interviewed said:

> We have made great progress in the development of bilingual intercultural education over the last years. The most important thing has been the inclusion of "traditional educators," who are people from the community who know and keep the Mapuche language and culture alive, and who work alongside teachers. They teach with methodologies typical of their culture, which were slightly disapproved by teachers at first, but they are in general respected by the school.

The contrast between the literacy policy with regards to teaching poor children and those with low literacy in their first language (traditional skills approach) and Indigenous children (balanced approach using Indigenous linguistic and cultural elements) is important to consider. Whereas the first group is seen as deficient, the second group is seen as different. For the first group, the literacy material is grounded on a deficit view of the children, who are perceived to need more decoding and grammar skills, whereas for the second group the literacy material opens up a different cultural context, of value not only to the child but also to the teacher. Thus, it is easier to hold onto balanced literacy philosophies and practices when teaching Indigenous Chilean children than when teaching those who are just poor.

Conclusion

It is certainly difficult to analyze the distance between discourse and practice in education. Concerning the hypotheses that can be advanced to account for this distance, we will formulate at least two. The first is based upon the work by the researcher Wertsch (2002) about the construction of collective memory (or collective remembering). Wertsch (2002) reflects on how, in some communities, a discourse is not accompanied by real or true events. Instead, the living of the experience is done through the discourse, especially when it is put in writing and starts being transmitted from generation to generation. This explains the Chilean case—the pervasiveness of the skills-based method for teaching literacy—in which the presence of the *cartilla,* the syllable primer, has influenced generations of students and teachers. It is then this that has become the critical issue to solve in Chilean education, given the disappointing results in literacy development in our country.

The second hypothesis is related to the dynamics of the formulation and application of public policies, especially in education. Here, the top-down format tends to become a hindrance for teachers' knowledge and implementation of certain policies, as exemplified in the new curriculum. Our interviews show that teachers learn about new approaches to literacy superficially. However, implementation of new methods involves years of small-scale intensive work, which is resisted, appropriated, and changed in ways portrayed in this chapter.

This chapter has shown how despite the efforts of a well-planned professional development program, a top-down reform that has the potential to transform literacy practices in Chile has not been fully implemented. The chapter shows how teachers cannot be considered passive recipients of policies. They will not follow top-down policies blindly or implement them appropriately, unless they respond to their own needs as teachers, and those of their children. In this regard, the chapter shows how teachers are active agents and how they negotiate policies according to their own teaching styles and those of their children. For educational policy to be fully effective, it must take into account the sociohistorical context and the educational traditions that precede it.

Discussion Questions

1   What is balanced literacy and what are its principles?
2   How did Chile carry out its language and literacy policy? How effective has it been?
3   Give examples from the chapter of teacher resistance and teacher adaptation to the governmental policy. Discuss each.
4   Compare the sociolinguistic and socioliteracy situation of Chile with that of other countries in this book.
5   What is the advice that you would give to language education policymakers in Chile regarding the way that the policy is being appropriated by the teachers?

Notes

1   The team is comprised of an academic group from Universidad Alberto Hurtado, with extensive teaching experience in primary classroom, wide-ranging political knowledge, and experience educating teachers for public schools.
2   Interview excerpts were translated from Spanish.
3   The Freinet approach follows five principles: (1) pedagogy of work, meaning that children learn by making useful products or providing useful services; (2) cooperative learning; (3) inquiry-based learning; (4) a natural method based on an inductive, global approach; and (5) following children's learning interests and curiosity. The Freinet approach is considered an alternative pedagogy. We interviewed those educators as a way to investigate another point of view about literacy teaching and learning.

References

Allende, F., & Condemarín, M. (2002). *La lectura: Teoría, evaluación y desarrollo* [Literacy: Theory, assessment and development]. Santiago: Andrés Bello.

Cassany, D. (2006). *Tras las líneas* [Beyond the lines]. Barcelona: Editorial Paidós.

Chauveau, G. (2000). *Comment réussir en ZEP: Vers des zones d'excellence pédagogique* [How to be success at school ZEP (Priority Education Areas)]. Paris: Editions Retz.

Chauveau, G. (2001). *Comprendre l'enfant apprenti lecteur* [Understanding the beginner reader]. Paris: Retz/HER.

Condemarín, M., Galdames, V., & Medina, A. (2004). *Taller de lenguaje* [Language workshop]. Santiago: Santillana.

Ferreiro, E. (1992). *Haceres, quehaceres y deshaceres con la lengua escrita en la escuela rural* [Doing, working and undoing in country school literacy]. Buenos Aires: Libros del Quirquincho.

Ferreiro, E. (2001). *Alfabetización. Teoría y práctica* [Literacy. Theory and practice]. México: Siglo Veintiuno Editores.

Freire, P. (1988). *La importancia de leer y el proceso de liberación* [Literacy importance and the freeing process]. México: Siglo veintiuno.

Linuesa, M. C., & Domínguez, A. (1999). *La enseñanza de la lectura* [Learning to read]. Madrid: Ediciones Pirámide.

Pressley, M. (1999). *Cómo enseñar a leer* [How to teach reading]. Barcelona: Editorial Paidós.

Snow, C. E., Griffin, P., & Burns, M. S. (Ed.). (2000). *Un buen comienzo. Guía para promover la lectura en la infancia* [Starting out right: A guide to promoting children's reading success]. México. Fondo de Cultura Económica.

Tompkins, G. (2001). *Literacy for the 21st century: A balanced approach.* Upper Saddle, NJ: Merrill Prentice Hall.

Walqui, A., & Galdames, V. (2005). *Manual de enseñanza del castellano como segunda lengua* [Teaching Spanish as a second language homework]. La Paz: PINS-EIB, PROEIB Andes and México: SEP, 2007.

Wertsch, J. (2002). *Voices of collective remembering.* Cambridge, UK: Cambridge University Press.

Part III

Moving Forward

Chapter 15

Stirring the Onion

Educators and the Dynamics of Language Education Policies (Looking Ahead)

Ofelia García and Kate Menken

The layers of the onion that make up the field referred to by different terms—*language planning* (Cooper, 1989; Eastman, 1983; Ferguson, 2006; Fishman, 1971; Fishman, Ferguson, & Das, 1968; Haugen, 1959, 1966; Kaplan & Baldauf, 1997; Kennedy, 1983), *language policy* (LP; Corson, 1999; Ricento, 2006; Shohamy, 2006; Spolsky, 2004; Tollefson, 2002), and *language policy and planning* (LPP; Fettes, 1997; Hornberger, 2006; Hornberger & Ricento, 1996) or *language policy and language planning* (LPLP; Wright, 2004)—have been well described by Hornberger and Ricento (1996). But it is time to stir the onion as it is cooked by those who "language," softening and blending the layers alongside each other. It is time, as Hornberger (2006) herself has said, to integrate perspectives. This book specifically looks at how educators stir the onion by locating ideological and implementational spaces within their own practices (Hornberger & Ricento, 1996), as it shifts the emphasis of the field from government official education policies that are handed down to educators to those that educators themselves enact in classrooms and in interaction with a myriad other factors.

The field of LP has evolved in the last half a century. Even from the beginning, the language-planning approach that focused on solving language problems of developing nations and finding solutions to social problems created by language differences (Fishman et al., 1968; Jernudd & Das, 1971) was questioned in the title of Rubin and Jernudd's influential book of 1971, *Can Language be Planned?* In defending the designation LPP, Hornberger (2006) reminds us that language planning—an activity to promote systematic linguistic change in a community of speakers and usually undertaken by government—and language policy—the ideas, laws, regulations, rules and practices intended to achieve planned language change in society (Kaplan & Baldauf, 1997)—are linked but yet have important and distinctive roles, even though their relationship is not linear. The complex dynamism between the components have led Spolsky (2004) to refer to the activity only as "language policy" with three components: (1) language practices or the habitual patterns of languaging; (2) language beliefs or ideology about languaging, (3) language management or planning as specific efforts to modify or influence languaging.[1]

Following Spolsky (2004), this book takes an integrative and dynamic approach to language policy, although concentrating specifically on the domain of education, an important concern of the field from its beginnings. We speak here of language education policies in the plural, focusing on the interaction between individual choices and sociopsychological possibilities and constraints, and thus engaging in an ecological approach to LP (Haugen, 1972). However, the main contribution of this book is its focus on educators as language policymakers, rather than just blind followers who implement policies mandated from above. It is educators who "cook" and stir the onion. The ingredients might be given at times, and even a recipe might be provided, but as all good cooks know, it is the educators themselves who make policies—each distinct and according to the conditions in which they are cooked, and thus always evolving in the process. It is thus the dynamics of language education policies as produced by educators in interaction with not only government officials and education bureaucracies, community, families, and students, but also with external sociopolitical contexts and resources, and internal experiences, beliefs, and ideologies that is at the core of this book. We start here by reviewing the role that education has played in the *LP* field so that we can then better understand the contribution that this book makes.

Education and Language Policy

Language Planning and Education

The Norwegian founder of the field, Einar Haugen, was aware that education was central for what he defined as the four areas of the enterprise: (1) selecting a language norm, (2) codifying it, (3) implementing its functions by spreading it, and (4) elaborating its functions to meet language needs. According to Haugen (1983), education is not only central to the implementation and elaboration of language and literacy functions, but it is also one of the most important reasons why the field emerged in the first place. It is the spread of schooling in the 20th century that precisely made language norms a social priority, for schooling is no longer solely controlled by elites who can spread their language norms with ease (Haugen, 1983). Joshua Fishman, a pioneer in the field, also viewed these education "problems," produced by the inclusion of linguistically different students in schools, as the catalyst for the formulation of what was then called language planning (Fishman, 1972).

From the early days, when language planning had to do with nation-building, education was seen as a most important component. In what perhaps is the earliest book on the topic, *Language Planning and Language Education*, Chris Kennedy, the editor, states:

> Nowhere is this planning more crucial than in education, universally recognized as a powerful instrument of change. At the focal point in educational language planning is the teacher, since it is the successful application of curriculum and syllabus plans in the classroom, themselves instruments of higher levels of language planning, that will affect the realization of national level planning. (Kennedy, 1983, p. 1)

Despite the fact that Kennedy's book mentioned the teacher as the focal point in educational language planning, education was only considered in the book as a societal issue, rather than as a local phenomenon enacted in teaching and learning. Thus, educators were ignored in much the same way as they have been mostly overlooked to date. The topic of education is also prominent in Eastman's 1983 book on language planning, but again, only as a societal phenomenon. She states:

> [E]ducation figures in LP when there is a need for bilingual training, establishing literacy, and learning a second language—all forms of education that are in some ways types of language planning. (Eastman, 1983, pp. 82–83)

Acquisition Planning

The theorizing of education as a type of language planning had to await the contribution of Cooper (1989). Cooper recognized what he called acquisition planning—increasing the number of those who language and in what ways—alongside the other two types of language planning that had been previously identified: (1) *corpus planning*, meaning the development of new linguistic forms, the modification of old ones, and standardization of others, and (2) *status planning*, meaning changes to increase the uses of a language. Although described as two separate processes, some scholars maintain that the distinction between corpus planning and status planning is clearer in theory than in practice as they are more effectively engaged in jointly (Fishman, 1979, 1983, 2006). We argue here that acquisition planning is also part and parcel of corpus and status planning, more likely to occur concurrently.

In defining a*cquisition planning*, Cooper refers to Prator (1967) whom he quotes (in personal communication) as saying:

> Language policy is the body of decisions made by interested authorities concerning the desirable form and use of languages by a speech group. It also involves consequent decisions made by educators, media directors, etc., regarding the possible implementation of prior basic decisions. According to this definition, the decision to emphasize in a language class specific skills or linguistic forms—even the choice of a textbook—could become a part of language policy. The latter should thus be one of the primary concerns of language teachers. The entire process of formulating and implementing language policy is best regarded as a spiral process, beginning at the highest level of authority and, ideally, descending in widening circles through the ranks of practitioners who can support or resist putting the policy into effect. (as cited in Cooper, 1989, p. 160)

But again, although the importance of LP for language teachers is highlighted in this definition, the role of the educator remains undertheorized. Cooper instead focuses on what he considers the three societal goals of acquisition planning—reacquisition of a language, maintenance of a language, and foreign second language acquisition. In so doing, he attempts to also develop a theory of social change by answering the question: What actors attempt to influence what behaviors of which people for what ends under what conditions by what means through what decision-making process with what effect?

Another important scholar in the field, Sue Wright, describes acquisition planning as "the term generally employed to describe the policies and strategies introduced to bring citizens to competence in the languages designated as national, official or medium of education" (Wright, 2004, p. 61). But again, the role of the educator is not seriously considered.

Language-in-Education Planning

Scholars in the field continued to point to the conscious influence of educational institutions on sociolinguistic norms as a form of language planning (Fettes, 1997). In their influential book on language planning, Kaplan and Baldauf (1997) introduce the term "language-in-education planning (LiEP)" to refer to what Cooper called acquisition planning. They add that language-in-education planning "is the most potent resource for bringing about language change" and that is the "key implementation procedure for language policy and planning" (Kaplan & Baldauf, 1997, p. 122). But in their conceptualization, Kaplan and Baldauf (1997) go beyond Cooper's definition of acquisition planning, for besides having as an objective increasing the number of users of particular ways of using languages, LiEP has to do with selecting the language media for education, the languages taught, and the varieties used in education. Kaplan and Baldauf (1997) argue that various forces—nonlinguistic and linguistic at the macro- and micro-levels—are at work in language planning, and that, therefore, the individual user cannot be isolated from the social, political, and economic conditions in which she or he lives and is educated.

Kaplan and Baldauf (1997) describe the six stages of language-in-education policy, which are separate and distinct from those of language policy:

1   Education Policy: the articulation of an education policy separate from the general policy;
2   Curriculum Policy: the description of what languages are to be used, when, for how long, how and for which students;
3   Personnel: the determination of the source for educators, how they would be educated, retrained, and rewarded, and who would educate them;
4   Materials: the consideration of what instructional material, space, and equipment are needed, how much, how soon, for what methodologies, and at what cost;
5   Community: the understanding of community and parental attitudes and the development of approaches to those attitudes, and the identification of funding sources;
6   Evaluation: the appraisal of curricula, student success, teacher success/interest, and cost-effectiveness.

Although these authors do not grant educators the vital role that they deserve in this enterprise, they voice the important idea that there is unplanned LPP that goes unnoticed and unrecorded, and that much microlanguage planning is unplanned (Kaplan & Baldauf, 1997, p. 299). This "unplanned microlanguage planning" has been the focus of Hornberger's work and especially of her important contribution on this topic—*Indigenous Literacies in the Americas: Language Planning from the Bottom Up* (1996). Hornberger's text, and her use of the phrase "bottom-up," remind us that LP does not always flow from the top to the bottom and that in struggling for language revitalization, education has a most important role, particularly in indigenous communities who most often turn to literacy education programs.

Language-in-Education Policy

In the past 20 years, a few important texts have focused exclusively on language-in-education policy, especially Corson (1999), Tollefson (2002), and Lin and Martin (2005). Although these contributions offer a critical perspective on language policy, the educator still does not figure prominently. Corson (1999) focuses on reversing negative attitudes and policies toward language minorities in schools and adjusting for political, economic, technological, and cultural changes. He defines LP as follows:

> [A] document compiled by the staff of a school, often assisted by other members of the school community, to which the staff members give their assent and commitment. It identifies areas in the school's scope of operations and programs where language problems exist that need the commonly agreed approach offered by a policy. A language policy sets out what the school intends to do about these areas of concern and includes provisions for follow-up, monitoring, and revision of the policy itself in the light of changing circumstances. It is a dynamic action statement that changes along with the dynamic context of a school. (Corson, 1999, p. 1)

According to Corson, the purpose of LP in schools should then be to consider how to best teach a national standard variety, give value to nonstandard varieties of languages, teach English, and maintain and revitalize community and heritage languages.

Tollefson's (2002) book continued his prior work on critical aspects of LP in which he pointed out how it is "one mechanism by which dominant groups establish hegemony in language use" (Tollefson, 1991, p. 16) and how this, in schools, often creates inequalities among learners (Tollefson, 1995). In his 2002 book, Tollefson's objective is to "move outward from educational concerns of the classroom toward broader social, political, and economic issues" (Tollefson, 2002, p. x). His text uncovers how language policies in education themselves shape social life. Again, the educator and her role in enacting policy are left out of the text.

Using postmodernism as its theoretical lens, Lin and Martin's text (2005) looks at local, situated, and contextual ways of understanding language-in-education policies by pointing out how power operates at the microlevel of diverse discourses and practices. Focusing on how English is appropriated by local agents, Lin and Martin rely on Pennycook's notion of postcolonial performativity (2000) by which local peoples appropriate English and penetrate it with their intentions. In so doing, their text gives voice to the educator and to others, describing their multiple investments in their acts, desires, and performances, especially in the classroom. But still, the focus of this text is not on the educator herself, but rather on language governmentality (Pennycook, 2006) and how decisions about languages and language forms are made across institutions and through a diverse range of mechanisms such as books and exams.

Language Education Policy

The progression in LP studies from the early focus on language itself to the role that language plays in social life was corresponded by the early interest in education as a way of increasing language users (acquisition planning), the role that education played in establishing sociolinguistic norms, and the social effects of these decisions (language-in-education policy). In 2006, Shohamy pointed to the important distinction between "overt policy"—having to do with the use of language to influence sociolinguistic use and norms and thus social life—and "covert or hidden policy"—not explicitly addressing language itself but relying on the discursive power of language to have the same social effects. In taking the focus off language in education itself, Shohamy (2006, p. 76) speaks of "language education policy" as the "mechanism used to create de facto language practices in educational institutions." Whereas language-in-education policy is concerned with decisions only about languages and their uses in school, language education policy refers to decisions made in schools beyond those made explicitly about language itself. Language is central in school, for it is through language that students learn and come to know, and educators teach and evaluate. Thus, most educational decisions are, in effect, language education policy, as Menken (2008) has convincingly shown us in the case of high-stakes assessments for emergent bilinguals in the United States.

Shohamy (2006, p. 76) views language education policy as "imposed by political entities in a top-down manner, usually with very limited resistance, as most generally schools and teachers comply." She sees educators as "soldiers of the system" (p. 76), "servants of the system" (p. 79), "bureaucrats that follow orders unquestioningly" (p. 79), and "main agents through which the ideology is spread" (p. 79). The evidence provided in our book, however, including Shohamy's own chapter, extends this position, arguing instead that educators are at the center of language education policies.

Language Education Policies

In speaking about language education policies in the plural, this book emphasizes the plurality and dynamism of the many choices that are available to educators, students, and communities, as they are constrained or liberated by different structures that are also changed through their actions. The emphasis on the educator as the stirrer of the onion means that the site of analysis here is the microinteractions in schools, usually within the classroom itself, as microactions and practices interact with macroactions in ways that stir and provide the dynamism of the processes that this book describes. This point is developed further in the sections of this chapter that follow.

The Dynamics of Language Education Policies

The spiral that Prator speaks about in Cooper (1989) is not a widening spiral that moves linearly from a narrow authoritarian top to a broader base of practitioners. Instead, the vortex constantly changes shape, as the behavior of both practitioners and authorities emerges from the interaction of its many components. Haugen (1972) early on introduced the ecology of language paradigm, arguing that there is an interaction between language and the psychological and sociological environment of its speakers. An ecological approach to language education policies in the 21st century must pay attention to the dynamism between what we have learned to call top-down, bottom-up, and side-by-side actions in education, stirring the different components as the direction of the interaction gains momentum. Furthermore, the relationship between acquisition, status, and corpus planning is a symbiotic one. In considering bilingual education policies, García (2009, p. 85) says:

> The interactive way in which language is planned (or unplanned) and dictated from the top down, and the ways in which it is interpreted, negotiated (or planned) from the bottom up makes it impossible to differentiate between one level and the other. And language beliefs and ideology interact with the two levels.

Language education policies exist only through the fluxes that feed them, as they change and adapt in response to feedback—both internal and external. This has to do with the interaction between internal cognitive ecosystems and external social ecosystems (de Bot, Lowie, & Verspoor, 2007). Because of this dynamism, there is much variability. The context, the here and now of sociological and psychological import, is an intrinsic part of language education policies, not a background against which action takes place. The educator's cognitive processes are also inextricably interwoven with their experiences in the physical and social world. For example, as these contributions attest, language use in the classroom is continuously adapted to take into account contextual factors. These adaptations, in turn, affect the context of use. At the same time that educators are operating in an agentful way, language education policies are being transformed beyond the conscious intentions of the educators.

It is difficult to then describe the steps that language education policies take, although it is clear that they are not static and are forever changing. The classroom is a complex dynamic system in which agents (educators and students) and elements (curriculum and resources) are interrelating (through many different sociological and psychological processes), connecting in turn to form the whole system. In studying complex systems in applied linguistics, Larsen-Freeman and Cameron (2008) describe how each thought that passes through a mind changes the system, how each point in a lesson builds on and differs from the previous moment, and how each new student alters the system. Dynamic language education policies coadapt, motivated by change in other connected systems.

Language education policies are the joint product of the educators' constructive activity, as well as the context in which this constructive activity is built. That is, language education policies provide a structure or text, which then engages educators in behaviors situated in their own local contexts. Language education policies are thus both structure and activity, much in the same way a spider web is the joint product of the spider's "constructive activity and the supportive context in which [the web] is built (like branches, leaves, or the corners of a wall)" (Fischer & Bidell, 1998, p. 473, as cited in Larsen-Freeman & Cameron, 2008, p. 159). As Sutton and Levinson (2001, p. 3) have said, individuals and groups "engage in situated behaviors that are both constrained and enabled by existing structures, but which allow the person to exercise agency in the emerging situation." Thus, both the structure and the activity are parts of a complex process of dynamic construction in multiple directions and with multiple stakeholders. Johnson and Freeman (this volume) explain the contradictions inherent in language education policies:

> Educators play a vital role in dynamic, interrelated language policy processes and are not merely "implementers" of some monolithic doctrine. Still, language policies are capable of hegemonically setting discursive boundaries on what is educationally normal or feasible.

The educator is sometimes motivated to stir the onion in ways that are in direct response to realities on the ground—because the pot is of a certain material or is of a certain shape or because the flame is too high. At other times, he or she stirs because of personal beliefs, experience, and knowledge. External conditions have much to do with the educator's actions in that the educator's actions are constrained or facilitated by the external conditions that the educator shapes in turn. Educators' external realities, driven by the social context in which they are educated, trained, supported, and teach, as well as their internal ideologies, beliefs, and attitudes, also have much to do with language education policies. Thus, as Creese reminds us in this book, it is possible for educators to choose to stir or not stir, in order to produce a different consistency every time.

Although educators may be the chefs, there are many sous-chefs in this enterprise. Many of the chapters in this book tell the story of the other stakeholders in language education policies. On the one hand, there are government officials and official policymakers, usually in ministries of education. On the other hand, there are communities and parents. There are also curriculum and textbook writers, test makers, and researchers. Finally, there are different students who have their own interpretations, negotiations, and needs.

There are also different pots and pans, of different materials and sizes—instructional materials and books; appropriate terminology for instruction; and sufficient financial support, to name but a few. Every kitchen staff is a team, with chef, sous-chefs, and the rest of the staff collaborating, and at the same time competing, as they turn to different tasks. In the same way, language education policies are collaboratively constructed out of complex relationships, even when the educator is given the responsibility to stir. Each interacts with the demands of the others, as well as with his or her own exigencies.

Dynamic Education Policies in this Book

What we see in the classrooms portrayed in this book is that despite the existence of official documents, language education policies are socially constructed and dynamically negotiated on a moment-by-moment basis. It is the French/Turkish bilingual student teacher in Hélot's chapter who expresses this most explicitly: "At that moment, being bilingual myself, I decided to intervene and to use Turkish, since I shared this language with the pupil."

There is never a single policy, but rather there are numerous, often competing ones; thus, our use of "policies" in the plural. Sometimes, as in the case of Ethiopia (Ambatchew), the written policy might be "ideologically noble," but, without teachers or materials to enact the written policy, only silence and chaos prevail. Other times, as in the case of Peru (Valdiviezo), the policy might be in direct contradiction with the history of marginalization as experienced by the educators and students. Policies, as either texts or discourses, are constructed, produced, and performed by individual human beings who appropriate them. As performed texts, they have the agency of their performers and are appropriated in unpredictable ways.

Perhaps one of the language education policies that seems more dynamically performed is that of language use in classrooms. Most language education policies, as handed down by bureaucrats and administrators, advocate against mixing languages. But the translanguaging (García, 2009)[2] that we witness by educators and students in the chapters that take place in South Africa (Bloch et al.), Lebanon (Zakharia), Peru (Valdiviezo), Ethiopia (Ambatchew), and India (Mohanty) offer evidence of how language education policies in classrooms are differently performed and dynamically negotiated for the purposes of sense making in a moment-by-moment basis. These classroom performances signal the disinvention of the concept of discrete standard languages (Makoni & Pennycook, 2007), substituting instead the idea of individual, multiple, discursive practices of teachers and students.

Other times, educators dynamically negotiate if and when languages, including English, are to be used in education. The chapters in this book have shown us how this occurs even in highly centralized education systems with explicit top-down language policies, such as Israel or France, as well as in decentralized education systems such as the United States, or in systems such as that of Lebanon, which has a centralized curriculum but highly decentralized schooling practices.

Even when the policy seems to be open and flexible with regard to multilingual education, such as in South Africa and Ethiopia, educators respond to the policy according to their own perspective—ideological, linguistic, cultural, educational, and pedagogical. The policy negotiation by teachers in South Africa (Bloch et al.) and Ethiopia (Ambatchew) offer cases in point.

This book also includes examples of language education policies that have to do with staffing models, such as partnership teaching in the United Kingdom (Creese) and the facilitator model in the United States (English & Varghese). When educators are assigned different roles within particular staffing models, this influences how they negotiate language education policies.

Another one of the language education policies most dynamically performed has to do with approaches to literacy and language development. Although the balanced literacy approach has become popular in the past decade, the chapters on the literacy campaign in Chile (Galdames & Gaete) and on the literacy efforts to teach Xhosa in South Africa (Bloch et al.) offer evidence of how teachers combine aspects of a given policy with their experience, their own conceptual ambivalence, and their philosophy, in order to appropriate and perform their own individual literacy education policies, despite enormous investment in professional development to "hand-down" a balanced literacy policy. The teachers in the chapter by Zhang and Hu also show teachers' different performances in their individualized responses to imposed task-based language teaching, prescribed by the national English curriculum in China.

Moreover, good educators do not blindly follow a prescribed text or march to an imposed language education policy but instead draw on their own knowledge and understandings in order to teach. As Zakharia says in this book, they reconstruct policy from preexisting elements handed to them, as well as new elements generated in the classroom in collaboration with students. Mohanty in this book summarizes these efforts by saying that teachers, though caught in the gulf between policy and practice, between what is prescribed by others and what is required for the children, innovate and find solutions. In so doing, the landscape of the classroom, and the policy as handed down, is in itself transformed. In describing the dynamism of the choices of educators, Johnson and Freeman say in their chapter: "The line of power does not flow linearly from the pen of the policy's signer to the choices of the teacher."

As this book brings to life, power in schools flows dynamically, and educators make choices. There is but one example in this book where the dynamism shapes a harmonious context with these flows responding to each other instead of competing. That context is Aotearoa/New Zealand, as described by Berryman et al. There, the national policy supports schools becoming self-governing. It is within this context that the Māoris have been able to enact policies and curriculum that are able to not only revitalize their language but, more importantly, reconnect to a Māori worldview of connection to families—as whānau (extended family)-centered, with everyone in the same waka (canoe). Despite the fact that in this case the educators' performances and those of the school and government authorities seem to move in the same direction, there are still many opposing forces. *Ako*, the balance of power between the roles of teacher and students through reciprocal activities, is an ideal, but it is, as Berryman et al. show, "only shared activities with more skilled performers." Thus, despite the more collaborative context, and the reciprocal and whānau-centered practices, language education policies are here, as in all cases, dynamic performances of educators that are contingent on their external and internal contexts and of those with whom they interact.

It may be time to dislodge the linearity of relationships between actors in language education policies as being top down, bottom up, or even side by side. Instead, what we propose in this book is that educators be given their rightful roles as stirrers of the onion, producing the dynamism that moves the performances of all of the actors. Status, corpus, and acquisition planning can only be interpreted and acted upon by human actors and thus understood through their actions. It is the educators' actions, as portrayed in this book, which enable us to understand language education policies as moment-to-moment, dynamic performances.

Notes

1 We use *languaging* to refer to the multiple discursive practices that individuals use, which extend beyond the sociopolitical constructions of a "language" as proposed by states (García, 2009; Makoni & Pennycook, 2007; Shohamy, 2006) and used in schools.
2 As per García (2009), *translanguaging* refers to the responsible use of hybrid language practices to educate and to enable effective communication in the classroom.

References

Cooper, R. L. (1989). *Language planning and social change.* Cambridge, UK: Cambridge University Press.

Corson, D. (1999). *Language policy in schools: A resource for teachers and administrators.* Mahwah, NJ: Lawrence Erlbaum.

de Bot, K., Lowie, W., & Verspoor, M. (2007). A dynamic systems theory approach to second language acquisition. *Bilingualism: Language and Cognition, 10*(1), 7–21 & 51–55.

Eastman, C. (1983). *Language planning: An introduction.* San Francisco, CA: Chandler and Sharp.

Ferguson, G. (2006). *Language planning and education.* Edinburgh: Edinburgh University Press.

Fettes, M. (1997). Language planning and education. In R. Wodak & D. Corson (Eds.), *Language policy and political issues in education* (pp. 13–22). Boston, MA: Kluwer.

Fischer, K. W., & Bidell, T. R. (1998). Dynamic development of psychological structures in action and thought. In W. Damon & R. M. Lerner (Eds.), *Handbook of child psychology, Vol. 1: Theoretical models of human development* (5th edn, pp. 467–561). New York: Wiley.

Fishman, J. A. (1971). The impact of nationalism on language planning: Some comparisons between early twentieth-century Europe and more recent years in South and Southeast Asia. In J. Rubin & B. H. Jernudd (Eds.), *Can language be planned? Sociolinguistic theory and practice for developing nations* (pp. 3–20). Honolulu: The University Press of Hawaii.

Fishman, J. A. (1972). *The sociology of language: An interdisciplinary social science approach to language in society.* Rowley, MA: Newbury House Publishers.

Fishman, J. A. (1979). Bilingual education, language planning, and English. *English World-Wide, 1*, 11–24.

Fishman, J. A. (1983). Modeling rationales in corpus planning: Modernity and tradition in images of the good corpus. In J. Cobarrubias & J. A. Fishman (Eds.), *Progress in language planning: International perspectives* (pp.107–118). Berlin: Mouton.

Fishman, J. A. (2006). *Do not leave your language alone: The hidden status agendas within corpus planning in language policy.* Mahwah, NJ: Lawrence Erlbaum.

Fishman, J. A., Ferguson, C., & Das, G. J. (Eds.). (1968). *Language problems of developing nations.* New York: John Wiley and Sons.

García, O. (2009). *Bilingual education in the 21st century: A global perspective.* Malden, MA & Oxford: Wiley-Blackwell.

Haugen, E. (1959). Planning for a standard language in Norway. *Anthropological Linguistics, 1*(3), 8–21.

Haugen, E. (1966). *Language planning and language conflict: The case of modern Norwegian.* Cambridge, MA: Harvard University Press.

Haugen, E. (1972). *The Ecology of language.* Stanford: Stanford University Press.

Haugen, E. (1983). The implementation of corpus planning: Theory and practice. In J. Cobarrubias & J. A. Fishman (Eds.), *Progress in language planning: International perspectives* (pp. 269–290). Berlin: Mouton.

Hornberger, N. (1996). *Indigenous literacies in the Americas: Language planning from the bottom up.* Berlin: Mouton de Gruyter.

Hornberger, N. (2006). *Frameworks and models in language policy and planning.* In T. Ricento (Ed.), *An introduction to language policy: Theory and method* (pp. 24–41). Malden, MA: Blackwell.

Hornberger, N. H., & Ricento, T. K. (Eds.). (1996). Language planning and policy [Special issue]. *TESOL Quarterly, 30*(3).

Jernudd, B. H., & Das, G. J. (1971). Towards a theory of language planning. In J. Rubin & B. Jernudd (Eds.), *Can Language be planned?* (pp. 195–216). Honolulu: University Press of Hawaii.

Kaplan, R. B., & Baldauf, R. B. (1997). *Language planning: From practice to theory.* Clevedon, Avon: Multilingual Matters.

Kennedy, C. (Ed.). (1983). *Language planning and language education.* London: George Allen and Unwin.

Larsen-Freeman, D., & Cameron, L. (2008). *Complex systems and applied linguistics.* Oxford, UK: Oxford University Press.

Lin, A. M. Y., & Martin, P. W. (Eds.). (2005). *Decolonisation, globalization: Language-in-education policy and practice.* Clevedon, Avon: Multilingual Matters.

Makoni, S., & Pennycook, A. (2007). *Disinventing and reconstituting languages.* Clevedon, Avon: Multilingual Matters.

Menken, K. (2008). *English Language Learners Left Behind: Standardized testing as language policy.* Clevedon, Avon: Multilingual Matters.

Pennycook, A. (2000). English, politics, ideology: From colonial celebration to postcolonial performativity. In T. Ricento (Ed.), *Ideology, politics and language policies: Focus on English* (pp. 107–119). Amsterdam: John Benjamins.

Pennycook, A. (2006). Postmodernism in language policy. In T. Ricento (Ed.), *An introduction to language policy. Theory and method* (pp. 60–76). Malden, MA: Blackwell.

Prator, C. H. (1967). The survey of language use and language teaching in Eastern Africa. *Linguistic Reporter, IX*, viii.

Ricento, T. (Ed.). (2006). *An introduction to language policy: Theory and method.* Malden, MA: Blackwell.

Rubin, J., & Jernudd, B. (Eds.). (1971). *Can language be planned?: Sociolinguistic theory and practice for developing nations.* Honolulu: East-West Center and University of Hawaii Press.

Shohamy, E. (2006). *Language policy: Hidden agendas and new approaches.* London: Routledge.

Spolsky, B. (2004). *Language policy.* Cambridge, UK: Cambridge University Press.

Sutton, M., & Levinson, B. (Eds.). (2001). *Policy as practice: Toward a comparative sociocultural analysis of educational policy.* New York: Ablex.

Tollefson, J. W. (1991). *Planning language, planning inequality: Language policy in the community.* London: Longman.

Tollefson, J. W. (Ed.). (1995). *Power and inequality in language education.* New York: Cambridge University Press.

Tollefson, J. W. (Ed.). (2002). *Language policies in education. Critical issues.* Mahwah, NJ: Lawrence Erlbaum.

Wright, S. (2004). *Language policy and language planning: From nationalism to globalization.* New York: Palgrave.

Chapter 16

Moving Forward

Ten Guiding Principles for Teachers

Ofelia García and Kate Menken

The diverse cases in this book place educators at the epicenter of the dynamic process of language policymaking, highlighting how they time and again act upon their agency to change the various language education policies they must translate into practice. We have seen how educators "stir the onion" by creating ideological and implementational spaces for multilingualism within their own practices, even in highly centralized contexts and educational systems that assert great control over educators and their languaging. We have also seen how educators can close off those spaces. At times educators' sense-making is directed by their prior experiences or personal identity, as individual cognitive forces shape their interpretations and enactment of language policies. At other times, it is instead external or situational forces that motivate educators' decisions and the policies they ultimately enact. As we have stated, variations in policy implementation are not a problem that should be avoided, particularly when policies hold the potential to marginalize language minorities. Instead, we simply need to gain deeper understandings of this variation to help educators negotiate this complex terrain when faced with their own policy decisions and to help policymakers who are working from outside of classrooms create policies that assume and allow for such variances.

In this final chapter, which reflects just the actual beginning, we speak to you who are educators—particularly teachers—and are faced with language policy negotiation, recreation, and implementation as policymakers in your own right. We draw upon the lessons learned in this book to offer you a set of principles to help you make sense of this complex terrain, to see yourselves as policymakers, and to act upon the agency and power that you have. As these principles reflect, we feel it is first necessary for you to turn inward before you can act outwardly. Thus, these principles focus on you as they spiral their way through the layers of the onion.

Ten Guiding Principles for Teachers

1   Understand your own sociolinguistic profile and language practices. Conduct a self-reflection by answering the following questions:

- How many languages do you understand? Speak? Read? Write? Sign? How well? How did you develop these ways of languaging?

- How would you describe your languaging at home? With different people?
- How would you describe your languaging in social situations?
- How would you describe your languaging in professional situations?
- How would you describe your languaging in your classroom as a teacher?

2   **Know the sociolinguistic profile and practices of the students in your classroom, school community, students' families, and the community surrounding the school.** By closely observing the activity of the classroom, school, families, and community, as well as conducting a sociolinguistic survey of the classroom, school and community actors, answer the following questions:

- What are the sociolinguistic practices of your *students* in *classrooms*?
- How do students language in classrooms? In what varieties? For what purposes? In what media? When and where?
- How do students language in the playground and cafeteria? In what varieties? For what purposes? In what media? When and where?
- What are the differences in languaging among students of different ethnicities? Genders? Socioeconomic class?
- What are the differences in languaging among individual students?
- How well do students language in different varieties and domains or contexts?
- In what ways are students encouraged or discouraged to language in your classroom in the ways that they language outside of school?
- What are the sociolinguistic practices of the *school community*?
- How do members of the school community, other than students, language? For example, how do principals and administrators, clerical staff, maintenance and cafeteria staff, support personnel, and others language? In what varieties? For what purposes? In what media? When and where? What, if any, are the differences between actors in their languaging, and what might be their motivations?
- To what extent do actors in the school community language in different varieties and do they do it well?
- What are the sociolinguistic practices of the *families of the students*?
- What are the languaging activities and varieties of the parents of students? Of their younger and older siblings? Of their grandparents and extended families?
- How do students language at home? In what varieties? When? Where? For what? With whom?
- What are the differences between the students' languaging with parents and with their older and/or younger siblings? With their grandparents and extended families?
- How well do family members language in different varieties?
- How well do students language within the family in different varieties?
- What are the sociolinguistic practices of the *community*?
- What languaging is heard or read around the block of the school? In other words, what is the linguistic landscape around the block? How

are people languaging in the street? In nearby stores and institutions? What are the languages and language varieties used in signs and bill-boards? What are the messages communicated in the different languages? Are different languages relegated to more official use in signs? Reflect on the reasons for the community's languaging.

- What languaging takes place in the larger community from which most students come? What languages are used in the larger stores and in important institutions? What languages are used in smaller stores and other institutions? What languages are commonly heard in the street? What are the languages and language varieties used in signs and bill-boards? What are the messages communicated in the different languages? Are different languages relegated to more official use in signs? Reflect on the reasons for the languaging used in the community.

3　**Know the societal language management policy.** Obtain information from the internet or other sources that would enable you to answer, with detail, the following:

- Do you live in a society that has an overt policy for language education? If so, what is it? Who determined the policy? Were all key stakeholders involved? Is it a national policy? If not, at what level has it been mandated? How do you feel about it?
- If there is an overt language education policy, how is it being implemented? When? By whom? Are there sufficient resources and support for it? What kind of teacher education or professional development plan has been instituted? Is it being supported by authoritative bodies? If so, what is their role? Are these bodies functioning at a national, supranational or sub-national level?
- Are there other mechanisms, other than overt policies, through which language policies are being encouraged? What are they? What are the *de facto* policies they create in schools? How do you feel about these?
- Is there ideological and implementation space for multilingualism in the policies?
- How well do these policies match the sociolinguistic profile and practices of your students, school staff, families, and community, as well as your own?

4　**Know the school's language education policy.** Reflect on your school language policy and then answer the following questions (if you're a new teacher, go through the school archives and/or speak with veteran teachers to learn about the policy):

- Does your school have an explicit language education policy? If so, what is it? How was it developed? Who participated? Was it a rigorously democratic venture in which all participated? Were there meetings with students, staff, parents, and community? Do all school stakeholders believe in, support, and act upon the policy?

- Does your school have an implicit language education policy? If so, what is it? How was it developed? What mechanisms are in place to support it? Do all school stakeholders believe in, support, and act upon the policy?
- Do all educators in your school interpret and implement the policy in the same way?
- What was the motivation for the policy? Was the motivation educational or otherwise?
- Has the policy been tested and adjusted over time? If so, what adjustments have been made? Why? How have these adjustments been made?
- What other educational policies must your school negotiate that impact language education? Do these support or undermine your school's language education policies?
- What other daily practices occur in school that can be considered mechanisms of language education policies? Are they hidden or overt? Do they support positive social change?

5   **Understand your beliefs, attitudes, ideologies, and motivations.** Conduct a self-reflection by answering the following questions:

- What are your beliefs about a standard language and/or other varieties?
- How would you describe your language identity? Are you and your students linguistically similar or different?
- What are your attitudes toward bilingualism? Do you believe there are cognitive consequences, and what might those be? Are there social consequences, and what might those be? If you had children, would you want your children to be bilingual or monolingual? Why?
- Do you hold any stereotypes of children who are linguistically different?
- Can you describe instances of linguicism you have witnessed?
- What are your beliefs about translanguaging in bilingual communities?
- What are your beliefs about translanguaging as a pedagogical tool?

6   **Understand the beliefs, attitudes, ideologies, and motivations of others.** Reflect on all of the information that you have gathered and answer the following questions:

- What are the attitudes of the school administration, the teaching and nonteaching staff, parents and families, and the community toward the present language education policy (or policies) that are being followed in the school? How does each of these stakeholders differ regarding the importance of the policy and its implementation?
- Is there a difference between those who favor the policy and those who oppose it? What might be the motivation for those differences?

7   **Know the staffing, organization, and leadership structure in your school.** Interview principals and teachers if necessary to make sure you can answer the following questions:

- How are classrooms in your school staffed? Is this adequate to meet the goals of the school's language policy and otherwise support effective language instruction?
- Is the leadership style in the school collaborative? For example, do teachers work together toward certain language goals?
- Are there shared values among the staff and is there an ethos of caring?
- Is the discourse used among the staff one of respect, collaboration, and inclusion of language differences? Are all staff members given a voice in school decisions that affect them?
- How is the relationship between school staff, parents, and community members?

8   **Understand how the curriculum and pedagogy are interrelated with language education policies, and the ways that you act as a policymaker in your school or classroom.** Read the sources in the bibliography and then reflect on what you know about the effect of your own curriculum and your pedagogy on social life.

- In what ways do you interpret the different language policies you negotiate in your classroom, and how do you implement them? In the process, how do you act as a policymaker?
- In what ways is the curriculum inclusive or exclusive of linguistic and cultural diversity? Does it convey the worldview of your students, their families, and their community?
- How do you plan for different ways of languaging to be allocated in the curriculum?
- Do you allow translanguaging in your classroom? Why or why not? When? And with what effects?
- What are the languaging arrangements that you make in your classroom to include different language practices? What are its effects?
- What are the strategies you use in teaching and how does this relate to students whose language practices are different?
- Do you scaffold instruction linguistically? Do you contextualize? Model? Bridge? Plan for multiple entry points? Use different grouping strategies that ensure each student has a voice?
- Do you plan curriculum and language objectives concurrently? Why or why not?
- Is biliteracy an important goal of your curriculum? If so, how do you develop it and sequence instruction? What pedagogies do you use to address this development? What other societal concerns do you have to keep in mind in order to implement literacy education policies?

9   **Understand how ways of assessing students are interrelated with language education policies.** Read the sources in the bibliography then reflect on what you know about the effect of your own assessment policies and practices on social life.

- What assessments are used in your school? What are the purposes of each assessment? Does the assessment match the purposes for which it was intended?
- Which assessments being used are high-stake tests imposed by educational authorities? What decisions are being made on the results? Does the test serve a gatekeeping function?
- Which assessments being used are formative assessments conducted by you? In what ways do they support your teaching and your students' growth?
- What language and cultural matters need to be kept in mind when developing assessments?
- What effects do different kinds of assessments have on you and your students, and what relationship do they have to language policy? Do the assessments have a positive or negative overall impact on your instruction and on your students' educational experiences? How do the assessments improve schooling for your students, if at all?

10 **Remain critical and aware of language education policies.** Understand the effects of language education policies on social justice and issues of inequality among linguistic groups and your own power as a policymaker.

- What are the effects of the present language education policy, as you enact it in your classroom, on equality among students? How is their languaging represented and included in your language education policy? In what ways have you as a policymaker carved our implementational spaces for multilingualism and muticulturalism in your classroom?
- Is your role in constructing language education policy acknowledged?
- What would you have to do to equitably build on, and use, the languaging resources of your students? Your school? Families and the community?
- How can you advocate for language education policies that are sound for your own students, and your school community?

Bibliography

Baker, C. (2006). *Foundations of bilingual education and bilingualism* (4th ed.). Clevedon, Avon: Multilingual Matters.

Canagarajah, S. (2004). *Reclaiming the local in language policy and practice.* Mahwah, NJ: Lawrence Erlbaum.

Corson, D. (1999). *Language policy in schools. A resource for teachers and administrators.* Mahwah, NJ: Lawrence Erlbaum.

Freeman, R. (2004). *Building on community bilingualism: Promoting multiculturalism through schooling.* Philadelphia, PA: Caslon Publishing.

García, O. (2009). *Bilingual education in the 21st century: A global perspective* (Chapters 12–15). Malden, MA & Oxford: Wiley-Blackwell.

Hornberger, N., & Ricento, T. K. (Eds.). (1996). Language planning and policy (Special issue). *TESOL Quarterly, 30*(3).

Hornberger, N., & Johnson, D. (2007). Slicing the onion ethnographically: Layers and spaces in multilingual language education policy and practice. *TESOL Quarterly, 41*(3).

Menken, K. (2008). *English language learners left behind: Standardized testing as language policy.* Clevedon, Avon: Multilingual Matters.

Nieto, S. (2002). *Language, culture, and teaching: Critical perspectives for a new century.* Mahwah, NJ: Lawrence Erlbaum.

Shohamy, E. (2006). *Language policy: Hidden agendas and new approaches.* London: Routledge.

Spolsky, B. (2004). *Language policy.* Cambridge, UK: Cambridge University Press (for general information).

Tollefson, J. W. (Ed.). (2002). *Language policies in education. Critical issues.* Mahwah, NJ: Lawrence Erlbaum.

Contributors

Michael Daniel Ambatchew is an Ethiopian educational consultant who has been working in education in Ethiopia for over two decades. He has his first degree from Ethiopia, his second from the United Kingdom, and his third from South Africa. He has worked for numerous organizations including the African Union and the United Nations.

Mere Berryman (Ngāi Tūhoe), New Zealand, Ministry of Education
Ted Glynn, University of Waikato
Paul Woller, New Zealand, Ministry of Education
Mate Reweti (Ngāti Porou), New Zealand, Ministry of Education.
These writers include two indigenous Māori women, both researchers with teaching backgrounds. One is an elder who is a native speaker of Māori language. The other two are non-indigenous, one a University professor, the other a researcher. All are bilingual. Collectively they form part of a research group who work collaboratively to support Māori students and their families in a range of Māori and English language education settings.

Carole Bloch is a former teacher and writer of several books for young children. She coordinates the PRAESA Early Literacy Unit at the University of Cape Town which helps to transform the way that early literacy and biliteracy is taught and learned in African multilingual settings. The Unit is involved in creating conducive environments for literacy development through teacher education, research, reading promotion and materials development.

Angela Creese is professor of Educational Linguistics at the University of Birmingham, UK. Her work is on educational inclusion, educational policy, multilingualism and community schooling. A particular focus is interaction in multilingual classrooms using approaches from linguistic anthropology. The processes of team ethnography is a current methodological interest.

Bonnie English is a graduate student at the University of Washington. She is interested in the role of classroom teachers as educators of English language learners.

Rebecca Freeman is director of the Language Education Division of Caslon Publishing and Consulting in Philadelphia, and adjunct professor at the University of Pennsylvania. She consults with educators on language education policy and programs, and is co-editor (with Else Hamayan) of *English language learners at school: A guide for administrators.* She is also author of *Bilingual education and social change* and *Building on community bilingualism.*

Rosa Gaete is a teacher at the Elementary Education School (in charge of primary school teacher training) at the Alberto Hurtado University in Santiago, Chile. She is deputy academic coordinator of the language team at the University that carries out, among other projects, the Technical Assistance in Language and Education project, a relevant project of the Chilean educational policy.

Viviana Galdames is director of the Elementary Education School (in charge of primary school teacher training) at the Alberto Hurtado University in Santiago, Chile. She is also responsible for the language team at the same university that carries out, together with the Ministry of Education, the Technical Assistance in Language and Education project, a project pertaining to the Chilean educational policy. She has published several books on the subject of teaching mother tongue and second languages, along with Mabel Condemarin and Aida Walqui.

Ofelia García is professor in the PhD program in Urban Education, Graduate Center of the City University of New York. She was formerly professor at Columbia University's Teachers College and Dean of Education at Long Island University. Her most recent book is *Bilingual education in the 21st century: A global perspective* (Wiley/Blackwell, 2009).

Xolisa Guzula is an early language and literacy teacher trainer and researcher with the Project for the Study of Alternative Education in South Africa (PRAESA) at the University of Cape Town. She is currently involved in a developmental research project on creating literate school communities. She has also been involved in translating a number of children's books and has written five of her own.

Christine Hélot is a professor of English at the University of Strasbourg (France) and a researcher in the field of bilingualism. She obtained her PhD from Trinity College, Dublin (Ireland). Her recent publications include: *Du bilinguisme en famille au plurilinguisme à l'école* (L'Harmattan, Paris, 2007) and *Forging multilingual spaces* with A.M. de Mejia (Multilingual Matters, 2008).

Guangwei Hu (PhD) is associate professor at the National Institute of Education, Nanyang Technological University, Republic of Singapore. His main research interests include bilingualism and bilingual education, language policy, language teacher education, psycholinguistics, and second language acquisition. He has published extensively in these areas.

David Cassels Johnson is assistant professor of Education at Washington State University. He investigates the interaction between language policy and educational equity from a sociolinguistic perspective. Recent publications appear in *Applied Linguistics, TESOL Quarterly,* and *Language Policy,* and he was the 2008 recipient of the National Association Bilingual Education's Outstanding Dissertation Award.

Kate Menken is an assistant professor of Linguistics at Queens College of the City University of New York (CUNY) and a research fellow at the Research Institute for the Study of Language in an Urban Society at the CUNY Graduate Center. Previously, she was a teacher of English as a second language, and a researcher at the National Clearinghouse for Bilingual Education. Her recent book is entitled *English learners left behind: Standardized testing as language policy* (Multilingual Matters, 2008).

Ajit Mohanty is a professor at Jawaharlal Nehru University and directs the National MLE Resource Centre and Project MLE *Plus.* He was Fulbright visiting professor at Columbia University and has published on *Psycholinguistics, Poverty,* and *Multilingual Education.* He is on the Editorial Boards of *International Journal of Multilingualism, Language Policy* and *Psychological Studies.*

Ntombizanele Nkence is an early language and literacy trainer and researcher with the project for the Study of Alternative Education in South Africa (PRAESA) at the University of Cape Town. She is currently involved in a developmental research project on improving literacy in schools and in teacher training. Ntombizanele has also been involved in translating a number of children's books and has written four of her own.

Rashim Pal is a research scholar at Jawaharlal Nehru University interested in education policy and schooling processes for disadvantaged children. With a Master's Degree in Psychology and M.Phil. in Educational Studies, she has taught in Delhi schools. Her current research is on classroom strategies for teaching English in India.

Minati Panda is an associate professor in Jawaharlal Nehru University. She is a cultural psychologist working on ethno-mathematics, school curriculum and education of tribal children. A Fulbright Senior Scholar at the Laboratory of Comparative Human Cognition, UCSD and Commonwealth Fellow at University of Manchester, she directs (with Ajit Mohanty) two major projects on Multilingual Education.

Elana Shohamy is a professor of language education at Tel Aviv University researching topics related to language policy, assessment and rights. Publications include *The power of tests* (2001); *Language policy* (2006); *Language testing and assessment* (ed. with Nancy Hornberger, 2008); *Linguistic landscape: expanding the scenery,* (ed. with Durk Gorter, 2009). She is the editor of *Language Policy.*

Laura Alicia Valdiviezo is assistant professor at the University of Massachusetts-Amherst. A native of Peru, Laura is a former bilingual educator interested in teachers' interpretations of language policy from a socio-cultural comparative and multicultural stance. Within global, national and local contexts, she studies

⌐agogic practices in linguistically and culturally diverse settings in turn ⌐ape education policy and theory.

⌐ka M. Varghese is an assistant professor of Language, Literacy and Culture at the University of Washington. Her primary research and teaching interests are in language teacher education, language teacher identity and access in higher education for linguistic minorities.

Zeena Zakharia is lecturer at Teachers College, Columbia University in New York. Her scholarly interests include language policy and educational practice within conflict/post-war and development contexts, particularly among minoritized populations. She has over fifteen years of experience in educational development practice and research among diverse communities in the Middle East and has published on related topics.

Yuefeng Zhang (PhD) is assistant professor at the Hong Kong Institute of Education, Hong Kong. Her main research interests include curriculum studies, English language teaching and learning, learning study and teacher education and has published in these areas.

Author Index

Subject Index